EMERGING STRATEGIC TRENDS IN ASIA

EMERGING STRATEGIC TRENDS IN ASIA

Editor

Uttam Kumar Sinha

INSTITUTE FOR DEFENCE STUDIES & ANALYSES
NEW DELHI

PENTAGON PRESS

Emerging Strategic Trends in Asia
Uttam Kumar Sinha (Editor)

First Published in 2015

ISBN 978-81-8274-823-1

Published by
PENTAGON PRESS
206, Peacock Lane, Shahpur Jat,
New Delhi-110049
Phones: 011-64706243, 26491568
Telefax: 011-26490600
email: rajan@pentagonpress.in
website: www.pentagonpress.in

Branch
Flat No.213, Athena-2,
Clover Acropolis,
Viman Nagar,
Pune-411014
Email: pentagonpresspune@gmail.com

In association with
Institute for Defence Studies and Analyses
No. 1, Development Enclave,
New Delhi-110010
Phone: +91-11-26717983
Website: www.idsa.in

Printed at Avantika Printers Private Limited.

Contents

Preface

Asian Geopolitics in the Coming Decade

Yan Xuetong

'Multi-polarisation' has been a buzzword since the collapse of the Soviet Union in 1991. However, the advocators for multi-polarisation have not currently identified any power possessing a nationally comprehensive strength which is similar to that of the USA. The financial crisis of 2008 dimmed the prominence of the USA as the only superpower; but it still did not bring about any bright future for multi-polarisation. Since China's GDP surpassed Japan's in 2010, the term 'bipolarisation' has been an alternative forecast, in contrast to the prediction of multi-polarisation. My latest book, The Inertia of History: China and the World in the Next Ten Years (2013), presented a structural analysis of the possible trend of bipolarisation. It will be very possible for all major powers to adapt their foreign policies according to that trend in a visible future.

Based on Deng Xiaoping's doctrine of 'keeping a low profile', the Chinese government has advocated multi-polarisation for more than two decades. It is obvious that multi-polarisation would provide better conditions for China's interest in preventing American containment efforts directed against it. Nevertheless, the trend of bipolarisation drove the USA to adopt a pivot/rebalancing strategy in East Asia in 2010. Some Chinese thought that the rebalancing strategy was merely a political technique used by the Obama administration for his election campaign, and hoped that the USA would still focus its strategy predominantly in the Middle East. Unfortunately, they were disappointed, for Obama clearly reiterated that the rebalancing strategy would not change under his administration. Faced with Obama's rebalancing strategy, China's new government, headed by Xi Jinping, changed China's foreign policy from the doctrine of 'keeping a low profile' to the principle of 'striving for achievement'.

With regard to bilateral relations, Xi Jinping suggested developing a new model of major power relations with the USA. After hard diplomacy, the USA officially accepted this idea in November, 2013, when Susan Rice delivered a speech at Georgetown University. This new model of major power relations between China and the USA is not characterised by a close relationship; but rather, it consists of a healthy or peaceful strategic competition. The positive aspect of this agreement to establish a new model of major power relations is that it supports these two countries working together while avoiding a repeat of the American-Soviet confrontation that occurred during the Cold War. The negative part of it is that, in the future, they will undoubtedly need to deal with more rather than less conflicts between them. Personally, I hope that China and India will develop cooperative relations rather than this new model of major power relations because the nature of the former is cooperation and the nature of the latter is competition.

Most of major powers, including India, have now adopted a policy to improve relations with China while managing their relations with the USA. In 2013, China further consolidated its relations with Russia, Germany, France and India while improving its relations with the United Kingdom. This phenomenon demonstrated that it is possible for most major powers to have good relations with both China and the USA at the same time. Nevertheless, Japan could be an exception. The Japanese Prime Minister, Shinzô Abe adopted a confrontational policy with respect to the rise of China. He has regarded China's rise as an opportunity for Japan to get rid of Article 9 of Japan's Constitution, and thereby transform itself into a military power. For the sake of achieving this goal, he purposely designed an official visit to the Yasukuni Shrine which honors 14 A-class war criminals of World War II, and has also adopted a confrontational policy on the territory disputes over Diaoyu Island. It is very possible that, during his governance of Japan, China-Japan relations will not only become much worse than those between China and the USA but could also well become the worst of all bilateral relations between major powers.

Japan's rightist policy will be as dangerous as North Korea's nuclear policy. These two problems have already become the two most important threats to regional stability in East Asia, which has enjoyed peace since 1991 when the Cambodian war ended. China adopted the principle of peaceful development; but that principle does not mean China will tolerate Japanese-initiated military attacks. According to historical studies, the weak initiate military attacks against the strong no less often than the strong do against the weak. Historical examples include the Japanese Navy's surprise military strike launched against the US' naval base at Pearl Harbor in 1941, and the Al-Qaeda's attack on the USA in 2001. When Abe's government works hard at organising an ideology alliance aimed at the containment of China, it is not a good sign for world peace.

The process of bipolarisation does not only have an impact on major power relations but also on regionalisation in Asia. Asian countries have experienced both of the recent major financial crises—during 1997-1998 and then from 2008 on. Bipolarisation will intensify the competition between the American Trans Pacific Strategic Economic Partnership (TPP) and Chinese regional cooperation. The Chinese government has announced three plans for economic regionalisation in Central Asia, South Asia and Southeast Asia. These plans involve the belt of the silk route in Central Asia, the economic corridor composing China, India, Bangladesh and Myanmar, and the maritime silk route in Southeast Asia. Unfortunately, Abe's confrontation policy makes it impossible to develop sub-regional economic cooperation in Northeast Asia.

Nevertheless, China-US competition for regional cooperation will benefit many countries economically in Asia. China will provide more capital to surrounding countries for regional cooperation, and the USA will provide a more favourable policy for Asian countries to access the American market.

Due to the strategic competition between China and the USA and the China-Japan political confrontation, it is very possible for East Asia to become the world centre within ten years. To become the world centre, Asia has to be the region where global competitors reside as well as be the most valuable place for them to compete. By 2023, the GDP of East Asia will be larger than that of the whole of Europe or North America. Meanwhile, East Asia may also have more tensions than the latter two regions. I am not a fatalist, and I think we still have a chance to make Asia better than in my forecast. My optimistic attitude is based on possible policy changes by Japan after Abe. Based on the rate of changing Japanese prime ministers after the Cold War, Abe will not stay in power for more than five years. After him, the world will have a chance to see a different Japanese government—one that will admit to Japanese crimes during World War II and will prefer cooperation rather than confrontation. In that case, we will at least defuse one of the two major danger problems of Asian politics and of the world; the Abe government and the nuclear issue in the Korean Peninsula.

Contributors

Uttam Kumar Sinha is a Fellow at IDSA and holds an adjunct position at the Malaviya Centre for Peace Research, Benares Hindu University. At IDSA, he is the Managing Editor of *Strategic Analysis* (Routledge) and edits the *Strategic Digest.* He leads the IDSA-PRIO institutional cooperation on peace and conflict studies and is also IDSA's lead researcher on the Asiarctic project with Norway. Since 2006, he has been a visiting fellow to the International Peace Research Institute Oslo (PRIO). In 2008 he was a Chevening 'Gurukul' Scholar at the London School of Economics and Political Science. From 2011-12, he was a CSCAP-India representative for the study group on water resources security. CSCAP is a Track 2 dialogue forum of ASEAN. In 2012, he was elected as Chair of Near East and South Asia Regional Network on Water Dispute Resolution Mechanism, National Defense University, Washington. A doctoral from Jawaharlal Nehru University, he worked in the daily *Pioneer* and wrote the weekly space, 'Strategic Eye'. His research areas focus on non-traditional aspects of security with particularly attention on climate change, transboundary water issues and the Arctic region. His recent work includes edited volumes, *Arctic: Commerce, Governance and Policy* (Routledge, 2015); *Non-Traditional Security Challenges in India: Approaches and Responses* (Routledge, 2015); and a monograph, *Climate Change Narratives: Reading the Arctic* (IDSA, 2013). He co-authored the IDSA Report on *India and Water Security: External Dynamics* (2010) and also the IDSA Report on *Security Implications of Climate Change for India* (2009).

Yan Xuetong is currently the Dean of the Institute of Modern International Relations, Tsinghua University, Secretary of World Peace Forum and the Chief Editor of *The Chinese Journal of International Politics*. He is Vice Chairman of both China Association of International Relations Studies and China Association of American Studies, and a member of Consultation Committee of Ministry of Commerce of PRC. He served as research fellow at the Institute of Contemporary International Relations during 1982-1984 and 1992-2000. He received his Ph.

D in political science from University of California, Berkeley in 1992. Xuetong Yan is the author and coauthor of a number of important books including *Inertia of History: China and the World in Next 10 Years* (2013), *The Analysis of International Relations-Second Edition* (2013), *Ancient Chinese Thought, Modern Chinese Power* (2011), *International Politics and China* (2005) and *American Hegemony and China's Security* (2000) and *Analysis of China's National Interests* (1996).

Takenori Horimoto is currently affiliated to the Graduate School of Asian and African Area Studies, Kyoto University and Open University of Japan. He was earlier professor of Contemporary South Asian Politics and US Asian Policy at Shobi University. He has authored and edited 11 books besides over 100 articles, and more than 170 lectures and presentations including Commentator on NHK TV. His recent books include: *India: The Big Elephant Globalizes*, Iwanami Shoten, 2007 (Japanese); (co-ed) *India as a Rising Military Power*, Askishobo, 2010 (Japanese); (co-ed) *Contemporary South Asian Politics,* Open Air University, 2012 (Japanese); (co-ed) *India-Japan Relations in Emerging Asia*, Manohar, 2013 English). His latest article has appeared in National Interest

Michael Wesley is a Professor of National Security at the Australian National University. He has extensive experience teaching, researching and communicating on Australia's international engagements, particularly in Asia. Wesley has published extensively and has authored several books on foreign policy, including *The Howard Paradox: Australian Diplomacy in Asia.* He won the 2011 John Button Prize for Best Writing in Australian Politics for his book, *There Goes the Neighbourhood: Australia and the Rise of Asia.* He was Executive Director of the Lowy Institute for International Policy from 2009 to 2012 and Professor of International Relations and Director of the Asia Institute at Griffith University from 2004 to 2009. Professor Wesley was an Assistant Director-General in the Office of National Assessments in 2003/04 and served as co-chairman of the Security and Prosperity working group at the Australia 2020 Summit in 2008.

Fumio Ota is a former naval officer and retired as the director of Defense Intelligence Headquarters at the rank of Vice Admiral in 2005. Earlier in his career he was the officer in charge of preparing the White Paper titled 'Defense of Japan 1987', for the Japan Defense Agency. He made his second retirement as a professor of the National Defense Academy in 2013. Ota has a PhD from the Johns Hopkins University in 2003. He has been a visiting fellow at the Center for International Security and Arms Control at Stanford University co-directed by William Perry, the former US Secretary of Defense. During this time, Ota also made the acquaintance of Condoleezza Rice, the former US Secretary of State, who was a fellow at the Center. Ota has a number of books both in English and Japanese including "The US-Japan Alliance in the 21st Century" (in English). He is an accomplished athlete and was a pentathlon candidate for the 1972 Munich Olympic Games.

Andrew Scobell is Senior Political Scientist at RAND's Washington, DC office and Adjunct Professor of Asian Studies at Georgetown University's School of Foreign Service. Prior to this he was Associate Professor of International Affairs at the George H.W. Bush School of Government and Public Service (with tenure) and Director of the China Certificate Program at Texas A&M University located in College Station, Texas. Scobell earned a doctorate in political science from Columbia University. He is author of *China's Search for Security* (Columbia University Press, 2012) [with Andrew J. Nathan]; *China's Use of Military Force: Beyond the Great Wall and the Long March* (Cambridge University Press, 2003), more than a dozen monographs and reports, as well as many journal articles and book chapters. He has also edited or co-edited more than a dozen volumes on various aspects of security in the Asia-Pacific region. Scobell was born and raised in Hong Kong and regularly makes research trips to the region.

Nguyen Hung Son is Deputy Director-General of the Institute for South China Sea/East Sea Studies, at the Diplomatic Academy of Vietnam. His areas of research include East Asia security and cooperation, particularly maritime security, East Asia regionalism and ASEAN affairs. He participated in Vietnam's delegation drafting the elements of the Code of Conduct for the South China Sea both at the official and informal tracks. Prior to his current designation, Hung Son was a full time diplomat. He was member of the Vietnam High Level Task Force delegation negotiating the ASEAN Charter. Nguyen Hung Son got a B.A degree from the National Economic University of Vietnam, an M.A degree on International Economic from Birmingham University of the United Kingdom, and a doctorate from the Diplomatic Academy of Vietnam.

Prakash Menon was the Military Adviser in the National Security Council Secretariat in the rank of Secretary to Government of India. An infantry officer he retired in 2011 as Lt. Gen. after nearly 40 years of service. During his military career he has had extensive operational experience at different levels having commanded a battalion, brigade and division in Central, North and South Kashmir. From 2009 to 2010, he was the Commandant of the National Defence College. For his distinguished services he has been awarded three prestigious awards including the highest distinguished services award, the Param Vishist Seva. Lt. Gen. Menon's civil qualification includes two post graduate degrees in Defence Studies and Management and also a PhD. He was been nominated by the Union Cabinet as a member of expert group for establishment of the Indian National Defence University. He is one of the Co-authors of *Non Alignment 2.0, A Foreign and Strategic Policy for India in the Twenty First Century.*

Hu Shisheng is a Senior Research Fellow and the Director of the Institute for South & Southeast Asian and Oceania Studies at the China Institutes of Contemporary International Relations (CICIR). He received his BA in Hindi and his MA in Sanskrit and Bali languages from Peking University. Hu did his PhD in International Politics & Relations with a focus in Ethnic and Religious issues from CICIR in 2006. In 2004 he was a Visiting Scholar at Johns Hopkins' School of Advanced International Studies (SAIS). His research areas include: the political and security situations in India and Pakistan, ethnic and religious problems in South Asia and the Tibet issue. Hu published a book *Tibetans in Exile: the Construction of Group Identities and its Embarrassment* (Center of China Tibetology, 2008). Hu's most recent research focuses on South Asia—particularly India, Pakistan and Afghanistan security issues.

Rajat Kathuria is Director and Chief Executive at Indian Council for Research on International Economic Relations (ICRIER), New Delhi. He has over 20 years experience in teaching and 10 years experience in economic policy, besides research interests on a range of issues relating to regulation and competition policy. He worked with Telecom Regulatory Authority of India (TRAI) during its first eight years (1998-2006). He has taught undergraduate economics at the University of Maryland and is currently on leave from the International Management Institute (IMI), New Delhi. He has worked with the World Bank as a Consultant and carried out project assignments for a number of organizations, including ILO, UNCTAD, LirneAsia, Ernst and Young, Consultancy Development Centre (CDC) and Standing Committee for Public Enterprises (SCOPE). He is a graduate from St. Stephens College, a Masters from Delhi School of Economics and a PhD degree from the University of Maryland, College Park.

Kristy Hsu is Associate Research Fellow and Section Chief at the Taiwan WTO Center, and Programme Director at the Taiwan ASEAN Studies Center, Chung Hua Institution for Economic Research (CIER), Taiwan (ROC). Her areas of research interest include international trade policy and economic/trade law, trade and development issues, regional integration, and gender issues. She is also Advisory Member to the Trade and Development Committee, ROC National Confederation of Industries, International Affairs Committee, ROC Chamber of Commerce, and adviser to the Chinese National Association of Industry and Commerce or CNAIC monthly publication CNAIC Magazine, and Standing Supervisor to Taiwan Women Film/Video Association. She was the Executive Secretary and associate research fellow at the Chinese Taipei APEC Study Center, Taiwan Institute of Economic Research (TIER) from 1999-2002; journalist of the Commercial Times in Taiwan from 1989-1998, and Correspondent in Tokyo for the newspaper in 1990.

Bobby A. Tamaela Wattimena is Senior Research Associate at Indonesian Institute for Energy Economics (IIEE) and Senior Energy Economist at in Quest Consulting. He was an executive director of IIEE and Pelangi Indonesia Foundation. He works in the field of energy economics and sustainable development. He has works with many national international agencies, such as Ministry of Energy and Mineral Resources, World Bank, Danida, IEEJ, and World Resource Institute. He is the principal developer of Integrated Indonesian Energy and Environmental Model (IIEEM). He received his Bachelor of Science in Petroleum Engineering from Trisakti University and Master of Science in Economics from University of Indonesia.

Yashika Singh is the India Economist at Rio Tinto, a world leader in finding, mining and processing the earth's mineral resources. She has over a decade's work experience in various facets of the Indian economy. Her current work involves analyzing the Indian economy's growth prospects and the evolving composition of the growth model, with a view to tracking the evolving resource consumption in the country. She also looks at the various supply side issues impacting the mining industry in India. Yashika has been with Rio Tinto for over 3 years now. Prior to joining Rio Tinto, Yashika headed the Economic Analysis, Research & Advisory functions at Dun &Bradstreet India, based out of Mumbai. She has completed her Masters in Economics from Jawaharlal Nehru University.

Mukul Sanwal joined the Indian Administrative Service in 1971, and as Joint Secretary in the Ministry of Environment and Forests represented India in the negotiations leading to the Climate Change Convention, the Forest Principles and Agenda 21, and co-chaired the negotiation group that developed the Rio Declaration, in 1992. He subsequently moved to the United Nations, in 1993, as Policy Adviser, first to the Executive Director of UNEP and later to the Executive Secretary of UNFCCC, and retired from the UN in 2007. He advised the Ministry of Science and Technology in the development of the National Action Plan on Climate Change, in 2008. He has been a member of a number of expert groups and has published extensively on sustainable development, multilateral treaties and conservation. He has a Masters in Public Administration from Harvard University.

Huang Ying is the Director for the Division of Financial Security Studies and an associate researcher with the Institute of World Economics Studies, China Institutes of Contemporary International Relations (CICIR). She earned a master's degree in Economics at China Academy of Social Science (CASS), and a doctoral degree in Law at CICIR. She stayed as a visiting scholar at the York Centre for Asian Research in the York University, Canada from 2007 to 2008. Her research interests cover resources security, international financial situation and cooperation, and regional integration. She has published many papers in the above areas.

Anup Singh was commissioned in the Indian Navy in 1973 and retired as Flag Officer Commanding-in-Chief, Eastern Naval Command in 2011. During his career, he commanded four warships: Matanga, Veer, Ranvir and Delhi. His last seagoing appointment was that of Flag Officer Commanding Western Fleet wherein he led Operation SUKOON, the evacuation of civilians from war-torn Lebanon in July 2006. His key appointments ashore included Assistant Controller of Warship Production/Acquisitions and Carrier Projects; Chief Instructor (Navy) at the Defence Services Staff College; Chief of Staff, Western Naval Command; Deputy Chief of Naval Staff; Deputy Chief of Integrated Defence Staff. He was the Sailing Master of the first ever square-rigged Sail Training Vessel in India, named 'Varuna', during 1980-82. He also skippered the Naval Yacht 'Samudra' for her Pacific crossing during the Tri Service round-the-world voyage in 1989.

You Ji is Professor at the University of Macau and also holds a Reader's position at School of Social Sciences, the University of New South Wales. He graduated from the Peking University and Australian National University. He is author of three books, including *the Armed Forces of China*, and numerous articles. His papers appear in journals such as *the Problem of Communism, the International Journal of Korea Unification Studies, the China Journal, the Pacific Review, Comparative Strategy, Asia Policy, Japanese Studies, Contemporary Southeast Asia, the Naval War College Review, Strategic Analysis, Journal of Contemporary China, Contemporary Security Policy* and *Issues & Studies*. You Ji is on the editorial board of *the China Journal*; *Provincial China; East Asia Policy; Asian and Middle East Studies, Issue and Studies, Sociology and Criminology* and *Journal of Contemporary China.*

Lan-Anh T Nguyen is Director of the Centre for Legal Studies of the Institute for East Sea (South China Sea) and Vice Dean of the International Law Faculty of the Diplomatic Academy of Vietnam. She was a research fellow and currently a global associate of the Center for International Law, National University of Singapore. Dr. Nguyen received her Ph.D. in International Law from University of Bristol, the UK, and L.L.M. from University of Sheffield. She has research interests in ocean law and policy, maritime security, and the South China Sea issues. Her main duties in the Diplomatic Academy of Vietnam include teaching for undergraduate students, postgraduate students and mid-career officials; doing research; attending national and track II international workshops on international relations and international law; and providing advisory opinions to Ministry of Foreign Affairs of Vietnam on ocean law and policy, particularly concerning the South China Sea issues.

Timothy Legrand is currently at the National Security College, Crawford School of Public Policy, Australian National University, Canberra. Legrand completed his PhD in Political Science at the University of Birmingham in 2008. His thesis, The Politics and Pathways of Policy Transfer, explored the processes by which policymakers learn from the experiences of their overseas counterparts. This research involved a series of interviews with policy officials in the UK, US, Canada, and Australia. He is the co-editor of a volume with Allan McConnell on International Perspectives in Emergency Policy (Ashgate). Prior to joining ANU, Legrand worked with the Griffith University, the UK Home Office, Department of Children, Schools and Families, Ministry of Justice and Department of Health as a specialist policy advisor.

Saskia Hufnagel is a Research Fellow within the 'Vulnerable Infrastructures' Project at the Australian Research Council Centre of Excellence in Policing and Security (CEPS). She has a PhD from the Australian National University and was previously employed as Assistant Professor at the University of Canberra. Within the 'Vulnerable Infrastructures' Project her work focuses on comparing legal frameworks in Australia and the EU, particularly in the field of mass gatherings, maritime and aviation security. She co-edited *Cross-border Law Enforcement - Regional Law Enforcement Cooperation - European, Australian and Asia-Pacific Perspectives* (Routledge, 2011). Hufnagel is a qualified German legal professional and accredited specialist in criminal law.

Simon Bronitt was appointed Director of CEPS at Griffith University in 2009. Prior to this appointment he was Professor of Law in the ANU College of Law in Canberra and Associate Director of the Australian Centre for Military Law and Justice, ANU. Between 2003-9 he served as the Director of the National Europe Centre – an EU funded Centre - in the Research School of Humanities at ANU. Drawing on comparative and interdisciplinary perspectives, he has published widely on criminal justice topics ranging across terrorism law and human rights, covert policing, family violence, and mental health policing. Simon Bronitt principal publications include two leading textbooks, *Principles of Criminal Law* (3rd ed, Thomson Reuters 2010) and *Law in Context* (4th ed, Federation Press, 2012).

Ashutosh Misra is Research Fellow/Associate Investigator at the *Australian Research Council Centre of Excellence in Policing and Security* (CEPS). Currently, he is developing two projects on 'the legality of drones under international law' and 'crime and corruption in international sport'. On the latter subject, he has successfully facilitated CEPS' collaboration with INTERPOL. He is also a visiting faculty with the National Security College at the Australian National University. Prior to migrating to Australia in 2007 he was a Research Fellow (2002-2007) at the Institute for Defence Studies and Analyses. He has published extensively including three books: *Pakistan's Stability Paradox*, (London: Routledge, 2012); *India-Pakistan: Coming to Terms* (New York: Palgrave Macmillan, 2010) and *Pakistan: Engagement of the Extremes* (New Delhi: IDSA and Shipra, 2008).

Introduction

Uttam Kumar Sinha

Is this Asia's Century or 'nobody's Century'?

Asia is the world's largest and most populous continent. With approximately 4.3 billion people, it makes up 60 per cent of the world's current human population. Asia's growth rate has quadrupled during the last 100 years and is currently the largest when measured in purchasing power parity. There is little doubt that Asia—stretching from the Eurasian landmass to the maritime reaches of Australia and the South Pacific—is experiencing a major shift in the global balance of power. Expressions like the 'Indo-Pacific' and 'Asia-Pacific', contested they maybe, capture Asia's expanse and dynamism. But for one brief and dramatic financial crisis in 1997, growth rates in Asia have been averaging well above the rest of the world. The rise of China along with the increasing global footprint of Russia and India in G20 and the ASEAN states soaring economies have made Asia the powerhouse and centre of gravity. Yet, Asia struggles with numerous conflicts in spite of its 'alphabet soup' of regional organisations and security structures.

A power shift from the West to the East is well under way. But what is not understood is how this global re-distribution of political, economic and military power will impact global and regional geopolitical order. International Relations experts warn us that power transitions of this magnitude can prove to be destabilizing. The argument that the world is interdependent to an unprecedented degree offers some hope that the transitions to new world order may turn out to be peaceful. The challenge before us is to take a measure of these changes and try to understand their impact on peace and stability. Interestingly, these changes are also changing the mindset of the people who are pushing for political reforms and accountability.

Is this China's Century?

Potentially, the global power shifts is also prising up Asia to confrontation as well as convergence as states compete. The resultant stress-lines and fault-lines expose Asia to many potential flash-points. Unresolved territorial issues stand between India and China, Vietnam and China, China and Russia, Russia and Japan. North Korea and Taiwan may trigger-off unmanageable crises. West Asia continues to be restive threatening to tear apart the socio-political fabric. Of the four Asian nuclear powers, North Korea and Pakistan are highly suspect nuclear proliferators involved in covert supply of missile technology. The China-Japan rivalry reveals dangerous chauvinism. At the same time, the two largest populated countries—China and India—referred to as 'planetary powers' surging need for energy and raw materials for its 2.5 billion people creates new areas of resource friction. Resource scarcity will not only be related to physical shortage but more possibly from failure of governance. China is an important piece of the puzzle and its rise is a defining line of the changing landscape. How will China define its national interest in the future? Will it pursue an assertive, even aggressive policy in Asia to back up its territorial claims? Or will China, assured of its great power status practice moderation and restraint? Importantly, how should India and other key states in Asia respond to China's continuous rise and influence—should the response be as a strategic competitor with a policy of confrontation or a containment approach through active cooperation?

Will it be a Century of Cooperation and Collaboration?

From a strategic grand view, the balance of power is uncertain in Asia. A sizeable US military presence continues and the Obama administration´s policy involves strengthening US military alliance and strategic partnerships and simultaneously repositioning forces. China would be far from assured that the 'rebalancing' is not directed towards it thus opening up the region to power play and rivalry in the East China Sea and South China Sea. A resultant increase in military expenditure and modernisation and a thrust towards new technologies will spur many countries.

Asia's economies are increasingly vital to each other and to the world with both the US and Europe continuing to post low GDP growth. The economic shift is shaping two different approaches to trade liberalisation in Asia. One paved by the ASEAN-led Regional Comprehensive Economic Partnership (RCEP) and the other by the US-led Trans-Pacific Partnership (TPP) and it has to be seen how these approaches will determine the economic choices in the coming years. While, at one level, certain investment and trade barriers will continue to hinder business in Asia, at another, poverty eradication will have to remain an essence of economic growth for Asian countries. The economies in Asia have to continuously grow fast along with being sustainable and inclusive. Other challenges that equally impact the economy are an increased number of natural disasters that interrupt the supply chain, security concerns emanating from terrorism and cyber security, where hacking, espionage and lack of privacy fuel concerns for companies as well as politicians and governments.

Asia is on the threshold of change—the known and unknown. Opportunities and uncertainties abound. Such times also offer an excellent chance to concentrate on the dynamics of change, to search for new ways of understanding, and to prepare for a future that is certainly set to surprise.

Will India be the 'fulcrum' and Lead the Way?

For India, the emerging geopolitical and geo-economic trends raise questions as to how it will lock into the new continental power matrix and how it will respond and reappraise to the changes. The big question is how India is responding to the strategic changes in Asia? China sits atop the power pyramid with its physical size, military capability and economic clout that combines to assert regional dominance. Powers like India would not like to easily cede the hegemonic space to China but, at the same time, would realise that its power is pervasive and difficult to counter balance. The arrangement possibly would be for India to trade and invest intensely with China while seeking a security alliance with the US. Will India follow this path? How is India as an emerging power looked at in the region? Can India be a guarantor/balancer or will it be seen as an opponent?

Conceptual Framework

A careful reappraisal of Asia's emerging strategic dynamics, a hard-headed assessment of what India's interests are and a considered approach to fulfilling these interests should deeply engage academia and policy makers. It is critical to explore the pillars on which India can build a more comprehensive, forward-looking and proactive Asia policy. Against this backdrop, the 16th annual Asian Security Conference (ASC) organised by the Institute for Defence Studies and Analyses, New Delhi, in February 2014 deliberated the emerging strategic trends in Asia and the accompanying challenges and opportunities. The 18 chapters of this volume are organised into six sections:

- I. Asia's Geopolitical Future
- II. Military Trends in Asia
- III. Economic Global Shift Toward Asia
- IV. Resource Stress in Asia
- V. Ocean Governance in the Indo-Pacific
- VI. Assessing Risks: Cyber and Critical Infrastructure

I. Asia's Geopolitical Future

Central to the future of stability in Asia is how the rise of China is impacting the balance of power. China is now strong enough to challenge US' leadership in Asia. But it is not clear as to what kind of new order would emerge. One possibility is a contested order framed by US and China strategic rivalry. The Chinese dominance might push other Asian powers into alliance with US making the landscape polarized. On the other hand, the US stays engaged in Asia, without being assertive and allowing for a 'concert of powers' as a counter weight to China's power in the Indo-Pacific. Regional institutions are important prescription for bolstering Asia's stability but raises doubts on whether such multilateral structures have the capability to absorb the shocks and resolve conflicts. The two chapters by Takenori Horimoto and Michael Wesley explore Asia's geopolitical future, the various scenarios that might emerge and the conditions for stability.

Horimoto's chapter 'Power Transition in Asia' focuses on the *status quo* states like the US, Japan and Australia, and revisionist states like China. The author says upfront that China, with its growth in power, has been inclined to question Asian power structures and has asserted that Indian Ocean cannot be just limited to India. This change in Chinese influence is propelled by its rise in power and economic growth. He further cautions that China's rise may not be peaceful and will test the US presence in the Western Pacific. Horimoto indicates that China views US engagement with India and Japan through the "containment of China" prism. He further elaborates that Japan has reasons to be anxious about US commitment given the latter's shift of focus to building a strategic relationship with China and its desire to operationalise the New Model of Major Power Relations (NMMPR).

Wesley's 'Restless Giants: Asia's New Geopolitics' highlights the importance of the maritime dimension and the emergence of Indo-Pacific as an important strategic realm in the heart of Eurasia, which, to the author, has given rise to two contradictory trends: economic interdependence and rising strategic rivalry. Wesley argues that China and India's exponential growth curves have led to changes in self-perception with a desire for greater prestige and status. He further indicated that China's rise has resulted in strategic rivalry in Asia, with tightening partnerships between Japan and South Korea, Japan and India, and an increase in the purchase of maritime naval systems in Asia. According to Wesley a new age of maritime economic dependence and maritime strategic competition has emerged in Asia in which instead of choke points and ports, three peninsulas and three bays will assume significance; namely, the Indo-Pacific, West Pacific, the South Asian peninsulas, and the Arabian, Bay of Bengal and South China Sea bays.

II. Military Trends in Asia

While Asia has seen a growth of regional institutions yet, Asian countries' military expenditures tell a tale of escalating security competition and the recent claims in South China Sea suggest that regional mechanisms don't necessarily lower the temperature. China's military budget accounts for nearly half of all the military spending in the region. Japan, on the other hand, has increased its defence spending, partly as a reality check to China and partly as a response to US defence cuts. Many of the US allies in Asia under US protection will have to accept more risks and boost their military capabilities. How will the Asian countries military modernisation impact the region? What are the perceived external threats and how is it impacting the military doctrines? What implications does the military expenditure have on future force structure and strategic posturing? The four well argued chapters in this section make for very interesting reading.

Fumio Ota, chapter, 'China's Military Expansion and Asian States' Reaction' scans the Chinese strategy from Deng Xiaoping "Hide our capabilities and bide our time" to Hu Jintao's "Active participation and acting on will." He points out that the Chinese military budget since 1989, as compared to Japan, has increased by 33 times. Ota makes the point of Chinese assertiveness by showing various incidences involving China and other nations from the South China Sea to the Western Pacific including the passing of Chinese naval ships and aircraft through Japanese territorial waters and airspace. He underlines the fact that Chinese assertiveness is bringing about a reaction from other nations who are also building up their maritime capabilities.

The following chapter by Andrew Scobell and Cortez Cooper 'What's Driving Asian Aircraft Carrier Programmes? The Case of China', describes the modernisation and expansion of navies and coast guards in Asia as an arms race. While touching on India's commitment to a three aircraft carrier force and the possibility of converting the new Japanese helicopter carrier to be able to operate short take off and vertical landing aircraft, the authors examine in detail the three drivers behind the Chinese aircraft carrier programme—bureaucratic push by the PLAN, prestige driven by nationalism and strategic planning. Scobell and Cooper, state that while the first two drivers had important roles, it is the third driver that is giving great impetus to the China's carrier programme. The authors express that the genesis of the programme are based on strategic thought process, growing economic might, protection of sea lines of communication (SLOC) and the view of US being a threat. All this according to the authors indicate that the Chinese are thinking beyond the Taiwan Straits scenario.

Nguyen Hung Son chapter 'Vietnam Naval Modernisation: Causes and Trends' interestingly observes that neither is Vietnam in any arms race nor is it reacting to Chinese military modernisation. The author explains that Vietnam's marine strategy 2020 sets out three broad strategic directions that looked at turning Vietnam into a strong marine country, integrate marine based economic development with national defence and explore all resources for social economic development accounting for 55 per cent of the nation's gross domestic product (GDP)—thus a need for a secure maritime environment and therefore the modernisation drive. Hung Son explains that as the acquisitions were taking place at the time of heightened tensions in the South China Sea, it was seen as if Vietnam was participating in an arms race and reacting to China. Hung Son concludes that Vietnam's naval modernisation is to achieve self reliance and build capacity to protect its maritime interest while staying non-aligned.

Prakash Menon's chapter 'India's Military: Modernising not Militarising', observes that militaries in a democracy plan and prepare for war based on guidance from the political leadership and resources made available. However, in the absence of such guidance mainly due to the existing civil military relations, a number of obstacles emerge between modernising and militarisation. In India's case, according to the author, modernisation was oft seen as militarisation. Menon examines the issue of civilian control and the misunderstandings on the issue that impinge on the arena of security. He highlights that the creation of CDS or Permanent Chairman Chief of Staff Committee would in a way diffuse the issue of 'too much control' in one person as it apparently was against the existing structure. This according to the author will enhance civilian control—control by politicians and not the bureaucracy. He also highlights that the Indian military had always remained subordinate to political control and therefore any notions of misadventure were misplaced. In conclusion, the author writes that though the character of civil military relations was changing there was a requirement for structural change.

III. Economic Global Shift Toward Asia

The world's economic centre of gravity has shifted to Asia with the rapid economic development seen in China, India and other Asian countries along with the economic problems experienced in Europe and the US. Urbanisation will be a key trend of the rapidly growing economies in Asia. The global economic shift is bringing forth opportunities and challenges. What are the responses of key economic and political institutions in Asia, particularly in India and China? Should India follow China's example and turn its attention towards boosting domestic consumption rather than foreign trade? Questions about how the old developed economies (the West) will react and whether Asia's current economic model is sustainable quite clearly emerge. Will there be a slowing with major adjustments or a collapse? What levels of impact will the changing demography particularly the growing middle class and the aging population have on the economy? The chapters in this section examine how these changes will shape the economic and business contours in Asia?

Hu Sheshing chapter, 'Economic Shift Towards Asia: Realities and Challenges' describes the intra and inter regional trades of East Asia which, according to the author, is becoming increasingly impressive, accounting more than the half of global trade in terms of trade volume. However, Sheshing observes that the global economic shift toward Asia, with East Asia in particular, has a long way to go. Interestingly, such a process could be stopped and even be reversed. The author notes that Asia still has to address critical challenges, in terms of reforming West-led economic orders and institutions; lacking the support of financial infrastructures; lagging in innovation capacity and importantly strategic mistrust even confrontations among Asian powers. The Cold War legacies, sovereignty disputes, regional power tussles, etc. have persistently disturbed the efforts of regional economic institutional cooperation, especially between China and India, among China, Japan and South Korea.

Rajat Kathuria, et al in their chapter, 'India and China: Benefits of Co-opetition' discuss the benefits of integration of the two economies of India and China, who have the capacity to change the dynamics of trade and investment in the region. The authors point out that as a part of the BRIC's conglomerate, both India and China are seen as leading the global economic revival but also very firmly argue that the possibility of peace through trade cannot materialize without considering security issues. The authors reaffirm that the strategic geo-political location of both India and China inevitably has consequences for the way trade and investment arrangements in the Asian region are developed. In 2012, India had the largest trade deficit with China of USD 39.41 billion. From an economic point of view, this isn't surprising. Trade balance is not a bilateral issue but a regional or global one especially when the world is coming to be dominated by global value chains and regional production networks.

Comparing India's and China's roles in the global value chains, Kristy Hsu chapter, 'India and China in Global Value Chain: Taiwanese Investors' Perspectives' expresses that the role and performance of Indian and Chinese economy in the global value chains varies significantly. While India is not counted among the highly popular investment destinations for manufacturing sector, China's manufacturing has earned a niche for itself in the global market and has succeeded in increasing its exports of higher value added products and services. Hsu analyses that relocation of Taiwanese firms towards Southeast Asia and China in post-1980 period was driven by scarcity of natural resources and escalating land and labour costs. Also given the political situation, the dependence on China is not merely an economic issue, but a national security issue. Hsu interestingly writes that India, for the Taiwanese investors, was perceived as an extension to the Southeast Asian region. The chapter through illustrations and figures describes that the Taiwanese perspective on Indian vs. Chinese economy was done with reference to nature of goods produced; raw materials or basic, intermediate and advanced goods, geographical location of projects, tariff barriers, etc.

IV. Resource Stress in Asia

One of Asia's major concerns centres on resource security. Food, energy, water and climate are intricately linked and further impacted by price, availability and quality. Population growth, urbanisation, and industrialisation are exacerbating resource-related stresses. Asia includes about 56 per cent of world's population and depends on 31 per cent of arable land and by 2030 the continent will have 5 billion people. Understanding the resource dynamics is useful to the political economy particularly as competition for natural resources among Asian nations intensifies. Will it bring the continent to a dangerous crossroads of dependence, geopolitical tension and environmental degradation? What trade-offs and at what appropriate scale (regional, national, sub-national) will be required to ease resource pressure? Is the framing of resource policies particularly complementary to rights-based development approaches? The four chapters in this section convincingly argue the resource complexity in Asia.

In his chapter 'Energy Security Challenges under Limited Resource Pressure in Asia' Tamaela Wattimena argues that due to the increasing economic and population growth, energy demand has grown exponentially. He underscores four objectives, namely the four A's—availability, accessibility, affordability and acceptability in situating the challenges in energy security. Each challenge complicates securing energy for Asia: stress on 'availability' results from uneven resource distribution across Asia despite being rich in resources, while stress on 'accessibility' results from the lack of energy infrastructure and investment connecting the supply lines to the demand centres. In the third A, i.e., 'Affordability', the author articulated that the need to control the price of energy resources led some countries to use subsidies resulting in higher demand for energy. Finally, 'acceptability', in his argument showed that renewable energy resources does not have high acceptance in the community as it affects population displacement, public interests, and governance issues. Wattimena suggests reforming domestic energy policies, developing third generation of bio-fuel resources and increasing regional cooperation to alleviate these concerns.

Yashika Singh and Shamika Joshi's chapter 'India's Resource Economy: Possible Choices and Probable Outcomes', describe India's policy approach to develop and utilise its resources. India's economy, according to the authors, is set to become more resource intensive over the next two decades as the composition and nature of India's GDP growth changes. Apart from the possible investment push, India's large and young population will continue to provide the impetus to consumption-led growth, the patterns of which will change as well. The authors draw on China as a comparison arguing that China had the level of GDP per capita comparable to that of India today when it started to sharply steepen its resource intensity curve. As China has adapted to this movement up the resource curve, it also had to adapt to issues of resource security, sustainability, environmental conservation, etc. India may well have to traverse similar paths, and the mining industry in India as much as the country as a whole will need to build capacity to handle these changed paradigms. According to the authors, policy, technology and management will need to intersect at an opportune point to deliver the most propitious outcome.

Mukul Sanwal chapter, 'Why Water Politics Matter?' emphasises the need to define the context in which the issue of water resource and scarcity is framed. The author conceptualises the emerging trend of urbanisation and the use of resources to facilitate it. Compared to the West, Sanwal argues that China has been relatively efficient in resource management given the trends of high use of natural resources linked to urbanisation. He makes a firm point that China has become a global power through its economic influence, not by its military projection. Therefore, the use and distribution of natural resources are important than framing it as scarcity. He underscored that South Asian and Southeast Asian countries rely on pre and post-monsoon instead of glacier melt from the Tibetan plateau, suggesting more scientific studies on glaciers in Asia and on building trust based rules and norms, as water is a transboundary issue.

Huang Ying chapter 'Urbanisation and Water Security in China' describes the challenges faced by China in securing water for its urban population and arguing that the shortage of quality water is the main problem. Huang analyses China's policy to tackle water challenges and identifies five categories: quality drinking water, fighting floods, food security, safe supply of fresh water, and safeguarding eco-systems. While illustrating such measures, the author gives insight into the implications in each of these policies. She also briefly describes the inadequacies of the water diversion projects against the rising water consumption in urban China. Efforts at desalination of seawater, according to the author, have gained importance in managing water resources in China though it is cost intensive. The measures to control water pollution and preventing industries moving into residential areas have moved industries from coastal areas to the hinterland. Huang suggests that China needs to play more active role in bilateral and regional cooperation in international rivers, information sharing, and move to develop domestic legal framework for protection of international rivers.

V. Ocean Governance in the Indo-Pacific

With the economic power shift to Asia, the Indo-Pacific region is fast becoming the centre of trade, investment and cooperation. The region contains close to half the world's population and provides several of the world's most important choke-points for global commerce including the Strait of Malacca. Clearly the region is recognised for its economic dynamism and geo-strategic importance. Many inter-state disputes are maritime in nature, both due to the many unsettled maritime boundaries as a consequence of the enactment of UNCLOS, and the tendency towards unrestrained exploitation of maritime resources with little regard for territorial jurisdictions. A legal framework and multilateral agreements are critical in managing communal global resources such as the high seas but fear of regional hegemony is likely to hinder support for the establishment of ocean governance, particularly among the weaker countries. The legal obligations, impact of institutional arrangements and strengthening governance over maritime resources are some of the critical questions that the three chapters in this section attempt to answer.

Anup Singh, in his chapter, 'Time to Discipline the Sea Lawyers' provides a useful overview of the evolution of norms of ocean governance, or international principles governing the maritime domain. In recent history, increased harvesting of fish and exploration of minerals led in early twentieth century to further revision in maritime thinking. The author describes the 1982 UNCLOS as one of the greatest UN Treaty or Convention, a total package including codification of all the principles concerning the maritime domain, i.e., territorial sea, contiguous zone, EEZ, etc. The author further discusses some maritime disputes predating UNCLOS like Cod Wars (England/Iceland), problems in Indonesian Archipelago waters, competing claims over the Senkaku/Diaoyou islands, and also disputes in South China Sea. He also briefly covered the case of Air Defence Identification Zone (ADIZ)-overlaps in the East China Sea. In conclusion the author writes that maritime issues can be addressed through mutual understanding and cooperation, but arguing that UNCLOS-IV will be difficult in view of the disputes about the convention itself. The author finally suggests a route through the United Nations Open-ended Informal Consultative Process on Oceans and the Law of the Sea in order to bring all UNCLOS members and stakeholders to evolve norms to deal with outstanding issues.

You Ji chapter "Meeting the Challenge of Maritime Disorder in the Indo-Pacific", attempts to clarify some of the misconceptions about the Chinese perspective. The author argues that it is important to lay emphasis on crisis prevention and crisis management rather than on conflict resolution. Focusing on the controversy surrounding nine-dotted line, which outlines the Chinese claims in the South China Sea, You Ji argues that the line was claimed by China way back in 1947. Hence, the line is 35 years older than UNCLOS. The author goes back into history and argues that United Nations Convention on the Law of the Sea (UNCLOS) could not be applied to deal with a problem which was 35 years older than it. According to You Ji, in 1992, in the United Nation General Assembly (UNGA), Jiang Zemin met Suharto to restore bilateral relationship. In the dialogue, Suharto raised the issue of nine-dotted line encroaching on Indonesian Exclusive Economic Zone (EEZ). Jiang Zemin clarified that the line applied only to the islands and the adjacent waters surrounding the islands. In 1993, China in its diplomatic notes to Indonesia explained its position on the nine-dotted line, hence the line, according to You Ji, does not cover all the waters, as it is being mistakenly held.

Lan-Anh T Nguyen chapter 'Quest for Effective Ocean Management in South China Sea' takes a counter perspective to You Ji's views, arguing that that South China Sea (SCS) is a sea of resources as well as a sea of disputes. She informs in her chapter that according to the US Energy Information Administration (EIA) estimates, SCS has higher potential than Europe as far as hydrocarbon reserves are concerned. Moreover, SCS has vast fishing potential as well. It is also one of the busiest maritime routes in the region. Therefore, the disputes in the region need to be addressed by the countries in the region. Lan-Anh further argues that China's declaration on nine-dash/dotted line in 1947 did not legitimize the Chinese claim. Vietnam also had similar claims in 1914. She argues forcefully that China had not made its stance on nine-dotted line clear enough which has created numerous problems. The author argues for UNCLOS as a legal basis to govern state behaviour to ensure international peace and that the waters claimed made by China in South China Sea lie within the continental shelf of Vietnam. The author stresses on the importance for China to participate meaningfully in the discussions in multilateral arrangements like Regional Cooperation Agreement on Combating Piracy and Armed Robbery against Ships in Asia (ReCAAP), Information Fusion Centre (IFC), Indian Ocean Naval Symposium and Western Pacific Naval Symposium.

VI. Assessing Risks: Cyber and Critical Infrastructure

In today's interconnected world, states share risks and vulnerabilities. Some of the biggest security challenges will come from the cyber space. Singapore and Indonesia have already taken steps towards setting up cyber commands. As cyber-attacks and hacktivism increase, challenges to information sharing will mount. Against this backdrop, how then will governments and policing bodies cooperate on law enforcement and sharing information? Policies towards preventions, precautions and preparedness plans will be critical.

In their chapter 'Risks and Resilience: International Approaches to Critical

Infrastructure' Tim Legrand and and Saskia Hufnagel explore the changing nature of 'threats' to the state and the new strategies pursued by governments towards increased informal modes of cooperation and collaboration with international and private sector partners to offset these threats. The authors argue that Governments around the world are confronted by a growing dilemma. While finance, manufacturing, food supply, energy and communications sectors, are increasingly internationalised (and digitised) in pursuit of greater efficiency gains, these processes often operate beyond the control of domestic governments. As a result, governments face a diminishing capacity to address emerging threats from organised crime, terrorism, turbulent financial markets, cyberspace, natural disasters, and so on. The authors draw on two sectors in particular: first, the use of international and Australian military and law enforcement networks to detect risks, destroy terrorist and criminal enterprise and respond to crisis; second, using the UK as a case study, the nascent efforts to tackle cyber-crime and cyber-terrorism by transferring risk into the private sector.

The lens shifts to civil-military cooperation and how 'calling out the troops' to combat emergencies occurs in countries. Simon Bronitt and Ashutosh Misra chapter, 'Use of Lethal Force and Military Aid to Civil Powers in India and Australia: Sharing Lessons in Counter Terrorism', focus on issues related to the use of emergency powers to combat terrorism and insurgencies through legal and constitutional frameworks such as those authorising the domestic deployment of the military in aid of civil power, and legislation authorising the military to use lethal force against hijacked planes pre-emptively to counter attacks similar to 9/11. They analyse how modern democracies like India and Australia could combat internal security challenges effectively, while remaining compliant with the relevant international treaties and conventions, constitutional and domestic laws relating to human rights, as well as fundamental liberal ideals related to the Rule of Law and separation of powers. According to the authors, the time is right for moving away from discourse of human rights and international law to comparative law. The moot question is how can modern democracies combat internal security challenges while remaining compliant with human rights and other laws within respective countries.

SECTION I

ASIA'S GEOPOLITICAL FUTURE

1

Power Transition in Asia

Takenori Horimoto

Introduction

There is little doubt that power transition is taking place in contemporary Asia where the leading actors are the U.S. and China, to say the least of Japan, Korea, ASEAN countries and India which are closely involved. The basic challenge confronting Asia is how to cope with the rapidly emerging and assertive China. All are compelled to delve into China's strategic behaviour to find suitable counter measures.

At the moment it is difficult to foresee exactly how the transition shall proceed. However, for Asian countries, such a transition should have a stable evolution without causing much trouble and tension. To achieve such a transition, how much the countries concerned need to invest to work out a feasible strategy? Probably, this aspect is the most crucial problem that Asia faces today. The main thrust of this essay is an examination of China's strategic objectives and how to cope with them.

How Power Transition in Asia is Taking Place

Probably no one would object to the argument that the world is witnessing a power transition. It might be designated as a transmutation of the geopolitical world map. One must bear in mind two points. First, at present, three power centres exist in the world in terms of economic and military power: the U.S.,

Europe (EU), and Asia. The shift is rapidly gaining momentum in favour of Asia. Second, emerging Asia shows a self-evident phenomenon of power transition in itself. If one were to apply a yardstick of status-quo powers and revisionist powers to the contemporary Asian scene, Japan and Australia, and the U.S. might be regarded among the former with the rapidly emerging powers of China and to some degree India for now, among the latter. Southeast Asian countries remain rather opaque if one were to try to specify a category to which they belong.

Regarding China as a revisionist power, one must then ascertain whether China is moving to a revisionist policy orientation or not. According to Ronald L. Tammen and Jacek Kugler, when a challenger has over eighty per cent of the capabilities of a dominant nation, it moves to challenge.[1] If China is the challenger and US, the dominant power in Asia, the application of the eighty per cent benchmark to the case of the US and China in terms of GDP and defence expenditure would suggest that China remains incapable of challenging the US at the moment, as the chart shows. The GDP and defence expenditure are more or less objective indicators that might be used to approximately measure the national power of any nation.

GDP and Defence Expenditure of Major Powers in Asia

	U.S.	*China*	*Japan*	*India*
GDP of 2012 (trillion US$*)	16.24	8.23	5.96	1.82
Defence Expenditure in 2012 (billion US$**)	682.0	166.0	59.3	46.1

*GDP (current US$)

Source: The World Bank (http://data.worldbank.org/indicator/NY.GDP.MKTP.CD)

**Military Expenditure (US$)

Source: The SIPRI Military Expenditure Database

http://www.sipri.org/research/armaments/milex/milex_database/milexdata1988-2012v2.xsls/view

However, as Joseph Nye points out, one must make a clear distinction between "power as resources" and "power as a behavioural outcome."[2] He explains, "For example, when people speak of the rising power of China or India, they tend to point to the large populations and increased economic or military resources of those countries. However, whether the capacity that those resources imply can actually be converted into preferred outcomes will depend upon the contexts and the country's skill in converting resources into strategies that will produce preferred outcomes."[3]

China's Emergence as a Predominant Power in Asia

Historic Preponderance of China

The central issue is whether China nurses an intention of aiming at power as a behavioural outcome. The answer might be positively judged by its historic development.

China has an extremely long history of more than two thousand years. It is an important cradle of great civilisations. As Stephen P. Cohen remarked, India is only one of two modern states—China being the other—that embodies distinct civilisations.[4] During its history, China has invariably been the centre in East Asia and Southeast Asia in terms of political and economic power along with its superior culture and civilisation. China's preponderance has produced its unique perception of Sinocentrism, particularly in the field of culture, which has tended to regard Chinese culture as superior to any culture and neighbouring countries as more or less its offshoots.

However, modern China has been subjugated to foreign domination by European countries and Japan. China's response to such domination has fostered indignation among the Chinese people and a tremendous upsurge against imperialism.

The Communist Party has been successful in throwing off foreign powers to create a new nation. In the past half-century China has established itself and strove to regain its lost glory as a superior country in Asia while getting its revenge against the rivals of its recent history. China conducted 2010 Beijing Olympic Games demonstrating its successful achievements in the various fields. The Olympic Games signified 'as the affirmation of a single nationalistic dream' which was soon followed by another major event, such as the Expo 2010 Shanghai China. And finally, China's GDP has surpassed Japan's GDP in 2010, making it the world's second largest economy after the U.S.

As a matter of fact, Xi Jinping recently held up the Chinese dream as achieving the "Two 100s": The material goals of China becomes a "moderately well-off society" by about 2020, the 100th anniversary of the Chinese Communist Party, and the goal of modernisation of China to a fully developed nation by about 2049, the 100th anniversary of the People's Republic.[5]

Consequently, briefly reviewing China's history, it is now no wonder that Chinese people tend to harbour a historic perception that China is a great nation and a predominant power. China might quite naturally seek to establish a preponderant position in the region. A popular proverb in China is that two tigers are not necessary on one mountain. Therefore, it would be more than natural that China aspires to establish a hierarchical power structure: first in Asia and then in the remainder of the world.[6]

Of course, China claims that its rise is peaceful. When one looks back the world history, one will see no instance to confirm the peaceful rise of hegemonic powers. History always shows us any emerging hegemonic power that tries to enrich its country, invigorate its political ambitions and exalt its prestige, then invest its wealth into expansion of military capabilities for power projections and finally has an eye on its supremacy in the region to which it belongs.

China's Implementation of its Preponderance

Moreover, the circumstances are favourable now against the backdrop of the gradual decay of the U.S. in term of national power (combination of economic and military power). Incorporating this situation into their strategic calculus, China has been pursuing its expansionist policy in Asia. At the moment, the main thrust is the western Pacific region, specifically into the East China Sea and the South China Sea.

To achieve their policy, China has first started to challenge Japan's interests: its claim to sovereignty over the Senkaku Islands—China has never claimed them until the early 1970s—by its declaration of an Air Defence Identification Zone that includes the Senkakus, its campaign against the perceived revival of Japanese militarism and historical revisionism under the Abe Government,[7] the periodic reiteration of its historical grievances against atrocities inflicted on China by Japan during the war years, and its persistent protests of Japanese leaders' visits to the Yasukuni Shrine.

Kanwal Sibal, former Foreign Secretary of India's Ministry of External Affairs has pointed out that these activities "are all part of a strategy to browbeat Japan, obstruct its resurgence as that will pose a challenge to the Asian hegemony that China seeks."[8] Beyond that, the activities are useful to test the U.S.-Japan relationship by making it appear that Abe is politically adventurous and that his policies can disturb the U.S.-China equilibrium in the making. The actual target of Chinese muscle-flexing is the American forward presence in the western Pacific because that prevents China from wielding untrammelled power in its neighbourhood and it constrains China's naval ambitions. China needs a strong navy to protect the sea lines of communication of its far-flung energy and trade interests.[9]

Hedging in the Indo-Pacific

US vs China and the Indian Ocean

In short, present power transition in Asia is taking place particularly in the western pacific. The protagonists are the U.S. and Japan as defenders as the status-quo powers and China as the revisionist power. Although China might not yet rival the U.S. in terms of national power, it appears to practice power as a behavioural outcome. A case in point would be its military activism during the past two decades to change the status quo unilaterally by force in the East China Sea and the South China Sea. China has been implementing various policies: The PLAN's expansion, the Island Chain strategy in the Pacific, and the String of Pearls operation.

The U.S. has been trying to cope with the assertive China. Its strategy is Rebalancing to Asia—initially a so-called Pivot to Asia. As a more concrete policy, the U.S. has propounded the Indo-Pacific idea with U.S. Secretary of State Hillary Clinton.[10] Her colleague, Secretary of Defense Panetta, announced in June 2012 that 60 per cent of U.S. naval forces would be deployed in the Pacific by 2020.

At a glance, it would appear that the Indian Ocean is not directly related to the ongoing tussle between the U.S. and China over supremacy in the Asian region, particularly in the western Pacific. However, the U.S. has shown tremendous interest in the Indian Ocean. Clinton noted, "The United States has a substantial interest in the stability of the Indian Ocean region as a whole, which will play an ever more important role in the global economy. The Indian Ocean provides vital sea lines of communication that are needed for global commerce, international energy security, and regional stability. Ensuring open access to the Indian Ocean will require a more integrated approach to the region across military and civilian organisations."[11]

Probably behind the U.S.' strategic calculus, its imperative is to widen its China front as wide as possible, for which India constitutes an extremely important component. The inclusion of the Indian Ocean in the front signifies the inclusion of India: the predominant power in the Indian Ocean.

India looks rather ambivalent towards the U.S. new strategic initiative of India-Pacific with accompaniment of both positive and negative effects. The initiative might help India to expand its influence in the East Asia and the Western Pacific and at the same time to counterbalance the China's string of pearls operation in the Indian Ocean whereas India's comparative predominance in the Indian Ocean might tend to be somehow diluted.

Quadrilateral Framework

At the moment, a tussle in Asia is apparently underway between the U.S., Japan, Australia, and, to a certain extent India and the Southeast Asian countries, and China. The U.S. and other countries are fundamentally implementing a so-called quadrilateral (quad) approach of combinations of the U.S., Japan, Australia, and India,[12] coping with emerging China, particularly in the Indo-Pacific region.

Since 2005 onward, a move was underway to construct a quad framework among the U.S., Japan, Australia, and possibly India. At the Sydney APEC Summit in September 2007, the heads of the U.S., Japan and Australia held a summit meeting for the first time. An Indian newspaper, the *Economic Times*, reported it by quoting the Japanese press secretary's statement that India has been asked to participate in such a meeting as a country with similar concerns of democracy and freedom.[13]

The quad approach died a natural death, especially after the exit of Prime Minister Shinzo Abe and Australian Prime Minister John Howard, in addition to fierce criticism from China. However, it remains alive in the form of bilateral arrangements as a part of a hedging policy. They are the Indo-U.S. defence agreement (June 2005), India-Australian defence MOU (March 2006) and the Joint Declaration of Security Cooperation (January 2009).

The Japan-India Joint Declaration on Security Cooperation (October 2008) was also released during Prime Minister Singh's visit to Japan. This was only the third such agreement that Japan has ever made, following those with the U.S. and Australia. Japan's Prime Minister Aso and Manmohan Singh emphasised that security cooperation should not target a third country. Dr. Singh clarified that the Indo-Japan economic partnership and security cooperation 'are not at the cost of any third country, least of all China'. There are allied relationships between the U.S. and Japan and the U.S. and Australia.

Although the quad process was put on the back burner, 'Japan's alliance with the U.S. and its new security ties, no matter how loose, with Australia and India sends the signal of a new security order in the region.[14]

The four countries regard the U.S. as a country that is a *sine qua non* to cope with China. The U.S., Japan and Australia are willing to revive the quad approach in the present Asian international situation. However, India is wary of such a joint front. The 2012 report, *Nonalignment 2.0* points out that "If China perceives India as irrevocably committed to an anti-China containment ring, it may end up adopting overtly hostile and negative policies towards India, rather than making an effort to keep India on a more independent path."[15] Perhaps a trilateral framework is apparently a maximum option for the involvement of India. The India-Japan-United States trilateral dialogue at the level of director-generals of ministries of foreign relations and defence started in December 2011 in Washington. Naturally China has shown its cautious response to the dialogue.[16] The fifth meeting was held in November 2013 in Tokyo. It looks that India plays a dexterous role between its relations with China and Russia through the BRICS summit and SCO and also its close cooperation with the U.S. and Japan in the India-Pacific Ocean.

In the strategic calculus of Asian countries including Japan, the U.S. could be designated as an indispensable ally to a greater or lesser degree. The U.S. has an intention to be a part of multilateral formations, as advocated clearly by a cable of May 5, 2006 from the U.S. Embassy in New Delhi to its home office.[17] Fundamentally, it is only barely possible to maintain an Asian balance of power without the U.S., as ex-Minister mentor of Singapore, Lee Kuan Yew, pointed out.[18]

At the moment, it is only the U.S. with which China engages seriously. A major Chinese policy orientation is *yǎng huì tāo guāng* (to maintain a low profile and to bide the time), which is only applicable to the U.S.[19] Put another way, China would not confront the U.S. directly.[20]

Shortly after the Second World War the U.S. has been the sole superpower with its GDP accounting roughly half of the whole world. Now the share of the U.S. has come down to about twenty per cent. In spite of its decline, U.S. maintains forty per cent of the world's total military spending. Naturally, such discrepancy produces financial bankruptcy in U.S.

It would be quite certain the military capabilities of the U.S. would be reduced at any time soon. The U.S. is facing the financial over-expansion and the imperial overstretch. Under such development, the U.S. has no alternative but to switch to offshore balancing[21] withdrawing from the Asian region as a sole regional order guarantor. I would not be surprised by the scenario that the U.S. accommodates the regional supremacy of China in its place. On November 20, 2013, National Security Advisor, Susan Rice remarked *"When it comes to China, we seek to operationalise a new model of major power relations."*[22] I would like to hastily add that the concept of *Asian Concert* propounded by Hugh White[23] tends to be too accommodative for China and not easily accepted by the Asian countries as a whole. Therefore, it might be the last moment now to utilise U.S. presence in Asia for creating the desired regional framework.

Importance of ASEAN Countries

Under the engagement and hedging policy orientation, one must bear in mind how ASEAN countries would be involved. The countries have shown their anxiety over China in terms of security and economy. For them, the U.S. annual defence cut from $ 600 billion, to $ 500 billion in the coming decade has presented the largest headache in the area of security for these nations.[24]

Additionally, ASEAN countries have been anxious about the omnipresence of China's goods and people in their respective countries, with the fear that their economies would be engulfed into the Chinese economy. Such concerns have come to constitute an important apprehension for Singapore and Brunei (both original signatories) and Malaysia and Vietnam (both under negotiations to join) as candidate countries of the Trans-Pacific Partnership (TPP) framework. These four countries face China's large and burgeoning economic might, although economic interactions with China present an inescapable reality.

Moreover, ASEAN countries such as Vietnam, Malaysia, Brunei, and the Philippines are facing standoffs with China over various disputes in the South China Sea. Those include not only the maritime boundaries and the territorial claims of the Spratly Islands and the Paracel Islands but also fishing zones, the potential exploitation of crude oil and natural gas and the strategic control of important shipping lanes.

Engagement and Mechanisms

However, a hedging policy that tends to produce China's counter-measures is expected to result in a more confrontational atmosphere in Asia. Military preparedness and formation of security in various countries might be only one way to cope with the present situation particularly vis-à-vis China. The present tit-for-tat mode is apt to cause an arms race in the region, with brinksmanship particularly on the high seas. In fact, that is occurring to a larger degree today.

Additionally, one must bear in mind the internal policy processes of China, which is governed by three major organs: the Communist Party, the PLAN, and the government. Among the triad, there might be moderates and hardliners. A hedging policy would tend to give much ammunition for the latter to pursue harder policies without giving space to take moderate policy orientations for the former. Even if such a distinction between moderates and hardliners were not existent in China and were simply an illusion or a wishful thinking, to pursue only a hard line policy would not produce a suitable space for mutual accommodations resulting in a chicken race. It would merely render an excellent excuse for a more steamroller-like policy orientation for China.

Regional Mechanisms

Therefore, two-fold orientation must be pursued simultaneously: hedging and engagement. A hedging-only policy would be antagonistic; engagement alone would yield only elusive results. By combining these two policies, one might expect an effective and sustainable situation in Asia. This policy framework of engagement and hedging should be pursued in a multilateral fashion. In such a framework, the basic concept should not be exclusive but inclusive and China must be included. Therefore, any strategic cooperation among Asian countries should be so oriented as to create an Asian environment in which any country would find it difficult to become a hegemon and would instead accept cooperation in support of a regional framework.

At present, multilateral and regional mechanisms exist in Asia. In the South Asian and the Indian Ocean regions, there are Bay of Bengal Initiative for Multi-Sectoral Technical and Economic Cooperation (BIMSTEC), the Indian Ocean Rim Association for Regional Co-operation (IOR-ARC), and the Indian Ocean Navy Symposium (IONS) aside from SAARC. Their basic characteristics are inclusive. We can expect that these organisations can develop into more full-fledged mechanisms.

The Southeast Asian region has many regional groupings such as the Association of Southeast Asian Nations (ASEAN), the ASEAN Regional Forum (ARF), and the East Asia Summit (EAS). The EAS is more or less moribund. Except for the Six-Party Talks (North Korean Nuclear Weapons Program), none of the above entity functions in finding a peaceful solution to security concerns.

Whatever organisations and associations exist, ways and means must be found to operationalise them for more solid and effective mechanisms in support of Asian stability and peace. This quest for countermeasures is particularly underway in the Western Pacific, where the concerned Southeast Asian countries and China are confronting each other, and also in the East China Sea. The western pacific has been transformed into the main stage of concern and rivalry between the U.S. (Rebalancing Asia policy[25]) and Japan (under the active defence policy under the Abe government), and China which are respectively metamorphosing from being land powers into nations with land and sea power in the past two decades.[26] The western pacific, and to a certain degree, the Indian Ocean, have become the main stages of naval activity in the world now that the pirate-infested Arabian Sea has gradually faded from popular attention.

United Nations Security Council

Upgrading existing regional mechanisms to create a new regional mechanism for stable and peaceful world would be difficult. But these must be explored even though it might require a hard process. An even more difficult pursuit would be the reform of the United Nations; in this reform, the main agenda should be to transform the Security Council into a more representative organ for which the inclusion of BRICS countries, particularly India, would be indispensable along with Japan, this is so because the centre of the world is gradually moving to Asia, and so they must get duly represented.

Conclusion

As Kondapalli and Mifune point out, "Asian vicissitudes to a large extent are dependent on how China evolves its relations with its neighbours—in mutually beneficial interdependence or ending and costly conflicts."[27]

When one country grows stronger, its relationships with other countries tend to evolve imperceptibly, reflecting their relative power shift. Such tendency allows a new order to emerge, absorbing an emerging country's ambition without conscious efforts of adjustments and concessions with concerned countries. Perhaps the world is undergoing such a transformation without a clear image of the outcome. This view could be neatly applicable to Asia as a whole.

In this regard, Indian Prime Minister Manmohan Singh's remarks are worth bearing in mind. He told the Japanese media on November 14, 2012, "*Japan and India have to work with China to ensure that the peaceful rise of China takes place in a manner which will be conducive to Asian security, Asian prosperity.*"[28]

Asia is gradually becoming the centre of the world. The crucial issue could be how we manage a stable transition in this region. Probably a policy of hedging and engagement are necessary for our times. Major countries such as Japan, India, South Korea, Russia, Australia, in addition to the United States and China have their respective compulsions and basic ethos to manage the present transition, particularly in the so-called Indo-Pacific Ocean region. Nevertheless, a stable and peaceful transition must be made.

Probably we are watching a power transition or geopolitical alteration in Asia. E.H. Carr argued in his classic *The Twenty Years' Crisis* that when there exists a gap between the distribution of position, prestige and leadership and actual distribution of power amongst major nations, we are urged to find a suitable answer.

NOTES

1. Ronald L. Tammen and Jacek Kugler, "Power Transition and China-US Conflicts," *The Chinese Journal of International Politics*, Summer 2006, athttp://cjip.oxfordjournals.org/content/1/1/35.full. More concretely, they argue that the conditions for parity are met when a challenger has more than 80 per cent of the capabilities of the dominant nation and that they cease when the challenger has exceeded the dominant nation's capability by 20 per cent—when it becomes the dominant nation. Previous research strongly suggests that the period of greatest danger is when the challenger manages to overtake the dominant nation and traverses the region between 100 per cent and 120 per cent.
2. Joseph S. Nye, *The Future of Power*, New York, Public Affairs, 2011, pp. 9-10.
3. Ibid.
4. Stephen P. Cohen, *India Emerging Power*, Brookings, Washington, DC, The Brookings Institution, 2001, p. 9.
5. "Xi Jinping's Chinese Dream," *The New York Times,* June 4, 2013. According to Kuhn, the Chinese Dream has four parts: Strong China (economically, politically, diplomatically, scientifically, militarily); Civilised China (equity and fairness, rich culture, high morals); Harmonious China (amity among social class); Beautiful China (healthy environment, low pollution).
6. An Indian expert on China interviewed in New Delhi on September 6, 2011 (Name not disclosed).

7. Hiroshi Hirabayashi, "China's anti-Japan campaign," *PacNet* #12 Thursday, January 30, 2014
8. Kanwal Sibal, "It is cherry blossom time in India-Japan relations," *Hindustan Times*, January 22, 2014.
9. Ibid.
10. Hillary Clinton, "America's," *The Foreign Policy*, October 11, 2011. She stated that the future of politics will be decided in Asia, not in Afghanistan or Iraq, and that the United States will be right at the center of the action.
11. Ibid.
12. Takenori Horimoto, "Strategic Convergence of Japan-India Relations and China's Emergence," in Lalima Varma (ed.), *India-Japan Relations in Emerging Asia,* New delhi, Manohar, 2013, p.60.
13. *The Economic Times*, September 7, 2007.
14. Purnendra Jain, 'Tokyo's Nexus with India Deepens', *Online Asia Times*, October 25, 2008.
15. Sunil Khilnai et al., *NONALIGNMENT 2.0, New Delhi:* Centre for Policy Research, 2012, p.14.
16. According to the *ZEE news* of December 20, 2011, "China on Tuesday reacted cautiously to the first-ever India-US-Japan meeting, hoping that the talks involving the three countries with "great influence" in the Asia-Pacific will be conducive to regional peace and stability", at http://zeenews.india.com/news/world/china-cautious-over-first-india-us-japan-meeting_747897.html
17. The cable pointed out that the stars aligned for closer trilateral relations among the U.S., Japan, and India. *The Hindu*, April 23, 2010.
18. *The Asahi Shimbun*, May 11, 2010.
19. Interview of Prof. Wang Jisi (王緝思) of Peking University *Asahi Shimbun*, October 2, 2012. *yang huì tâo guâng* has been advocated by Deng Xiaoping.
20. Seiichiro Takagi, *"What China seeking under the new type of major power relations," Toa,* January 2014 (in Japanese).
21. Christopher Layne, "The (Almost) Triumph of Offshore Balancing," *The National Interest,* January 27, 2012. Layne points out "But, American "exceptionalism" notwithstanging, the United States is not exempt from the historical pattern of great-power decline. The country needs to adjust to the world of 2025 when China will be the number-one economy and spending more on defense than any other nation."
22. Suzan E. Rice, "America's Future in Asia (Remarks As Prepared for Delivery by National Security Advisor Susan E. Rice) at Georgetown University on November 20, 2013, at http://www.whitehouse.gov/the-press-office/2013/11/21/remarks-prepared-delivery-national-security-advisor-susan-e-rice (Accessed January 14, 2014).
23. Hugh While, *The China Choice,* Black Inc, Place of Publication, 2012.
24. 'Asian Anxiety', *The New York Times,* October 25, 2011.
25. U.S. global policy has shifted from *War on Terror* to *Counter to China.*
26. Takenori Horimoto, 'Major Country of South Asia and Japan', in Nishihara and Horimoto, eds., *India as a Rising Military Power,* Askishobo, 2010 (in Japanese), pp. 22-32.
27. Srikant Kondapalli and Emi Mifune, "Introduction," in Srikant Kondapalli and Emi Mifune ed., *China and its Neighbours,* New Delhi, Pentagon Press, 2010, p. xiii.
28. His trip was cancelled because of the dissolution of Japan's parliament on November 16, 2013.

2

Restless Giants: Asia's New Geopolitics

Michael Wesley

Introduction

Every generation believes it is living through the most dangerous and turbulent decade in history. Variations on that phrase occur with striking regularity in the defence planning documents of Australia and many other countries, stretching back to before the Second World War. In what has become a process of inter-generational gloom rivalry, the conceptions of risk and turbulence of competing eras are compared and debated over—and ultimately left unresolved. The whole process, it strikes me, is rather pointless. All eras are beset by turbulence, uncertainty and risk. Whether one era is more uncertain, turbulent or risky than another is largely irrelevant—in each era it is the job of defence planners to assess risks and uncertainty as best they can, and assign responses and resources as best they can to address them. In the absence of an ability to apportion defence resources through time, each generation is obliged to use what resources it has to best offset risk and uncertainty in the present and foreseeable future.

Surely a more useful form of temporal comparison should be to ask: what is distinctive about the era we are entering? What are the new drivers of turbulence, uncertainty and change? How do these new factors challenge our strategic environment, and how best can we use our defence resources to respond to these? Of course, these questions give rise to different debates about how new the changes actually are, and how challenging they are to the established order. But even these debates can generate productive avenues of thought and discussion for defence planning.

I contend that, in the current period—the first quarter of the twenty-first century—is being shaped by two vectors of turbulence: the rapid enrichment and empowerment of Asia's largest societies, and the rapid advance and spread of communication technologies. The future of both of these vectors is attended by significant uncertainties: in trajectory, dynamics and consequences. But there is mounting evidence that each of these is generating new upside and downside risks for defence planners. While there are undoubtedly connections between both vectors, I will focus on the first and its impact on Asia's emerging geopolitics.

Wealth, Power and Turbulence

There are two predominant and opposed narratives concerning the rapid enrichment and empowerment of Asia's largest societies. One is that all will be well and that, by mid-century, Asia will be a prosperous and peaceful continent; the other is that wealth and power will lead to competition and war, both hot and cold.[1] But there are strong signs that the actual consequences of rapid empowerment and enrichment in Asia will be much more complex. There are three compelling reasons why I believe that wealth and power changes in Asia will cause turbulence, but not necessarily lead to sustained conflict.

First, the overwhelming weight of history shows that economic growth is not secular, if by secular one means that growth can occur without affecting a society's perceptions and beliefs. Wealth and power are two fundamental locators of a state's roles and rights in international relations; those with more wealth and power invariably have a more expansive sense of their rights and prerogatives—and often of the moral rectitude of their actions—than those with less. History shows that larger societies tend to be more moralistic in their interpretations of international affairs: wealth and power require a sense of moral rectitude, both in order to be amassed and used, and to justify the actions of the wealthy and powerful. Smaller and poorer societies of necessity view international affairs more pragmatically and, more often than not, do not share the virtuous self-perceptions of powerful and wealthy states.

Hence, sudden shifts in wealth or power cannot but alter the self-perceptions, expectations and beliefs of societies. The recent histories of colonialism and domination—along with the deeply hierarchic logics of their social relations and worldviews—in many Asian societies means that relatively sudden adjustments in wealth and power will acquire great significance in terms of rights, prerogatives and perceptions of justice. Asia's two largest societies each have a long tradition of looking at international affairs through a moralistic lens; it would be odd indeed if their sudden rise has not been interpreted in terms of virtue and prerogatives.

Secondly, Asia's economic growth has brought a rapid expansion in the external dependence and vulnerabilities of its societies. Industrialisation and urbanisation have created a massive demand for energy, raw materials and consumer markets for rapidly growing economies. Between 1990 and 2007, China's oil consumption tripled, and India's increased by over two-and-a-quarter times. The International Energy Agency estimates that, by 2030, China's energy thirst will have doubled again, and India's will have grown by two-and-a-half times. A second form of economic interdependence overlays the first, flowing from Asia's enthusiastic participation in an increasingly sophisticated system of distributed manufacturing, or global production sharing. Research shows that in no other region has global production sharing advanced so far as in East Asia—to the extent that between 70 per cent and 80 per cent of the growth in manufacturing in East and Southeast Asia has come from global production sharing. This makes the manufacturing sector in East and Southeast Asia—the rapidly expanding heart of these economies —highly vulnerable to disruptions in the supply chain in other countries.

One recent study found that the March 2011 Fukushima disaster in Japan, which cut Japanese automobile production by 47.7 per cent and electrical component production by 8.25 per cent, also caused a 19.7 per cent drop in Thai auto manufacturing, a 24 per cent drop in auto manufacturing in the Philippines, and a 6 per cent drop in Indonesian auto manufacturing; it also affected the electrical sectors in the Philippines by 17.5 per cent and Malaysia by 8.4 per cent.[2]

Thirdly, rapid wealth and power increases in Asia's largest societies have raised the prospect of one or more of them contemplating regional dominance. Previously, during the second half of the last century, no Asian power was large or wealthy enough to realistically dominate all others, or to challenge American power in the Pacific. Asia's giants were poor and internally weak while Asia's wealthy countries were small and geographically isolated. Japan, a wealthy country of relatively large population size, could not contemplate regional dominance because of its controversial recent history and the unwillingness of its own population to support a vigorous foreign policy.

Now, China appears increasingly able to both dominate its region and challenge American power in the Pacific. This is a prospect that has stimulated a number of different reactions among its neighbours. In strategic affairs, it does not matter whether a country actually contemplates dominance: what matters is that other countries consider its size and strength enough to make its bid for dominance viable. Surrounding China is a series of second-tier powers that are either its long-term rivals, or have current disputes with Beijing, or both. These include countries like Japan, Vietnam, Indonesia, India and perhaps Russia.[3] Acquiescing to China's regional dominance would be unacceptable in terms of hard interests as well as prestige and self-respect. As a result, these powers have been reaching out to each other and to the USA, building economic and security partnerships to offset China's rise. The rise and increased security activism of these second-tier powers has in itself alarmed a series of third-tier powers that have, traditionally, had difficult relationships with the second-tier powers. Some of these countries are reaching out to China to help offset their worrying neighbours: Cambodia and Thailand in Southeast Asia, Pakistan and Sri Lanka in South Asia.

Consequently, the neat set of reinforcing trade, investment and security dynamics that once existed around the Pacific Rim has been superseded by a growing bifurcation between the security interests of states and their economic connectivities. Globalisation and the dynamics of manufacturing investment have re-established China as the East and Southeast Asia's economic hinterland. The closeness of this integration can be seen in the rest of the region's close tracking of China's economic fortunes during the global financial crisis. Consequently, China has become a major trading partner of regional economies: currently 6 of APEC's 21 members have China as their major trading partner, another five have China in their top 3, and a further 4 in their top 5. More and more of China's neighbours are gaining a greater interest in China's economic, social and political performance and cohesion.

However, growing economic integration has not led to a growing trust of China—in fact, it is quite the opposite. Most of China's significant neighbours have been establishing strategic connections with each other, and with the USA as a way of hedging against China's growing power, while at the same time deepening their economic linkages with the Chinese economy.

The result is an escalating rivalry between the interdependent states of the Indo-Pacific. And, this condition seems to be self-accelerating: interdependence leads to growing wealth, which leads to expanding expectations, which leads to growing rivalry. The stakes involved in such deep and complex interdependence mean that the rivalry cannot be brought to a head in a physical contest of arms that could jeopardise economic enrichment. At the same time, the rivalry and lack of trust among regional countries means that economic interdependence cannot drive the sort of political integration that has led to the creation of what Robert Cooper called 'post-modern states' in Europe.[4]

Psychology of Interdependence

In purely structural terms, these three changes have resulted in three developments in Asia's strategic and economic geography. The first is the emergence of an Indo-Pacific economic and strategic realm. The consolidation of British dominance over the Indian subcontinent in the mid-nineteenth century had the effect of dividing the Indian Ocean from the Pacific as strategic realms. Britain's Indian

Empire was dominant from the Suez Canal to the Malacca Strait; but beyond the Malacca Strait the Pacific was vigorously and continuously contested. No local or outside power was able to establish dominance in Pacific Asia. The result was almost continuous warfare between 1842 and 1975, rivalries and alignments along Asia's eastern coast, a string of anchoring American post-war alliances along the western Pacific coast, and the eventual integration of insular and peninsula East Asia into a virtuous trade and investment cycle that produced the astonishing growth rates of the original Asian economic miracle.

A combination of factors—the energy thirst of the Asian giants, the emergence of regional great power rivalry, the regionalisation of supply and production networks, overlaid by the sudden collapse of European and American consumption in 2008—has begun to link the Indian ocean and Pacific ocean into a single Indo-Pacific economic and strategic domain. The trade figures alone tell the story. East Asia's trade with South and West Asia grew by six-and-a-half times between 1990 and 2007. Intra-Asian trade grew by 240 per cent in the 1990s, and by 280 per cent in the following decade. This means that for North Asia's industrial giants, the Straits of Hormuz have become as crucial to their stability and viability as the Straits of Malacca. The Indo-Pacific has become not only a source of enrichment, but also a realm of vulnerability for Asia's jostling giants.

The second development in Asia's strategic-economic geography is the opening of a pronounced geographic separation between Asia's centres of consumption and Asia's centres of production—particularly in minerals and energy. Asia's industrialising and urbanising giants represent the greatest growth trajectory in the demand for energy and minerals in the world today, and it will probably continue to be so in the foreseeable future. It is a demand growth that is both insatiable and structural—meaning that if the demand is not met with dependable supplies at sustainable costs, it will threaten social, economic and political cohesion in Asia's rapidly industrialising societies. This is particularly so with regard to energy. There is only one source of sustainable supply in the world that can hope to meet the demand: West Asia's hydrocarbon reserves. For many West Asian producers, the security of demand provided by East and South Asia's energy thirst is as structurally compelling, for without the continued robust demand for energy and reliable flows of export dollars, the stability of their own mostly autocratic societies would also be threatened.

The third development in Asia's strategic-economic geography is the development of a region-wide manufacturing system, and the rapid end to the prospects of autarchic industrialisation—where all or most elements of manufacturing and consumption occur within a single national economy. With regional and global manufacturing becoming ever more footloose, this has made considerations of comparative advantage among countries and companies more fleeting and more fraught. China and several Southeast Asian countries have become increasingly worried about being caught in the 'middle income trap', where their cost of labour rises but the local manufacturing sector is unable to innovate up the value chain.[5]

While both processes have undoubtedly led to rapid increases in power and wealth as well as the modernisation of Asian economies, they have also been disconcerting for some. This has been so particularly for countries with histories of self-sufficiency, import-substitution, and autarkic policy settings. The sudden and irreversible expansion of their economic dependence on the outside world has led to increasing anxiety, particularly as the global economy seems to be gripped by periodic instability with increasing frequency. The combination of a sense of increasing vulnerability to flows and supplies located outside the country's borders, growing strategic rivalries, and competition touched off by China's ascent have led to a growing sense of strategic claustrophobia, especially among Asia's larger powers. This strategic claustrophobia manifests itself in the growing anxiety that rivals will play out their strategic designs by manipulating vulnerabilities and dependencies; and that the only way to counter this is to position one's own country to be able to manipulate the vulnerabilities of its rivals.

Claustrophobia and Rivalry

The arrival of an era of rivalrous interdependence has led to some distinct changes in the Indo-Pacific's strategic dynamics. The first can be termed the 'normalisation' of Asian security. On gaining independence, most Asian countries inherited colonial boundaries that included a great deal of diversity and rivalry; and many also soon acquired communist insurgencies. The result was ethnic and political instability, and a consequent preoccupation with domestic security in a way that crowded out serious external security preparation or competition.

Over the past decade, security spending in the Indo-Pacific has shifted decisively in favour of external security. While few of those countries which, in the past, have been preoccupied with internal security would admit that their domestic concerns have been completely resolved, their shift in favour of external security reflects intensified strategic competition in the region. Thus, despite its internal security budget being larger than its military budget, China's arms spending continues to grow strongly.

The growing strategic rivalry across the Indo-Pacific can be read from basic arms acquisition statistics. In 2012, SIPRI reported that the period from 2007-2011 saw a 200 per cent higher volume of arms transfers into Southeast Asia than there had been between 2002 and 2006. This volume of imports was the highest since the end of the Vietnam War. Naval weapons formed the bulk of these purchases, with ships and maritime weapons accounting for 52 per cent of the total, and another 37 per cent accounting for weapons with a possible maritime role. SIPRI reports that a similar level and profile is evident in weapons acquisition intentions also.[6]

As a result, Asian countries on the whole are becoming more able to prosecute their own external security interests and, as the ability grows, willingness follows closely. The Indo-Pacific is becoming a more militarised realm, with a greater number of consequential security actors. The options for both rivalries and coalitions have expanded, as have the chances of conflict occurring among militaries whose capabilities exceed their doctrine or maturity.

Another change appears to be developing in strategic doctrine. The growing rivalries and capabilities in the region have coincided with a wariness about direct confrontation and escalation, particularly of the sort that could disrupt the lucrative interdependences of the region. A result of this reluctance has been a growing awareness of the options for 'horizontal escalation'—that is, responding to confrontation in one location by threatening to exploit a rival's vulnerabilities in another location. So, for example, a USA unwilling to risk a direct naval confrontation with China in the Taiwan Strait could threaten to shut down the Strait of Hormuz to China-bound oil tankers. Or China, in order to build pressure on Japan over the Diaoyus/Senkakus, could start harassing Japanese ships in the South China Sea. Or India, under pressure from China on their mutual land border, could threaten to squeeze off access through the Andaman Sea to Chinese ships. Looked at from this perspective, the sudden flaring up of maritime territorial disputes looks much less like being driven by localised demands and rivalries, and much more about strategic positioning for the evolving rivalries across the Indo-Pacific.

Geography and Strategy

In the context of an increasingly contested Indo-Pacific domain, the particular geographic features of Asia's southern and eastern coasts begin to take on particular strategic significance. At the heart of manipulable dependence lies Asia's east-west energy trade: the disruption of no other commodity or supply could wreak such widespread damage as that of hydrocarbons. The physical properties of these energy commodities means that the bulk of them must be transported along a concentrated and non-redundant sea route—from the Gulf, through the Indian Ocean, the Straits of Malacca, and the South and East China Seas.

As the weapons acquisition statistics in Southeast Asia attest, the sea along this singular corridor has become a symbol of vulnerability and opportunity for Asia's jostling powers. As C.E. Calwell notes, the coast always exists as a potential frontier between belligerent states, with the scale and timing of the threat rarely being able to be anticipated or planned for.[7] Calwell has particularly noted the strategic advantages and disadvantages presented to maritime powers by two particular geographic features: peninsulas and bays. He argues that peninsulas, by definition, lack strategic depth; they are the very opposite of a land-based salient into enemy territory.

> The salient land frontier does not necessarily place troops within the salient at a strategical disadvantage; because they may be in a position to strike; and there are two different directions in which they can strike. But an army in a salient girt by the sea cannot from the nature of the case strike if the enemy has command of the sea...[8]

Bays, on the other hand, offer a completely different set of advantages.

> As, in time of war, the frontier of that nation which enjoys the maritime control is the coast line of the enemy, it follows that when the coast line takes the shape of a giant gulf or bay, the army of the power dominating the sea can strike either to the left hand or to the right, while the adversary is compelled to divide his forces.[9]

With these observations in mind, it is necessary to suggest another way of thinking about Asia's geopolitics than the control of the sea lines of communication or choke points. The threat to close a particular choke point has two disadvantages: it offers, at best, a short term strategic advantage. Moreover, it is likely to be undiscriminating—inconveniencing rivals and allies at the same time. One must also keep in mind Sir Julian Corbett's observation that 'the most common situation in naval war is that neither side has the command [of the sea]; that the normal position is not a commanded sea, but an uncommanded one.'[10] Particularly in a situation with several rising rivalrous naval powers, it is more likely that they will try to strive for enduring political and strategic preponderance over key geographic features of maritime Asia, and to forestall the preponderance of their rivals.

From this perspective, there are six alluring possibilities for preponderance that offer themselves to Asia's jostling powers. Conveniently, these divide into three bays and three peninsulas. The three Bays are the Arabian Sea, the Bay of Bengal, and the South China Sea. The geography of the bays interacts with power as well as the strategic imagination of rising powers in peculiar ways: bays are enclosed bodies of water that engage the territorial imagination. One can imagine 'owning' a bay much more easily than one can imagine 'owning' a sea or an ocean. Maritime Asia's three Bays are historical trade hubs, with abundant historical—and therefore contemporary civilisational—overlays. Before European conquest, Asia's maritime trade route was neatly divided into three 'circuits', each with a different pattern of monsoonal trade winds. The South China Sea circuit was dominated by Chinese traders; the Bay of Bengal by Indian traders; and the

Arabian Sea by Arabs.[11] It is not hard to see why these bodies of water might so engage the romantic and strategic imagination of these peoples. Each of these Bays is subject to territorial disputes and expansive great power sovereignty claims. Each is bordered by one big and several smaller claimants, with the USA as the anxious guarantor of the maritime commons in the background. Each Bay is attended by complex politics and strategy around its egress and ingress points: does the control of a Bay confer or negate control of a choke point? Does the control of a choke point confer or negate the control of a Bay?

The three peninsulas are the South Asian Peninsula, the Indo-Pacific Peninsula, and the West Pacific Peninsula. Peninsular geography also interacts with power and the strategic imagination in peculiar ways: it constrains, concentrates, funnels and bundles power. Strategic shifts in one part of a peninsula are likely to cascade through to its other parts. Peninsulas tend to be strategically stable if dominated by a single set of strategic interests; but once a contrary strategic interest gains hold, they become extremely unstable. Two of the Indo-Pacific's peninsulas—the South Asian and West Pacific peninsulas—hold the key to India's and China's strategic claustrophobia. Each is held in full or part by rival entities; each contains parts of India's and China's historic sense of wholeness; each is a site of the strategic footholds of major rivals. For China to gain control of the West Pacific Peninsula, or for India to become supreme on the South Asian Peninsula, would represent major advances in their regional and global power capabilities. The Indo-Pacific Peninsula—running from northern Thailand through the Malay Peninsula and the Indonesian archipelago to northern Australia—is just as crucial. Here, the land divide between the Indian and Pacific Oceans is a vital frontier between American power and Indian and Chinese ambitions. Any one, or combination, of powers that gain supremacy over the Indo-Pacific Peninsula would hold the key to the broader Indo-Pacific.

The Indo-Pacific chessboard is larger and more complex than the Pacific: its stakes are higher, and the consequences of miscalculation are enormous. The USA is the only power capable of exercising dominance across the Indo-Pacific realm, a state of affairs that necessarily provokes countervailing action on the part of China. China and the other powers only have the capacity to assert dominance over parts of the Indo-Pacific: for instance, China in the South China Sea, and India in the Bay of Bengal. These two great rivals realise that their mutual vulnerability achieves a potentially stabilising rough balance; however, how their naval strategy fits in with that of the USA introduces significant uncertainty.

Conclusions

Three Peninsulas, three Bays—to find a Mackinderian formula, *the Peninsulas hold the key to the Bays; the Bays hold the keys to the Peninsulas*. So, for example, the further expansion of Chinese influence down the Indo-Pacific Peninsula will further split ASEAN solidarity, allowing the continuing advance of Beijing's claims in the South China Sea. Creeping Chinese control over the South China Sea brings it closer to its goals in the West Pacific Peninsula—what the Chinese strategists call the First Island Chain—including by ramping up the pressure on territorial disputes with Japan in the East China Sea. If India is able to draw Pakistan, Bangladesh and Sri Lanka into its own growth dynamic and thereby neutralise them as strategic concerns, it can build influence in the Arabian Sea and Bay of Bengal. India's growing presence in the Bay of Bengal and into the Malacca Straits can act as a counter to Chinese control over the Indo-Pacific Peninsula—and even into the South China Sea. China's ability to establish a permanent presence in the Arabian Sea—perhaps at Gwadar—will decisively counter India's position in the South Asian Peninsula and the Arabian Sea.

Arguably, this geopolitical perspective on Asia's future raises more questions than it answers. Many of these developments are nascent. Big unknowns abound. To what extent will the USA be able to maintain maritime supremacy against the naval build-ups of so many southern tier states? What are China's and India's abilities to build geopolitical influence on the Peninsulas while establishing supremacy over the Bays? To what extent will peninsular and littoral states forge a strategic common purpose? Or be divided and dominated by their giant neighbours?

For the countries of the Indo-Pacific, there are some clear implications. First and foremost, we must get used to the fact that we are an integral part of the Indo-Pacific realm, and cannot escape the escalating competition for it. Secondly, we must stop thinking tactically and start thinking strategically about the region. Instead of priority relationships as the foundation of our foreign and defence policies, we need to think in terms of three bays and three peninsulas. The outcome in each will have profound implications for us, and we need to think hard about all possible permutations. Thirdly, neither multilateralism nor bilateralism will provide a way forward. The great powers will—and already are—using the region's institutions as instruments in their rivalry. Staking our future on Asia's institutions being able to mitigate this scale of rivalry will be a mistake. Neither will cultivating good bilateral relations with the major powers be enough. Instead, we need to find a flexible, plurilateral approach to the region, in which we place an equal or even greater emphasis on building common cause and understanding with countries closer to our own size.

Be it in the Bays or the Peninsulas, it is the choices of medium sized and small states that will hold the key. These are a natural caucus group when the great powers are locked in an escalating rivalry. In particular, the roles of the peninsular swing states—Japan and Indonesia—will be crucial. Much depends on their choices among the escalating rivalries which, in turn, will be shaped by their strategic visions for the peninsulas and bays. One thing is certain: the Asian Century will almost certainly not be benign for Asia if we continue to be strategically naïve about how rapid economic growth affects security dynamics. But by thinking geopolitically about Asia as a whole—Indo-Pacific power highway, with its bays and peninsulas—we can survive and prosper in the Asian century.

NOTES

1. An example of the panglossian school is the Australian government's 2012 White Paper, 'Australia in the Asian Century'; of the Hobbesian school is Aaron L. Friedberg, 'The Geopolitics of Strategic Asia, 2000-2020' in Ashley J. Tellis, Andrew Marble and Travis Tanner (eds.), *Strategic Asia 2010-2011: Asia's Rising Power and America's Continued Purpose*, Seattle: NBR, 2010.
2. Linghe Ye and Masato Abe, 'The Impacts of Natural Disasters on Global Supply Chains', ARTNeT Working Paper Series No. 115, Bangkok: UNESCAP, June 2012
3. On the complex and ambiguous Sino-Russian relationship, see Bobo Lo, *Axis of Convenience: Moscow, Beijing and the New Geopolitics*, London: Chatham House, 2008.
4. Robert Cooper, *The Breaking of Nations: Order and Chaos in the Twenty-First Century*, London: Grove, 2003.
5. Shekhar Aiyar, Romain Duval, Damien Puy, Yiqun Wu, and Longmei Zhang, 'Growth Slowdowns and the Middle-Income Trap', IMF Working Paper, WP/13/71, Washington D.C.: IMF, March 2013.
6. Siemon T. Wezeman, 'The Maritime Dimension of Arms Transfers to South East Asia, 207-11' in *SIPRI Yearbook 2012: Armaments, Disarmament and International Security*, Oxford: Oxford University Press, 2012.
7. C.E. Calwell, *Military Operations and Maritime Preponderance: Their Relations and Interdependence*, Edinburgh: William Blackwood and Sons, 1905, p. 264.
8. Ibid., p. 266.
9. Ibid., pp. 266-7.
10. Julian S. Corbett, *Some Principles of Maritime Strategy*, Annapolis: Naval Institute Press, 1988 [1911], p. 91.
11. Janet L. Abu-Lughod, *Before European Hegemony: The World System AD 1250-1350*, NY: Oxford University Press, 1989, p. 252.

SECTION II

Military Trends in Asia

3

Chinese Military Expansion and Asian States' Reaction

Fumio Ota

Introduction

Even though there are transnational threats in Asia such as cyber-attacks and the proliferation of Weapons of Mass Destruction (WMD), most of these transnational threats are supported by states like North Korea, Russia and China in Asia. The chapter will describe China's expanding strategy, its assertiveness and territorial claims.

North Korea

DPRK does not possess enough resources to acquire a large number of modern weapons. Therefore, they have concentrated on special areas in order to conduct asymmetric warfare such as, long-range artillery, ballistic missiles, special forces, cyber-attack capabilities and weapons of mass destruction especially nuclear weapons.

DPRK has been developing various ballistic missiles from short to very long range. Scuds were developed to target the ROK and U.S. forces on the Korean peninsula. Rodong was developed to target Japan. Taepodong 1 was tested in August 1998. However, this missile has not been mass-produced and was likely only a step in the development of the much longer range missile, Teopodong 2. The missile, which can reach the continental U.S., was tested in July 2006, August

2009, April 2012 and December 2012. Musudan was probably developed to target the U.S. Strategic Bomber bases in Guam. Finally, KN-08 is a new probable Inter-Continental Ballistic Missile (ICBM) that appeared in the military parade in April 2012. One notable aspect of the KN-08 is the transportable erector launchers (TEL) that were exported from China. As mentioned at the beginning, most transnational threats such as proliferation in Asia are supported by states themselves.

One of military trends for ballistic missiles is that they are developing solid propellant. Liquid fuelled ballistic missile launch preparations are easily detected by satellite because its launch requires hours of preparation, so DPRK is seeking a more ready solid propellant. Iran succeeded with a solid propellant medium range ballistic missile test in November 2008. Due to strong military technology relationship between Iran and DPRK, it is only a matter of time until DPRK possesses solid propellant ballistic missiles. In order to prepare to defend against those ballistic missile threats, Tokyo has constructed Ballistic Missile Defenses composed of AEGIS ships and Patriot-III missile systems. According to the latest National Defense Program Guidelines, Japan Maritime Self Defense Force (JMSDF) will be increasing AEGIS destroyer's order of battle from six to eight. Updated AEGIS destroyers are capable of shooting down those ballistic missiles. The Republic of Korean (ROK) Navy also has AEGIS destroyers.

DPRK has developed nuclear weapons that they intend to modify for installation into ballistic missile warheads and have reactivated 50kw nuclear plant in 2013 to produce additional nuclear material.

Special Forces are largest in the world and are estimated to number about 200,000. DPRK possess various vehicles used by Special Forces such as mini-submarines which attacked ROK Navy corvette *Cheonan*, disguised fishing boats containing water scooters, semi-submersible boats, hover craft, An-2 aircraft and Mi-17 helicopters. Since Jang Sung-taek, who had strong connections with China, was executed in December 2013, it will be expected to have a much stronger autonomous military policy.

Russia

Since the demise of the Soviet Union, Russian military activities have been at a very low level. However after the turn of this century, Russian military activities were revitalised because of her financial improvements. From 2003 to 2012, Russian Defense Budgets increased 5.12 times which is even greater than China's increase of 3.51 times.[1] Since the beginning of 21st century, Russia conducted many exercises/training and real missions, especially joint exercises simulating various types of conflicts.

As for military units, two *Mistral*-class amphibious assault ships constructed by France will be operational in the Pacific Fleet very soon. Japanese concern is whether or not *Borey*-class SSBN will be stationed in the Pacific Fleet. If that is realised, the associated protection capabilities such as air, surface and subsurface defense, will also be revitalised because one of wartime fleet's missions is area defense of SSBN operating areas.[2]

Due to the demographic problems of a shrinking Russian population since the demise of the Soviet Union and due to Russian economy which does not rely on modern industries and has a GDP synchronised to the price of oil, Russia will not be a major threat in foreseeable future.

China

Expanding Strategy

Since the Tiananmen Square incident in 1989, Chinese Military strategy was based on the Deng Xiaoping twenty four character phrase 'Hide our capabilities and bide our time'. However since that year, Chinese annual defense budgets have increased at double digits rates up till today. There are also many hidden defense expenditures. For example, defense research and development outlays are included in the education and science budget, weapon production and purchase is counted in the national foundation construction budget and armed police administration is included in the administrative management budget. All of the above are counted as central government finances and not included as part of the defense budget. Additionally, draft and civil military support are included in Regional Finance. Weapon purchases from abroad, such as Russian Su-27/30 as well as *Kilo*-class submarines and *Sovremenny*-class destroyers are included in the Foreign Foundation budget, and military products like food are not listed as part of military budgets.[3]

Therefore, Chinese military buildup is at an exceptional pace. According to the *Military Balance 2012/2013* issued by the International Institute for Strategic Studies (IISS), People's Liberation Army (PLA) Air Force created ten fourth generation fighter squadrons during 2011-2012. This is the same as the entire Japanese Air Self Defense (JASDF) fourth generation fighter squadrons. The Chinese built 16 new submarines during 2001 to 2005, which is the number of submarines in the current Japan Maritime Self Defense Force (JMSDF) order of battle. The subsequent five year period saw the Chinese increase their building rate and they produced 22 submarines between 2006 and 2010. The number equals the total number the JMSDF is planning to build up to according to the latest National Defense Program guidelines.

In July 2009, then-General Secretary of the Communist Party of China, Hu

Jintao added 'Active participation and acting at will' to Deng's 'Hide our capabilities and bide our time' at the eleventh overseas mission conference.

Although Chinese Maritime strategy had been "coastal defense" since the PLA Navy was established in 1982; Admiral Liu Huaqing, the then-PLA Navy commander with strong support from Deng Xiaoping, shifted the strategy to Offshore Defense. In 1992, China defined almost all of South and East China Sea as their territorial waters by the Law on the Territorial Sea and the Contiguous Zone. In April 2009, Hu Jintao declared in a speech at the 60th anniversary of the PLA Navy that offshore defense should shift to Far Seas Defense.

At a strategic level, it appears that China always fills the power vacuum created by a retreating super power. While the U.S. was retreating from Vietnam, China advanced to the Paracel Islands in 1974. Following the reduction in Soviet Navy ships in Vietnam's Cam Ranh Bay starting in 1984, China advanced into the west side of the Spratly Islands from 1987 to 1988. After the 1991 U.S. withdrawal from Clark Air Force Base and Subic Naval Base in the Philippines, China advanced into the eastern side of the Spratly Islands and occupied Philippines-claimed Mischief Reef in 1994. From these precedents, it should be expected that China will invade the Senkaku Islands if the U.S. retreats from Okinawa.

The tactical pattern for China's maritime territorial encroachment is as follows. First, China declares territorial rights. The example is the Law of the People's Republic of China in its Territorial Sea and the Contiguous Zone of 1992 in which China claimed the Senkaku Islands as her territory. Second, China usually conducts maritime surveillance in the area where she declared her territorial rights. Third, China makes its presence known by dispatching naval forces/combatants. As a final step, China makes its final *de facto* occupation. While China has followed this pattern in the South China Sea, it has also advanced till the third step in the East China Sea.

That Chinese strategy is derived from *Sun Tzu*, namely '*Army may be likened to water, for just as flowing water avoids the heights and hastens to lowlands.*' in Chapter VI (Weaknesses and Strengths). Therefore, we have to create strong hedges against Chinese expansion.

In 2003, the Chinese Communist Party Central Committee and the Central Military Commission endorsed the "three war-fares" concept which consisted of Legal, Psychological and Media warfares. A PLA publisher issued 100 examples each for Psychological, Media and Legal Warfares after that. The Psychological Warfare 100 examples cited Sun Tzu thirty times, the Media Warfare 100 examples cited him six times and the Legal Warfare 100 examples cited him three times. A PLA political article in December 2003, wrote "Conduct Media, Psychological, and Legal Warfare, and develop to maneuver for disintegrating an enemy force."

(Chapter 2 article 14(18)). This would indicate that one of purposes for the Three Warfares is to disintegrate an enemy force. Later, the PLA publisher issued *Disintegration Warfare* in 2010. There is a famous *Sun Tzu* phrase in Chapter ? (Offensive Strategy), "*To subdue the enemy without fighting is the acme of skill*," that appears on the cover of *Disintegration Warfare*. Those warfares are completely non-military.

Chinese Assertiveness

After the successful 2008 Beijing Olympic games, China had strong confidence and proceeded with assertive actions in the South China Sea as well as the East China Sea and even in the Sea of Japan. In October 2008, four warships including two *Sovremenny*-class destroyers imported from Russia passed through Tsugaru Strait. This was the first time Chinese warships passed through Tsugaru. In the next month, four warships, including a *Luzhou*-class destroyer, passed through the Miyako Strait. In December 2008, two Chinese State Oceanic Administration (SOA) ships invaded Japanese territorial water surrounding Senkaku islands for about ten hours. Beijing insists that Senkaku issue was triggered by Japanese nationalisation (note that was merely an ownership transfer). But this is not true. Japanese nationalisation of Senkaku happened in September 2012. In truth it was triggered by China in 1992 when Beijing announced a Territorial Sea and the Contiguous Zone Law, declaring that her territorial water not only included almost all of the South China Sea but also much of the East China Sea. This law was followed by many intrusions into the territorial waters surrounding the Senkaku islands. In March 2009, USNS *Impeccable* was harassed in the South China Sea. USNS *Victorious* was also harassed in the East China Sea two months later. In June 2009, five PLAN warships, including *Luzhou*-class destroyer, were deployed to the north of Okinotorishima. In December 2009, Vietnamese were arrested by a PLAN ship.

In March 2010, six PLAN ships including *Luzhou*-class destroyer were deployed to the Pacific. In the next month, ten PLAN warships including two *Kilo*-class submarines were deployed to the Pacific. At that time, PLAN helicopters made low flights near JMSDF *Suzunami* at a distance of 90 meters and an altitude of 30 meters. The same month, a Chinese vessel in the South China Sea chased Malaysian ships. In May 2010, a Japanese Coast Guard cutter was expelled by Chinese SOA ship. From May to June in 2010, Indonesians were arrested by Chinese paramilitary ship in the South China Sea. In June, Vietnamese were arrested near Hainan Island. In July 2010, two PLAN warships including *Luzhou*-class destroyer deployed to the Pacific. In September 2010, a Chinese fishing boat rammed into a Japanese Coast Guard cutter two times in waters near the Senkaku Islands. In this case, fortunately no one was killed. In December 2010, however, same type of incident occurred involving a ROK vessel and several Koreans were killed in that case.

After March 11, 2011 when Japanese people suffered the effects of the Great East Japan earthquake and the resultant huge Tsunami, Chinese Y-8 approached the Senkaku Islands and JASDF reacted by scrambling fighters. In the same month, China harassed Philippine gas exploration activities. In May 2011, China constructed poles near the Philippine's Palawan Island. In May and June 2011, Chinese vessels harassed Vietnamese seismic survey ships by cutting their wires. In June 2011, eleven PLAN warships were deployed to the Pacific. In August 2011, two PLAN warships entered Wonsan in North Korea. In same month, Chinese Fisheries Law Enforcement Command (FLEC) vessels invaded Japanese territorial waters surrounding the Senkakus. In November 2011, two Chinese fishing boats were observed in the Japanese territorial waters of Torishima in Nagasaki prefecture and also Chinese fishermen threatened ROK Maritime Police with axes and knifes. In the same month, six PLAN warships, including *Sovremenny*-class destroyer, deployed to the Pacific. In February 2012, a Japanese Coast Guard ship was harassed by Chinese SOA ship. In the same month, a Vietnamese ship was fired at by a Chinese warship. In May 2012, ROK fishermen were injured. In the same month, North Korea captured Chinese fishermen. From April to July 2012, China and the Philippines confronted each other over Scarborough Reef. In July 2012, the Russian Coast Guard fired on Chinese illegal fishing boats in Sea of Japan. Since September 2012, many Chinese Coast Guard ships invaded Japanese territorial waters surrounding the Senkakus. In January 2013, Chinese warships locked their fire control radars onto Japanese naval vehicles. Although it seemed that China denied that but this was just another deception. In July 2013, five PLAN warships passed through the Soya Strait (also called La Perouse Strait) for the first time. In the same month, a Y-8 approached the Senkakus. In September, two H-6 PLA Air Force bombers advanced into the Pacific and an Unmanned Aerial Vehicle approached the Senkakus. In October, all three PLAN Fleets conducted a Joint exercise beyond the First Island Chain. In December, a Chinese warship nearly collided with a U.S. Navy guided missile cruiser, USS *Cowpens* 30nm south of Hainan Island. In January 2014, China enforced the New Fishing rule inside her nine dash lines to obligate other states for reporting fishing activities in the South China Sea. This is another example of legal warfares. The U.S., Philippines, Taiwan and Vietnam strongly reacted against that. In the same month, Chinese two frigates and an amphibious ship intruded Malaysian claimed James Shoal.

It is important to remember that Beijing uses paramilitary, namely maritime militia, aggressively. When China took Paracel Islands from Vietnam in 1974, China used disguised fishing boats. In 1978, over one hundred Chinese armed fishing boats surrounded the Japanese Senkaku Islands. When the Philippines Mischief Reef was occupied by China at the beginning of 1990s, China used disguised maritime militia, saying that they needed safe refuges for fishermen. Should Japanese naval vessels attack those maritime militias, it should be expected that China will issue propaganda stating that the JMSDF killed innocent civilians. Should China invade the Japanese Senkaku Islands, she will use those maritime militias as a spearhead.

In their 1999 book *Unrestricted Warfare*, two Chinese colonels advocated the use of cross border measures such as cyber-attack,[4] but also using non-military meant including disguised fishing boats as well as merchants. For example, China reduced rare earth exports to Japan after a Chinese fishing boat rammed into Japanese Coast Guard cutters and restricted banana imports from Philippines after the Scarborough Reef incidents. In addition, the China Coast Guard unified four out of five dragons, which are former Coast Guard, Fisheries Law Enforcement Command, Marine Surveillance and Customs in March 2013. This new organisation will apparently lead the way. China plans to increase Maritime Security Forces personnel from current nine thousand to fifteen thousand by 2020. Its air arm will increase from current nine to sixteen aircraft and its surface ships from current 260 to 520.[5] Examples such as skirmish over Senkaku or Scarborough Reef, are called gray zone situation indicating to the ambiguity and that the area remains unaffected by the stagnant war and peace situation. Air assertiveness has also intensified. The number of JASDF scrambles against Chinese aircraft finally exceeded the number in reaction to Russian aircraft in the last year.

Territorial Claim

Xi Jinping told President Obama during the U.S.-China summit in June 2013 that Pacific Ocean has enough space for both U.S. and China. This was similar to when a Chinese admiral suggested to American Admiral Keating, then Commander USPACOM, that they divide the Pacific in 2007.

Everybody knows about the Chinese first and second islands chains. In 2004, the Chinese map/chart publisher traced a third island chain that included the Hawaiian Islands. The Singapore Economy dated December 1, 2012 reported that then-Secretary of State Hillary Clinton revealed China's "claim to territorial rights in Hawaii."[6] The Think Tank of the People's Liberation Army, the Academy of Military Science, issued 'Strong Military Strategy' in which noted that China should protect her national interests effectively over the sea west from 165 degree west longitude and north from 35 south latitude which includes the entire Indian Ocean. Remember, the Chinese "String of Pearls" include Gwadar in Pakistan where a Chinese company took on the port-management task in February 2013[7] and Myanmar where Beijing wants to carry energy into Chinese continent without passing through the Strait of Malacca which is controlled by western states. The background is that China became a net oil importer after 1993, the second largest oil importer exceeding Japan in 2003, and the largest oil importer in the world exceeding the U.S. in 2013.

The above facts indicates that China is an imperialistic expansionist even though they say in *China's National Defense 2012* that China will never seek hegemony or behave in a hegemonic manner.[8] There is a great inconsistency between what China said and what China has done in the past. This is clearly deceptive and in line with *Sun Tzu*'s chapter I (Planning).

The Chinese idea for their state boundary is defined by the extension of their national power and is not based on modern international law. There are major differences between Japan and China over territorial claims in the East China Sea. China insists that the Chinese Exclusive Economic Zone (EEZ) extends to the Okinawa Trough due to the location of her undersea continental shelf. The Japanese position is that the Chinese continental shelf extends to the Ryukyu Trench due to the soil survey, but there are some islands in the southeast that are Japanese territory on the Chinese continental shelf, and therefore we should draw a middle line between both side's territory. There are submerged energy resources in this contested area. The middle line concept has been used by international courts since the mid-1980s to settle similar territorial conflicts.

PLAN launched new aircraft carrier, *Liaoning*, in 2012; marking the beginning of a major transition in naval doctrine and will provide Beijing with tremendous capabilities and flexibility. A Chinese carrier could pose a serious threat to Japanese territorial integrity. Chinese aircraft carriers increase the PRC's tactical abilities and the chances of a strategic overreach. Surrounding states in the region should be worried.[9] China started the second aircraft carrier which will commission by 2018, and will possess four aircraft carriers by 2020.[10]

Currently, China is not only claiming Senkaku islands but is also saying that Okinawa's sovereignty is not solved yet in *People's Daily* as well as in *Global Times* in May 2013. The Chinese *Global Net* dated September 17, 2012 reported "According to the referendum conducted on March 4, 2006, 75 per cent of Okinawan requested the independent and free traffic with China. It stated that the remaining 25 per cent did not require independence and wanted to belong to Japan with self-governance."[11] This is completely false. There was no referendum on March 4, 2006. Due to the survey conducted by the prefecture in November and December 2012, in reverse, 89 per cent of Okinawans had an unfavorable impression of China. This is the typical Chinese disinformation or fabricated information warfare based on *Sun Tzu*'s Chapter XIII (Intelligence). The truth is that the majority of Okinawans support belongs to Japan.

As for the Senkaku Islands, Japanese Government carefully investigated whether or not any country had sovereign power over Senkaku before 1885. Tokyo found that nobody controlled the islands and were declared sovereign before the end of Sino-Japan War. Before World War II, the Senkaku Islands had a Japanese dried bonito factory where several people lived. Beijing never claimed sovereignty until 1971 right after the Economic Commission for Asia and Far East (ECAFE) in the United Nations announced the possibility of submerged energy resources near the Senkaku Islands in 1969.

Additionally, Beijing claims Okinotorishima, which is located between the first and second island chains, and is merely a rock and not an island which warrants an EEZ, so that China insists that the Japanese 200nm EEZ surrounding Okinotorishima is not authorised. However, a United Nations' committee indirectly authorised Japanese EEZ surrounding there in April 2012.[12]

Anti-Access/Area-Denial

China has increased its military buildup, especially anti-access/area-denial (A2/AD) weapons such as submarines and ballistic/cruise missiles as well as developing cyber-attack capabilities.

Submarines are invisible objects that are difficult to detect on a daily basis. Sometimes, however submarines accidentally surface because they have a fire or need to pass through international straits. I have plotted those incidents since the last ten years. In May 2003, a *Ming*-class submarine had an accident in the Yellow Sea and the entire crew was killed. Another *Ming*-class submarine passed through Strait of Osumi in November 2003. In November 2004, when I was the director of Japanese Defense Intelligence Headquarters, a *Han*-class nuclear submarine invaded Japanese territorial waters. In May 2005, another *Ming*-class submarine surfaced in the South China Sea because of a fire. In October 2006, a *Song*-class submarine surfaced near USS *Kitty Hawk* within torpedo firing range east of Okinawa. In November 2007, *Jin*-class nuclear ballistic missile submarine (SSBN) moored at Sanya in Hainan Island, where PLAN constructed an underground secret base in order to conceal operations from spy satellites. In October 2008, unknown submerged object was detected at Bungo Channel. American AEGIS destroyer, USS *John S. McCain*'s towed array sonar was hit by a submarine near Subic Bay, the Philippines, in June 2009. In April 2010, two surfaced *Kilo*-class submarines and eight surface warships passed through Miyako Strait. In October 2010, two *Shang*-class nuclear attack submarines (SSN) moored at Sanya, Hainan Island. Probably, PLA Navy deployed one of the *Shang*-class SSNs to the Indian Ocean at the beginning of 2014 for the first time.

In August 2011, *Yuan*-class new Air Independent Propulsion (AIP) submarine surfaced in the East China Sea. In May 2013, several submarines were detected near the Okinawa islands. As noted earlier, those submarines were accidentally detected and are likely to be many in number. These areas are important Japanese sea lines of communication carrying energy from Middle East.

Regarding ballistic missiles, China is targeting American carriers as well as JMSDF destroyers. Chinese ballistic missiles have been shifting from liquid fuel to solid fuel in order to improve readiness and improving their accuracy. Additionally, they are decreasing the Circular Error Probability (CEP) using Chinese GPS named *BeiDou* that will be a complete network of thirty-five satellites, for global coverage by 2020.[13] If you install the *BeiDou* terminal, however your vehicle position would be reported to the Chinese authorities.

Most Chinese Ballistic Missiles are transportable and based underground. The Chinese have been extending the range of the Short Range Ballistic Missiles named DF-15/11 that are aimed at Taiwan. In December 2013, China conducted DF-41 test firing which will reach the continental United States. Finally, China is developing a second strike capability utilising long range submarine launched ballistic missile named the JL-2 on board *Jin*-class SSBN.

The construction of the *Houbei*-class missile armed fast-attack craft also has been significant, with perhaps sixty to eighty now in commission.[14]

As for PLA Air Force (PLAAF), China has produced fourth generation fighters and is developing fifth generation fighters such as J-20 and J-31. PLAAF also obtained air refueling capabilities as well as Airborne Warning and Control System (AWACS) capability, like four KJ-2000s in order to expand their operational area.

In November 2013, Chinese Defense Department established her Air Defense Identification Zone (ADIZ) which covers Japanese territorial airspace in the Senkaku Islands as well as the disputed EEZ with Japan, disputed Socotra Rock with ROK, and overlaps the Taiwan ADIZ. China obligated to report flight plans and stated, 'it would take defensive emergency measures if aircraft did not follow its instructions'. In other words, Chinese ADIZ actually interferes with freedom of flying over the international waters. This action was probably requested by the PLA Air Force, namely General Xu Qiliang, Vice Chairman of the Central Military Commission who made many statements regarding ADIZ in the past. This is an another challenge for the current status quo. ROK responded by expanding her ADIZ to include Socotra Rock. This is another example of 'Three Warfare' which meant to establish ADIZ legally followed by media warfare in which PLA spokesman said Japan established ADIZ 44 years ago, ignoring the submitting process and the fact that the Chinese ADIZ is completely different with the international standard, and to create psychological pressures such as division of Japan and other states civil air reactions.

Cyber and Space Warfare

Sun Tzu stated "*An army avoids strength and strike weakness.*" in Chapter VI (Weaknesses and Strengths). Chinese *Unrestricted Warfare* must be based on this phrase. The western countries are heavily reliant upon information systems including computer networks and space surveillance. Therefore, Beijing wants to attack those weaknesses using cyber-attacks as a soft means and anti-satellite weapons as hard means.

According to American think-tank, Project 2049 Institute, there are 130,000 soldiers working for Signal Intelligence (SIGINT) under the PLA General Staff Department (GSD) Third Department.[15] Among those, Unit 61398 is based in Shanghai and targets the United States. It made a cyber-attack against *New York Times* in October 2012 when it reported that Wen Jiabao's relatives had tremendous financial assets in America.[16] Beijing put tremendous pressure on the New Citizen's Movement in China and on mass media, such as *Reuters*' and *Bloomberg* who were going to disclose Chinese leaders' financial assets.

During the U.S.-China Defense summit in August 2013, Chinese Minister of Defense, General Chang, baldly denied that China was a major source of pervasive global computer hacking. It has long been acknowledged that China is the greatest source of cyber war against the West.[17] This is exactly what *Sun Tzu*'s meant when he wrote, "*When active, feign inactivity.*" in Chapter I (Estimates)—same as denying locking Chinese frigate *Lianyungang*'s fire control radars onto the Japanese naval vessel, *Yuudachi*. It was reported that there were cyber-attack exchanges between China and Philippine when they confronted each other over the Scarborough Reef. I am sure if China invades the Senkakus, Beijing would use cyber attacks simultaneously. In December 2013, we found that on using Chinese software *Baidu*, all input information leaks out.

Regarding Space warfare, China established a Space Strategy, which is the integration of Air Force and Space Developments and includes both Offence and Defense. China conducted anti-satellite attacks using DF-21 in 2007/2010 and probably May 2013. According to the LIGNET, real time analysis of CIA, China launched three probable ASATs which were Chuangxin-3, Chiyan-7, and Shinjian-15 approaching each other with arms under the possible Satellite Destruction Program in July 2013. Beijing launched eleven of those ASTAs in 2012 and will launch more than 100 ASATs by the end of 2015.[18]

China has also been increasing their satellite capabilities for targeting and communications by launching large numbers of GPS and communications assets. Beijing is proceeding with manned space flight projects in a three-stage development strategy: the first, launching *Tiangong* 1 and docking *Shénzhou* 8/9/10 by 2010; the second, launching *Tiangong* 2/3 and constructing the Space

Laboratory by 2016; and the third, constructing a manned Space Station by 2020.[19] In December 2013, China's first lunar rover landed on the moon. Those technologies could be adapted to the military. For example, Intercontinental Ballistic Missiles could be improved due to high power propulsion engines development, improved missile accuracy using docking technologies and better materials created for the reentry.

Generally speaking, not only Army, Navy, Marine Corps and Air Force but also Space and Cyber should be integrated today. In that sense, warfare must be of jointmanship.

Reactions

China is the unilaterally Status Changing Power by force while other Western states are Status Quo Power.[20] Therefore, other surrounding states are counteracting Chinese military developments, especially the drastic increase in its submarine force. For example, Australia decided to possess 12 submarines by 2030 from current six, Vietnam purchased six *Kilo*-class attack submarines from Russia by 2016, Russia also has an increasing number of SSNs,[21] Taiwan wants to acquire new submarines, Malaysia acquired two submarines, Indonesia purchased three submarines from Republic of Korea (ROK), ROK intends to increase her AIP submarines from current three to nine by 2018 in addition to nine *Chang Bogo*-class, the Indian Navy planned five nuclear powered submarines by 2020 in addition to acquiring French-built *Scorpene*-class submarines with at least fifteen conventional submarines, Singapore recently acquired two AIP submarines from Sweden,[22] the U.S. Navy increased SSN stationed at Guam from three to four, Myanmar is going to build up a submarine by 2016, Thailand is planning to buy submarines in the next 10 years military build-up plan and Japan will increase to 22 submarines from current 16. Even the Philippine navy is discussing the acquisition of submarines.[23]

The U.S. Department of Defense (DOD) published its *Strategy for Operating in Cyberspace* in July 2011. Every state established or prepared the cyber command center. Tokyo created the ASEAN-Japan Ministerial policy meeting on cybersecurity cooperation in September 2013. In that sense, the warfare must be formulated in coalition and inter-agency.

Some examples of coalitions are, emerging Philippine-Australian military training agreement, a similar agreement between Singapore and India, a long-standing pact between Singapore and the Philippines, an Indonesia-Singapore submarine rescue pact,[24] and expanding Japan-Russian joint exercises decided by two plus two (Foreign and Defense Ministers) in November 2013.

The U.S. is also a Pacific nation. The U.S. Department of Defense published *Sustaining U.S. Global Leadership* which defined rebalance to Asia-Pacific followed by the *Joint Operational Access Concept* which is designed to counter A2/AD in January 2012. General Norton A. Schwartz, then-Chief Staff of Air Force, and Admiral Jonathan W. Greenert, Chief of Naval Operations, published *Air-Sea Battle* in February 2012. U.S. Army and Marine Corps published *Gaining and Maintaining Access* in March 2012. The Air-Sea Battle Office of the U.S. Department of Defense published *Air-Sea Battle* in May 2013. The U.S. deployed Littoral Combat Ships (LCS) to Singapore and a Marine Air-Ground Task Force (MAGTF) to Australia. Those forces are increasing combined exercises/training, including the Cooperation Afloat Readiness and Training (CARAT) series, with the Philippines, Australia, ROK, Japan and even India and ASEAN. They are also accessing Vietnam and Perth (Stirling Naval Base) in Australia. Those are a counteraction against Chinese military developments, especially A2/AD capability.

Japan decreased her defense budget eleven years in a row until 2012, but has increased that since 2013. In December 2013, Tokyo established a National Security Council, revised the National Defense Program Guidelines of 2010, published the first National Security Strategy, relaxing the arms export ban including ten Coast Guard cutters to the Philippines by the Official Development Assistants (ODA). Tokyo also intends to revise the guidelines for Japan-U.S. Defense Cooperation by the end of 2014, which was authorised in 1997. Prime Minister Abe processed the Proactive Contribution for Peace and legislated the Special Secrets Protection Act. He further accelerated relocation of Futenma and the U.S. Marine base in Okinawa and also revised the interpretation of the right of collective self-defense.

Last, but not least, the Indian Navy is planning a 74 per cent budget increase in 2013, due to the Look East policy, the build-up of naval facilities in the Andaman and Nicobar Islands and the newly constructed SSBN, INS *Aribant* joining the navy in 2015 with twelve short-range *Shaurya* ballistic missiles capable of carrying a nuclear warhead to a range of 435 miles, which would reach far into China.[25] In December 2013, Indian Navy and Japan Maritime Self Defense Force (JMSDF) conducted joint exercise in the Indian Ocean and followed then by Malabar that also included the US in 2014.

In conclusion, military trends in Asia are summarised by Chinese military expansion and other Asian states' reaction.

NOTES

1. Defense Of Japan 2013, Annual White Paper, Ministry of Defense, Government of Japan. http://www.mod.go.jp/e/publ/w_paper/e-book/2013/index.html#122.
2. Alexander Muraviev, "Russian Naval Power in the Pacific: Today and Tomorrow", Working Paper 15, Canberra, ACT, Australia Sea Power Center, 2003, pp. 4-5.
3. Ikuo Kayahara, *Chuugoku Gunjiyogo Jiten*, SoSo Sha, October 2006, pp. 178-179.
4. Colonel Qiao Liang and Wang Xiangsui, *Unrestricted Warfare, Import*, 2002.

5. "China to Strengthen Maritime Forces amid Disputes", in *People's Daily*, June 17, 2011.
6. "Clinton Reveals China Claim to Territorial Rights in Hawaii", *Singapore Economy*, Saturday. December 1, 2012.
7. "*Pakistan Hands Management of Strategic Gwadar Port to China", Reuters,* February 18, 2013.
8. *China's Defense White Paper, 2012. See Xinhua News Service, April 2013. http://english.chinamil.com.cn/special-reports/2013-04/17/content_5305617.htm*
9. Fumio Ota, "The Carrier of Asia-Pacific Troubles", *Wall Street Journal*, August 11, 2011.
10. *Sunday Morning Post (China)*, January 19, 2014.
11. http://mil.huanqiu.com/history/2012-09/3122927.html
12. "Tairikudana 31 man heiho kiro kakudai—Okinotorishima hoppo nado," *Yomiuri Shimbun*, April 28, 2012.
13. "The Construction of BeiDou Navigation System Steps into Important Stage", *China National Space Administration*, May 19, 2010.
14. Bernard D. Cole, *Asian Maritime Strategies*, Naval Institute Press, 2013, p. 100.
15. Mark A. Stokes, Jenny Lin and L.C. Russell Hsiao, *The Chinese People's Liberation Army Signals Intelligence and Cyber Reconnaissance Infrastructure*, Project 2049 Institute, November 11, 2011, p. 4.
16. *Sydney Morning Herald*, February 20, 2013.
17. Richard D. Fisher Jr., China's 'New Relationship' Trap, *Washington Times*, August 26, 2013, p. B4.
18. Yoshihisa Komori, 'China aims Japan by the terrible New Weapons', *THEMIS*, November 2013, pp. 50-51.
19. *People's Net*, March 4, 2011.
20. Fumio Ota, "In My View", *Naval War College Review,* Autumn 2013, 66(4), pp. 147-148.
21. "Russian Naval Developments in the Far East". Paper presented at Conference on Asian Navies, Center for Naval Analyses, Alexandria, Virginia, 9 August 2012.
22. Bernard D. Cole, *Asian Maritime Strategies*, Naval Institute Press, 2013, pp. 88, 118, 123, 127, 128, 130, 137, 138 and 203.
23. Jon Grevatt, "Philippines Eyes Submarine Acquisition by 2020," *IHS Jane's*, May 18, 2011.
24. Vivek Raghuvanshi, "India to Continue Training Singapore Troops," *Defense News*, July 12, 2012, "Philippines Ratifies Australia Military Pact," *Defense News*, July 24, 2012, and Koh Swee Lean Collin, *Indonesia-Singapore Submarine Rescue Pact*, RSIS July 24, 2012.
25. Bernard D. Cole, *Asian Maritime Strategies*, Naval Institute Press, 2013, pp.138 and 140.

4

What's Driving Asian Aircraft Carrier Programmes? The Case of China

Andrew Scobell and Cortez Cooper

Introduction

According to some respected analysts, Asia is experiencing an arms race.[1] Perhaps the liveliest arena for this alleged on-going military competition is in the maritime realm. Geoffrey Till observes that Asian '[n]avies are modernising at an unprecedented extent,' and suggests that the region may be experiencing a 'slow-motion' arms race.[2] All along the Asian littoral, countries seem to have embarked on sustained modernisation, enhancement, and even expansion of their navies and coastguards.

A significant component of this naval modernisation is an eagerness to develop indigenous aircraft carrier programmes. The decision to pursue such a programme is not to be taken lightly because it requires a massive commitment of resources and extended time horizons. Aircraft carriers are expensive complex systems that require sustained effort, substantial funding streams, and considerable technical and professional competencies. Carriers are a luxury that few countries can afford to commission. Even fewer countries have the shipyards, the engineering expertise, and associated infrastructure to build these vessels. Moreover, there is some question as to the enduring strategic and operational utility of aircraft carriers in the second decade of the 21st century. Some analysts suggest that carriers are becoming obsolete.[3]

The authors are with the RAND Corporation.

For many years aircraft carriers were the purview of the European powers and the two superpowers. The USA pioneered the construction and employment of carriers. In recent years, only a small number of other states have possessed operational carriers: Brazil, China, France, India, Italy, Russia, Thailand, the United Kingdom, and the USA.

Today, carrier expansion seems concentrated in Asia. India's navy is officially committed to a three aircraft carrier force structure.[4] And Japan, currently, has in service a helicopter carrying destroyer capable of being reconfigured to handle short take off and vertical landing aircraft. However, perhaps the greatest attention has focused on China. The entry of the People's Republic of China (PRC) to this exclusive club has played out in a slow motion series of low keyed and secretive developments over the past several decades. This sequence of events culminated in that country's first aircraft carrier sea trial in August 2011, and subsequent official commissioning of the People's Liberation Army Navy's first carrier, the *Liaoning* in September 2012. Since that date the *Liaoning* has undertaken training missions in the East China Sea and South China Sea.

This essay is a case study of China's acquisition of aircraft carriers, and the many questions that have been raised by this development. These include: What has been driving this development? What does it mean for India and the rest of Asia? What is driving this naval build up in Asia? What has triggered what one might call 'Asia's aircraft carrier arms race'?

One can conceive of the factors driving naval modernisation as being in one of five 'buckets.' The first bucket contains domestic political drivers. This is suggested by some scholars, especially those who study China's naval modernisation.[5] A second bucket of drivers contains external security dynamics. A number of scholars who have analysed naval build ups in East Asia emphasise the importance of these drivers.[6] A third bucket holds economic drivers—a thriving economy provides both the resources for naval modernisation and the logic of expanding maritime interests to justify the build up.[7] A fourth bucket of drivers contains developments in military technology.[8] A fifth bucket holds strategic and doctrinal drivers.[9] Ideally, a state would only undertake a naval build up after careful study and analysis: a strategic assessment of the security environment, national interests (including economic ones), and an examination of the grand strategic goals identified by the country's political leaders. The outcome of this analysis would then determine a state's appropriate naval strategy, available resources, the naval posture, and a weapon system adequate to implement it.

Case of China

Various explanations have been floated for the PRC's aircraft carrier programme, including that it is: (1) the result of a persistent bureaucratic push by the People's Liberation Army Navy (PLAN); (2) a prestige project driven by nationalism; and (3) the outcome of coherent strategic planning.

The earliest explanation posited for driving the People's Republic of China (PRC)'s maritime ambitions was bureaucratic interests.[10] This was initially identified with reference to the South China Sea. This has been advanced as the key driver for the aircraft carrier programme by scholars such as Ian Storey and You Ji.[11] There have long been voices within the PLAN calling for the acquisition of carriers, and the emergence of an actual carrier programme suggests the growing influence of the navy. Certainly, the maritime service has enjoyed an unprecedented rate of modernisation in recent decades. However, the dominant service in the PLA continues to be the ground force and, in comparison, the air force and navy have been very much the junior partners. Moreover, the programme's key champion appears to have been an individual rather than a bureaucracy. However, the PLAN's second rate status is changing and, since 2004, the commander of Beijing's navy has had a seat on the Central Military Commission (CMC)—the apex of military power in the PRC, and a body roughly equivalent to the US Joint Chiefs of Staff.

A second and more recent explanation is that the PRC's carrier programme is driven primarily by nationalism. This approach is perhaps most closely associated with Robert Ross.[12] Ross persuasively demonstrates that a carrier programme has strong public support. Clearly, an aircraft carrier would provide the PRC with the high profile accoutrement of great power status. A carrier demonstrates global power projection—or at least extended off-shore reach—and the possession of multiple carriers epitomizes the overwhelming naval dominance of the USA. The acquisition of aircraft carriers is considered important by a country's leaders to signal the arrival of a state to great power or superpower status. This was certainly the case with the Soviet Union, which struggled to build, and put into service, carriers modelled after those operated by the US Navy.[13]

According to Ross, Beijing's national security needs do not justify a carrier. Such a programme is extremely costly, and the necessary funds could be better spent on more pressing defence needs. In addition, Ross contends that a PRC carrier would unduly alarm neighbouring states. However, he does not allow for the possibility that there is a strategic rationale for acquiring a carrier, and Ross appears to argue that all PRC aircraft carrier proponents are rabid nationalists.[14]

A third possibility is that the carrier programme may be driven by an overarching strategic logic and/or part of a coherent maritime strategy. This alternative appears to be the explanation offered by Bernard Cole as well as Andrew Erickson, Abraham Denmark and Gabriel Collins.[15] They argue that the PRC is pursuing a naval strategy first set out thirty years ago by Admiral Liu Huaqing whereby the PLAN would gradually extend its reach outward into the Pacific Ocean in three phases.

This sea power road map grew in significance as China's economy underwent rapid growth and major expansion in seaborne trade during the 1980s and 1990s. This maritime strategy has gained greater traction in the 21st century as the PRC perceives itself under growing threat from the USA. Particularly since the terrorist attacks of 11 September 2001, Beijing views Washington's behaviour around the PRC's periphery as being aimed at containing or encircling it.[16] From the PRC perspective, the USA has become increasingly assertive in the near seas, especially in the South China Sea.

Thus, one can ask again: What is driving the PRC's aircraft carrier programme? Is it the outcome of a sustained bureaucratic push by the PLAN to enhance its political power and status vis-à-vis the other services? Is the carrier programme best seen as a prestige project aimed at assuaging the nationalist fervour of the Chinese people? Or, is the programmeme a part of a coherent maritime strategy? How well does the carrier programme fit into the PRC's maritime plans and aspirations? What capabilities does a carrier programme provide the PLA, and how does a carrier affect the security situation in the Asia-Pacific?

We suggest that an overarching strategic logic has propelled the PRC's carrier programme inexorably forward. While nationalist impulses and bureaucratic lobbying have played important roles, the push for a Chinese carrier could not have been sustained across many decades unless the programme was driven by a larger strategic rationale and fit within the context of a coherent overall maritime strategy. This essay first examines the genesis of the PRC's carrier programme over the passage of fifty years. An analysis of the historical record suggests that the critical driver was strategic. While nationalism was certainly an important contextual factor, and the lobbying by PLAN leaders was significant in keeping the idea of a carrier programme alive, ultimately the decisive driver was strategic logic and operational importance. Indeed, the reason for the programme's lengthy gestation and the repeated failure to gain traction early on is attributable to the absence of a strategic imperative until quite recently. The emergence of this strategic imperative and the operational demands for a carrier in the 21st century correspond to a rise in PLA and PLAN thinking and planning beyond a Taiwan scenario.[17] This matter is analysed in the second part of the essay. In conclusion, the implications of the carrier programme for the balance of military power in the western Pacific and beyond will be evaluated.

Genesis of China's Carrier Programme

China's carrier programme has evolved remarkably over five decades. In a span of forty years, the programme was transformed from one man's elusive dream in 1970 (see below) to sea trials of an actual aircraft carrier in 2011 to commissioning one in 2012. The programme found it hard to gain traction, and languished for many years because it lacked a strategic imperative. But the idea of an aircraft carrier never died completely because of the persistence of a key PLAN leader, Liu Huaqing (1916-2011), who gradually rose to the highest post in the uniformed military hierarchy—Vice Chair of the CMC in 1989. In addition, the idea slowly captured the imagination of political leaders as well as the ordinary people who came to view a PLAN aircraft carrier as the ultimate symbol of full-blown Chinese military power.

The 1970s: One Man's Dream

The origins of the PLAN's aircraft carrier programme are intimately intertwined with the career of one prominent military figure: Liu Huaqing. He is justifiably considered the most important and certainly the most dogged champion of the programme. Liu is often dubbed the 'father of China's aircraft carrier'.[18] According to his memoirs, Liu floated a proposal to his military superiors as early as 1970 for China to begin preparations to acquire an aircraft carrier.[19] However, it does not appear that his suggestion received any support within the PLA hierarchy.

But this is hardly surprising, since the PRC had nothing remotely resembling a blue water navy in the 1970s, and its main threat at the time was overland invasion or attack from the Soviet Red Army, which could come anywhere along its several thousand mile extended and very exposed common border. And the most logical maritime scenario—an attack on or invasion of Taiwan—did not appear to get any serious attention at the time. In short, there was no compelling strategic or operational rationale for the development of a PLAN carrier programme in the 1970s. Moreover, nationalism did not even come into play in that decade.

The 1980s: A Vision

In the early post-Mao Zedong era, the idea of an aircraft carrier seemed a more plausible if still remote possibility. While the PRC's primary military threat remained land-centric—the Soviet Red Army—the 'reform and opening' policy of Deng Xiaoping significantly altered its national security calculus and defence priorities. As the PRC embraced foreign investment and expanded international trade links, Beijing began to attach much greater weight to maritime matters. PRC leaders not only had to be concerned with the security of their land borders but also with coastal and off-shore defence—a sharp change from 'near shore' (*jinan*) to the 'near seas' (*jinhai*).[20] Moreover, territorial claims in the South China

Sea and the unresolved matter of Taiwan provided added impetus for modernising the PLAN. In the mid-1980s, the PLA shifted from preparing for an imminent all-out global conflagration, likely to involve nuclear and conventional conflict between China and one of the superpowers, to a limited, localised conventional war fighting scenario.

Such geostrategic reorientation and doctrinal transformation produced a new strategic logic that was more conducive to the idea of aircraft carriers. A carrier might come in useful in signalling the shifting balance of military power in the Taiwan Strait, and in demonstrating the PRC's strengthened commitment to its maritime claims in the East China and South China Seas. Liu Huaqing reportedly held such a view, and insisted others also did so. Liu recalls in his memoirs that in November 1986, he chaired a seminar comprised of leaders and experts from both inside and outside of the PLA. Liu writes:

> Many comrades expressed the view that from the standpoint of our strategic mission of safeguarding the country's maritime interests, including the recovery of the Nansha [Islands], and the reunification of Taiwan, the navy should develop aircraft carriers. My own thinking was consistent with this view.[21]

The purchase of the decommissioned Australian Navy carrier, the *HMAS Melbourne*, in 1985 by a PRC company ostensibly for scrap signalled Beijing's growing interest in a carrier programme. The flight deck was kept intact; but the rest of the vessel was scrapped after reportedly being scrutinised by Chinese engineers and naval architects.[22] In 1982, upon being promoted to commander of the PLAN, Liu commissioned a study on the feasibility of carriers. He instructed a research institute in Shanghai to examine carrier design and construction. Three years later, Liu directed the Guangzhou Naval Academy to initiate a training course for aircraft carrier commanders.[23]

The 1990s: A Serious Debate

By the mid-1990s, maritime challenges had moved at the forefront and centre of Beijing's national security concerns. The collapse of the Soviet Union prompted much soul-searching in the PRC, and was viewed as a mixed blessing. Overall, however, it improved China's security environment. The Soviet breakup created three new contiguous land neighbours in Central Asia; but Beijing moved swiftly and deftly to recognise these states, resolve territorial disputes, and demilitarise border areas. With the PRC's inner Asian borders more secure, its rulers could focus greater attention on the security of China's coastal regions and its unresolved maritime territorial disputes. Moreover, the PRC was increasingly becoming enmeshed in the global economic system, of which the lion's share of trade was seaborne. In 1993, the mainland became a net importer of petroleum. All this signalled the PRC's growing dependence on the sea lines of communication radiating through the 'Near Seas', and out beyond the ' First Island Chain.' Additional attention to the maritime realm came as a result of tensions in the South China Sea (in 1995) followed by a crisis in the Taiwan Strait (1995-1996).

It was probably no coincidence that during a three-year period, PRC entities made three separate purchases of Soviet era aircraft carriers: the *Minsk* and *Varyag* (both in 1998), and the *Kiev* (in May 2000). These buys not only represented a sizeable amount of funds expended reportedly totalling some US$ 33.4 million— but these acquisitions came within a relatively short time period. All of this suggests some degree of high-level coordination. Moreover, a number of the circumstances surrounding the purchases were suspicious. For example, the buyer of the *Varyag*, the Chong Lot Tourist and Amusement Agency, reportedly had several retired PLAN officers on its board of directors. The alleged intent of the company was to turn the *Varyag* into a floating casino in the gambling mecca of Macau; but the waters around the former Portuguese colony were too shallow to accommodate the vessel, and no application for a gambling permit ever appeared to have been filed with Macau's gambling authority. Moreover, when the *Varyag* arrived in China in early 2002, it docked well away from Macau—in the northern port of Dalian.[24] In addition, during the mid-1990s, Chinese entities reportedly made considerable efforts to acquire blue prints for an aircraft carrier from a Spanish shipbuilder which was constructing a carrier for the Royal Thai Navy, and showed far less interest in placing a purchase order with the European company.[25]

This flurry of activity indicates that Beijing was engaged in a serious debate about the viability of acquiring an aircraft carrier. The evidence suggests that the option most seriously being considered was to build the carrier indigenously using one of the frames purchased overseas rather than buying a completely fitted foreign-made carrier. This tends to support the report that, in the mid-1990s, CMC Chair Jiang Zemin gave the PLAN the green light to commence work on designing a carrier.[26]

The 2000s: A Decision is Made

With the dawn of a new century, Beijing's maritime domain loomed ever larger in strategic significance. This prompted a 'paradigmatic change' (*zhuanxing*) in naval thinking from the 'near seas' (*jinhai*) to 'far seas' (*yuanhai*) according to an authoritative overview of PLAN history.[27] PRC aircraft as well as surface and sub-surface vessels routinely found themselves operating in the same vicinity, and often at very close quarters with US platforms. These encounters prompted what appeared to be a growing number of incidents. One of these incidents escalated into a crisis when a PLAN J-8 fighter collided with a US Navy EP-3 surveillance aircraft some 75 nautical miles south of Hainan Island. The crisis was defused with limited loss of life (one PLAN fighter pilot died when his aircraft crashed into the South China Sea); but this and other incidents signalled to Beijing that there was a growing threat from a perceived strategic encirclement by the USA, and the swift emergence of the Near Seas as a zone of US-China contestation.

The decision to go ahead with the construction of an actual PLAN aircraft carrier appears to have been made by the CMC in 2004 or 2005.[28] The decision was almost certainly made in conjunction with, or shortly after, CMC Chairman Hu Jintao's December 2004 declaration of a revised set of military strategic guidelines (*junshi zhanlue fangzhen*) for the PLA. The importance of these guidelines is hard to overstate. They function as a 'rolling national military strategy' that provide the key guidance and direction for PLA planning and force development.[29] There have only been five sets of guidelines issued in the entire sweep of PRC history, most recently in 1993. However, these guidelines are periodically amended, and hence evolve over time. Hu's remarks constituted an important modification to the 1993 guidelines.[30] Addressing the CMC on 24 December 2004, Hu outlined what became known as the New Historic Missions. He sketched out four broad brush missions for the PLA: (1) protecting the 'ruling position' of the CCP; (2) guaranteeing 'national development'; (3) safeguarding 'national interests'; and (4) maintaining 'world peace.'[31] Hu subsequently reportedly endorsed the concept of 'far sea operations' (*yuanhai zuozhan*). Together, these pronouncements provided a strong doctrinal rationale for the PLAN's acquisition of aircraft carriers.

And yet, despite the apparent decision and work getting underway during the mid-2000s in a Dalian shipyard to prepare the *Varyag* for eventual duty as an operational aircraft carrier, no official public statement was forthcoming from Beijing. The PRC was equipping a major naval surface combatant but keeping mum about the matter. Noteworthy was the absence of any mention of the PLAN's carrier project in China's defence white papers of 2004, 2006, 2008 and 2010. However, in 2006 and 2007 several senior military officials did publicly comment that the PRC had decided to develop an aircraft carrier programme with the goal of building them indigenously. Finally, in March 2009, PRC Minister of National Defence General Liang Guanglie is reported to have declared that the PLAN was preparing to build its own aircraft carriers.[32]

The 2010s: Commissioning a Carrier

The early years of the second decade of the 21st century seemed only to underscore the growing importance of sea power to the PRC. Tensions emerged with the USA and China's neighbours in the Near Seas. In 2010, China accused the USA of meddling in the South China Sea, and then engaged in heated protests against a planned US-Republic of Korea joint military exercise scheduled in the Yellow

Sea. Tensions also rose in the East China Sea over the disputed Diaoyu/Senkaku Islands. Beijing claims a 200 mile Economic Exclusion Zone in all these areas, and insists that other countries cannot operate military vessels or aircraft without the prior approval of the PRC.

Thus, the strategic logic for an aircraft carrier became more apparent: it was needed in order to cope with the PRC's expanding array of maritime interests. Accompanying these growing interests are operational demands.[33] The aircraft carrier can provide much needed air protection for the PLAN's surface fleet and submarines operating several hundred miles beyond the coastline. The most obvious region for such operations would be in the southern portions of the South China Sea, some 900 miles from Hainan Island—that is, well beyond the routine patrol range of PLAN land-based aircraft. Indeed, this is reportedly the area that Liu Huaqing felt an aircraft carrier would prove its worth.[34]

Against this backdrop, the *Varyag* undertook its first sea trial in August 2011. The vessel cruised in the Bohai Gulf and Yellow Sea for four days before returning to port. Further sea trials followed. Then, in late September 2012, the *Varyag* was officially commissioned as the *Liaoning*. The *Liaoning* was also ceremonially 'christened' by Hu Jintao barely two months before he stepped down as Chair of the CMC. As a result, Hu will go down in history as the leader responsible for the PRC's first operational aircraft carrier even though knowledgeable experts contend that the carrier will not become fully operational until 2015, at the earliest.[35]

Grand Strategic and Naval Strategic Logic

Traditionally, China has had modest oceanic interests and limited naval capabilities. Despite a long history of a thriving and colourful maritime subculture—replete with fishermen, seafarers, and pirates—China has never been a major naval power. Historically, external threats have come overland, and not from the sea. Moreover, most scholars insist that contemporary China is heir to a civilisation that is deeply rooted in a continental, agrarian, and sedentary existence. This tradition is often contrasted with Western civilisation which tends to be depicted as maritime, mercantilist, and expansionist.[36]

Nevertheless, in the modern era, successive rulers have recognised that China requires a significant naval capability to be able to defend itself from other states which possess substantial naval forces. Moreover, as China has become more engaged in global maritime commerce, and its economy become more dependent on international trade—especially in the post-Mao era—its leaders are giving greater thought and attention to developing a more robust navy.

By the early 1980s, the PLAN had articulated a grand strategic vision—widely attributed to Admiral Liu Huaqing—for a phased expansion of Chinese sea power. In the first phase, by 2000, the PLAN was to extend its area of operations in the Near Seas (South China Sea, East China Sea, and Yellow Sea), out as far as the so-called First Island Chain—the Kuril Islands, Japan, the Ryukyus, Taiwan, the Philippines, Borneo, and Natuna Besar. In the second phase, by 2020, the PLAN aimed to project its operational reach out to the so-called Second Island Chain—the Bonins, the Marianas, and the Carolines. In the third phase, by 2050, China would become a global sea power, and hence on a par with the US navy. In fact, the PLAN's activities and power project efforts have so far kept pace with the timeline Liu had projected.

The increasing importance of the maritime domain for China, and the PLAN's aspirations to evolve into a significant blue water navy together provide potent strategic logic for the development of an aircraft carrier programme. Carriers offer significant enhancement of power projection capabilities, not just in sea power but also in air power. The New Historic Missions articulated by Hu Jintao back in December 2004 provide the strategic and doctrinal logic for naval force modernisation, both broadly and implicitly, for the appearance of several aircraft carriers. Two of the four missions outlined by Hu are currently protecting China's 'national interests', and safeguarding 'world peace.'[37] The former mission has been defined ever more broadly to include China's maritime territorial claims inside the First Island Chain, as well as its 'overseas interests' well beyond. The latter mission provides the rationale for the PLAN to play a greater global role in a broad spectrum of activities, including patrolling the sea lines of communication as well as contributing to international humanitarian assistance and disaster relief efforts.[38]

A Hybrid Approach? Or a Transition to a Carrier Navy?

Despite these ambitious aspirations, the *Liaoning* will primarily serve as a training platform for the first three to five years, and most likely within the First and Second Island Chains. It will take time for the air wing and rotary aircraft to become operationally competent, and for the carrier to exercise in tandem with other PLAN surface and subsurface vessels. Moreover, although additional aircraft carriers are almost certainly in the cards, these are likely to come on line gradually—over the course of the next two decades. At least the second carrier will, very probably, mirror the first in terms of design and capabilities, although subsequent carriers could be heavier.[39]

It does not appear that the PLAN is building a future force with aircraft carriers at the core. Such a goal would require a complete order-of-battle overhaul. Instead, current doctrine and naval modernisation efforts suggest that the PLAN is aiming for approximately 3-5 carriers.[40] In short, China's navy appears to have adopted a hybrid approach, encompassing both carrier and surface action groups for mission specific operations.

In addition, such an approach more closely comports with political and fiscal realities. Aircraft carriers are extremely expensive systems. Whether the hull is acquired from abroad, or indigenously built, does not necessarily make much difference in the overall cost of the carrier (both can be expensive), and follow-on carriers may not be appreciably cheaper if they are of a different design or possess different subsystems. Moreover, while the PLAN has increased its power and influence vis-à-vis the other services in the past decade or so, the ground force remains the dominant service, with the preponderance of political clout. And, the Navy must compete with the Air Force which has greater representation on the CMC—an unprecedented two seats are held by PLAAF generals (Xu Qiliang as one of two uniformed CMC Vice Chairs, and Ma Xiaotian as Commander of the Air Force) selected at the 18th Party Congress in November 2012.[41] While the defence budget has continued to grow in double digits annually, overall military spending is carefully monitored, and continued increases presume further economic growth. In short, there are limits to the size of the defence budget and constraints on funds allocated to PLAN acquisitions.

Operational Rationale for Carriers

The most pressing operational logic for aircraft carriers is their value-add in war time. Most significantly, carriers offer extended blue water capability, an improved capacity for anti-submarine warfare (ASW), and airborne early warning (AEW) support. This can extend the PLAN to reach out to the Second Island Chain, and beyond. A fully operational aircraft carrier can provide the PLA's first steps toward an extended air defence cover for regional contingencies, and an incremental extension of the air defence umbrella in tandem with advanced escort combatants. However, vulnerabilities in ASW and AEW remain too great for the *Liaoning* to be successfully employed in high-intensity maritime combat. In short, there are limitations to what one aircraft carrier can do, especially when operational experience has been very limited.[42]

What difference would one or two aircraft carriers make in a contingency inside the First Island Chain? In a South China Sea clash, the *Liaoning* would be able to provide an extra air power projection against opposing combatants, especially in the southernmost reaches of that body of water; however, it would also present adversaries with a nice big target. One or two carriers would also offer little in an East China Sea battle. As for a Taiwan contingency, carrier air would add little to a direct fight, although there would be some possible utility as a diversion in the more easily protected approaches away from Taiwan and Japan.[43] The use of an aircraft carrier would tend to severely complicate the PLA's current doctrinal approach: missile-centric firepower strike and counter-intervention ops, supported by advanced information war capabilities. This would be especially true in a Taiwan contingency. The absence of catapults or a ski jump means that there is a limit to the size and weight of an aircraft that can take off from the deck. This limits the payload and the amount of fuel that a jet can carry.

Non-Combat Operations

An additional rationale is the contribution an aircraft carrier can make to peacetime operations. Indeed, this non-combat dimension has received considerable attention in recent years in China. Moreover, the PLA has neither had recent war fighting experience; nor does it anticipate significant combat operations in the near future. Thus, the *Liaoning*—and any subsequent aircraft carriers—can expect considerable non-combat operational experience. Since at least 2008, China's armed forces have emphasised military operations other than war (MOOTW) as an important doctrinal component for the PLA.[44] While there is a significant domestic dimension to MOOTW with Chinese characteristics, this body of doctrine also includes substantial overseas elements as well, and the PLAN appears poised to play a central role. These MOOTW missions include extended SLOC protection and humanitarian assistance/disaster relief flat-deck operations. China became acutely aware of the value of an aircraft carrier during the US navy's response to the Southeast Asian tsunami in 2004.[45] Moreover, recent experiences with non-combatant evacuations in places such as Libya have highlighted the value of air and naval assets.

Also, in peacetime, a carrier can provide a high profile presence where ever it steams. It can symbolise Chinese power and commitment without necessarily raising fear or alarm. However, the challenge in the not-too-distant-future will be how to operate a carrier close to home without being perceived as threatening by China's neighbours. While a carrier is much more likely to be warmly welcomed outside of the First and Second Island Chains than within them, the vast distances involved in Far Seas operations will also provide the greatest challenges to Chinese carriers.[46] A carrier operating off the coast of Africa or Latin America would be a strong symbol of Chinese national pride and could also serve as a goodwill ambassador whether in port visits or in patrolling the global commons.

Conclusion

This essay contends that PRC's carrier programme has been driven forward by an overarching strategic logic. While nationalism and bureaucratic interests have played—and will continue to play—important roles, the push for a Chinese carrier could not have been sustained across many decades, and ultimately triumph, without the impetus of a larger strategic rationale and the emergence of a coherent maritime strategy. The programme's lengthy gestation and repeated failure to gain traction are attributable to the absence of a strategic imperative until the end of the Cold War. The emergence of this strategic imperative and the operational demands for a carrier in the 21st century correspond to a rise in PLA thinking beyond a Taiwan Strait scenario. This is because while the PRC's military was narrowly focused on operations against the island of Taiwan, an aircraft carrier did not make much sense. However, the operational value of a carrier is more evident in other scenarios, including the protection of the South China Sea and beyond the First Island Chain. Moreover, the strategic and operational value increases as the PLAN expands its horizons beyond the First and Second Island Chains.

While the PLAN is still years away from being able to project and sustain significant naval power—especially an aircraft carrier—out of these areas, Beijing is intent on the goals of being able to play a greater role in patrolling SLOCs further afield. Given China's dependence on imported energy and the importance attached to energy security, a logical priority location for increased PLAN operational activity is the Indian Ocean. Although China has paid great attention to overland routes for oil and gas (witness the construction of pipelines in recent years from Central Asia, Russia, and Myanmar), the PRC remains reliant on seaborne energy, especially petroleum from fields in Africa and the Middle East.

If we can generalise from the case of China, then Asia's aircraft carrier arms race appears to be propelled forward by multiple drivers. While all the buckets identified at the outset of this essay seem to be necessary for a country to successfully launch an indigenous aircraft carrier programme, the first bucket—domestic political drivers—seems particularly important (namely nationalism and bureaucratic politics), and the fifth bucket—strategic and doctrinal logic (namely the need to protect expanding maritime interests and address evolving operational challenges)—has also acquired significance in recent years. What does this particular arms race means for Asia? It heralds a more congested and heated maritime environment, and probably higher operational tempos for the navies of the major regional powers. Moreover, the carrier race may also exacerbate the extant multiple security dilemmas that crisscross Asia and the Pacific.

NOTES

1. Andrew T.H. Tan, *The Arms Race in Asia: Trends, Causes, Implications* (New York: Routledge, 2014). According to the International Institute for Strategic Studies, 'Asian defense spending…[is] increase[ing] strongly.' IISS, *The Military Balance 2013* (Routledge, 2013), p. 250.
2. Geoffrey Till, *Asia's Naval Expansion: An Arms Race in the Making?* (London: International Institute for Strategic Studies, 2012), pp. 35, 241.

3. Captain Henry J. Hendrix, USN, *At What Cost a Carrier?* (Washington, DC: Center for a New American Security, March 2013); and Robert C. Rubel, 'The Future of Aircraft Carriers', *Naval War College Review* Vol. 64, No. 4 (Autumn 2011), pp. 12-27.
4. Till, *Asia's Naval Expansion*, pp. 93-94.
5. See, for example, Eric Heginbotham, 'The Fall and Rise of Navies in East Asia: Military Organisations, Domestic Politics, and Grand Strategies', *International Security* Vol. 27, No. 2 (Fall 2002), pp. 86-123; and scholars of the PLAN cited below.
6. See, for example, Paul Bracken, *Fire in the East: The Rise of Asian Military Power and the Second Nuclear Age* (New York: HarperCollins, 1999); and Aaron L. Friedberg, 'Will Europe's Past be Asia's Future?' Survival Vol. 42, No. 3 (Autumn 2000), pp. 147-159.
7. Kent E. Calder, *Asia's Deadly Triangle: How Arms Energy, and Growth Threaten to Destabilise the Asia-Pacific* (London: Nicholas Brealey, 1996); and Desmond Ball, 'Arms and Affluence: Military Acquisitions in the Asia-Pacific Region', *International Security* Vol. 18, No. 3 (Winter 1993/94), pp. 78-112.
8. Barry Buzan, *An Introduction to Strategic Studies, Military Technology, and International Relations* (London: Macmillan, 1987).
9. The doctrinal for a carrier program is emphasised by Rubel, 'The Future of Aircraft Carriers', op. cit.
10. John W. Garver, 'China's Push through the South China Sea: The Interaction of Bureaucratic and National Interests', *The China Quarterly*, No. 132 (December 1992).
11. Ian Storey and You Ji, 'China's Aircraft Carrier Ambitions: Seeking Truth from Rumors', *Naval War College Review* Vol. 57, No. 1 (Winter 2004), pp. 77-92.
12. Robert S. Ross, 'China's Naval Nationalism: Sources, Prospects, and the U.S. Response', *International Security* Vol. 34, No. 2 (Fall 2009), pp. 46-81.
13. The Soviet navy faced considerable challenges in this endeavour, and it was only after several decades of effort that it was able to launch operational aircraft carriers (in the 1970s and 1980s)— although large ships with limited capabilities were launched in the 1960s.
14. See the critique by Michael A. Glosny and Phillip C. Saunders, 'Correspondence: Debating China's Naval Nationalism', *International Security* Vol. 35, No. 2 (Fall 2010), pp. 161-169.
15. Bernard D. Cole, *The Great Wall at Sea: China's Navy in the Twenty-First Century* 2nd ed. (Annapolis, MD: Naval Institute Press, 2010); Andrew S. Erickson, Abraham N. Denmark, and Gabriel Collins, 'Beijing's 'Starter Carrier' and Future Steps: Alternatives and Implications', *Naval War College Review* Vol. 65, No. 1 (Winter 2012), pp. 15-54.
16. See, for example, Andrew J. Nathan and Andrew Scobell, 'How China Views America: The Sum of Beijing's Fears', *Foreign Affairs* 91:5 (September/October 2012), pp. 32-47.
17. Roy Kamphausen, David Lai, and Andrew Scobell (eds.), *Beyond the Strait: PLA Missions Other Than Taiwan* (Carlisle Barracks, PA: U.S. Army War College Strategic Studies Institute, 2009).
18. See, for example, Bai Ma, 'Zhanwang Zhongguo haijun de hangmu shidai [The prospects for China's navy in the era of aircraft carriers]', *Jianchuanzhishi* (Naval and Merchant Ships), March 2011, p. 18. Liu is also often called 'China's Mahan'.
19. Liu Huaqing, *Liu Huaqing Huiyilu* [Memoirs of Liu Huaqing] (Beijing: Jiefangjun Chubanshe, 2004), p. 477.
20. Tang Fuquan and Han Yi, 'Renmin haijun yanzhe dang zhiyin de chuanxiang polang qianjin [People's Navy advances along the course set by the Party]', *Zhongguo Junshi Kexue* [China Military Science], no. 4 (2009), pp. 13-14.
21. Liu Huaqing, *Liu Huaqing Huiyilu*, p. 478.
22. Storey and You, 'China's Aircraft Carrier Ambitions', p. 79.
23. Storey and You, Ibid., p. 78.
24. Storey and You, Ibid., pp. 81-84.

25. Storey and You, Ibid., p. 80.
26. Cole, *The Great Wall at Sea*, p. 88.
27. Tang Fuquan and Han Yi, 'Renmin haijun yanzhe dang zhiyin', p. 14.
28. Author interviews with civilian and military analysts in Beijing and Shanghai indicate that a decision was made in this timeframe.
29. David M. Finkelstein, 'China's National Military Strategy: An Overview of the Military's Strategic Guidelines', in Roy Kamphausen and Andrew Scobell (eds.), *Right Sizing the PLA: Exploring the Contours of China's Military* (Carlisle Barracks, PA: U.S. Army War College Strategic Studies Institute, 2007), pp. 69-140.
30. Andrew Scobell, 'Discourse in 3-D: The PLA's Evolving Doctrine, Circa 2009,' in Roy Kamphausen, David Lai, and Andrew Scobell (eds.), *The PLA at Home and Abroad: Assessing the Operational Capabilities of China's Military* (Carlisle Barracks, PA: U.S. Army War College Strategic Studies Institute, 2010), pp. 100-101.
31. The text of Hu Jintao's speech has never been made public; but it has been widely cited. For a concise overview, see Daniel Hartnett, 'China Military and Security Activities', *Hearings before the US-China Economic and Security Review Commission* 111 Cong. 1st sess. March 4, 2009 (Washington, DC: Government Printing Office, April 2009), pp. 45-55.
32. Cole, *The Great Wall at Sea*, pp. 88-90.
33. See, for example, Tang Fuquan and Han Yi, 'Renmin haijun dang yanzhe dang zhiyin', p. 14.
34. Storey and You, 'China's Aircraft Carrier Ambitions', op. cit., p. 86.
35. Erickson, Denmark, and Collins, 'Beijing's "Starter" Carrier', pp. 21-24. https://www.usnwc.edu/getattachment/647f61ae-c554-4475-b344-6e3b8c3d551f/Beijing-s—Starter-Carrier—and-Future-Steps—Alte
36. See, for example, Yao Youzhi and Peng Guangqian (eds.), *The Science of Military Strategy* (Beijing: Military Science Publishing House, 2005), pp. 72-77; and Andrew Scobell, *China and Strategic Culture* (Carlisle Barracks, PA: U.S. Army War College Strategic Studies Institute, 2002).
37. For more on the New Historic Missions, see Daniel Hartnett, 'China's Military and Security Activities Abroad', *Testimony before the U.S.—China Economic and Security Review Commission*, 111th Cong. 1st sess., 4 March 2009 (Washington, D.C.: Government Printing Office, April 2009), pp. 5-55.
38. See, for example, Andrew Scobell and Gregory Stevenson, 'The PLA (Re-) Discovers Non-traditional Security', in Lyle J. Goldstein (ed.), *Not Congruent but Quite Complementary: U.S. and Chinese Approaches to Non-traditional Security*, China Maritime Studies Institute Papers (Newport, RI: U.S. Naval War College, 2012).
39. Recent news reports citing PLAN officials suggest this may not be the case. See, for example, 'China's 2nd Aircraft Carrier Will be "Larger"', *China Daily*, 24 April 2013; and Pete Sweeney, 'China to Build Second, Larger Carrier: Report,' *Reuters*, 23 April 2013.
40. RAND estimates. See also, Richard D. Fisher, Jr., 'Dalian official says Chinese planning four aircraft carriers,' *Jane's Defense Weekly*, 21 January 2014.
41. See James Mulvenon, 'The New Central Military Commission,' *China Leadership Monitor*, no. 40 (January 2013), pp. 1-10.
42. See the discussion in Erickson, Denmark, and Collins, 'Beijing's Starter Carrier', pp. 33-35.
43. See the discussion in Erickson, Denmark, and Collins, Ibid., pp. 35-40.
44. See, for example, Scobell, 'Discourse in 3-D', pp. 99-134.
45. See the discussion in Erickson, Denmark, and Collins, 'Beijing's Starter Carrier', pp. 37-38.
46. See the discussion in Erickson, Denmark, and Collins, Ibid., pp. 39-41.

5

Vietnam Naval Modernisation: Causes and Trends

Nguyen Hung Son

Introduction

Vietnam naval modernisation was only brought to broad international attention and scrutiny after news of a deal to build 6 Kilo class submarine for Vietnam was leaked and reported by a Russian newspaper in April 2009. The deal reportedly worth $1.8 billion seemed oversized compared to the modest $ 91 billion GDP of Vietnam, and a defense budget of only $ 3.6 billion.[1] Observers quickly saw it as Vietnam's hasty reaction out of fear to the heightened tension in the South China Sea and military modernisation going on in Asia with some analyst suggesting the deal might further increase the tension and trigger a new arms race in the region.[2] When the first submarine was delivered to Vietnam in December 2013 and the official commissioning of the boat started in January 2014, new warning of such competitive arms procurement in Asia were revived.[3] While it might be intuitive to assume Vietnam's naval modernisation was primarily driven by maritime security developments in the region, a deeper look into the drivers and trends of Vietnam is needed to better understand the nature of such modernisation.

Drivers of Vietnam's Naval Modernisation

To Provide Security Assurance to National Maritime Development Agenda

One of the first criteria to judge the motivation and legitimacy of country's naval modernisation is if the country's legitimate maritime interests merit such naval enhancement. As for Vietnam, despite often being described geo-politically as a continental South East Asia country or an Indochinese country lying within the sphere of influence of two giant continental powers, the country has always been a very maritime obsessed nation and has always depended on the sea for its citizens' livelihood. This geo-political characteristic has long influenced the Viet's economic and security thinking. Vietnam's long stretched, thin territory, mostly mountainous and rough terrain of the western part means that the country and its people have to look out to the eastern sea and depend on the sea for its economic development. Vietnam faces the sea on three sides, has 28 coastal provinces out of a total of 64 (almost half), and a 3000 km coast line, which is estimated to generate more than 1 million km2 of exclusive economic zone under UNCLOS 1982, a maritime zone three times as large as the country's territory itself. Vietnam is among the top ten in the world with the most kilometer of coast line per square kilometer of land territory. About 25 million people live along the coast, 31per cent of the country's population. By 2020, it will be 30 million. It is believed that along the coastline there are 100 suitable sites for sea port development; 125 nice beaches, among them 20 meeting international standards. Vietnamese are deeply aware of the strategic importance of the South China Sea and believe in the great economic potential of this semi enclosed sea, in particular its bio-diversity, its oil and other mineral reserves, therefore the people are also very susceptible of foreign intention to dominate it and to exploit its richness.[4]

From the early 90s, particularly since the 7th Communist Party Congress in 1991, Vietnam decided that developing the ailing economy was the nation's top priority and urgent task, hence it started opening up its economy, adopted market economy and expanded foreign economic relations. Under market economy and foreign investment, both natural and human resources were better utilised for economic development and the country's potentials slowly began to turn into real economic progress. Vietnam's vast marine potentials were quickly placed high on Vietnam's development agenda. On September 22, 1997, the Politburo of the Vietnamese Communist party, the most authoritative body within the Vietnamese political structure, issued an order to enhance the country's marine based economy towards industrialisation and modernisation. The order marked the beginning of Vietnam's most recent effort to transform itself into a country with strong marine capabilities, where the social and economic development of the country's islands and marine areas will be placed in the overall context of national economic development, national defense as well as regional and international economic integration.[5]

On February 9, 2007, the Communist Party Central committee approved Resolution 09-NQ/TW on "Vietnam's marine strategy towards 2020", recognising that "the 21st century belongs to the ocean", and set out three broad strategic directions for Vietnam's marine related economic development towards 2020:

(i) the target is to turn Vietnam into a strong marine country which can derive strong benefits from marine richness and potentials, with a fully developed marine's based economy;
(ii) integrate marine based economic development with national defense, international cooperation and the protection of marine environment;
(iii) to explore all resources for social-economic development, to effectively conduct international cooperation and attract foreign investment while firmly protect national sovereignty and territorial integrity.

The resolution set the target that by 2020, marine based economies will account for 53-55per cent of the country's GDP, and 55-60 per cent of total export volume.[6] The most important sectors of the marine based economies are fisheries, oil and other minerals exploration, marine transportation, services and tourism. In 2005, marine's sectors started contributing about half of the country's GDP (48 per cent), and a major source for revenue ($ 7 billion from oil; $ 2.7 billion from fishery).

With more than half of annual projected income from marine related economic activities, it is expected that Vietnam will want a secure maritime environment, and a strong defense policy to protect those interests. The Resolution spelled out that the defense policy should "*combine political, diplomatic, legal, economic and military... (based) on a strong military, the core being the navy, air force, marine police, coast guard, paramilitary... to effectively support fishermen, marine resources exploratory and other activities*".[7] The XI Communist Party Congress in January 2011, a five yearly gathering of top policy making body of the Vietnamese Communist Party, resolved that protecting territorial integrity is a fundamental national interest and a top priority for both national security and foreign relations. It directed the government to enhance national defense, especially to remote border areas, including the sea and islands. It also directed the government to settle remaining border issues with relevant countries on the bases of international law and regional codes of conduct.[8]

Prime Minister Nguyen Tan Dung statement on June 8, 2011 on the World Ocean Day and Vietnam's Sea and Island week, further elaborated the tasks to implement the resolution of the XI Communist Party Congress as follows:[9]

- To resolutely protect with highest determination Vietnam's sovereignty, sovereignty right and jurisdictional rights of the Motherland's sea and islands.
- To further develop the policy and legal foundation with regards to the sea, island, and marine's resources, with the view of enhancing

management capability.

- To integrate economic and defense activities; to integrate the development of marine economic zones with urban development planning towards industrialisation.
- To enhance marine research for sustainable resources development, environmental protection, and to effectively cope with climate change, rising sea level, and to preserve bio-diversity and other marine ecological system.
- To enhance international cooperation on marine's related issue on the bases of mutual respect to sovereignty and international law, protecting security and safety of navigation and for regional peace and stability.
- To enhance education to raise awareness on the importance of Vietnam's marine's sovereignty, rights and strategies, on the need to preserve marine's environment.

The passing of the Law of the Sea on June 22, 2012 was an important milestone, laying the legal foundation to implement the Communist Party resolution. The underlying objective of the Vietnam's Law of the Sea was to codify the letters and spirit of UNCLOS into national legislation with the aim of aligning Vietnam's claims and legislation to international law. The Law also codified the objectives and principles of marine's resources development and protection into concrete policies and charged respective government agencies with specific duties.

The above analysis proves that Vietnam naval enhancement originated first and foremost internally from a comprehensive national development strategy with strong emphasis on marine based economy, which has been long planned and systematically implemented along with other economic, administrative, legislative measures.

To Respond to Developments in the External Security Environment

External treat perceptions are also seen as strong influencing factors on Vietnam defense strategy and consequently its military strategy. Vietnam's Defense White Paper in 2009 although saw the Asia Pacific region becoming increasingly important, at the same time posed several challenges to national security and defense. It identified hotspots which can easily burst into conflicts, increasing territorial disputes, competition for resources and new emerging non-traditional security as the most prominent security risks. It further emphasised territorial disputes; disputes over sovereign rights and jurisdiction in the East Sea[10] are seriously affecting people's life and the development of country's marine based economy.[11]

The mild language of the Defense White Paper did not fully capture the country's off-shore insecurity. It was widely reported that the number of ships and vessels (both surface and underwater) illegal infringements of the country's exclusive economic zones and territorial waters have been on the rise. There were increasing cases of foreign vessels ignoring the safety zone of the country's offshore oil exploration and installations, threatening its safety and security. More seriously were reports of foreign ships undertaking exploratory activities within the clear exclusive economic zones (EEZ) of Vietnam.[12] Fishing activities also faces critical challenge as fishermen reported increasing cases of clashes with foreign ships within their traditional and regular fishing zones, increasing "hit, rob and run" cases by un-known foreign ships. Vietnamese fishing ships that were captured by foreign authority were also reported to have been asked for more ransom that is a "fine" to be paid in order to be released. Many fishermen were captured more than once. A fisherman in Quang Ngai province of Vietnam were captured four times while fishing in his family traditional fishing zones for generations, each time he was confiscated of all his belongings.[13] On top of all are unresolved issues of sovereignty disputes over the Spratlys and Paracels, maritime zones and continental shell delineation in the region.

The insecurity is further helped by greater awareness among the Vietnamese people on the importance of the sea and its benefit, better reporting of incidences, and growing concern of insufficient capability of the authority to ensure security in a maritime zone three times as large as the country itself. In fact, this weakness have been publicly admitted by Vietnamese naval authorities,[14] especially under public pressure to conduct better search and rescue operations, as well as to act more timely and efficiently on other emergency issues. Reviewing the most recent development in Vietnam's external security environment, the political report of the XI Communist Party Congress in 2011 admitted that despite the effort to integrate economic and defense activities, the efficiency of combining these two activities in "strategic areas" is still lacking. The defense industry still falls short of the requirement of the armed forces.[15] The congress further highlighted the increasing complexity of regional maritime competition while noting that there has been new ways of forming alliances with clear effect on regional overall stability.

Heightened tensions in the South China Sea in 2011 and 2012 were due to some serious incidences. Most notably was the "Cable cutting incidence", when Chinese vessels harassed by cutting off seismic surveying cable being operated by the Vietnamese Binh Minh 02 vessel, which were undertaking seismic survey 120 miles off the Vietnamese coast, deep within Vietnam's EEZ. Another incidence was the opening for bidding by China's national off-shore oil company (CNOOC) ofnine oil blocks under Vietnam's EEZ after Vietnam adopted its maritime law. These incidences, which happened in undisputed area deep within Vietnam's EEZ, further highlighted the eminent threat from China, ignited a major surge of nationalism sentiment in Vietnam and placed the government under further pressure to counter the threat to the national territorial integrity. For the first time, the Prime Minister of Vietnam was questioned publicly on measures to defend territorial integrity by the National Assembly. The failure of ASEAN to issue statements on the South China Sea in Phnom Penh in July and November 2012, which were broadly perceived in ASEAN as a deliberate Chinese attempt to disunite ASEAN on the South China Sea further exposed the China's threats in the South China Sea. These events have contributed to convince the government, the ministry of defense and the public on the need to expedite and enhance efforts to modernise the national naval capability to protect its interests.

To Enhance the Vietnamese Government's Legitimacy Amid Rising Nationalism

Domestic politics is another key driver for Vietnam naval modernisation, by enhancing national unity, prestige and legitimacy of the government and the Communist Party of Vietnam. The interaction between the Vietnamese peoples, both living inside and outside of the country, and the government has had strong influence on the government actions in the South China Sea, including its naval enhancement. Like other people across the region, the Vietnamese peoples are also experiencing rising nationalism amid rising territorial tensions. The people place heavy pressure on the government for transparency on the South China Sea and actively participate in the discussions among themselves and with the government on how Vietnam should respond. The government legitimacy is highly placed on its ability to act to protect national interests and territorial integrity is one of the core interests. Vietnamese diaspora, whose regular objectives is to de-legitimise the Communist Party and the government also found the South China Sea as a good reason to unite among them and to use it as a pretext against the government.

In response, the Vietnamese government has been making efforts to de-mystify, de-sensitise as well as socialise the issues to the public with the aim of keeping national unity and managing nationalism. Previously regarded as a highly sensitive issue that the uninformed public may not be able to discuss, the government has steadily encouraged public awareness and participation. The government started feeding mainstream information to the public through various channel, such as opening official websites,[16] encouraging the media to carry columns on the subjects etc. The national assembly started questioning officials on the territory and maritime boundary. The Prime Minister of Vietnam, Nguyen Tan Dung, even discussed with the national assembly the government's policies and measures to protect its maritime interests which were broadcasted live on TV. The government took steps to encourage scholarly studies of the South China Sea and scholars are increasingly invited to formulate policies; Vietnamese diaspora were actively engaged. Dissidents who vocally opposed the government's policies on the South China Sea were invited to return to Vietnam and visit the sites to provide hands on experience and understanding of the issue.[17] Through its naval procurement and modernisation program, the Vietnamese government clearly wanted to prove that it is fully responsible and capable of handling the South China Sea issue as well as other national interests. Announcement of the 6 Kilo class, which came in 2009 was at the critical timing ahead of the five yearly Communist Party Congress in 2011, when the Communist Party and the military must appear fully capable of protecting the country so as to ensure their legitimacy against the backdrop of rising nationalism.

It could be shown from the analysis of the most important drivers of Vietnam's naval modernisation, that external factors is neither the only nor the most prominent cause of Vietnam's naval enhancement in recent years. It could be argued that Vietnam increased seaward looking and economic dependence were the forefront reason for the increase in defense services, especially in the maritime domain. The increased threat perception due to recent geopolitical development in the region as well as increased nationalism, however, did play acceleratory roles in pushing the government to speed up the pace of naval acquisition, effort which was enabled by relatively high economic growth of the Vietnamese economy.

Vietnam's Naval Modernisation Trends

The trends of Vietnam's naval modernisation may provide another clue to the actual Vietnam's motivation and objectives. According to the 2009 Defense White Paper, Vietnam naval force is charged with managing and controlling the maritime zone under Vietnam jurisdiction, the EEZ under Vietnam's sovereign rights, islands under Vietnam's sovereignty, keeping security, protecting the normal activities of the people, ensuring safety of navigation, participating in search and rescue activities, and fight off all foreign invaders from the sea.[18] The Defense White Paper recognised that the Navy is currently only equipped enough to perform search and rescue function, and will need to be further strengthened with modern weaponry to successfully undertake the duty of protecting national sovereignty and other interests at sea.[19]

Vietnam defense has traditionally focused on land rather than the sea. Most of the country's recent wars were fought on land. The Navy, as a result was poorly equipped. While there is little public information about the current Vietnamese navy fleet, it is widely believed that the fleet consists of about 50 decades old, mostly Russian made vessels from the 60s and 70s and some western made vessels captured after the fall of Saigon. Economic difficulties during the 80s and early 90s mean that little or no new procurement took place for decades and not much maintenance is performed on the aging fleet. It is therefore, believed that the number of vessels still in service are much less, not to mention their combat capability. Vietnam, however, does make some small vessels for military use. Among the most important vessels in the Vietnamese navy fleet are the Petya-II and III class frigates, Osa-II, Tarantul I and BPS 500 class missile boats, Shershen and Turya class torpedo boat, Yurka class mine sweeper; SO 1 class patrol boats, Svetlyak class high speed patrol boat.[20]

The current fleet is considered too thin, too slow and too old for its duties. The leading fleets are not designed for sustained and deep off-shore operations, thus are considered not capable of undertaking combat operations in areas where Vietnam has territorial disputes. To reach the potential combat areas alone may take these frigates and missile boats almost two days at full speed. With loads, they will be much slower. Some of the vessels are already too old to risk sailing too far off coast. The support and supply vessels are also weak and old. Without good and efficient support, sustaining operations at sea is very difficult. A Vietnamese fisherman's wife in Da Nang observed that "*At sea, we all have to look after ourselves. When there are storm, the border defense force would radio us to inform, that's all. There is no protection out there.*"

The Navy chief commander, also Deputy Minister of Defense, Nguyen Van Hien, spelled out the following target and strategies for Vietnam's naval modernisation:[21]

- The broad target is to strengthen and fully develop the naval organisation, including its equipment and infrastructure in order to meet the new demand and responsibility.
- The Navy's organisation and equipment must enable it to undertake modern, high tech warfare; and allow it to act independently, sustainably, continuously for long days in both near and far waters; the force must be highly dynamic and also integrate well with other defense forces.
- To realise the target, the Navy will need to transform itself towards fineness, compactness and forcefulness; dynamic and mobile, highly balanced and synchronised, balanced between the standing force and reserves, balanced between forward combat force and back end support. The Navy also needs to strengthen its organisation into strong naval areas;
- Modernise the Navy's equipment and weapon while maximising utilisation of the current assets; invest in research and application of new technological advancement to the development of modern weapons; undertake international cooperation to modernise equipment and technological infrastructure of the Navy.
- To spare no effort and resource to build the Navy into a modern force which will be capable of ensuring security at sea; in tandem with national economic development, the Navy should take steps to equip itself with

all fundamental elements of a modern navy, including ships, submarines, navy air force, marines, defense force at island and island groups.

The implementation of such targets and strategies has seen the following trends in recent years:

Equipment modernisation: Russia continued to be the main source for Vietnam weapon modernisation with flagship procurement being the purchase of the Kilo submarines, Gepard frigates and Su-30 fighters. Vietnam ordered six Kilo class submarines from Russia, the first delivery of the "Hanoi" Kilo took place in December 2013, which was officially commissioned by the Vietnamese Navy from January 15, 2014. The second Kilo, named after "Ho Chi Minh city" is at the time of this writing, being transported to Vietnam and the other four Kilos is expected to be delivered at the speed of 1 delivery a year.[22] The sales package includes provision for training and maintenance. Admiralteiskye Verfi, manufacturer of the 6 Kilos has sought to open a representative office in Vietnam, supposedly to support its maintenance programme. Russia has also constructed a training center for naval officer in Viet Nam. Two Gepard 3.9 frigates from Russia, built at Tartarstan's Gorky Ship building Plant, both have been delivered by 2010 and 2012,[23] and Vietnam has ordered two more such frigates in December 2011, to be delivered in 2016 and 2017. In 2007, Vietnam bought high speed missile boats Molnya (Tarantul I), and Russia plans to license Vietnam to have its own production of the boat,[24] some report stated that production of first batch of 10 is already underway [25] under close supervision of the Russian manufacturer. In 2002, Vietnam bought 2 *Svetlyak* patrol boats from Rusia, and in 2009 ordered 4 additional. [26] Two of the four *Svetlyak* patrol boats were delivered to Vietnam in 2012, a year behind the schedule due to delayed supply of 76mm AK-176 cannon.[27] After completion of the delivery of 20 Sukhoi-30 fighter jets to Vietnam in 2012, Vietnam has contracted another 12 additional Su-30, to be delivered in 2014-2015.

Establishment of a naval air force with anti-submarine capability: The Navy established its air arm to boost its power in July 2013, a move made due to lack of coordination between the Navy and the Air Force.[28] It was reported that the air wing would initially be equipped with 12 Ka-28 ASW helicopters, 2 EADS-CASAs and 6 Viking Twin Otters for marine patrol.[29] The Vietnam's People Army paper reported that the main tasks of the air wing is anti-submarine warfare, military transportation, air surveillance and search and rescue at sea.[30]

Diversification of platforms and providers: Apart from diversifying its capability by varying its platform to transform the Navy into a three-dimensional force, the Navy is also seen to diversify its source of procurement to reduce over reliance on one provider and to widen its adaptability with different technology and platforms.

Although Russia continues to be the most important source, Vietnam now also buys from other sources, including the European Union and the U.S. Though may not be directly related to the Navy and its air force, Vietnam has expressed interests in acquiring French helicopters and transport airplane.[31] The *Janes' Defense Weekly* reported that Lockheed Martin might be selling P-3C Orion anti-submarine aircraft to Vietnam. Vietnam ordered two Sigma 9814-class corvettes from the Damen Shipyards Group of the Netherlands, which is to be equipped with the French made Exocet MM40 Block 3 anti-ship missiles. Vietnam is also seeking to modernise its short and medium range missile capability, ordering modern missile systems from Russia (Bastion/Yakhont and Brahmos),[32] India (Prithvi),[33] Israel (the Extended Range Artillery Monition system)[34] and others.

Indigenising the defense industries: The Molnya high speed missile boats were among the first major landmark of Vietnam's effort to indigenise the defense industry. In 2005, Vietnam bought license to domestically construct 10-12 Molnya worth $ 1 billion. Construction for the first Molnya started in October 2010 under close supervision of Russian technicians and experts. In October 2013, the first two Vietnamese made Molnya went into testing. Also under Russian support, Vietnam will indigenise the anti-ship missile Kh-35 production, to be equipped for the Gepard frigates.

Widening international defense cooperation: The Hindu of India reported that Vietnam is seeking help from India to upgrade its defense capability, particularly its naval force. In President Truong Tan Sang visit to India from October 11-15, 2012, the president asked for help from India to modernise Vietnam capability in four areas: (i) to train a submarine crew to man the Kilos bought from Russia; (ii) to train pilots for the Su-30; (iii) to upgrade Vietnam's strategic ports (especially Nha Trang sea port near Cam Ranh) and to transfer some medium sized frigates (1000-1.500 tons) to Vietnam; (iv) to supply Vietnam with BrahMos missiles. According to this news, India is "actively" training Sukhoi pilots for Vietnam. India had experience training pilots for the Malaysian airforce.[35] Sweden, on the other hand, might supply Vietnam with unmanned drones in the near future. In a recent trade fair, it was reported, Sweden has agreed on a three pronged project to supply these equipment to Vietnam. The Magic eye 1, weighing 40kilograms with operating time of six hours at maximum speed of 200km/h at the range of 100-200 km is the prime focus of the project.[36] Vietnam further expanded defense industry cooperation with several partners, including those form the former Soviet block as well as "new partners" like South Korea, Spain and the United States.

De-militarise the national coast guards: the Vietnamese "marine police" is an armed force under direct control of the ministry of defense. In recent years, this force has also been strengthened with more modern and specialised ships to suit its duties, in particular search and rescue, anti piracy and smuggling. Since 2013, the force was renamed "coast guards" and placed under direct control of the minister of defense, a move to further highlight its civilian nature and lessen the military connection of the force, a preparatory step to fully detach this force from the military in the near future.

Focusing on both "hardware" and "software": According to Admiral Nguyen Van Ninh, Deputy Chief of Naval force Commander, aside from modernising its equipment, Vietnam is paying much attention to the human factor by re-organising its forces, investing on training and military tactics, in order to archive a highly efficient force. New war fighting skills are being taught including anti-submarine tactics, training on new radar and surveillance system, on new high precision and mobile weapons systems suitable for marine environment. A new salary system for highly skill naval personnel is being proposed. A future naval colonel serving on submarines might have two times as much salary as admiral serving on the surface ship. Naval infrastructure including factories, military ports and training sites were to be reviewed and re-organised.[37]

It could be seen that current Vietnam's naval modernisation focused heavily on complementing the Navy current most critical weaknesses, which is its capability to defend national interests further off-shore in the outer areas of its 200 miles EEZ and beyond. The modernisation path seems to be diversification of both the platforms and the sources. There is little evidence, apart from it seeking anti-submarine capability to suggest that the choices of Vietnam procurement and modernisation was in direct response to other regional competitors military modernisation. No action-reaction type of dynamics exists in Vietnam's recent naval procurement and acquisition. While Vietnam continues to base its military strength on Russian support, it clearly does not want to form any military alliance or rely on a single weapon or country to defend its critical interests, hence, it tends to invest in diversification of platforms and defense partners. These trends reflect that Vietnam's self-reliant and non-aligned defense and foreign policy are not provocative to the regional security environment and do not instigate any arms race. While pursuing its naval modernisation, Vietnamese leaders showed understanding to the complexity and sensitivity of the regional security environment and tried to be transparent about its intention and procurement objectives as well as defense policies. On several occasions, Vietnamese leaders have publically clarified its defense policies to the domestic as well as regional and intentional observers. The Vietnamese Prime Minister, for example, in response to the question as to whether the region is going through an arm race, and weather Vietnam is jointing such a race, commented: "*Vietnam pursues a peaceful and cooperative foreign policy, but also need a strong army for self-defense. The human factor is decisive, but equipment is very important. When economic condition allows, we need to modernise the military. This is a very usual business, every country does it. I want to emphasise that Vietnam modernise the military in accordance with the economic condition, not because we want to race with any country*".[38] Phung Quang Thanh, the Minister of Defense of Vietnam, said that Vietnam naval modernisation is in line with global trends as well as the national economic development. He does not see the modernisation as an arms race but an effort to enhance "*national defense force responsibility to protect national sovereignty, contributing regional peace and stability. This is a normal activity of every country, including Vietnam*".[39] Nguyen Chi Vinh, Deputy Minister of Defense, also said Vietnam did not modernise its army in response to other country's modernisation. He explains Vietnam military modernisation comes obvious given the country's economic progress in recent years. He stressed that while the region was severely affected by the economic crisis, Vietnam's economy recovered rather rapidly, thus allowing the country to afford some modernisation, and that in the future, Vietnam's modernisation will be according to the country's economic development, but will be below 1.8 per cent of GDP, much less proportionately to GDP than many other regional countries.[40] Vietnam's self-reliance and non-aligned foreign and defense policy is most clearly reflected in Nguyen Chi Vinh insistence of Vietnam's "3-nos" policy: no military alliance, no foreign military base in Vietnam's soil, no military cooperation against a third country.[41]

Conclusion

If the definition of an arms race is a country competing to stay ahead of another country militarily with no specific goal, Vietnam for certain does not seems to be in a mood nor has any interest to join one. Vietnam naval modernisation is neither offensive nor provocative to the regional security environment. On the contrary, it was clear that Vietnam naval modernisation is defensive and the recent procurement of naval equipment is fully in line with Vietnam's systematic implementation of her *Marine Development Strategy Towards 2020*, enabled and accelerated in part by the economic boom of the past five years, especially the period of 2007-2008, after Vietnam was admitted to the WTO and as a consequence received record high foreign direct investment in the subsequent years, boosting the country's dollar reserve, enhancing its confidence and purchasing power.

Vietnam's recent procurement can hardly trigger a regional arms race as some have feared because the country's navy is not directed to nor threatens its neighbouring country to provoke a response. In fact, several countries in the region started modernising earlier than Vietnam and spent more money than Vietnam both in absolute terms and as a proportion to their GDP. Vietnam's choice of equipment for modernisation, however, does seem to take into account the regional security context, the status of Vietnam's relations with some of the most important equipment suppliers as well as the status of regional security cooperation. Therefore, Vietnam's choice for procurement was the outcome of careful calculations and balance between geo-strategic, economic as well as political-security factors facing the region and Vietnam, and not a mere response based only on any particular country or countries modernisation plan. The military modernisation plan, seen in perspective and in conjunction with Vietnam's development strategy and foreign policies, highlights Vietnam's desire to protect its national interests while remain independent, self-reliant and at the same time broaden its international cooperation and integration regionally and globally.

NOTES

1. Joseph Abrams, "Vietnam Orders Fleet of Russian Subs, Sending Message to China", July 5, 2009, at www.foxnews.com, (Accessed December 21, 2010)
2. "Rethink this arms buildup", *Bangkok Post's Opinion*, December 21, 2009.
3. Christian Le Mière, "The Spectre of an Asian Arms Race", IISS, at https://www.iiss.org/en/publications/survival/sections/2014-4667/survival—global-politics-and-strategy-febraury-january-2014-e67d/56-1-11-le-miere-ca5b
4. Lieutenant General Cao Thuong Luong, "Vietnam's marine and the protection of Vietnam's sovereignty", *Vietnam Military Science* Journal, (3), 2008.
5. Ta Quang Ngoc, "To make Vietnam a strong and rich marine nation", *Communist Review Journal*, 13 (133) 2007.
6. Introduction to Communist Party documents section of the Vietnamese Communist Party website. (http://www.cpv.org.vn/cpv/Modules/News/NewsDetail.aspx?co_id=30463&cn_id=239397)
7. Ibid.
8. Communist Party Economic and Social Development Strategy for 2011-2020, reported at the Communist Party official website. www. cpv.org.vn
9. At http://giaoduc.net.vn/Xa-hoi/Tin-nong/Tuyen-bo-danh-thep-cua-lanh-dao-Viet-Nam-ve-bao-ve-chu-quyen/4304.gd
10. Vietnam calls the South China Sea by the name "East Sea"
11. Vietnam Defense White Paper 2009, Ministry of Defense of Vietnam, p.17
12. Tran Hien, Deputy Director-General of Vietnam Petro, "Improving overall strength in protecting sovereignty, and oil exploratory activities", *People's Defense Journal*, July 2009.
13. "How long do Vietnamese fisherman have to suffer?",at http://www.rfa.org/vietnamese/in_depth/Stories-of-a-fisherman-returned-from-Hoang-Sa-05062010071515.html
14. Interview with Tran Van Hinh, Chief Naval Commander, reported on http://vnexpress.net/GL/Xa-hoi/2009/11/3BA152CA/
15. The XI Communist Party Political Report, reported on the Vietnam Communist Party official website.
16. www.biengioilanhtho.gov.vn
17. A delegation of 60 oversea Vietnamese from more than 30 countries participated for the first time on a trip to the Spratlys in June 2012, reported by the Voice of Vietnam at http://vov.vn/Nguoi-Viet/Cam-nhan-Truong-Sa-sau-chuyen-ra-dao-cua-ba-con-Viet-kieu/211499.vov
18. Vietnam Defense White Paper 2009, Ministry of Defense, p. 71
19. Ibid., p. 72.
20. "Current state of Vietnam's Navy", www.vndefense.info

21. Nguyen Van Hien, "To further promote its tradition, build a strong People's Navy to protet national sovereignty", *Military Research Journal,* (5), 2007.
22. "Vietnam to receive first Kilo sub in 2013", at http://vietnamdefence.com/Home/tintuc/Nam-2013-Viet-Nam-nhan-tau-ngam-Kilo-dau-tien/201010/49803.aspx
23. "Russia floats out second Gepard class frigate for Vietnam", http://en.rian.ru/mlitary_news/20100316/158215375.html
24. http://www.bbc.co.uk/vietnamese/vietnam/2009/12/091215_russia_frigate.shtml
25. For example, http://vietnamdefence.com/Home/tintuc/Viet-Nam-dong-o-at-tau-ten-lua-Molnya-Projekt-12418/201010/49794.aspx
26. http://rusnavy.com/nowadays/concept/opposite/vietnamcontracts/index.php?print=Y
27. http://quocphong.baodatviet.vn/Home/QPCN/Hai-tau-phao-Svetlyak-len-duong-ve-Viet-Nam/20128/228777.datviet
28. Robert Karniol, "Naval air arm to boost Viet offshore power", *The Straits Times,* Singapore, September 14, 2009
29. http://www.vietnam-about.com/forums/showthread.php/1768-Plans-for-Vietnamese-Navy-Modernization
31. http://www.rfa.org/vietnamese/VietnameseNews/vietnamnews/Vietnam-wants-France-to-help-with-military-modernization-07262010164828.html
32. "Vietnam receive Bastion missile system", at http://vietnamdefence.com/Home/phantich/Viet-Nam-nhan-2-he-thong-BastionYakhont-va-trang-bi-BrahMos-cho-Su30MK2/20107/49411.aspx
33. http://www.monthlyreview.org/0306rupe2.htm
34. Robert Karniol, "Vietnam bolstering Spratlys firepower", *The Straits Times,* Singapore, May 10, 2010
35. http://quocphong.baodatviet.vn/Home/QPCN/4-linh-vuc-hop-tac-quan-su-Viet-Nam—An-Do/201111/177216.datviet
36. http://www.vietnamplus.vn/Home/Thuy-Dien-giup-VN-che-tao-may-bay-khong-nguoi-lai/201211/169620.vnplus
37. http://tuoitre.vn/Tet-Online-2012/Tet-Viet-2012/473963/Dien-mao-moi-cua-Hai-quan-Viet-Nam.html
38. Interview of the Prime Ministers, at http://vietbao.vn/Xa-hoi/Thu-tuong-Viet-Nam-khong-chay-dua-vu-trang/11144855/157/, on July 1, 2010
39. http://tuoitre.vn/Chinh-tri-Xa-hoi/449577/Dai-tuong-Phung-Quang-Thanh-Xay-dung-hai-quan%C2%A0hien-dai.html
40. Interview with Nguyen Chi Vinh, "Vietnam does not accept dependent peace", at http://vietbao.vn/Xa-hoi/VN-khong-chap-nhan-nen-hoa-binh-le-thuoc/11200697/157/
41. "Vietnam reiterates 3-nos policy", *Vietnam News,* at http://vietnamnews.vn/Politics-Laws/202996/Vietnam-reiterates-3-nos-defence-policy.html

6

India's Military: Modernising not Militarising

Prakash Menon

Introduction

This chapter examines the relationship between India's military modernisation and the dangers of militarisation in the context of India's national security imperatives. The theoretical framework is set within the existing dynamics of the civil-military relationship in India, and the emerging threat perspective. It argues that India's military plays a stabilising role in a turbulent neighbourhood, but its Modernisation is handicapped by the concomitant and acknowledged necessity to preserve civilian control over the military. The focus is on India in the context of its disputes with China and Pakistan.

The strategic behaviour of nation states is influenced by belief systems that are internalised, both culturally and structurally. Culturally, the conflation of geography and history produce the essential geo-political contours that frame a nation's ideas on the use of force, both internally and externally. The other influential dynamics in the use of force are the existing structures of decision-making. The issues of force application relating to the adversary, the purpose, the timing and the method lie more in the realm of political decision making, though not exclusively so. How to use force falls more within the military domain—but again, not exclusively, especially because of the presence of nuclear weapons. In democracies, militaries direct growth and force development process plans in accordance with the envisaged political objectives and, thus, prepare for war according to the guidance and the resources provided by the political leadership. This continuous process is commonly understood as Modernisation.

The growth of the armed forces even in established democracies like India must guard against what has been a primal fear—the fear of the military as an institution usurping political power. Hence, the concentration of military power in the military elites must be avoided. Though the character of civil-military relations has been changing, the Indian military has remained steadfastly subordinate to political control. Although some of these changes may be inevitable and positive, the effects of other changes, while strengthening the modernisation process, must necessarily be compensated by structural changes that should weaken the danger of militarisation, however remote its possibility. In essence, it should not only help to strengthen democracy, but also increase our capacity to protect India against anyone seeking to use force to resolve disputes.

Since a nation's cultural predilection to use force is rooted, in some unknown degree, in the influence of the military in the highest levels of decision-making, it is therefore a possibility that authoritarian states are more inclined to use force. This is not to say that democracies refrain from using force. Military minds, through an acculturation process, are naturally inclined to believe in the effectiveness of the military as an instrument to resolve disputes. This faith is deepened mostly through training and experience. In times of crisis, military men are naturally inclined to reach for the gun, and their advice would normatively reflect a deep rooted conviction regarding the utility of the military instrument. Historically, military leaders may have promised a quick victory, but normally delivered less. When General Krishnaswamy Sundarji assured the Indian Prime Minister that he would wrap up the LTTE speedily, it was certainly misplaced confidence though our judgment is based on hindsight.

Nuclear Context

Current military Modernisation in Asia has, as one of its architectural components, the nuclear overhang that is expected to keep conflict at levels that should not put the nuclear threshold and operational shibboleths to test. So, while operational concepts like Anti Access Anti Denial (A2AD) are impressive for deterrence, they could be rendered ineffective both by counter measures and the 'friction' of battle, thus making it unlikely that it will survive the practical test. The danger, however, is when civil political decision makers, being unduly persuaded about their military effectiveness, overplay their hand during times of crisis.

War cannot escape the elements of uncertainty and chance. Described by Carl von Clausewitz as 'friction', it has—and will remain—the major factor in war's unpredictability. The current fashion of believing that technology has made the battlefield transparent and, therefore, any target can be neutralised swiftly requires an injection of reality. Data overload is also a major problem. It must also account for the fact that adversaries are as crafty as us, and are equally apprehensive of their survival. An added dimension is that machines, however hi-tech, require to be operated by human beings who, under stress, are susceptible to all kinds of strange behaviour because of which judgments are often impaired. Human error as a natural phenomenon will endure. Both machines and humans, individually and in combination, contribute to 'friction' which has, so far, remained impervious to advancements in technology. Of course, friction can sometimes be overcome by preponderant superiority. But such superiority is unlikely to be obtained in the Indian context. However, it could be achieved between China and the smaller countries of East and South East Asia if force application remains bilateral.

The temptation for the political leadership to utilise the military instrument to resolve disputes is, in contemporary times, circumscribed by the presence of nuclear weapons. Though such circumscription applies more to nuclear powers, they are also applicable to most of the American allies who are under its nuclear umbrella. The presence of nuclear weapons has, so far, driven levels of conflict to lower levels—often described as the 'Security-Insecurity Paradox'. Nuclear powers have avoided direct major conflict even though they prepare for the 'big fight' in the name of deterrence. They also know that such an encounter could speedily deteriorate into mutual suicide, driven primarily by friction from which there could be no escape—unless of course one is willing to gamble with one's own survival. Postulations of intra-war nuclear deterrence are based on a misplaced faith on the ability to control nuclear exchanges. Fortunately, no country has moved beyond the rhetoric of nuclear war, and put these illusory notions to test.

With the advent of the nuclear weapons, war prevention rather than decisive military victory has become the predominant theme. The acquisition of photogenic weapons with the promise of effectiveness, combined with esoteric operational buzzwords, certainly strengthens deterrence at the psychological level. An industry for buzzwords has been created, most of which pretend to portray an old concept as new, or promise to create a revolution that, unfortunately, can just as easily be nullified by a wily adversary. Asymmetric Warfare, Effects Based Warfare, Net Centric Warfare and Hybrid Warfare are a few that illustrate the point that they are all old wine in new bottles, meant to impress the gullible, and probably also an opportunity to launch several 'theses'. The danger is when an issue cannot be unilaterally resolved, and the military sells the promise of a quick victory to the political leadership. This brings about a situation fraught with uncertainty.

Asian Context

Ever since the Indian economy started on its present trajectory of economic growth, the Indian military, in tandem with the heightened military related activity in Asia, has been on the Modernisation path. This trajectory of Modernisation has been driven by the contours of geo-politics in its strategic neighbourhood that includes mainly the sub regions of South Asia, West Asia, Central Asia, South East Asia and the Indian Ocean. The main impetus that drives the geo-politics of the Asian region is the shift of economic power from the West to the East, as also the turbulence in West Asia where India has to protect its interests. The economies of China, Taiwan, Japan, India, South Korea and the ASEAN countries have been major contributors in the shift of economic power. The pace of growth of China's economy for the last three decades, complemented by a concomitant build up in its military capacity, has reverberated across Asia, thus triggering the classical phenomenon of the 'Security Dilemma'.

In line with its aspirations of being a global power during and after the Cold War, the USA considered the Asia-Pacific region as having been pacified. However, with China's enhanced military capacity, the USA is finding its hold on the Asia-Pacific region being increasingly challenged, and has reacted by rebalancing towards the Asia-Pacific region. The USA and China are now the two main powers whose struggle for dominance in this contest is casting its shadows over the Asian geo-political landscape. Although the rivalry is also marked by their mutual economic dependence, it is also regarded as a competition between an existing hegemon and a challenger who envisages a return to its historical place of glory amongst the comity of nations. China refers to it as the 'Chinese dream'.

The impact of the US-China rivalry has been felt by all countries in China's periphery and has rekindled historical, land and maritime border disputes. In nearly all the cases, the expression of Chinese claims, and the counter-claims by other nations have resulted in an increase of tensions. The nations impacted by China's claims have, in recent times, described the Chinese military and para-military activities as being 'assertive'. Nearly all the nations in the Western Pacific have sought to balance China's growth through US support. It also means that any major conflict in the region will be fought under the nuclear overhang of USA and China, and hence, only 'limited force'—also described as assertiveness used for limited purposes—is already being played out in China's periphery.

At another level, though all these countries have China as their major trading partner, unlike the Sino-US situation, the balance of trade is in China's favour and it, therefore, holds the economic upper hand. While the military balance at a collective level in the Western Pacific currently remains in favour of the USA and its allies, doubts about the reliability of the USA to come to their aid in limited crises have gained ground as China has pushed the envelope only marginally—enough so as not to provide sufficient stakes for US intervention.

Indian Context

Since India has unresolved disputes with China and Pakistan, and all are nuclear armed, the use of force to resolve disputes will have to be circumscribed by the nuclear factor. This is not to say that it is the only factor; but it underscores the point that its influence on the use of force cannot be wished away, especially if one is talking of the 'big fight'. Beyond the rhetoric, all political and military leaders are convinced that nuclear wars cannot deliver victory even though nuclear weapons can be useful for the deterrence of nuclear engagement. The resolution of the Sino-Indian and Indo-Pak disputes are not any more resolvable through the use of massive force. Force application will have to be contained, and the form of conflicts restricted to changing the status quo at best, through a process of applying limited force for limited objectives.

India has also been experiencing the assertiveness of China through some increase in the activity pattern on the disputed Sino-Indian border, and in the Indian Ocean region. The Depsang incident of 2013 has been the most prominent in recent times. China has, over the last decade or more, built an extensive infrastructure in Tibet that has enhanced its capability for supporting military options on the Sino-Indian border. It has developed roads very close to the Line of Actual Control (LAC) and, therefore, stepped up their patrolling activity in some places. The overall military balance, especially on the disputed Sino-Indian border, is in favour of China. However, the military balance in the Indian Ocean favours India due its geographic location and the fact that it is supported by a sizable naval capability that is also expanding.

Towards the West, India is also saddled with territorial disputes with Pakistan. It has fought four wars in the last sixty-six years and has had numerous skirmishes on the border, especially along the Line of Control (LOC). The lingering effects of US-Soviet tensions have also impacted the Indo-Pak situation during the Cold War through the legacy of the US using Pakistan to fight the Soviets in Afghanistan. It has accelerated the rise of extremism and the jihadi culture now being witnessed in full bloom. The use of terrorism as a foreign policy tool has been the hallmark of a proxy war against India, which Pakistan has continued to support since the late 1980s. Pakistan has also used the USA and China to balance India. China has had a long and enduring relationship with Pakistan that has deepened in military terms along with the growth of China's military power. China has also been the main contributor to the build-up of Pakistan's missile and nuclear capability. In the present situation, Pakistan's relationship with China remains steadfast, while its relations with the USA is maintained, however tenuously, due to the leverages it has regarding the US presence in Afghanistan and the support required for its planned withdrawal. Post the US withdrawal, the leverage will be weakened.

Despite the adverse balance of power with China and the large commitment of military forces against Pakistan, India continues to seek the management of the situation bilaterally. Though Pakistan has persisted in internationalising disputed issues, India has resisted most such attempts. The Indian thrust has been to develop an independent capability to defend its interests, not be part of any military alliance, avoid the game of military balancing and, through the development of friendly relations based on mutual respect, seek the resolution of the disputes without the use of force. In its ideas regarding the use of force resides the role India has chosen in a turbulent strategic neighbourhood. It is a role that has a stabilising effect on the Asian ambience, which is pregnant with possibilities of conflict.

India has successfully managed to create conflict resolution mechanisms with both China and Pakistan. With China, five agreements have been signed; in 1993, 1996, 2005, 2012 and 2013. These agreements have ensured that the border dispute is not resolved through the use of force, and local military tensions are resolved through suitably evolved mechanisms at various levels. It also covers various confidence building measures. These agreements have, despite occasional tensions, kept the borders peaceful without change in the status quo even as differing perceptions exist on the actual alignment of the Line of Control. The last incident when violent force application took place was in 1967. At the political level, the Sino-Indian dialogue on the border issue has, however, remained static since 2005 when the agreement on the political parameters and the guiding principles of a possible settlement was signed. Dialogue continues without much progress. The boundary problem is being managed; but resolution is not yet in sight.

The Indo-Pak ceasefire agreement was signed in 2003, and though the ceasefire continues to be disrupted from time to time, overall, it has provided a useful framework that has at least managed to keep at least an uneasy and intermittent peace. At the political level, the composite dialogue continues to meander through the maze of issues it seeks to address, and is often disrupted by the terrorism emanating from Pakistan. Disputes with Pakistan continue to be unresolved; the situation is being managed through the bilateral mechanisms that have been instituted. This is because India firmly holds the view that its disputes with China and Pakistan cannot be resolved through the use of force.

China and Use of Force

China and Pakistan have both been inclined to use force more liberally than India, both internally and externally. China has been culturally inclined to use force to resolve disputes. According to Western sources, China has resorted to violence in varied forms in 72 per cent of its foreign policy crises as opposed to 18 per cent in the case of the USA, and 27 per cent in the case of the Soviet Union.[1] These statistics are misleading as they mask greater use of force in absolute terms, but still indicate the general propensity regarding use of force. However, China's methodology for the use of force is different from the Clausewitzian paradigm. According the Clausewizian paradigm, the use of force must be directed to the centre of gravity of the adversary by applying maximum force. The Chinese, based on Sun Tzu, direct their effort at the minds of the adversary, and believe in achieving the objectives through either no use of force or only the minimum use of force. The route to success is the exploitation of emotion rather than the sheer use of physical power. China's growing assertiveness is better explained in the context of Sun Tzu. The Sun Tzu style is also eminently suitable for the nuclear age. Thus, the creation of doubt regarding the reliability about its major ally—the USA—amongst the South East Asian and East Asian nations through assertiveness is Sun Tzu in action. India's military planners must learn from it, and prepare most for the small dosages of force that China might apply periodically.

At the structural level of China's decision making process, the open source indications are that the trend has been to reduce the role of the military in political decision making. The move to restructure the military regions to facilitate inter-service integration will reduce the clout of its army, and power could diffuse towards its navy and the air force. For sure, the growing maritime capability of China is being reflected in its representations in various higher level bodies. The concentration of power in the army is being diluted, with the size of the army reduced, and its non-military involvement (like the agricultural battalions) dismantled. Overall, though the military retains its presence in various high level decision making bodies, there is a shift that could be assumed to indicate a dilution of the military's influence. However, as long as the structural construct of the armed forces being directly answerable to the Communist party remains, the influence of the military on decision making could be substantial. The recent trend has been the increasing role of force in its relations with its smaller neighbours. Thus, the more accurate assumption would be that China's cultural proclivity to use force has been strengthened with military growth; but force application will be moderated by political forces that could be acting within Sun Tzu's paradigm of directing the threat or application of force at the adversary's mind, in small doses, with each dose meant to create the intended psychological effect.

Pakistan and Use of Force

Pakistan's evolved style regarding the use of force has been its reliance on terrorism that provides it some deniability and yet impacts the dispute resolution process. Deniability as a predominant characteristic was witnessed with the tribal invasion of 1947, infiltrators in 1965, regulars in the garb of militants in Kargil, and its proxy war using terrorism as the means of applying force. The character of the threat from Pakistan is terrorism. Catering against such a threat should inform planning and preparations.

At the structural level, Pakistan has had 32 years under military rule in sixty-six years of its existence. It indicates the pervasiveness of Modernisation. The military continues to play a preponderant role in shaping both the foreign and security policies. However, with civilian rule since 2009, military preponderance has become diluted to a limited degree even as it retains its grip on policy issues that impinge on its autonomy and corporate interests. The ISI continues to be answerable to the Army, and even undertakes some activities without the knowledge of the civilian government. Terrorism directed against India could be expected to continue even as the civil government talks peace. In essence, the current structural dynamics in Pakistan have followed a trend of decline in the military's pre-eminence in some areas of domestic politics, but continue to shape its foreign policy by using terrorism as its instrument of choice. The on going internal turmoil against home grown terrorist groups could increase civil-military tensions, especially if the Army views the civil government's actions as compromising its corporate interests. Sustaining the India threat by arming itself can be expected to continue, with the availability of resources being the only constraint.

India and the Use of Force

Having achieved independence through a non-violent struggle, India has been reluctant to use force except as a last option when all other means for achieving justice have been exhausted. This doctrine has been reflected in all the occasions when India has used force. In the early period after Independence, the newly created Indian Union used force to liberate Junagadh, a tiny princely state in Western India, where a Muslim minority ruler remained recalcitrant despite the majority population wanting to accede to India. But force was used only after prolonged negotiations and when all other means were exhausted. The situation was similar with the incorporation of Hyderabad in 1948 and later in Goa in 1961 against the Portuguese. Even when tribal invaders swarmed into Jammu & Kashmir (J&K) in October 1947, India's action to rush troops was taken as a defensive measure to save the state from the Pakistani tribals. However, this was done only after having obtained the Instrument of Accession from the ruler of J&K. The Sino-Indian War of 1962, the Indo-Pakistan Wars of 1965 and 1971, and the Kargil Conflict of 1999 were all forced upon India, with either China or Pakistan being the aggressor. In the popular imagination of most Pakistanis, India is considered to have been responsible for the break-up of Pakistan in 1971. However, the fact is that Pakistan had unleashed genocide in East Pakistan, which resulted in several million refugees fleeing to India. The speedy withdrawal of the

Indian troops after the establishment of the Bangladesh government headed by Mujibur Rehman provides ample indication of India's role in the War. The dispatch of an Indian Peace Keeping Force (IPKF) to Sri Lanka in the 1980s was the aftermath of the agreement between the Sri Lankan Government and the Liberation Tigers of Tamil Eelam (LTTE). The swift dispatch of troops to the Maldives in November 1988 to save the government of President Abdul Gayoom, then under threat from mercenaries, was undertaken at the request of the elected government of that country. Indian troops immediately withdrew once the mission was accomplished.

The Indian restraint displayed in the aftermath of the terrorist attack on Mumbai on 26 November 2008 perhaps personifies India's belief that force must be used only after all other means have been exhausted. It would not be too far off the mark to state that very few nations would have shown the restraint that India has shown in dealing with terrorism that emanates from Pakistani soil that is also abetted by elements of the Pakistan state. The fact that Indian political decision-makers could display restraint despite popular clamour for revenge is sufficient proof of political wisdom prevailing over strategic logic. India's rulers are convinced that force has utility, but the contextual vectors that encompass a particular situation must determine its utility. Force, Indians believe, is certainly required to defend territory and interests; but it may not always be the appropriate instrument of statecraft[2] except as a last resort.

India's Stabilising Role

The critical question that Indian strategic and defence planners will have to confront in the coming years is how India will deal with the changing strategic landscape occasioned by the emergence of power struggles in its strategic neighbourhood, and the continued use of terrorism as a foreign policy tool. As the Indian economy grows, demands that India take up 'greater responsibilities' are increasing; in fact, there are actual hints that India must be ready to use force to keep order in the region. Others have suggested that India become part of military alliances, an idea that is anathema to most Indians. The Indian political establishment has also shied away from such options, preferring instead 'strategic partnerships' with select countries. An overview of these partnerships will indicate that they tend to be issue-based and contextual. Thus, India can comfortably partner China on climate change or trade talks, while also partnering with the USA on nuclear non-proliferation. This approach is also evident in the Indian policy of committing the armed forces only under the banner of the United Nations. This is an expression of a deeply held belief that force must be used multilaterally—that is, only under the United Nations flag. It would be difficult for any democratic government to convince the Indian public that the Indian armed forces operate elsewhere without an international multilateral umbrella. As the world's most populous democracy and an economic power, it is perhaps fortunate that doctrinally, India will always view the use of force as the last resort. India, thus, views itself as a stabilising force in an uncertain world, and is in the process of a major military Modernisation programme, a major component of which is the development of its maritime capability that is expected to facilitate the role of becoming a net security provider in the region.

Military Modernisation

Modernisation is not merely the acquisition of the latest weapon systems; it has to be supplemented by the evolution of doctrinal changes that drive—and are driven by—structural changes and acquisition programmes. This, however, has not been the case. No overarching written security doctrine or strategy guides India's military preparations. While political guidance is provided through the Defence Minister, it is subject to differing individual inter-service interpretations due to the inadequacies in the structure that are required to harmonise inter-service differences, resulting in the lack of inter-service synergy—an imperative to plan, prepare, and fight modern wars.

In recent years, India's defence modernisation has been the 'trending story' in defence industry circles. The planned military Modernisation is formidable in numerical terms (about US$ 100 billion for the 12th Five year Plan period), and was to include the procurement of 126 multi-role combat aircraft, armed helicopters, aircraft carriers, conventional and nuclear powered submarines, heavy and light artillery, heavy lift aircraft and air defence equipment, *inter alia.* While the press played up the fact that India was Asia's largest importer, there was little appreciation of the fact that nearly all of this modernisation was replacement driven. A few facts may be cited to buttress the argument regarding the replacement driven modernisation process. Following the collapse of the Soviet Union, the Air Force experienced a drop in its total number of squadrons: from 45 to 42. In 2009, this fell further to 32, and a delay in new acquisitions may lead to a further reduction to 29. The long delayed MMRCA (Medium Multi Role Combat Aircraft) project and the selection of the Advanced Jet Trainer have seen severe delays. Similarly, considerable portions of the Indian Army's major weapon systems, which are due for replacement, have unfortunately been delayed as it is an issue that is mired in the pathologies of the defence acquisition system. This also highlights the lack of a sound defence industrial base required to support India's growing defence requirements. The potential of the private sector remains under-utilised even as the inefficiencies of the public sector continue to exist. The dependence of the Indian military on imports, even though jeopardising strategic autonomy, continues to be around 60 per cent, and while the country has achieved self-sufficiency in the field of long-range missiles, it has paradoxically failed to fully capitalise on it.

When viewed against similar enhancements taking place in the neighbourhood, the advantages in most areas are, admittedly, marginal rather than overwhelming. However, the prime impulse for armament up-gradation has been the 'security dilemma' posed by the process of the global economic power shift from West to East. The Indian challenge for defence planners remains providing the requisite security posed by the 'security dilemma' without upsetting the apple cart of India's development process, and requires the optimum utilisation of resources.

As Indian economic growth has faltered, plans for modernisation have already come under pressure as is evident in the reduction of over Rs. 140 billion (late 2012) from the funds earmarked for procurement, and the shift of allotment from the capital to the revenue budget. In nominal terms, defence allocation increased by 5.3 per cent, a far more modest growth in comparison to previous years (17.6 per cent and 11.6 per cent in 2012 and 2011, respectively). After taking the average inflation rate—estimated at between 7.6 per cent and 10 per cent—into account, the actual growth of the budget is estimated to be in the negative: by about 1.3–3.7 per cent. This negative growth is further worsened by a high exchange rate.

Structural factors in the budget are equally dismaying. Long delays and poor procurement policies have led to committed liabilities absorbing major portions of the budget, thus minimising future procurement options. A second factor is the high percentage of resources swallowed up by revenue, with the Army the worst hit being a personnel heavy service. Inadequacies in services planning is apparent from the fact that the gap between the expectations (capital projections) and the actual allocation rose from around 11 per cent (2009-2010) to over 30 per cent in the financial year 2013-14. The 2014-15interim budget constraints bring home the point that military growth priorities need to be reworked. Despite the prioritisation of the development of naval capacities, it is challenged by competing demands from the other Services due to joint service structural inadequacies. The extant inter-service structures and the lack of adequate integration between the Services and the Ministry of Defence, pose obstacles to the prioritisation problem. At the heart of resolving these twin issues of inter services synergy and the MoD-Services integration is the issue of India's civil-military relationship that is frame-worked within the issue of Modernisation.

Modernisation

The question of whether Asia is militarising is often posed these days. This is because if there is a calculable and clearly perceptible rise in military spending across parts of Asia, there are also assertive—and at times openly threatening or nationalistic statements—from leaderships in various countries, thus adding such simmering disputes to the milieu. An overview of the literature on conflict analysis indicates that these developments are often seen as the underlying symptoms of a trend towards modernisation. Prominent analysts describe these symptoms as 'a rush to armaments, the growing role of the military establishment in national and international affairs, the use of force as an instrument of supremacy and political power, and the increasing influence of the military in civilian affairs'.[3] In the past, 'Modernisation', and its associated term 'militarism', has been associated too often with Fascism and Nazism, and the associated horrors that were wrought by them.

There are, however, significant differences in the characteristics of modernisation from country to country, depending on whether the purpose/objective/reason is to deter an invasion or attack, to engage in war, or to gain prestige. At the same time, modernisation may also have an internal dimension where militarism may be seen as the systemic disruption in terms of repressive measures, and the seizure of civil competencies by the military. Militarism can, therefore, be understood as a dynamic process, operating at both the national and international levels, to mobilise people and resources for organised warfare which acts in such a way as to expand the role of the military over civilian affairs. Even though tensions in the civil-military relationship continue to simmer, India's well-entrenched democratic systems have very successfully kept militarism at bay.

Civil-Military Relations

At the time of Independence, civil-military relations in India, though they never met all the stipulations, were more akin to Samuel P. Huntington's 'objective control' which, by carving off a sphere of action for it which was independent of politics, was a form of civilian control based on efforts to increase the professionalism of the officer corps. It was, in Huntington's view, the preferred form of civil-military control that delivered the best military effectiveness. The armed forces were viewed as a separate institutional entity of the state, whose professional expertise in the 'management of violence' gave them a separate status from the civilian establishment. The military leadership viewed officer-ship as being different from any other vocation, upholding a sense of responsibility to one's work which while transcending monetary rewards, underlined the importance of a sense of community feeling and commitment to the members of one's group.[4] Wartime control, however tenuous, also followed the guiding principle of objective control. During the wars of 1947-48, 1965 and 1971, once the broad political objectives were identified, wartime control followed, in general, the principle of guided military autonomy, It was never total autonomy—as indeed it shouldn't be—but the issue was that the professional judgment of military leaders must prevail in spheres that were considered to be purely military in nature.

However, the 1962 war witnessed a severe dilution in the application of the principle of military autonomy. In contemporary times, there is a blurring of the purely military domain due to the conflation of external and internal threats, an emergence of newly contested domains—like space and cyber—that are constituted more by civilian entities but whose protection requires a high degree of civil-military coordination. The concept of a purely military domain has reduced in relevance. Consequent to its emergence as a nuclear power, pervasive war time oversight of the military would be required, thus encroaching further on what the military has traditionally considered its exclusive sphere.

Over time, the civil-military equation has gradually changed to what appears to align more to the description of being under 'subjective control' which, according to Huntington's theory, means that civil control over the military is exercised by civilianising the military and controlling it from within by transplanted civil elites. With greater control being established by the civil elite (bureaucracy) of the Ministry of Defence, and most of its values mirroring societal norms, the Indian military appears to have become more civilianised. The main problem with this shift, however, is that India does not derive the full benefit that should accrue from our military being the third largest in the world, thus necessitating an examination of why the shift from objective control to subjective control has not translated into desirable benefits.

Civilianisation of the Military

The apolitical character of the Indian military is founded on institutional non-involvement in politics. Hence, the ultimate impact of the civilianisation of the military is the erosion of its apolitical character, a long term effect that is already being felt. The symptoms and the causes of civilianisation are being exposed with time, and most of the leadership of the armed forces no longer consists of people whose sense of responsibility transcends monetary compensation for one's work. Earlier, the military profession did not look upon itself as one meant for the creation of wealth; 'high thinking and plain living' was the motto given to newly commissioned subalterns. Cantonments provided exclusivity for a lifestyle that was plain in taste and dignified in manner. At this time, India had not been smitten by the consumer revolution, and the atmosphere of camaraderie could still be found; high professional standards prevailed and more than made up for the lack of material comforts. Now, materialism—the prime driver of the consumer revolution—has shifted the weight of values to material possessions. Perhaps this shift could not have been stopped, as it was part of a larger societal trend to which the armed forces were not immune despite the fact that they continue to be ensconced in exclusive military cantonments/air force and naval bases. The effect of the consumer revolution in diluting the insularity of the military from the civil, in tandem with the armed forces prolonged deployment on internal security duties has only served to deepen the institutional urge for comparisons with other civil service institutions, thus civilianising the military.

The Pay Commissions, especially from the Third Pay Commission onwards, have realised that the existent unfair comparison is a constant source of angst amongst the armed forces and its pensioners. The larger internalised narrative has been that the armed forces have a justified claim to exclusivity which, not having been given the cognizance it deserves, no desired special treatment has ensued. Public dissatisfaction expressed by the military leadership after Sixth Pay commission signified that the notion of parity is the essential benchmark between the civil services and the armed forces. In essence, it not only dismissed the concept of exclusiveness, but therein confirmed the loss of an important parameter that provided the rationale for objective control

The sustained deployment of the armed forces in counter insurgency duties and internal security situations in J&K and the North East has diverted attention and resources from its main role. Worse yet, this, essentially 'policing role' has impinged on military values through their exposure to the underbelly of domestic politics leading inevitably to a certain degree of politicisation both at the collective as well as the individual level. Working in close proximity to the police forces has also resulted in the adoption of some practices which the army can ill afford. The unfortunate part is that though the Central Armed Police Forces have expanded significantly—with the raising of more units on the anvil—their effectiveness is stymied by the lack of concomitant reform in the local police forces coupled with other organisational pathologies, especially the quality of leadership at most levels. Hence, the army has not been sufficiently thinned out even from areas where the levels of violence have declined over several years. A gradual reduction of the army from internal security duties should be a strategic objective, not only to regain focus on its primary tasks, but also to preserve its professional exclusivity so much required for improving its military effectiveness as also to restore, to some degree, its apolitical character.

In recent times, the threat to the apolitical character of the army has also emerged from the community of veterans which has staged public protests, returned their medals, taken the government to court as a collective, and is now even trying to enter the arena of politics as a collective body. Disabled soldiers have been forced to seek remedy from the court, with the Ministry of Defence appealing to the Supreme Court and losing a number of cases. Veterans keenly feel a sense of victimisation from an unsympathetic government. While it is not possible to go into the causes of such a situation, the fact is that India's veteran community is getting more and more politicised as a collective body, in contrast to previous trends in which politicisation happened at the individual level. Some veterans are also taking up issues affecting serving soldiers, thus politicising them. This is not a healthy trend, as it could have a long term harmful impact on the apolitical character of the armed forces. Because the serving community has umbilical linkages, the politicisation of veterans cannot be viewed in isolation from the long term danger of the politicisation of the armed forces.

Political Control and Decision Making

The political control of the military is a necessary though not a sufficient condition for democracy to flourish. Unlike most of the armed forces in the developing world, the Indian armed forces have an exemplary record in their commitment to the democratic foundation of the state. This has been possible due to the political control exercised through Parliament, the Cabinet Committee on Security (CCS), and the Defence Ministry. Parliamentary oversight is exercised through debates on defence issues, the approval of the defence budget, questioning the executive in the Parliament, and the deliberations of the Defence Committee of the Parliament. The Committee examines all issues regarding security, and has the power to question the members of the executive branches of the government. The Committee can examine any issue it deems necessary, and most committees have made valuable recommendations. Unfortunately, many of these recommendations have not normally found favour with the Ministry, and *status quo* has prevailed. Also, defence issues are hardly debated except during crises or consequent to some incident. Not much debate takes place about the defence budget. Parliamentary oversight has, therefore, remained low and instead, the executive in the form of the Ministry of Defence has filled the gap.

The CCS, through the Ministry of Defence, exercises political control over budget allocation, expenditure, promotions and high-level appointments, *inter alia*. The Strategic Policy Group (SPG), constituted after 2001, with the National Security Adviser (NSA), the Cabinet Secretary, the Service Chiefs and the Secretaries of all major ministries as its members is the body below the political level that is tasked to examine cross cutting strategic issues and strategy formulation. Not only has the SPG rarely met, a former Foreign Secretary was not even aware of its existence! There has also been an illogical demand that the Chiefs must be part of the CCS. Such a dispensation will mean military inclusion in a political body, which is neither desirable nor feasible in India.

The problem of a greater military input in decision making has, however, a different colour. One of the foremost problems is that Service Headquarters have no effective mechanism to harmonise differences amongst themselves, and is coupled with the fact that the Defence Ministry is saddled with reconciling the differences without adequate in-house professional military expertise. Military advice, as is given, may lack objectivity as it is based on an individual service outlook. Thus, the structural inadequacies in the higher military leadership compel the Ministry of Defence to arbitrate unresolved inter-service issues that actually require to be resolved by military professionals. A typical example is the issue of service ownership of armed helicopters. The Ministry of Defence finally ruled upon the resolution of the issue, which required reconciliation at the level of the Chiefs of the Army and the Air Force. The failure of arbitration at the professional level was due to the structural inadequacies of the higher military leadership.

The current system mandates that for all requirements, whether it be force development, training, maintenance and all major related activities, the armed forces need to obtain sanction—one that is usually financial in nature—from a civilian bureaucracy under the Minister of Defence, which administers such control. Since the military domain is a specialised one, the requirement for some military expertise to adequately facilitate the decision making body in the Ministry of Defence has been a long felt need. Following the Kargil conflict in 1999, though the Group of Ministers Report recommended that a system of training the civil services for duties in the Defence Ministry be put in place, it has not yet been effectively incorporated, and the civil services officers continue to depend mostly on learning on the job. Several parliamentary committees in the past and, most recently, the Naresh Chandra Committee, have recommended an evolution of mixed staffing system to make up the lack of military expertise in the Ministry of Defence.

The higher military leadership, exercised through the Chiefs of Staff Committee (COSC) which consists of the three chiefs (with the senior most chief donning the additional hat of Chairman) is a system prone to dysfunction regarding the resolution of inter service issues as the Chairman, but naturally, cannot be expected to take an unbiased stance. The longevity of the Chairman's tenure, which has ranged from one month to a year, depends upon the balance of service at the time of appointment. In 2001,the frequent change prompted the Group of Ministers to recommend the creation of the post of a Chief of Defence Staff (CDS). Apart from political reticence, the recommendation was not implemented due to the opposition from the Indian Air Force. Although an Integrated Defence Staff was created, it has not resolved the original problem of lack of synergy at the apex level of the military leadership. Here too, the Naresh Chandra Committee has recommended the creation of a Permanent Chairman for the Chiefs of Staff Committee.

In the absence of a Permanent Chairman or any other such entity, and from a purely military professional requirement point of view, the capability of the armed forces to prepare, fight, and win future wars is being impaired. With the existing structure of the higher military leadership, a slew of issues that call for reform at the inter services level cannot be carried out due to the difficulty of arbitration at the existing COSC level. Major reforms—such as the integrated commands that are required to fight modern wars—can be examined and implemented only after structural changes takes place. Integrated commands is a 'big ticket' reform that is urgently needed not only to improve military effectiveness, but also to save resources by doing away, where possible, with service specific command headquarters that are geographically separated at present. While balancing the development of continental and maritime capability, the prioritisation of hard power development is also required; however, this has been difficult to achieve due to the inability of the COSC structure to harmonise differences. Another example is the development of a dedicated amphibious capability, which being a tri-service capability, has no dedicated ownership. Many such reforms that demand action cannot be successfully undertaken because of the existing structure of the higher defence leadership. The creation of a Permanent Chairman is not the silver bullet to resolve inter-service issues; rather, it is a necessary, though not sufficient condition for essential reforms to materialise. This is, however, a purely Services perspective. The real catch lies at the political level.

While in theory, the biggest internal threat to Indian democracy could emanate from its armed forces, in reality India's democracy has been supported by the armed forces, which have never threatened its subordination to civilian political control. To be sure, there have been instances when civil-military relations have been through rough patches; but those were over individual disagreements between a Chief and the political authority. There has never been any instance of the military as an institution defying political authority or attempting to usurp political power. Instances of episodes with General K.S. Thimmayya, Admiral Vishnu Bhagwat, and General V. K. Singh were all individual runs-in with political authority. It is natural to expect that these cases would, in some manner, have left their mark on the psyche of India's political leadership, coming as they do in the face of the record of most militaries in the developing world. The political leadership cannot but be conscious of the latent threat that all armed forces pose to democracies, and that India can be no exception. Institutional safeguards must remain a concern and, on that account, one of the major concerns must be prevention of the concentration of power within the military hierarchy. It could be surmised that the non-implementation of the earlier recommendation on CDS may have been rooted in the political apprehension that it may concentrate too much power in one individual. While seemingly genuine, the apprehension is completely misplaced.

The fact is that with the apolitical character of the armed forces being threatened, the creation of a Permanent Chairman will diffuse power which, in the present arrangement, is skewed in favour of an individual Service, principally the Army Chief, who commands a body of nearly 10 lakh personnel. Nowhere in the world does such a concentration of military power exist under a single individual. In theory at least, such a concentration of power is the biggest threat. Thus, politically, the requirement is to reduce such a concentration of power and not emasculate it by pervasive oversight and supervision, because doing that would only serve to impact military effectiveness.

The creation of a Permanent Chairman, or any such like entity, will be a political solution to the problem because the diffusion of power in several Joint Service Commands will provide the necessary safeguard should its apolitical character get further eroded. It will also facilitate the enhancement of military effectiveness through efficient and integrated planning, and enhanced capacity to conduct war. With integrated commands, the Chiefs will focus on individual service training, administration of personnel, and the equipping of their own particular service. This solution converges not only with the military requirement of generating synergy, but meets the political condition of the prevention of a concentration of power within the military. In the course of time, an Indian model for integrated military structure will evolve. Considering India's security panorama, the creation of the Permanent Chairman is only an essential first step, and a reform that is long overdue.

Conclusion

India's historical record regarding the use of force, its refusal to join military alliances, and its economic and military power, imbue the armed forces with the capacity for their role as a stabilising force in the changing geo-politics of the global and Asian landscape. Effective military capacity requires the politically guided development of hard power through sustained modernisation. But India's ability to fully undertake the role of a stabilising force is hampered by the pace of its Modernisation due to the lack of structural reforms in the higher defence structure as well as the deficiencies in its defence industrial base.

India's military modernisation requires better direction, and be fast tracked. It is, in some ways, hostage to a structure of higher defence leadership that is unsuited to plan, prepare, and execute its role of optimally providing the military element of India's defence. The modernisation effort is, in a way, paradoxically stumped by its own strength of remaining a steadfast institutional support for India's democracy even though the concentration of power continues to exist within the military structure. The existing concentration of military power under the Army Chief requires diffusion through major structural reforms (like Integrated Commands) that are also necessary for improved operational effectiveness. Such reforms are not feasible under the existing COSC system. The reforms suggested in the existing COSC system are meant to break the present impasse, and to enable other reforms that are necessary to ensure a better utilisation of the nation's scarce resources and improve its military effectiveness. In the process, military power will be better aligned to political objectives and, more importantly, provide further additional safeguards against modernisation that lurks, however remotely, in the barrel of the gun. Presently, there is a convergence of political and military interests that should be grasped with alacrity as dark clouds of uncertainty, in the context of Asian and global geopolitics, hang ominously overhead.

NOTES

1. Alistair Iain Johnston, 'Thinking about Strategic Culture', *International Security*, Vol. 19, No 4, Spring 1995, pp. 23-64.
2. Prakash Menon, 'Military as Stabilizer', in Rajesh Basrur, Ajaya Kumar Das and Manjeet Pardesi (eds.), *India's Military Modernisation*, Oxford, Oxford University Press, p. 283. 2014.
3. Mathews George Chunakara, Militarisation of Politics and Society, Daga Press, Chapter one, Dec 1994, http://www.daga.org.hk/press/military/military01.htm
4. Samuel P Huntington, *The Soldier and the State: A theory of Politics in Civil Military Relations*, Massachusetts, Belknap Press, 1981, p. 68.

SECTION III

Economic Global Shifts Toward Asia

7

Economic Shift Towards Asia: Realities and Challenges

Hu Shisheng

Introduction

Ever since the beginning of this century, with the rapid rise of India and China and the recovery of East Asia as a whole from 1997's financial crisis, the global economic center of gravity has visibly shifted toward Asia, with East Asia in particular. Forecasts by various well-known institutions in the world have regarded the prospect of a rising Asia, where China, India, Japan, South Korea, and ASEAN are standing high on the world economic plateau. Especially after the 2009 global financial crisis and its concomitant economic recession, economic global shift toward Asia has become much more evident.

Economic shift toward Asia: Measurement

In terms of GDP scale, in 2012 in $,[1] China is 8.22 trillion, Japan 5.96 trillion, India 1.82 trillion, South Korea 1.15 trillion, ASEAN 2.31 trillion, while in comparison, the GDP of EURO countries stood at 13.8 trillion, and the U.S. 15.68 trillion. In 2012, the combined GDP of East Asian alone could be around $ 18 trillion USD, accounting about 25per cent of the world GDP ($ 71.70 trillion), and 119 per cent of the GDP of the U.S. However, in 2006, the combined GDP of East Asia was around $ 9.63 trillion, accounting for 72 per cent of U.S. GDP ($ 13.33 trillion); in 2002, the combined GDP of East Asia stood at about $7.13 trillion, accounting about 64 per cent of U.S. GDP ($ 10.98 trillion). The shift is quite outstanding.

In terms of trade volume, the intra and inter regional trades of East Asia have been becoming more and more impressive, accounting more than the half of global trade. In particular, according to the statistics issued in 2012 by the U.S. commerce department and China's Ministry of Commerce, China's trade volume was $ 3.87 trillion, while the U.S. was $ 3.82 trillion.[2] China has overtaken the U.S. as the world's largest trading nation. Moreover, China became the largest trading partner of 124 economies by 2011, compared with 70 in 2006, which meant that it overtook the United States as the biggest trading partner of most nations. The U.S. which was the largest trading partner of 127 economies about five years ago, meanwhile, has seen a decrease in that number to 76, according to figures from the *Associated Press*, released December, 2012.[3] In 2012, China's share of global trade (with $ 34.8 trillion) increased to 11.1 per cent in 2012 from 10.4 per cent a year earlier, while Japan's about 4.7 per cent ($ 1.643 trillion), South Korea's about 3.0 per cent ($ 1.067 trillion), India's about 2.2 per cent (with $ 780 billion).

In terms of regional economic arrangements, Asia with East Asia in particular is also full of dynamics. The most outstanding regimes are five bilateral FTA arrangements between ASEAN and its six partners (China, Japan, South Korea, India, Australia, and New Zealand). Now all the countries involved are making efforts to optimise and even upgrade the five FTAs into RCEP, with the purpose of building up new regional free trade regime with higher quality. RCEP, once established by the end of 2015, will become the largest FTA regime (in terms of population) in the world, including 3.3 billion population, and the total GDP of about $ 19.3 trillion. Besides, It is significant that China, South Korea and Japan are promoting very hard trilateral FTA negotiations and monetary cooperation, though disturbed every now and then by the sovereignty disputes and historical legacies. In terms of GDP in 2012, the club of these three countries alone could defeat EURO countries and overhang the U.S.

In terms of foreign exchange reserve, East Asia has more than 70 per cent of the world foreign exchange reserve, among which 70per cent are USD assets; also 70 per cent of the money purchasing the U.S. treasury securities have come from East Asia. That is to say, East Asia has been a most major pillar in supporting the USD dominant regime in the world.

However, the above global economic shift toward Asia and East Asia in particular, is still a process and has a long way to go. Also, since such a process could be stopped and even be reversed, Asia and especially East Asia has a lot of hard homework to do instead of feeling complacent about the above achievements. In this sense, Asia needs to address the following challenges with success.

First of all, in terms of policy making powers and sayings in setting up or reforming economic orders and institutions, the U.S. and EU still play dominating roles. In recent years, there have been some modest reforms in the existent international economic regimes and institutions. For example, China's shares and voting powers in IMF have been increased from 3.72 per cent to 6.384 per cent and from 3.65 per cent to 6.07 per cent respectively, just second to the U.S. and Japan. After the reforms of World Bank (WB), China's voting powers have increased from 2.77per cent to 4.42 per cent, also second to the U.S. and Japan. Also, the voting powers and shares in IMF and WB have been increased accordingly for anther emerging large economic community—India. However, the old dominant powers still dominate the economic system. This reform still needs the U.S. Congress to approve to come into force. More significantly, the U.S. alone still has the veto power in blocking any major decisions made by IMF and WB, since the U.S. holds about 17 per cent voting powers in these institutions. The reform has been at the cost of EU and Japan.

What is more alarming is that, the existent dominant powers centered with the U.S. has kicked off a set of new initiatives to prevent the economic global shift from the old center U.S.-EU to Asia with East Asia in particular. In recent years, after the global financial crisis, the international community has witnessed that the U.S. has let three sets of big international negotiations. The successful conclusion of the Trans-Pacific Partnership talks and the parallel Transatlantic Trade and Investment Partnership negotiations would definitely cement the dominant positions of U.S. and EU in global economy. To complete the patchwork, the U.S. and EU are also leading the talks between more than 20 advanced and rising economies to liberalise trade in services. All these efforts from the U.S. and EU shows that the old global powers have become more and more determined in giving up on the grand multilateralism (with WTO as its outstanding symbol), which has been regarded by the west as the powerful facilitator in empowering the visible global economic shift toward Asia during the Postwar era. In all these revolutionary economic reforming efforts, featured with the so-called "midi-lateralism",[4] none of the Asian rising powers, who are the main driving forces behind the current visible global economic shift towards Asia, is actively involved. As a matter of fact, the obvious sideline of both China and India is more than a coincidence. Each of the proposed new agreements could significantly strengthen the West's grip on global standards and norm-setting and reduce the East's bargaining positions in rule-making and policy-making in world economic activities. In general, the global economic leaders in rule-making and policy-making are still composed of old faces, like the U.S.

Second, the economic performance of East Asia still lacks the solid support of financial infrastructures. Although the Chinese RMB is fast becoming the dollar's major competition for dominance in global trade, but the U.S. dollar still functions as the bedrock of the global financial system. The Society for Worldwide Interbank Financial Telecommunication, better known as SWIFT, reported on December 3, 2013 that China's RMB was used in 8.66 per cent of global trade finance transactions in October 2013, and RMB has become the number two most widely used currency for trade finance, supplanting the EURO, which is used in 6.64 per cent.[5] However, the USD still accounts for more than 81per cent of global trade finance. Asian currencies are still used in a negligible quantity. Moreover, there is still no Asian Central Bank; there is no financial power or powerful financial infrastructure in Asian countries to match their economic might and dynamics in the global trade; there is no parallel financial capital in Asia in par with London or New York. Although UK has lost its super economic power status 100 years ago, London is still the world famous financial center, witnessing each year the world largest bond transactions. This has still endowed with UK significant influence in the world economic interactions. Moreover, the Wall Street controls the global money transactions and major commodities trading.

The U.S. and EU have hence enjoyed unparallel privileges and dominance in the world economic arena via dominating the international clearance currency. In line with the IMF statistics, during 2007-2012, the USD rate of usage in international commerce has been kept at 67 per cent, EURO at 23 per cent. While Asian currencies have legged quite behind, other RMB or Yen have been much used in financing trade even within Asia, let alone globally. There is only about 15per cent of China's foreign trade that has been undertaken in using RMB. Although Chinese economy ranks second in the world, the free flow of capital in and out of China is still under much restriction, the modern bond markets in China are still under-developed, the free convertibility of the RMB still has a long way to go. Although Japanese economy had ranked second for more than 30 years (from 1978 to 2009) and still ranks the third in the world, the high fluctuations of Japanese Yen in its value has prevented Japan to play the role of a financial giant. Although Singapore has become one well-known financial center in the world, the competitiveness of Singapore in allocating international financial assets still need more promotion.

In one world, the global financial power is still controlled in the hands of old centers, not the rising powers. The US and EU has not only controlled the trading-pricing power, but also the trading rules.

Third, Asia's innovation capacity still lags behind that of U.S. and EU. Although the number of patent applications and science papers published by Asian countries have witnessed increase, especially in China and India, and more and more high-tech companies have mushroomed in Asian countries with South Asia and Japan in particular, the capacity to lead and to undertake technological, scientific and industrial revolutions is lacking in Asia. The significant innovations and inventions, which have profound impact upon human lives and economic activities in the areas like new materials, big data, Automatic driving vehicle, living energy, internet of things (IOT), 3D Printing, bio-tech etc., have mainly been created from the U.S. and EU. An impressive number of innovative companies and talents are proactive in the U.S., while Asia with China and India in particular is still the major exporters of high-educated talents. Asia still needs much solid infrastructures to support its innovation. And the recent round of efforts by the U.S. and some EU countries in rejuvenating their industries and real economies, with more advanced technologies and competitive energy prices are also posing new significant challenges to manufacturing powers in Asia.

Fourth, the internal strategic mistrust even confrontations among Asian powers have been disturbing the regional economic integration efforts. The World Wars and Cold War legacies, sovereignty disputes and regional power tussles have persistently disturbed the efforts of regional economic institutional cooperation especially between China and India and between China, Japan and South Korea. For example, the sovereignty and historical disputes have greatly disturbed the negotiations among China, Japan and South Korea in formulating FTA arrangements and in inking currency swap deal.

It can be imagined that, if without the disturbance of geopolitics, the scale of Northeast Asia FTA alone could be as large as EU; if Taiwan, Hong Kong, Singapore and Four Small Tigers (Indonesia, Philippines, Malaysia and Thailand) be included, the East Asia FTA could be the world largest economic community, amounting to a total GDP of $ 30-40 trillions, much larger than the EU ($ 27 trillion) and the U.S. ($ 24 trillion. If by the end of 2015, RECP could be reached and even use local currencies in regional economic transactions, the dominance of USD will be weakened dramatically. Only then, it could be said that the center of global economic gravity genuinely has shifted to Asia, and especially East Asia.

If the shift of global economic gravity towards Asia is not to be disturbed or even not reversed, all Asian countries need more unremitting efforts. In general, whether the shift is completed largely depends upon whether China, Japan and India could overcome their disputes and differences and make joint efforts with success in the same direction.

NOTES

1. Refer to the data issued by IMF in April, 2013.
2. China Trade Report, 2012, http://www.iwep.org.cn/upload/2013/03/d20130307160336894.pdf
3. Bao Chang, "China continues to increase influence on global", *China Daily*, November 1, 2013, p.17, at http://www.chinadaily.com.cn/cndy/2013-01/11/content_16104315.htm
4. "midi-lateralism" mainly refers to "coalition of the willing". See Philip Stephens, "Trade trumps missiles in today's global power plays", November 21, 2013, at http://www.ft.com/cms/s/0/69fc0970-51f8-11e3-adfa-00144feabdc0.html#axzz2pQcgf67z
5. Neil Irwin, "This one number explains how China is taking over the world", *The Washington Post,* December 3, 2013, at http://www.washingtonpost.com/blogs/wonkblog/wp/2013/12/03/this-one-number-explains-how-china-is-taking-over-the-world/

8

India and China: The Benefits of Co-opetition

Rajat Kathuria, Samridhi Bimal and Devyani Pande

Introduction

International trade and cross-border investment is integral to the process of globalisation. Over the years, countries have increasingly liberalised their economies to international trade, both through multilateral trading arrangements and regional cooperation. The benefits of trade liberalisation are enormous. Trade has allowed countries to benefit from specialisation and economies to produce at a more efficient scale (OECD, 2011; WTO, 2013). Trade has raised productivity, facilitated the flow of technology and knowledge, and has proved to be the driving force for economic growth and development. Apart from economic benefits, another major consequence of trade is peace. A much debated issue has been whether trade can buy peace or is peace a way forward for trade. In today's global economic order where sub regional and bilateral regional economic cooperation and integration have security implications, it is plausible that trade can be a means of attaining peace. There is literature to suggest that an increase in bilateral trade, interdependence, and global trade openness significantly promotes peace. The effects of trade on peace may vary depending on the geographical proximity of countries. The peace promotion effect of bilateral trade integration is significantly higher for contiguous countries that are likely to experience more conflicts (Lee and Pyun, 2009).

Given the post-crisis scenario of slow growth and high unemployment in countries, and the failure to advance in multilateral trade liberalisation (Doha Round), regional economic integration is now seen as a 'second-best' alternative to sustain growth dynamics in middle-income countries. Following the global trend, Asia has also witnessed a shift in regional trade strategy from multilateral to sub regional and bilateral trade agreements. India and China are the two Asian superpowers that are crucial for the integration of the South-East Asian region. Both countries have specific characteristics that have been instrumental in shaping their role and significance in the global landscape. Trade between both countries has been growing but remains below the potential. Bilateral trade has a potential to reach US$ 100 billion by 2015.[1] This would create huge and unprecedented opportunities for businessmen and investors of both countries in recent years. However, India's burgeoning trade deficit with China has been a matter of concern, especially among policy makers. An important question that naturally arises is whether the magnitude of the trade deficit has or will be a problem for India in the near future, mainly from a political economy perspective.

The integration of the economies of India and China has the capacity to change the dynamics of trade and investment in the region. Being a part of the BRIC's conglomerate, both countries are seen as leading the global economic revival. In terms of trade, China had a trade to GDP ratio of 51.84 in 2012. The corresponding figure for India was 55.36 in the same year. The trade-GDP ratios of both countries have been among the highest in the Asian region. India-China trade is among the fastest growing bilateral trade relationships in the world, but insignificant compared to size of their economies. In the age of mushrooming growth of regional trading blocs, there are few alternatives to further liberalising trade, especially in the absence of a multilateral push. Therefore, the signing of a free trade agreement between both the countries is the need of the hour, and can herald a new era of economic cooperation for the entire region. An India-China FTA would foster outward-oriented development, and generate economic and social benefits. The bilateral FTA can serve as a bridge between South and East Asia, and could facilitate formation of the Asian Economic Community (Bhattacharya and Bhattacharyay, 2006). This could also lead to peaceful relations between the countries, and the region as a whole.

The possibility of peace through trade cannot materialise without considering security issues that are pertinent on a wider Asian and global canvas. In fact, it is fundamental in the current post-Cold War logic of international relations that a cooperative security engagement between countries with unsettled issues can be a confidence building measure (CBM) (Suryanarayana, 2013). Although there are many areas of India-China cooperation, the scope of engagement on the unresolved border issue needs to be deepened.[2] The present climate of India-China relations has been generally peaceful and an addition of economic dimension to the goal of mutual security trust would greatly enhance the association.

Trends in India-China Trade

Trade between India and China has been growing rapidly since the mid-1990s. In 1996, India's export to China was US$ 0.61 billion, which grew to US$7.18 billion in 2005 and registering a figure of nearly US$15 billion in 2012. India's exports to China have been growing at a much faster rate than its total trade. India's imports from China have shown a similar increasing trend over the last 2 decades. India's import from China skyrocketed to US$ 10.16 billion in 2005 from US$ 0.7 billion in 1996, showing growth of 12.43 per cent. India's imports from China stood at US$ 54 billion in 2012. In 2012, total bilateral trade stood at around US$ 80 billion, with an exponential growth of 23 per cent over the period 2010-11. The potential is achievable, and less than the potential figure of US$ 100 billion that the countries intend to reach by 2015. The potential of US$ 100 billion is still less compared to the potential India has set for trade with the USA standing at US$ 500 billion by 2015 and US$ 572 billion for trade with the EU by the same period.

Graph 1: India's Trade with China

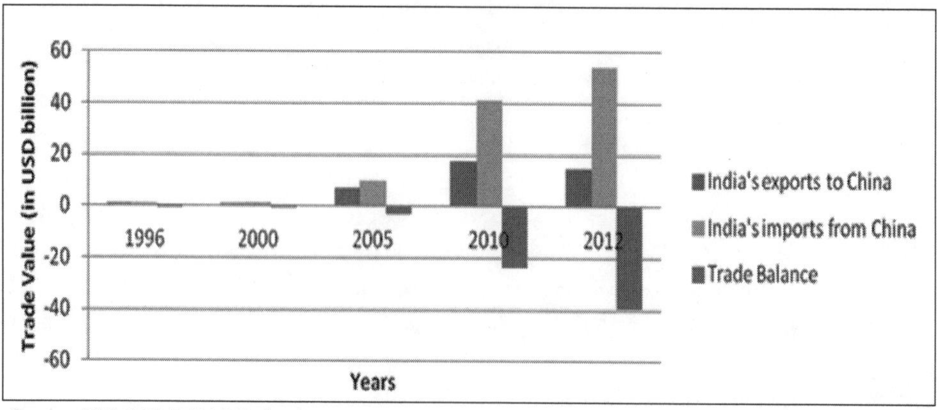

Source: UN COMTRADE database.

Trade data reinforces the dominance of Chinese exports. India's exports to China were US$ 14.72 billion and its imports valued US$ 54.74 billion in 2012. The fact that India's imports from China were 10 per cent of its total imports from the world, points to China's significance as a trade partner. India's main imports from China have been electrical equipment, machinery, nuclear reactors, organic chemicals, and iron and steel. Its top export items to China include cotton, copper articles, organic chemicals, plastic articles, and iron and steel (Annex 1 and 2). The export basket of Indian items to China consists mainly of intermediate and consumer goods and, contrary to popular opinion, China is not predominantly exporting consumer goods to India. Indian imports from China are mainly intermediate goods and are, therefore, an important driver of production costs. Table 1 below shows the classification of India's exports to, and imports from China in 2012 as raw material, intermediate goods, consumer goods, and capital goods.[3]

Table 1: Classification of Indian Exports to, and Imports from China (2012)

Classification	*Share of Indian exports to China (per cent)*	*Share of Indian imports from China (per cent)*
Raw Materials	7	6
Intermediate goods	37	41
Consumer goods	32	32
Capital goods	24	21

Source: HS Standard Product Groups Classification, World Integrated Trade Solution, World Bank; Author's calculations.

The share of raw materials in India-China trade has been negligible as compared to trade in other segments. Trade is mainly concentrated in intermediate and consumer goods between both the countries. With 41 per cent of Indian imports from China being intermediate goods, a major chunk of the Indian trade with China is in this segment. Capital goods is another segment in which trade between the two countries takes place, accounting for 24 per cent of India's exports to China, and 21 per cent of India's imports from China.

Apart from the threat of a Chinese invasion from imports, another popular concern has been the trade balance in China's favour. In 2012, India had the largest trade deficit with China: of US$ 39.41 billion. From an economic point of view, this is not surprising. Given the size of China which covers 3.5 per cent of the world's land area, is endowed with natural resources, and has established a decent manufacturing base, running a trade deficit with it is inevitable. Trade balance is not a bilateral issue but a regional or global one, especially when the world is coming to be dominated by global value chains and regional production networks.

China has captured the advantages of integrating into global value chains (GVCs) in recent times. On the other hand, India has not been able to capitalise on this phenomenon, despite its proximity to the East Asian economies. Electronics and electrical goods have been the prime mover of global production networks in East Asia (Athukorala 2013). Multinational firms set up offshore labour intensive manufacturing plants in China, and have benefited from China's processing trade regime (Ma and Assche, 2011). However, India has failed to attract investment from these larger companies due to an unfavourable business climate, fears of supply delays and disruptions that could bring the production network to a standstill. India can benefit from China's import dependent participation in the global production network for IT and electronics. Exporting IT and electronics intermediates to China can provide a boost to India's domestic manufacturing, and lead to its eventual integration into the value chain for IT and electronics. Moreover, services such as business services, transport and logistics, account for over 30 per cent value creation in GVC in China (OECD Council, May 2013).

Both India and China are relatively open economies, with trade to GDP ratios exceeding 50 per cent. The trade engagement of both countries is geographically dispersed and, therefore, addressing the trade balance at a bilateral level is neither feasible nor desirable. Moreover, trade theory teaches us that the current account deficit is not necessarily a sign of weakness, just as surpluses are not symbols of strength.[4] An FTA between India and China should, therefore, not be viewed from the narrow lens of bilateral trade, but from the perspective of issues related to growth and development.

Box 1: Tackling High Trade Deficit: India's Response

Trade deficit is not a new phenomenon for the Indian economy. India has been recording sustained trade deficits since 1957. Today, India has trade deficits with over 80 countries, and for the year ending March 2013, it recorded a trade deficit of US$ 87.8 billion. A trade deficit simply represents outflow of domestic currency to foreign markets. A large and unsustainable increase in the sale of domestic currency can drive value of domestic currency down, thereby making imports more expensive. India runs a trade deficit with two kinds of countries. Under Category 1, we have countries that are rich in petroleum, oil and natural resources—the demand of which is inelastic for a country like India. Under Category 2, we have countries like China, Taiwan, and South Korea from which we import high-tech machinery to raise productivity levels in India, and hence are desirable.

The foremost reason for the rise in trade deficit is due to the increase in imports of gold and petroleum products. In the recent times of increasing trade deficit, the policy response of the Indian government has been to tax imports, and tighten import financing. These policy decisions have been successful in reducing the demand for gold. Gold imports were around 60 tons in quarter 2 of the financial year 2013-14, representing a steep fall from 335 tons in quarter 1 of the same year. In September 2013, the trade balance registered a US$ 6.8 billion deficit. This was significantly less than US$ 17 billion shortfall reported in the same month last year, and represents the lowest deficit since

March 2011. The declining trend is expected to continue in the future. The government has also set an export target of US$ 325 billion for the current fiscal year—that is, 2013-14. In order to achieve this goal, the government announced a package of US$ 550 million which is intended to stimulate country's exports. Increasing exports and curbing the import of gold has been a successful means of filling the trade deficit gap.

The Case for an India-China Free Trade Agreement

Across the globe, there is an expanding network of free trade agreements (FTAs). High quality, comprehensive free trade agreements can play an important role in supporting global trade liberalisation, and are explicitly allowed under the rules of the World Trade Organisation (WTO). Under these agreements, parties enter into legally binding commitments to liberalise access to each other's markets for goods and services, and investment. FTAs also typically address a range of other issues, such as intellectual property rights, government procurement, and competition policy (Department of Foreign Affairs and Trade, Australian Government).

A pertinent question is why countries enter into free trade agreements. The answer is obvious: FTA is the best way to open up foreign markets to domestic importers. They help in reducing barriers, and protect the interests of traders, thus leading to a more stable and transparent trading and investment environment. Trade agreements also open markets to both countries, and provide a range of good quality products to consumers, thus increasing consumer welfare. Increased market accesses can also benefit producers who have a competitive advantage in the other country, thus increasing producer surplus. Overall, an FTA tends to increase welfare gains in both trading countries.

Both India and China have entered into several trade agreements, both at a bilateral and regional level. As of February 2014, India has entered into 19 trade agreements,[5] whereas China has signed 11 free trade agreements.[6] India has signed agreements with countries like Afghanistan, Bhutan, Malaysia, Japan, Korea, Chile, Nepal, Singapore, Sri Lanka. China has FTA's with Pakistan, Chile, New Zealand, Singapore, Peru, Costa-Rica, Iceland, Switzerland and ASEAN. Both countries are currently negotiating agreements with several other partners.

Given the power both India and China command in the global trade scenario, it is mildly surprising that India and China have not entered into a bilateral free trade agreement till now. In 2003, China and India established a Joint Study Group to examine the potential for economic engagement between the two countries. In October 2007, the Joint Task Force finalised its report on the feasibility of a China-India Regional Trading Arrangement (RTA). According to the feasibility report, a China-India RTA will be mutually advantageous. Both sides welcomed the conclusion of the feasibility study on an RTA between the two countries, and agreed to explore the possibility of commencing discussions on a RTA that meets the common aspirations of both countries, as also bring benefits to the region. The possibility of this happening is still under consideration.

Against the background of benefits of FTA and concerns about the rising trade deficit, it would be interesting to examine the position of other countries which have entered into trade agreements with China.

Table 2: Trade Balance of Countries Engaged in Trade with China and India

	Countries	*China's Trade balance 2012 (USD billion)*	*India's Trade Balance 2012 (USD billion)*	*Whether India has an FTA/ RTA with the country*
Countries that have FTA with China	Singapore	12.22	5.75	Yes
	Pakistan	6.13	1.13	Yes
	Iceland	0.006	0.02	No
	New Zealand	-1.94	-0.45	No
	Peru	-3.12	0.21	No
	Costa Rica	-4.36	-0.14	No
	Chile	-8.03	-1.84	Yes
	Switzerland	-19.37	-27.54	No
Countries for which FTA with China is under negotiation	Australia	-46.83	-10.29	No
	Norway	-0.047	-0.67	No
	GCC	-46.45		No
Countries for which FTA with China FTA under consideration	India	28.88[7]	-	
	Korea, Democratic People's Republic of	1.02	-9.59	Yes

Source: UN COMTRADE database; China FTA Network & Department of Commerce, Ministry of Commerce & Industry, Government of India.

Table 2 shows the trade balance of both India and China with countries that China has an FTA with; and those agreements which are under negotiation and consideration. China runs a trade deficit with most of the countries with which it has an FTA, and same is the case with India. This can be attributed to the fact that trade between countries is principally determined by the comparative advantage of the exporter country. For instance, China's imports from Peru are mainly items whose production involves the use of natural resources. The GCC countries are mainly oil exporting countries. This refutes the claim that all bilateral agreements must result in a sum game. In a world where multilateral arrangements co-exist with bilateral arrangements, a zero-sum game, while politically convenient, is an economic impossibility. Thus, the issue of a very high trade deficit must not impede the possibility of signing an FTA between the two countries. Essentially, a high trade deficit with one country can be countered by a trade surplus with another country, and so on. Thus, one must view bilateral trade deficit/surplus in a more general framework—that is, by keeping the country competitive advantages in the background.

The operation of an India-China FTA would have world-wide consequences. It would be the largest FTA in the world since it would cover two-fifths of the world's population (Bhattacharya and Bhattacharyay, 2006). India has a comparative advantage in services; but it significantly lags behind China in the manufacturing sector. It could also provide a competitive boost to our manufacturing sector. India's strength in software and services can complement the hardware and manufacturing prowess of China. India's exports of services to the world were US$ 141.20 billion in 2012 as compared to China's exports to the world of US$ 191.43 billion. Thus, the international competitiveness of China's manufactured goods is of great concern to India, and even China would have much to gain from India's comparative advantage in services.

The time is ripe for an India-China FTA given the increasing trade engagements of countries in the world, and especially in Asia. This should be done keeping in view the trade complementarities between both the countries. China is much ahead of India in terms of its degree of openness. It had initiated the process of liberalisation in 1978—much before India started its in 1991. The amount of FDI flowing into China has been far greater than that into India. China even out-places India in terms of the World Bank ease of doing business indicators: in 2013 China was ranked 91, and India was far behind at 132 in terms of the ease of doing business. India's association with China will help attract FDI, and improve its business prospects.

Security Issues

To view the relationship between the two countries in a holistic manner, the issue of security cannot be overlooked. Against the backdrop of a dynamic global scenario, security becomes a major factor in the enhancement of trade and investment between India and China. Border and maritime security issues are the primary matter of concern in the Asian region.

The strategic geo-political location of both India and China inevitably has consequences on the way trade and investment arrangements in the Asian region are developed. China is the only country to be a crucial actor in four separate regional subsystems: Northeast Asia, Southeast Asia, South Asia, and Central Asia. India, on the other hand, commands a similar position in South Asia, and is an important link between the fast growing South-East Asian countries and Central Asia.

The border disputes between India and China are generally seen as the biggest hurdle to improving bilateral ties. Disagreements such as that over the Arunachal Pradesh border, the westernmost Aksai Chin region, and construction on the Brahmaputra river that flows from Tibet to China have been at the fore. China proposed making use of the existing mechanism of Special Representatives to strive for a fair and rational solution framework acceptable to both sides, and prevent the issue from affecting bilateral trade relations (Suryanarayana, 2013). However, inertia in the India-China relationship has been generated by their prolonged failure to resolve the border disputes. Recognising the importance of partnership for peace and prosperity to serve the fundamental interests of the people of the two countries,[8] India and China signed the Border Defence Cooperation Agreement in October 2013. Entering into an economic agreement might not completely solve these problems; but it would be a step ahead in improving cooperation between the two countries.

One of the top foreign policy priorities of China has been to maintain sufficient military and economic strength. The fact that it is ranked above India in the nuclear material security index reinforces the policy goal.[9] The recent setting up of an air identification zone by China across islands—the jurisdiction of which are disputed between China, Japan and Taiwan—has also been a cause of concern for its neighbours.

The 'String of Pearls' approach is another noted strategic move that China has undertaken in the recent years. It refers to the network of Chinese military and commercial facilities along its sea lines of communication. With the use of the 'string of pearls' strategy, China has been able to establish a series of nodes of military and economic power throughout the South Asian region. So far, the 'pearls' in this 'string' include Bangladesh (Chittagong), Burma (Sittwe and Coco Island), Sri Lanka (Hambantota), Pakistan (Gwadar), and Tanzania (Bagamoyo).[10] The origin of this strategy can be traced to China's rapid economic development, and its dependence on foreign sources of energy. This has enabled China to set up naval bases extending from the South China Sea to the Indian Ocean. It is quite evident that China has been using economic incentives to strengthen its strategic control over South Asian countries. To what extent trade can assist in overcoming security problems between India and China, especially in energy security, is a matter that needs to be explored.

Triangular Dynamics: India, China and Pakistan

There is another pair of countries in the South-East Asian region that bears close resemblance to the relationship between India and China. Keeping the India-China in the background, the relations of India-Pakistan are quite similar at a micro level. The dynamics of the India-China and India-Pakistan relations are comparable in issues of trade, investment and security. Trade between India and Pakistan has always been inextricably linked to the political relations the two countries share, rather than being governed merely by economic factors. Relations between India and Pakistan have been strained due to a number of historical and political factors. In 1996, India accorded Most Favoured Nation (MFN) status to Pakistan, thereby offering it the same trading regime it offers to any other country in the world. Pakistan, on the other hand, continued to allow imports of a limited number of items from India, collectively known as the positive list, in which the number of items has increased gradually. The grant of MFN was linked to the resolution on the Kashmir issue (Taneja et al., 2013).

The process of trade normalisation was finally set in motion in 2004—during the Commerce Secretary level talks on Commercial and Economic Co-operation between India and Pakistan. In this comprehensive dialogue, trade negotiations were to be discussed, along with a dialogue on several other issues. In recent years, the two countries have made several efforts to delink trade from other political and security issues. India and Pakistan are members of the South Asian Free Trade Area (SAFTA) Agreement,[11] the aim of which was to integrate the South Asian region economically by offering preferential treatment to its members. However, with the two largest countries in the region not trading under normal WTO rules, SAFTA remains a virtual non-starter till date. The bilateral trade between India and Pakistan stands at US$ 2.6 million—much below the potential of US$ 10.9 billion. The trade normalisation process will unleash trade opportunities for both India and Pakistan. Trade has also been viewed as being the instrument of improving political relations between the two countries. Recently, an innovation in nomenclature was introduced in the Commerce Secretary level talks between the two countries. MFN was rechristened the reciprocal 'Non-Discriminatory Market Access' (NDMA) to overcome the politics linked to the translation of MFN in Urdu.

There is a stark similarity between the India-Pakistan relationship and the India-China relationship. The economic engagement between India and China can be viewed through the same lens at a macro level. Similar to India-Pakistan trade relations, trade relations between India and China have been viewed cautiously against a background of security concerns. In both cases, the bilateral relationship is under the broader ambit of a multilateral agreement. India and China are members of Asia-Pacific Trade Agreement (APTA), which is a preferential trade arrangement formerly known as the Bangkok Agreement;[12]

whereas India and Pakistan are members of the regional South Asia Free Trade Agreement.

Figure 1: The India-China-Pakistan Dynamics

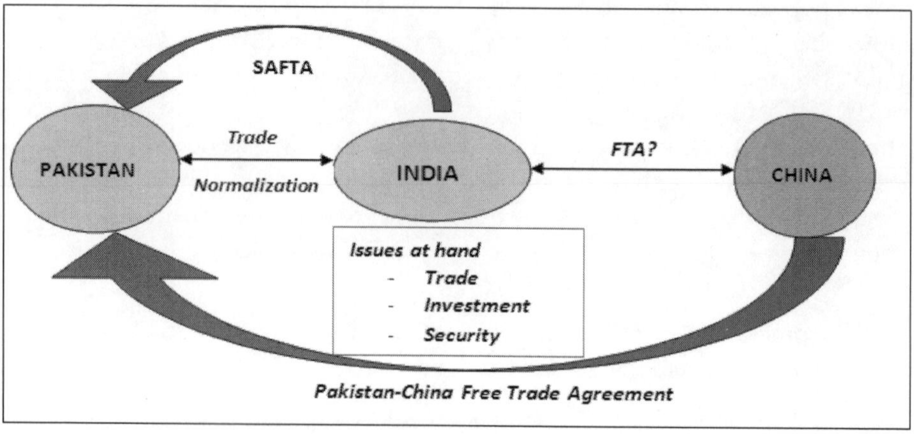

In both cases, serious concerns have been raised regarding the growing trade deficit. In the India-Pakistan trade scenario, industries in Pakistan are worried about the influx of items from India, once trade opens up. In India, there is apprehension among stakeholders that since India's tariff level is much higher than China, any reduction in tariff will open the floodgates of cheaper imports from China (Bhattacharya and Bhattacharyay, 2006).This did not happen, for instance, when China became a member of WTO, although there were apprehensions. Similarly, the Pakistan industry has not been overwhelmed by Chinese imports, post FTA. Also, trade is governed by the principle of comparative advantage, and a country would import only those items in which the partner country has an advantage. This would also provide consumers greater variety, and ensure cheapest and best quality goods. Also, from the consumers' point of view, the availability of cheaper goods would lead to an increased consumer surplus. Hence, market benefits are seriously undermined if the argument of there being an influx of goods from China is accepted.

Just like India is pursuing trade normalisation with Pakistan, despite the fact that Pakistan runs a trade deficit with India, it should also pursue case of trade liberalisation with China despite it running a trade deficit with it.

Conclusion

Trade, investment and security issues are the front runners of cooperation between countries today. Economies, world over, have recognised the importance of the comparative advantage theorem, and realised that the goal of 'self-reliance' is impractical. With economic growth and development as an objective, foreign policy goals have also undergone changes. Trade agreements are not entered into only by economic logic; political logic is also a big consideration. It is in a similar sense that an FTA between India and China should be carried out.

China's sheer size and volume of production has enabled it to play an active role in production networks and accessing the markets of the world. An FTA between India and China would be a chance for India to participate in global production networks worldwide. In turn, through the collaborations in research and development, India would be able to explore China's strengths, and incorporate them into its own system.

Economic interdependence can be a driver of improving relations between India and China. Security concerns have come to the fore since the recent setting up of an air defence identification zone in East China which has, subsequently, generated wide attention in the region. In response, China has also expressed a pro-India stand, declaring that it would not establish an air defence zone near the Indian border. Such efforts would go a long way in establishing mutually respectful relations. Nonetheless, one cannot lose sight of the fact that, in a post-WTO regime world, bilateral relations are affected by multilateral engagements too. In this context, India would have to strike a balance with China in terms of economic benefits and security concerns.

Clearly, co-operation and competition are two sides of the same coin for India and China. An FTA may act as a catalyst to strengthen their bilateral relationship under the multilateral ambit of the WTO, and towards formation of the Asian Economic Community. Cooperation and integration in trade, investment, and infrastructure development can foster outward-oriented development, and generate economic and social benefits. Integration will bring reduced transaction costs; greater productive infrastructure services; lower trade barriers; faster communication of ideas, goods and services; and rising capital flows. Integration requires a strong political will not only at the national level, but also at the regional level (Bhattacharyay and De, 2005). The environment for a FTA has never been better between China and India, and to reap the fruits of economic integration, India and China must enter into an economic engagement at the earliest. However, while signing a trade agreement, it would be important to consider issues of unfettered market access and security.

NOTES

1. Shri Anand Sharma, Minister of Commerce and Industry, Government of India; at a meeting with the Governor of Xinjiang province of China, Mr. Nur Baki. Press Information Bureau, Ministry of Commerce, 3 November 2011.

2. 'Despite cooperation, India-China border is issue: Foreign secretary', Sujatha Singh, Foreign Secretary; at the India-China Media Meet Forum, *DNA*, 16 September 2013.
3. According to WTO, products are classified as raw materials, intermediate goods, consumer goods and capital goods.
4. Paul Krugman, 'The Competition Myth', *New York Times*, January 23, 2011. Accessed at http://www.nytimes.com/2011/01/24/opinion/24krugman.html?_r=0
5. Department of Commerce, Ministry of Commerce and Industry, Government of India. Accessed at http://commerce.nic.in/trade/international_ta.asp
6. China FTA Network accessed at http://fta.mofcom.gov.cn/english/index.shtml
7. India's trade surplus with China is US$ 39.41 billion; however China's trade surplus with India is US$ 28.88 billion. The data mismatch could possibly be due to various reasons: difference in valuation of exports (f.o.b) and imports (c.i.f), different trade recording systems, exchange rate fluctuations etc. For more details, please see 'Mirror Statistics of International Trade in Manufacturing Goods: The Case of China', UNIDO [February 19, 2014] (http://www.unido.org/fileadmin/user_media/Publications/Research_and_statistics/Branch_publications/Research_and_Policy/Files/Working_Papers/2009/WP%2019%20Mirror%20Statistics%20of%20International%20Trade%20in%20Manufacturing%20Goods-%20The%20Case%20of%20China.pdf)
8. First Post, India. 'Key India-China border defence pact signed'. Accessed at http://www.firstpost.com/india/full-text-key-india-china-border-defence-pact-signed-1188753.html?utm_source=ref_article
9. India has been ranked below its two nuclear-armed neighbours—Pakistan and China—in the list of countries with a weak nuclear material security in the world, according to a US-based think-tank. Source: India ranked below Pakistan, China in nuclear material security index, *First Post*, January 9, 2014. Accessed at http://www.firstpost.com/india/india-ranked-below-pakistan-china-in-nuclear-material-security-index-1330827.html
10. D. James, 'The String of Pearls that is Choking India', Strategy Page. Accessed at http://www.strategypage.com/dls/articles/The-String-Of-Pearls-That-Is-Choking-India-4-30-2013.asp
11. Bangladesh, Bhutan, Nepal, Maldives are members as the least developed countries, and India, Pakistan and Sri Lanka are the members as the non-least developing countries of SAFTA.
12. Signatories to the Agreement include China, Bangladesh, India, Lao, Republic of Korea and Sri Lanka.

REFERENCES

Boilot Joseph, Jean and Labbouz Mathieu, *India-China Trade: Lessons Learned and Projections for 2015, Economic and Political Weekly*, Vol. 14, No. 26 (June 30–July 7, 2006).

Bhattacharya K., Swapan, and Biswa Bhattacharyay N., *Free Trade Agreement between People's Republic of China and India: Likely Impact and Its Implications to Asian Economic Community*. Working paper, ADB Institute, 2006. http://www.adbi.org/files/dp59.free.trade.agreement.pdf.

China FTA Network. Accessed at http://fta.mofcom.gov.cn/english/index.shtml

Copeland Dale C., '*Economic Interdependence and War: A Theory of Trade Expectations*', *International Security*, Vol. 20, No. 4 (Spring 1996).

D. James, 'The String of Pearls that is Choking India'. Strategy Page. Accessed at http://www.strategypage.com/dls/articles/The-String-Of-Pearls-That-Is-Choking-India-4-30-2013.asp

Department of Commerce, Ministry of Commerce and Industry, Government of India. Accessed at http://commerce.nic.in/trade/international_ta.asp

Devadason, Evelyn Shyamala, 'Establishing Regional Identities in East Asia: An Assessment of Trade Strategies of China and India'. 30 June 2013. Available at SSRN: http://ssrn.com/abstract=2287440 or http://dx.doi.org/10.2139/ssrn.2287440

'Despite cooperation, India-China border is an issue: Foreign secretary', DNA, 16 September 2013. Accessed at http://www.dnaindia.com/world/report-despite-cooperation-india-china-border-is-issue-foreign-secretary-1889864. Accessed 7 February 2014.

First Post, India, 'Key India-China border defence pact signed'. Accessed at http://www.firstpost.com/india/full-text-key-india-china-border-defence-pact-signed-1188753.html?utm_source=ref_article

First Post, India, 'India ranked below Pakistan, China in Nuclear Material Security Index'. Accessed at http://www.firstpost.com/india/india-ranked-below-pakistan-china-in-nuclear-material-security-index-1330827.html

'Globalisation, Comparative Advantage and the Changing Dynamics of Trade', OECD 2011.

Krugman P., 'The Competition Myth', *New York Times*, 23 January 2011. Accessed at http://www.nytimes.com/2011/01/24/opinion/24krugman.html?_r=0

Lee J. and Pyun J., 'Does Trade Integration Contribute to Peace?' ADB Working Paper Series on Regional Economic Integration, No. 24, January 2009.

Li, Quan, and Rafael Reuveny. "Trading for Peace? Disaggregated Bilateral Trade and Interstate Military Conflict Initiation." Journal of Peace Research(2008): 137-164.

Mirror Statistics of International Trade in Manufacturing Goods: The Case of China, UNIDO Research and Statistics Branch, Working Paper 19/2009. Accessed at http://www.unido.org/fileadmin/user_media/Publications/Research_and_statistics/Branch_publications/Research_and_Policy/Files/Working_Papers/2009/WP%2019%20Mirror%20Statistics%20of%20International%20Trade%20in%20Manufacturing%20Goods-%20The%20Case%20of%20China.pdf

Nathan, J Andrew and Ross Robert S., *The Great Wall and the Empty Fortress: China's Search for Security*, (New York: W.W. Norton, 1997).

Pillai, Rajeshwari, 'Why China, India Clash', *The Diplomat*, 9 March 2012.

Press Information Bureau, 'India China to Achieve Trade of US$ 100 Billion by 2015'. Last modified 3 November 2011. Accessed 7 February 2014 at http://pib.nic.in/newsite/erelease.aspx?relid=76986.

Suryanarayana, P. S., *India-China Talks: Full Scope Security is Potential Issue*, Manuscript, Institute of South Asian Studies, 2013.

Swain D. Michael, and Ashley Tellis J., *Interpreting China's Grand Strategy: Past, Present, and Future*, RAND Corporation, 2000.

Taneja, N., *Normalising India-Pakistan Trade Relations*, Working paper, ICRIER, 2013. http://www.icrier.org/pdf/working_paper_267.pdf

ANNEXURES

ANNEXURE 1

Top 10 Exports of India to China (2012)

HS Code	*Description of Items*	*Share of items in total trade*
520100	Cotton, not carded/combed	18%
740311	Cathodes and sections of cathodes	15%
260111	Iron ores and concentrates	15%
251611	Granite, crude/roughly trimmed	3%
390210	Polypropylene, in primary forms	3%
151530	Castor oil and fractions thereof	2%
720241	Ferro-chromium, containing by weigh	2%
520524	Cotton yarn, single (excl. sewing)	2%
130232	Mucilages and thickeners	2%
271011	Light petroleum oils and preparations	2%

ANNEXURE 2

Top 10 Imports of India from China (2012)

HS Code	*Description of Items*	*Share of items in total trade*
999999	Commodities not specified according	8%
851712	Telephones for cellular networks	6%
851770	Parts of telephone sets	3%
847130	Portable digital automatic data processing machines, weighing not more than 10 kg, consisting of at least a central processing unit	3%
310530	Diammonium hydrogenorthophosphate	2%
310210	Urea, whether/not in aqueous solution	2%
710812	Gold	2%
847330	Parts and accessories of the machines	1%
294200	Organic comps. n.e.s. in Ch.29	1%
851762	Machines for reception	1%

9

India and China in Global Value Chains: Taiwanese Investors' Perspectives

Kristy Hsu

Introduction

India and China are two rising economic powers in Asia and share a lot of characteristics in common. However, despite considerable amount of research aimed at comparing these two powerhouses on political, military, economic, cultural or other aspects, any attempts to make a genuine and comprehensive comparison would fail to precisely capture the differences of these two countries.

Having said that, in recent years increasing attention is drawn on how India and China have responded to economic development challenges and have shaped their policies of participation in economic globalisation and integration. Among the increasing volume of research, one focus is on India and China's respective roles in the global value chains (GVCs) and how they have and will hence be affected in the future.[1]

Taiwan has been an active investor in the region since the 1980s. Both India and China are important trading partners and investment destinations for Taiwanese firms. China is currently the largest host country of Taiwan's Foreign Direct Investment (FDI) outflows, estimated volumes of direct and indirect (FDI through third country) Taiwan—owned or—dominated investment reaching $ 250 to 300 billion. India is on the rise of receiving FDI from Taiwan, estimated direct and indirect investment from Taiwan ranging between $ 1 to 1.2 billion.

This chapter aims to make comparable analysis of India and China in their economic development and participation in the globalised economy and regional integration by examining their positions and roles in global value chains. The paper then presents the analysis from Taiwanese investors' perspectives, addresses the motives, decision making and assessment of the investment environments of the two countries and suggests policy recommendations for Taiwan and India to work together to encourage more Taiwanese investment in India and jointly promote India's position in GVCs.

India and China: FDI Flows and Participation in Global Value Chains

Economic Performance and FDI Activities in India

Indian economy experienced three decades of low and volatile growth after its independence, with annual GDP growth rate registered at less than 2 per cent in most years in this period. In 1991 India adopted economic reforms and since then the compound economic GDP growth rate averaged at 6.6 per cent until 2010, putting India among the fastest-growing economies in the world. 2011 and 2012 saw the turn of Indian economic performance which registered the lowest in the past ten years. However, in contrast with the economic growth momentum, the average annual growth rate in GDP per capita of India was only around 3.5 per cent in the 1980s, 3.7 per cent in the 1990s, and 5.5 per cent in the 2000s.

Despite the economy continues to register positive growth, India faces enormous challenges in sustaining satisfactory economic growth. Other challenges include expediting socio-economic reforms, overcoming institutional and infrastructure bottlenecks and addressing health, education and other human development issues while the country pursues economic development in the age of globalisation.

India also needs to increase efficiency in the agricultural sector and develop more value-added manufacturing and services sectors. The average share of agriculture in India's GDP decreased from around 55 per cent in the 1950s to 21.8 per cent in the 2000s, and further to 14.4 per cent in 2012. The share of industrial sector increased from around 14 per cent in the 1950s to 20.4 per cent in the 2000s, but decreased again to 19.8 per cent in the 2012 due to economic slowdown. The service sector demonstrates the strongest growth, increasing from 29.8 per cent in the 1950s to 53.7 per cent in the 2000s, and further to 65.8 per cent in 2012.

To respond to the call to develop manufacturing sectors, the Indian

Government adopted a series of economic schemes with the goal to develop a stronger manufacturing sector. In 2011 New Delhi passed the new manufacturing policy, envisaging establishment of mega-manufacturing hubs to attract foreign investment. The goals were to create 100 million jobs in 15 years; grow manufacturing sector about 3 per cent faster than GDP so that its contribution to GDP can increase from 16 per cent to 25 per cent by the year 2020. The policy, though failed to receive enthusiastic response in the local as well as foreign business communities. Recently, Prime Minister Narendra Modi's administration announced his new economic policy to "put India on a world map as a manufacturing hub."[2] The new government points out three pillars for bringing out transformation in manufacturing: improving business environment, enabling manufacturing and opening foreign direct investment (FDI) in key sectors.

India launched a "Look East" policy in 1991 at the start of its economic liberalisation by trying to enhance economic ties with Japan, China and some Association of Southeast Asian Nations (ASEAN)[3] countries. In 1991, India suffered from stalled economic growth of its agro-based economy where the industrial sector accounted for less than 15 per cent in the composition of the GDP. Therefore, one of the objectives of the "Look East" policy was to learn from China and other export-oriented ASEAN countries, such as Thailand and Malaysia, their experiences and models of developing manufacturing sectors as a growth engine in their economy.

However, when the New Manufacturing Policy was adopted 20 years later after the launch of the "Look East" policy, the share of the industrial sector in India's GDP remained relatively small, increasing only by around 7 per cent points to 22 per cent. India still suffers from stagnant performance of manufacturing industries and widening gap of its participation in Global Value Chains (GVCs) from China and other ASEAN peers. In this regard, the new government not only has to continue and strengthen previous government's policy to promote the manufacturing sector, it also needs to increase technological depth and value addition in the manufacturing sector in order to enable the country to "climb up the value chain ladder".[4]

In contrast to India's political and economic system, China is a socialist country with strictly controlled economy for three decades until in 1978 when its then Communist Party leader Deng Xiaoping[5] began to implement economic reforms and adopted a more market oriented economic system. After enjoying impressive economic growth for some decades, China furthered its programs of reforms under the guidelines of "Socialism with Chinese characteristics". In its latest 12th Five-Year Plans (2011-2015),[6] the key economic targets are to among others, grow GDP by 7 per cent annually, to increase urbanisation from 47.5 per cent to 51.5 per cent, to increase service contribution to GDP by 4 per cent points, namely from 43 per cent to 47 per cent, and to increase spending on R&D to 2.2 per cent of GDP. Instead of emphasis on 2-digit growth rate, Chinese political leaders made a turning point to prioritise sustainable and inclusive growth. Under this guiding theme, the Plan sets a clear goal to "move up the value chains", transforming China from being the "World Factory" to R&D hubs, high-end manufacturing and knowledge-based services sector.

There are various benchmarks in comparing India with China. In economic terms, ranked as the world's first and second populous countries, both countries have enjoyed strong economic growth than most other developing and emerging economies since the 1990s. In 2012, China's GDP at current price was $ 8.35 trillion, GDP at Purchasing Power Parity (PPP) was $ 12.47 trillion, only next to the US and EU and ranked as the third in the world. India's GDP at current price was $ 1.84 trillion GDP at PPP was $ 4.79 trillion, ranked as the fourth in the world. In the same year, two-way trade of China totaled $3.87 trillion, making it the largest exporter and the second largest importer in the world. China's share accounted for 11.13 per cent of the world's total exports and 9.78 per cent of the total imports. With respect to India, India's total trade volumes reached $785 billion, ranked as the 19th largest exporter and the tenth largest importer. India's share in international trade is much smaller than China. It accounts for only 1.60 per cent of the world's total exports and 2.63 per cent of the total imports (WTO 2013).

The most alarming difference between China and India trade pattern may lie in the trade balance. China has continuously enjoyed merchandise trade surplus with most of its major trading partner. In 2012 China's trade surplus reached $ 230 billion. Its constant trade surplus with the United States has received criticism for the White House and pressure to appreciate Chinese currency Ren Min Bi (RMB). India, on the contrary, has had a chronic trade deficit after its independence. Despite India tried to manage the deficit within certain limits of its current account deficit, the volume has increased to $ 192 billion in 2012 which is a historic record. In order to address the widening trade imbalance, India's policy makers prioritised various schemes to promote export, diversify export markets, and even restrict import activities. However, so far the result has not been satisfactory (Pal, Mukherjee, and Hsu 2013).

Foreign Direct Investment (FDI) is another aspect to analyse China vis-a-vis India in their economic development models. China began to relax limited sectors for FDI in the 1980s, while India began to actively attract FDI since 1991. Both countries put forward comprehensive policy frameworks and incentive schemes to attract FDI. Though foreign capital and technology have played an important role in both countries, FDI inflows and sectoral distribution demonstrate a different scenario.

Both China and India are among the most important FDI recipient countries in the world. The inward FDI stock in China reached $ 832.9 billion, while that of India reached $ 226.3 billion. FDI stock in China was about 3.7 times the volumes of Indian FDI stock (UNCATD 2013). In terms of FDI inflows, China continued to top all developing countries in receiving FDI from the world. In 2012, China received $ 121.1 billion of FDI inflows, a decrease by two per cent points compared with $ 124 billion in 2011. In the same year, FDI inflows in India registered only at $ 25.5 billion. India experienced its slowest economic growth in the past few years. The flat growth in FDI inflows since 2010 reflected the low investors' confidence in Indian economy.

On the other hand, both China and India are active investors in the world. Chinese enterprises began their outward investment activities in early 2000s, following Chinese Government's "Go Out Policy",[7] about two decades before India's large and outward-looking enterprises' movement in the world. However, China's FDI outflows surpassed India's both in volumes of FDI and number of projects. In 2013, China's FDI outflows reached $101 billion, which is a historic high and growth of 16 per cent points from $87.8 billion in 2012 (UNCTAD 2014).

Compared with China's upward outward FDI, Indian enterprises, on the contrary, tend to take a less outward-looking approach in the past years. In 2013, India's FDI outflows totaled $ 16.8 billion, a further decline from $ 84.9 billion in 2012. It represented only around 15 per cent of the average FDI outflows before the global financial in 2008/2009.

Figure One demonstrates common uptrend of both India's and China's inward and outward FDI stock. Both countries have seen continuous growth in their inward as well as outward FDI. China's inward FDI flows began to take off after early 1990s, while it took ten more years for India's inward FDI flows to see significant growth after mid-2000s. There is a positive correlation between China's inward and outward FDI stock. When China received increasing inward FDI at home, most significantly after mid-2000s, Chinese firms were also actively investing around the world. A similar correlation also appears between India's inward and outward FDI stock, though with much less growth momentum compared with China.

Figure two also shows a positive correlation between China's inward and India's inward FDI flows. Both countries saw their inward FDI flows continue to grow after the 1990s and both declined after the global financial crisis in 2008, but though picked up in 2010, they shrank slightly in 2012. However, figure two demonstrates quite different trends between China and India in their enterprises investment behaviors. China's outward FDI flows registered strong growth after mid-2000s and a further jump after the financial crisis, while India's outward

FDI flows showed a much mild growth until 2008 when it began to decline. Furthermore, since early 1990s when China received increasing inward FDI flows at home, Chinese enterprises also actively set foot in the world. While in case of India, after the global financial crisis, India not only saw a sharp decline in its inward FDI flows, its outward FDI flows also went down significantly. One reason to explain the opposite trends is Chinese Government's policy guidance affecting its enterprises' overseas investment activities which was hardly found in India and led to extremely different results.

Figure 1: Inward and Outward FDI Stock of India and China (1980-2013)

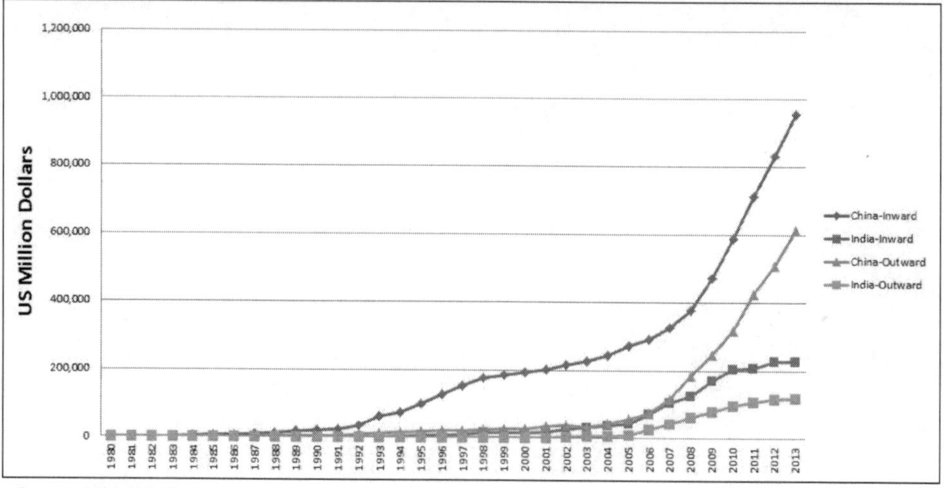

Source: UNCTADstat.

Figure 2: Inward and Outward FDI flows of India and China (1980-2013)

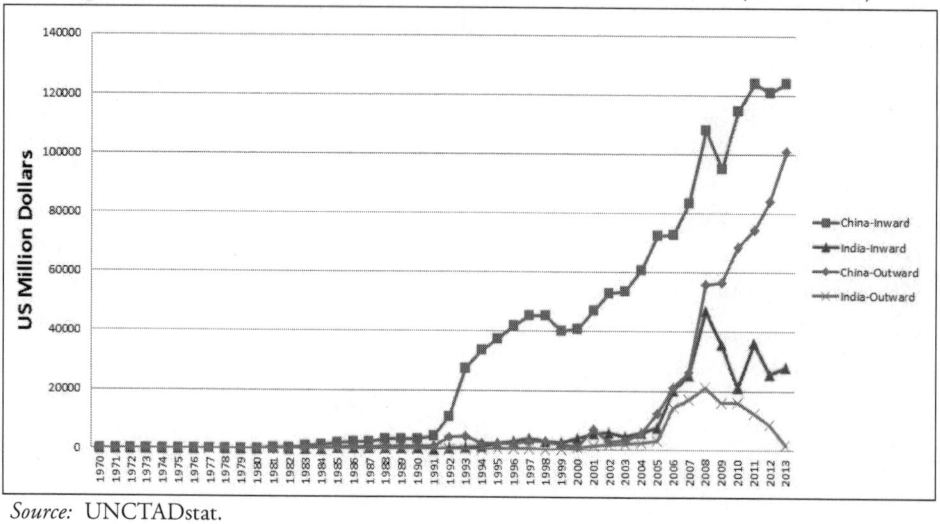

Source: UNCTADstat.

Comparisons of India's and China's Roles in the Global Value Chains

The studies of Global Value Chains (GVCs) have almost been a global phenomenon. Some studies argue that in 21st century, the global economy can be characterised by GVCs.[8] According to the World Bank, the conceptual operation of GVCs is that intermediate goods and services are traded among countries with different production processes. The operation or application of GVCs can be explained in the context of regional or global collaboration of the traditional ideas of comparative advantages to stages of production rather than final goods. The main differences between the comparative advantages applied today and in ancient times are the large number of countries and enterprises involved and the sophistication of the stages of production nowadays[9] (ADB 2014).

Furthermore, these processes are usually coordinated, and in most cases, dominated, by Trans National Corporates (TNCs). It is estimated that TNC-coordinated GVCs may well account for around 80 per cent of global trade.[10] As GVCs contribute to economic development, it has become one of the most popular policy goals in a lot of developing countries (UNCTAD 2013).

In general, it is believed that the GVCs development or links can significantly contribute to GDP, employment and trade growth. Most developing countries are increasingly participating in GVCs, while a lot of them are still at an early stage of GVC development. According to an UNIDO study of GVCs, one of the reasons for the popularity with GVCs is that there are fewer prerequisites needed for the development of activities within value chains than the prerequisites needed for complete industrial development. In the long term, GVCs will also support the build-up of productive capacity through technology dissemination and skill upgrading and industrial development (UNIDO 2011).

However, participation in GVCs may not necessarily deliver the desired benefits. According to UNCTAD study, a lot of developing countries have remained locked into low value added activities. In some cases, there could also be a reduction in domestic value added trade share (UNCTAD 2013). In addition, full participation in GVCs may hinder developing countries' strategic goals and capabilities to develop their own industries, and thus becoming overly dependent on TNCs which may weaken governments' autonomy in policy making. Some developing countries may also expose their people under poor working conditions and worsening social and environmental standards.[11]

Both India and China are key players in GVCs, yet their roles and performances in the GVCs provide two totally different stories, reflecting their distinct policy choices and results in participating in the global economy.

Compared with China and some other ASEAN countries such as Vietnam and Thailand, India is not among the highly popular investment destinations for those foreign investors seeking to establish manufacturing facilities in Asia.[12] According to Department of Industrial Policy & Promotion (DIPP), Ministry of Commerce and Industry of India, in terms of sector wise FDI equity inflows in the April, 2000 to April, 2013, six out of the top ten sectors that have received the most shares of FDI are services sectors, including services, constructions, telecommunications, computer software, hotel and tourism. The only four manufacturing sectors among the tensectors are drugs/pharmaceuticals, chemicals, automobiles and metallurgical industries. During the same period, FDI inflows in services sectors (including financial, banking, insurance, business, outsourcing, R&D, courier, tech. testing and analysis, etc.) reached $ 37.47 billion, while FDI inflows in construction development reached $ 22.22 billion.[13]

It is interesting to compare India *vis-à-vis* China in their positions and roles in GVCs. China's rapid economic development has been supported by its strong export growth since the 1980s. After some decades of manufacturing and industrial development, China has reduced the share of labour intensive products such as clothing, textiles, footwear, furniture and toys, in its exports, and successfully increased exports of higher value added products and services. This was made possible with the huge volumes of FDI going into China involved in the more complicated processes of value chains. Increasing investment in R&D by the government and private sector also contributes significantly. For example, FDI in electromechanical industry has been a catalyst and helped China expand into more high-tech export-oriented activities and knowledge-based services exports (UNCTAD 2013).

India, however, has not experienced the same development. According to UNCTAD study, when calculating a country's exports by level of technological sophistication, 35 per cent of India's exports are in the "resource-based" sector, while 15 per cent and 10 per cent are in "low-tech manufacturing" sector and "mid-level manufacturing" sector, respectively. "Sophisticated manufacturing" only accounts for 5 per cent of India's total exports. A very unique characteristic that makes India distinct from other developing countries in participation in GVCs is that India has 25 per cent share in "knowledge-bases services" export, a larger share even when compared with most developed countries (See Table 1).

In the case of China, China has 10 per cent in its shares of exports of "resource-based" sector and 25 per cent in "low-tech manufacturing" sector, respectively. Its share in "mid-level manufacturing" and "sophisticated manufacturing" sector is 20 per cent and 30 per cent respectively, much larger than those of India. However, in involvement in services in GVCs, China has only 5 per cent share in "knowledge-bases services" export, significantly smaller than that of India (See Table 1).

The two more advanced countries in the region, Malaysia and Singapore, demonstrate quite different compositions. Similar to India, Malaysia, as an oil and natural gas exporting country, also depends heavily on "resource-based" sector, which accounts for 30 per cent of Malaysia's exports. Both Malaysia and Singapore have larger shares in "mid-level manufacturing" and "sophisticated manufacturing" sector. For Malaysia, the share is 15 per cent and 30 per cent respectively. For Singapore, the share is 15 per cent and 35 per cent respectively. As for services, Malaysia has only 5 per cent in "knowledge-bases services", while Singapore has 15 per cent in the share (See Table 1).

Table 1 Participation of India and China in GVCs at Different Levels, 2010

(in per cent)

Country	*Resourced-based*	*Low-tech manufacturing*	*Mid-tech manufacturing*	*Sophisticate manufacturing*	*Knowledge-based service*
India	35	15	10	5	25
China	10	25	20	30	5
Malaysia	30	10	15	30	5
Singapore	20	5	15	35	15

Source: UNCATD analysis, 2013 World Investment Report.

Increasing studies reveal that integration of a country in the global economy nowadays is often closely linked with its participation in the GVCs. India participates strongly in GVC manufacturing in certain industrial sectors, such as chemicals and electrical equipment. Further, more than one third of the value of India's manufacturing exports is in the services sector.

The OECD, WTO and some other international organisations recognise the importance of technology and trade liberalisation in enabling participation in GVCs, for both can significantly reduce trade and operational costs in GVCs (OECD 2013). This may shed light on India's policy makers if the new government is determined to strengthening manufacturing industries in the country and improve India's position in the GVCs. For example, in the 2014-2015 Global Competitiveness Report (GCP), India ranks as the 71st out of 144 countries/economies, the lowest ranked among the BRICS countries (Brazil, Russian Federation, India, China and South Africa). The report analysed India's poor performance and addressed the need for India to move the country up the value chains so as to ensure more sustainable and predictable growth.[14]

Taiwanese Investment in East and South Asia: Characteristics and Trends

The government-led FDI outflows into Southeast Asia and Firms-driven FDI outflows into China. Since the 1980s, scarcity of natural resources and increasing land and labour costs had driven Taiwanese firms to relocate their manufacturing facilities in Southeast Asia and China. At the same time, Taiwan began to undertake industrial re-structuring and upgrading by promoting ICT and electronics industries and more value added services at home in order to differentiate from its competitors in the Asia Pacific region.

In 1990, outward FDI stock of Taiwan was reported at $ 30.36 billion. In 2012 the volume increased to $ 226.1 billion, around 7.4 times the volume of 1990. If compared with inward FDI stock, it is around 4 times the volumes of inward FDI stock.

Due to political rivalry across the Taiwan Straits since 1949, Taiwan government had not opened up investment to China until 1992 when the then President Lee Tung Hui decided to officially relax ban on cross straits economic exchanges and allowed trade with and indirect investment in China.[15] During the period 1990-2012, the government had approved more than 40,000 investment projects in China, total reported volumes reaching $ 124.5 billion. It is informally estimated that, if unreported or indirect investment is included, investment in China by Taiwanese firms may well reach $ 250 to $ 300 billion, accounting for more than 70 per cent of Taiwan's total overseas investment. The high concentration, together with the fact that exports to China (including via Hong Kong) comprises of around 40 per cent of Taiwan's total exports, indicates the dependence on China is not only an economic issue but also a national security issue.

The production networks or value chains established by Taiwan-invested manufacturing operations in China and Southeast Asia not only created millions of jobs across those countries but also helped develop manufacturing industries and made possible economic restructuring in some host countries. For example, in the 1990s, more than 200 Taiwanese electronics firms invested in Penang, Malaysia and helped established one of the most important electronics industrial clusters in Southeast Asia at that time.

In China, Taiwanese firms have also contributed significantly to the development of several industries, ranging from textiles and garment, footwear, toys to electronics and electrical machinery. Benefitted from capital, technology and management knowhow brought by Taiwanese firms, China was hence able to establish production networks which later became the base for its successful development of GVCs today.

Taiwanese Investment in India

Since the 1990s, the "Go South" policy had targeted Southeast Asian countries, particularly Thailand, Indonesia and the Philippines, as major investment destinations.[16] India was added in the 2000s when the policy was further expanded to include South Asian region. However, to most Taiwanese firms, India in these years was considered mainly as an extension from the Southeast Asian region instead of a separate potential market.

It is important to note that there is a close correlation between Taiwan's interests in India and Taiwan's relations with China. Starting from mid-2000s when investment environment in China began to appear less favorable, some Taiwanese firms began to look outside China in search of both overseas investment destinations and new markets in order to diversify dependence on China. Wage increase, shortage of labour in Southeast coastal provinces of China and enforcement of new labour and environmental laws all drove an increasing number of Taiwanese firms away from the once "World Factory". India and some Southeast Asian countries, such as Vietnam and Indonesia, hence became emerging attractions with their abundant workforce and relatively low wages. The sharp growth contrasted with the consecutive decline of FDI flows to China since 2009 implying that Taiwanese firms are "returning" to Southeast Asia.

The total volume of FDI inflows from Taiwan to India has although remained very small. According to DIPP statistics, total investment amount has been only around $ 66 million, representing 0.03 per cent of total investment flows received by India during the period of January 2000 to December 2012.[17] It is noteworthy that the FDI inflows to India from Taiwan in the past four years (2009-2012) also demonstrated a significant increase. FDI volume in these four years reached $ 46 million, comprising around 70 per cent of the total accumulated FDI since April 2000. While Taiwanese firms are "returning" to Southeast Asia, some FDI moves to India. In this context, India receives growing attention from Taiwan.

India vs China: Taiwanese Investors' Perspectives

Taiwan is known to be a hub of ICT production and innovation. Taiwanese firms produce more than 80 per cent of the notebook computers and their peripherals worldwide. Most of the production is outsourced to China or Southeast Asian countries, while major R&D function maintains in the headquarters of the enterprises or mother companies in Taiwan. Having operations in different countries, Taiwanese contract manufacturers, such as Foxconn and Compal Electronics,[18] collaborate with their clients (brand owners) in coordinating the GVCs in China and other countries. While for other Taiwanese enterprises that are brand owners themselves, such as smart phone maker HTC Corporation and

Notebook computer maker acer, they manage direct operations across the countries.

The aforementioned operations in China/Southeast Asia are different from the operations of Taiwanese FDI in India. As India has not yet been able to develop comprehensive electronics industrial clusters, if Taiwanese firms (and other foreign firms) invest in India to manufacture electronics products, usually they need to import raw materials from other countries and other intermediate goods for their production and assembly in Indian operations. This has hindered Taiwanese electronics enterprises to seek further extension of their current marketing or services operations in India to possible investment opportunities or manufacturing cooperation. Furthermore, though Department of Industrial Policy and Promotion, Ministry of Commerce and Industry of India targeted Taiwanese electronics/ICT industry as potential investors when the Indian Government finally allowed foreign investment in single brand product and multi brand product retail trading in India, the response was not positive.

According to DIPP, if investment in single brand/multi brand product retail trading involves foreign ownership beyond 51 per cent, the principle of sourcing of 30 per cent of the value of goods purchased needs to be done from India.[19] This is the so called local sourcing or local content requirements used very often in developing countries aimed at developing domestic industry through FDI policy. However, it would be very difficult or expensive for Taiwanese firms to satisfy the 30per cent local sourcing requirement as the supporting electronics industry is not yet in place in India. The lack of strong industrial foundations and very complicated central and state-level tax and legal systems make manufacturing across states in India difficult and cost intensive when compared with China and most Southeast Asian countries.

Another obstacle for establishment of production networks or GVCs in India deals with the "trade barriers" faced by Taiwanese firms. India's high tariff rates on intermediate goods and raw materials make the operation of GVCs more difficult than China and some Southeast Asian countries. Given the fact, that most ICT products are already subject to zero tariffs under the Information Technology Agreement (ITA), this has become the major reason why Taiwanese electronics/ICT enterprises hesitate to invest in India.[20] This was also the reason for countries like Japan and Korea to negotiate FTAs with India. FTAs will allow Japanese or Korean investors to import materials, components and automobile parts under preferential or zero tariffs for their production or assembly in India.

According to a survey by Chung Hua Institution for Economic Research (CIER) of Taiwan in 2012, Taiwanese firms in India tend to focus on resource-based or low to mid-level manufacturing for domestic market or exports. So far no high tech firms could make presence by investing in big-scale manufacturing facilities, though almost all ICT brand owners have set up their sales or services centers in India. If India wishes to invite more Taiwanese technology enterprises to establish manufacturing facilities in India, the problems faced by Taiwanese firms have to be effectively addressed.

Due to difficulties in domestic sourcing, manufacturers have to import from other countries raw materials or semi-finished products, key components and parts for production. If Taiwanese enterprises can integrate suppliers from upstream and downstream industries needed in the GVCs, more vertical investment can be made possible. India can also realise its policy goals to develop a strong manufacturing sector.

For example, India is well known for its comparative advantages in software and services, while Taiwan is a dominant producer and exporter of ICT goods. There is huge potentials of benefits if two countries can collaborate in ICT industry. However, Taiwan's interest in India is fairly recent. A large number of Taiwanese ICT enterprises set up their services or sales and distribution offices in India, yet none of them seriously consider investing large-scales manufacturing facilities in the country.

India's failure to develop diverse and strong manufacturing industry has to a large degree become an obstacle to the country's economic restructuring and pursuit of further economic growth. It is also the main reason behind the constant deficit of balance of payment, trade deficit and high unemployment rate. Moreover, as the East and Southeast Asian countries are accelerating negotiations for further economic integration, India needs to consider further trade and investment liberalisation and integration into the regional economy.

Make GVCs work in India: Conclusions and Some Policy Recommendations

It has been a policy choice for most developing countries to participate in the GVCs with more value addition in recent past. If a developing country plays an important role in certain GVCs and upgrades its exports structure by capturing larger value-added share in trade, it can significantly benefit from growth of GDP, trade, FDI and employment. However, over dependence on GVCs may also create problems such as poor working condition, worsening social and environmental standards, vulnerability to relations with TNCs and inability to promote industrial upgrading, etc. Policy makers also need to take these factors into consideration.

This paper examines and compares India with China in their economic development, trade and investment activities in order to understand their participation in the GVCs. India and China have different policy goals and approaches in economic development and foreign investment policies. TNCs also have different decision making mechanisms as to whether and how to invest in these two countries. After decades of enforcing export-oriented policy and close relations between TNCs and their contract manufacturers, China is more advanced in developing GVCs; trade structure is also upgraded by developing high tech and more value added share in trade. India, given the same measurement, lags behind China as around 50 per cent of Indian trade is still in resource-based and low-tech manufacturing sectors.

In order to attract FDI inflows into important manufacturing sectors, the Indian Government has put forward various policy schemes. Building an investment environment for manufacturing of electronics and electrical products can be a key policy for India to improve manufacturing capacities and reduce dependence on imports. India has negotiated with Japan and Korea to allow country-specific industrial parks or industrial zones within the Delhi-Mumbai Industrial Corridor (DMIC) for Japanese and Korean investors. These efforts explained that, in order to develop GVCs and improve value addition, governments have to provide a welcoming and facilitating environment to encourage TNCs and domestic companies to invest.

This chapter suggests the following policy direction for making GVCs work in India:

Preparing Sufficient Skilled Human Capital

In order to promote higher value added activities in supply chains, such as electronics and ICT products, a large supply of skilled and experienced work force will be needed that can handle a full range of supply chain functions. This also involves training and skill enhancement of the workers in resource-based and low-level manufacturing sectors towards more technology and management sophisticated activities. Taiwan has experienced similar transformation when it began to upgrade its industrial structure from labour intensive industry to technology-based industry in the 1980s. Taiwan and India can share experiences and create joint efforts to promote human resource development in India.

Removing Trade Barriers that Hinder International Trade and Foreign Investment Activities

Increasing studies indicate that tariffs and non-tariff barriers, such as rigid product standards and customs practices not in compliance with international standards, may become significant impediments to trade of intermediate goods and the functioning of GVCs. Due to severe competition in electronics industry leading to very low profit margin for mass-produced electronics parts and components, even very low tariffs would hinder related trade activities. This explains why a lot of GVCs are developed among countries that have FTAs to provide zero tariffs and other facilitating treatments for trade of intermediate goods among them. By removing tariffs and non-tariff barriers that apply to all foreign investors, India can encourage more TNCs to consider investment in India.

Creating a Supportive Business Climate and Providing Investment Incentives

The Indian Government can create a supportive and welcoming environment and business friendly climate for investment. Moreover, India can also consider providing investment incentives to encourage TNCs and domestic firms to invest in certain strategic sectors of GVCs. Some Southeast Asian countries, such as Thailand and Vietnam, have successful experiences in promoting FDI inflows and are now important participants in electronics/ICT GVCs.

In addition to the above, there are other factors that may affect TNS's decisions to invest in GVCs. For example, currency fluctuation nowadays is becoming a critical factor in deciding which country to invest. Other factors include political stability, policy consistency, government efficiency, infrastructure, etc. India needs to improve its rankings in global competitiveness on ease of doing business and investment friendliness in order to demonstrate its determination to actively participate in GVCs.

From Taiwanese investors' perspectives, India and China present different investment environments and opportunities and challenges. Taiwanese firms started investing in China in the 1980s and have played an important role in helping China to develop its manufacturing industries, including labour intensive industries, light consumer industries and technology-based industries. On the other hand, Taiwanese firms are new comers in India. Tariffs, non-tariff barriers and policy environment in India are hindering trade and business operations. Therefore, so far Taiwanese firms have not yet developed value chains or supply chains in India, though most ICT brand owners have their sales and service centers in the country.[21] Taiwan and Indian Governments should work closely together to encourage more high tech Taiwanese FDI outflows to India. In addition, Indian Government should also consider reduction of tariffs and removal of non-tariffs barriers for it will help develop a stronger manufacturing sector in India.

India and Taiwan can work together in the regional production networks. The past three decades of industrial development and overseas investment in the region have enabled Taiwan to stand at a strategic position in the GVCs. As an increasing number of Taiwanese firms are relocating their manufacturing bases away from China and considering India as a potential new "Factory of Asia", India and Taiwan can work together to improve productivity and quality in India's manufacturing sector. India and Taiwan can develop a comprehensive partnership that covers cooperation in areas such as high value added manufacturing industries and knowledge based services, R & D collaboration and joint human resource development, among others. Moreover, Taiwan's active outward investment activities in China and Southeast Asia in the past decades can play a critical role in connecting India with East Asia, helping India to further integrate into the East Asian regional economy.

NOTES

1. World Bank, WTO and Asia Pacific Economic Cooperation (APEC) have engaged in related study of different research scope and objectives.
2. The Modi Government announced "100 days of the new government: the making of manufacturing driven economy". http://dipp.nic.in/English/default.aspx
3. The Association was created in 1967 out of a need to enhance political and security cooperation in the Southeast Asian region, ASEAN membership includes Brunei, Cambodia, Indonesia, Laos, Malaysia, Myanmar, Philippines, Singapore, Thailand and Vietnam.
4. DIPP, Ministry of Commerce and Industry, FDI Statistics, at http://www.dipp.nic.in/English/Publications/FDI_Statistics/FDI_Statistics.aspx
5. Deng Xiaoping was the leader of the Communist Party of China (CPC) from 1978 to 1992 and led China through far-reaching market economic reforms. Deng is considered "the architect" of China, opening the country to foreign investment and world market and introducing limited private competition with China's state-own institutions.
6. The 12th Five-Year Plan was endorsed by the National People's Congress on March 14, 2011. The Plan has three main priorities: sustainable growth, industrial upgrading and the promotion of domestic consumption
7. China adopted a "Go Out Policy" in early 2000, encouraging its state-owned enterprises and private enterprises to invest overseas.
8. The concept of GVCs first appeared in development studies. The first references to the GVC concept date from the mid-1990s, echoed in the World Bank's reports of the East Asian export-led economies' success stories in economic development.
9. A more up-to-date explanation of the GVCs in Asia can be found in the Asian Development Outlook 2014.
10. However, GVCs cause the problem "doubt-counting in trade", as intermediate goods are counted several times in world export. It was estimated that about 28 per cent or $5 trillion of global exports has the "double counting" problems.
11. Such issues may include humane working conditions, legal labour rights, public health, etc.
12. A survey of Taiwan firms operating in India done by Chung Hua Institution for Economic Research, 2011, also reflects similar conclusions.
13. Department of Industrial Policy and Promotion (DIPP), Ministry of Commerce and Industry, Government of India, *Annual Report 2012-2013.* http://dipp.nic.in/English/default.aspx
14. G-20 Leaders Summit, "Implications of Global Value Chains for Trade, Investment, Development and Jobs, OECD, WTO, UNCTAD, August 6, 2013. http://www.oecd.org/sti/ind/G20-Global-Value-Chains-2013.pdf
15. The government of Taiwan had adopted a No-Engagement policy with China since 1949 until present Lee relaxed the bans and allowed Taiwanese citizens to visit China and indirect trade and investment in 1992.
16. The "Go South" policy was first adopted in 1994 and then expanded several times. The purpose is to provide information and resources to the private sector, research institutions and businesses.

17. According to an informal survey conducted by the Taipei Economic and Cultural Center (TECC), if taking a broader definition of "Taiwanese firms operating in India" and including both direct and indirect investment by Taiwanese firms, realised and planned investment may be around $1.0~1.2 billion.
18. Foxconn (Hon Hai Group) and Compal are Taiwan-based ICT companies producing motherboards, Notebook PCs, LCD, smart phones, tablets, etc., for clients or under own brands. They are among the largest five electronics contract manufacturers (ODM manufacturers) in the world; Foxconn ranks as number one and is also the largest export in China. Both companies have operations in China, Southeast Asia, Americas and Central Europe.
19. DIPP, Ministry of Commerce and Industry, Consolidated FDI Policy. http://dipp.nic.in/English/Policies/FDI_Circular_2014.pdf
20. The ITA is a plurilaterial agreement under the WTO providing preferential tariffs (zero tariffs) for ICT related products. Currently there are 70 signatory countries, including India, Taiwan, and most developed countries and China and other East Asian countries.
21. The brand owners include HTC, ASUS, acer, BENQ, etc.

REFERENCES

Alajääskö, Pekka, Peter Boegh Nielsen, Samuli Rikama and Johanna Sisto, "Global value chains—international sourcing to China and India.", *Eurostat*, European Commission, March 2011.

APEC Policy Support Unit, "Global Supply Chain Operation in the APEC Region: Case Study of the Electrical and Electronics Industry", July 2013.

Asian Development Bank, *Asian Development Outlook 2014 Update*, Manila: ADB, 2014.

Baldwin, Richard, "Global Manufacturing Value Chains and Trade Rules", *The Shifting Geography of Global Value Chains: Implications for developing Countries and Trade policy*, 16-17. Geneva: World Economic Forum, 2012.

Bhunia, Abhirup, "Export-oriented FDI can jumpstart Indian manufacturing." *East Asia Forum.* http://www.eastasiaforum.org/2014/07/11/export-oriented-fdi-can-jumpstart-indian-manufacturing/

Department of Commerce, "100 days of the New Government: the making of manufacturing driven economy". http://dipp.nic.in/English/default.aspx

Dimaranan, Betina, Elena Ianchovichina and William J. Martin, China, India and the Future of the World Economy: Fierce Competition or Shared Growth?¡¨*Policy Research Working Paper*, August 2007. http://elibrary.worldbank.org/doi/pdf/10.1596/1813-9450-4304

DIPP, Ministry of Commerce and Industry, "Consolidated FDI Policy". http://dipp.nic.in/English/Policies/FDI_Circular_2014.pdf

Hoda, Anwarul and Kumar Rai, Durgesh. "Revitalising India's manufacturing industry", *East Asia Forum.* http://www.eastasiaforum.org/2014/09/24/revitalising-indias-manufacturing-industry/

Klaus Schwab (ed), "Measuring Competitiveness¡¨, *The Global Competitiveness Report 2014-2015*, World Economic Forum, 2014 Year

Mukherjee, Arpita and Tanu M. Goyal. "FDI in Services and India," *Foreign Trade Review*, 8(3), pp. 413-430.

OECD, WTO and UNCTAD, "Implications of Global Value Chains for Trade, Investment, Development and Jobs¡¨, Paper prepared for the G-20 Leaders Summit, Saint Petersburg, Russian Federation, September 2013.

Pal, Pathapratim, Arpita Mukherjee, and Kristy Hsu, *Enhancing Trade, Investment and Cooperation between India and Taiwan,* New Delhi, Academic Foundation, 2013.

Sturgeon, Timothy J. and Olga Memedovic, *Mapping Global Value Chains: Intermediate Goods Trade and Structural Change in the World Economy,* Vienna: UNIDO, 2011.

UNCTAD, *World Investment Report 2013—Global Value Chains: Investment and Trade for Development,* Geneva: UNCTAD, 2013.

UNCTAD, *World Investment Report 2014—Investing in the SDGs: An Action Plan,* Geneva: UNCTAD, 2014.

WTO Secretariat, "Country-Trade Profile: India." http://stat.wto.org/CountryProfile/WSDBCountryPFView.aspx?Language=E&Country=CN

WTO Secretariat, "Trade Policy Review: India". http://www.wto.org/english/tratop_e/tpr_e/tp349_e.htm

SECTION IV

Resource Stress in Asia

10

Energy Security Challenges Under Limited Resource Pressure in Asia

Bobby A. Tamaela Wattimena

Introduction

The Asian region has experienced high economic growth during the last few decades. During 1985-1995, the GNP per capita for developing East Asia grew more than 7 per cent per annum. In the same period, the economies of India and China grew at 3.2 and 8.3 per cent per annum (Soubbotina and Sheram, 2000). For 2013, the World Bank estimated that economic growth would be higher than 7 per cent, although at slowing pace (World Bank, 2013). Nevertheless, the region's contribution to world economic growth was still high, and had a significant share in global trade. The five biggest economies in the region are China, India, Japan, South Korea and Indonesia.

Besides its economic strength, the Asian region is also the most populous in the world. In 2012, the Asian population was around two thirds of world population, with China, India and Indonesia being the most populous.. In general, most of the Asian population lives in rural areas, and relies on an agriculture based economy. However, increasing industrialisation across the region in the last few decades has created non-agriculture employment that is usually concentrated in the urban areas.

The author would like to thank the IIEE for providing valuable data and information for writing this essay. Also, the author would to thank Ms. Nataliawati Siahaan from the IIEE for providing research assistance.

One of the direct consequences of economic and population growth is increasing energy demand. The energy consumption in 2010 was 1.545 million ktoe, which was primarily fossil-based energy. IEA has estimated that in 2030 the total energy demand in Asia will be doubled (IEA, 2012). The largest energy consumers are China, India, Japan and South Korea, while ASEAN countries[1] contribute around 13 per cent of the total consumption. The high demand growth, however, was overshadowed by the fact that some developing countries in the region still have low rural electrification ratio and low energy service quality. IEA has estimated that, in 2010, the average rural electrification rate in developing Asia was 74.2 per cent (IEA, 2012). However, this figure varied across the countries. For example, the electrification ratio in Myanmar was 28 per cent, while Singapore and Malaysia is already 100 per cent electrified. The electricity generation is mostly through fossil fuels, notably coal. Some countries, like China, India, Japan and Pakistan, also generate electricity from nuclear plants. Hydropower is the largest renewable energy resource in the region, while geothermal energy is located around the 'Ring-of-Fire' areas, such in Indonesia and Philippines. In general, the role of renewable energy is still limited, but showing an increasing share across the years.

Meanwhile, fossil energy resources can be found across the region. Oil and natural gas can be found in the Western Asia (Arabian Peninsula), Central Asia, Southern Asia, and to Southeastern Asia. Asia is the largest coal producer in the world, of which China, India and Indonesia are the largest. For increasing natural gas supply and decreasing dependency on oil, some Asian countries, such as China, India, Indonesia and Vietnam, have already started the development of unconventional gas sources (shale gas and coal bed methane).

While available fossil energy resources and their indigenous production in the Asian region seem adequate to fulfill the demand—at least in the short run—in the long run the region will depend on other resources, which may be derived from other places. Even now, some Asian countries are already becoming net energy importers due to unavailable domestic resources. Thus, countries like Singapore, South Korea, Armenia and Japan import at least 50 per cent of their energy supply (ADB, 2012). Another example is Indonesia—previously a net oil exporting country and OPEC member—has already become a net oil importer for the last few years.

Conditions such as high economic and population growth, dependency on fossil fuels, and the depletable nature of fossil fuel will eventually affect the energy security of these countries, and the region as a whole. How these conditions impact resource availability, accessibility, and affordability as well as social/environmental issues will be discussed in the following sections.

Energy Security Challenges

The exploration of energy security at the regional and country level are based on four obectives known as the 4A's: availability, accessibility, affordability and acceptability. These have been developed by APERC and are based on the WEC approach (Hughes and Shupe, 2010). In a broader definition, the availability objective concerns the supply of energy, including resources, as well as indigenous production and imports, both for fossil and renewable energy. Accessibility refers to how the resources can be utilised to supply the demand, which includes infrastructure availability and access to energy markets. The affordability objective concerns the price, thus the cost, of providing and consuming the resources. Finally, the acceptability objective focuses on the environmental and social impacts of utilising energy resources.

Availability

Asia is fortunate to have a considerable amount of hydrocarbon, with the region having the largest oil and natural gas reserves as well as coal reserves in the world. A new discovery of natural gas reserves in offshore Sri Lanka will add to current gas capacity in the region. In terms of production, a steady growth has been identified in Asia, with West Asia dominating the oil production, and North Asia (that is, the Russia Federation) in natural gas production. A similar trend is also visible in coal production, with China as the main producer (BP, 2013).

On the consumption side, it is evident that the consumption of energy commodities has been increasing steadily over the last decades. China and India have been the largest energy consumers in the region, followed by Japan and South Korea. On the whole, energy production and consumption in the region were sufficiently balanced. However, at the sub-regional level, there was a problem of unbalanced supply and demand. For example, the natural gas consumption in East Asia in 2012 reached 32.6 BSCF. If the consumption here is to be supplied by the nearest regions of Southeast Asia, with total production of 20.5 BSCF, then supply will fall short. The gap will be even greater if domestic consumption is considered in the producing region. The supply gap will eventually be filled by imported fuels. Countries like Japan, South Korea, and Taiwan are net primary energy importers in the region due to the lack of domestic energy resources, while still others have already started to become dependent on imported fuels as their domestic resources are depleted even as their demand continues to rise. In other words, except in the Western part of Asia, the diversity index of primary energy supply in the region has started to decline.

For meeting demand, especially petroleum fuels and electricity, the region has increased the production capacity of its petroleum refineries and power plants. The refinery capacity in Asia and Pacific has increased 2.4 per cent per annum

(CGAR)—from 25,923 thousand BOPD in 1990 to 44,128 thousand BOPD in 2012. China, Russia, Japan and India have the largest refinery capacity in the region (EIA, 2013). At the same time, the refinery fuel consumption has increased from 25,694 thousand BOPD to 41,716. In electricity generation, the total generation has shown more than 6 per cent growth per annum (CAGR)—from 3,039 TWh in 1990 to 11,338 TWh in 2012 (BP, 2013). Most of the electricity generation comes from coal, natural gas, oil and renewables such as hydro, geothermal and nuclear. Hydro power plants can be found in China, Southern and Southeastern Asia, while geothermal power plants are mainly located in Indonesia and Philippine. Nuclear power generation can be found in Northern, Eastern and Southern parts of Asia. While there are no existing nuclear power plants in Southeast Asia, countries like Indonesia, Malaysia and Vietnam are planning to build them in the near future.

The diversity index of final energy supply is, generally, much better in the region. Most of the countries can produce domestically almost all of the refinery fuels and electricity. However, due to slow investment on new capacity, the diversity index may change in the short and medium term.

Accessibility

The accessibility issue in energy security includes (1) how to access the available indigenous energy resources, and (2) access to the international, or regional, energy market for acquiring imported fuels to fill the supply gap. The main issue in terms of access at the national level is lack of investment, geographical conditions, and government regulations. The investment needed for exploring and producing the primary energy, especially fossil fuels, has been increasing in the last few decades as new discoveries have moved away from traditional and low cost reserves to more high risk remote and frontier areas. Moreover, as domestic reserves decline, exploration and production activities move to other countries or regions—as has happened in oil production. As government regulations in various countries differ, the risks also differ. If the growth of demand outpaces investment in new capacity, the number of unserved demands will increase, lead to low quality of service, and increase the possibility of needing to import from outside of the country. This has already happened in several countries in Asia—as for example in Indonesia. In this country, the capacity growth in electricity generation, oil refinery, and natural gas infrastructure could not row fast enough to meet the demand.

The geographical conditions in Asia are another barrier for increasing access to modern energy services. Mountainous regions and scattered small islands are typical in this region. Low density population in many of these areas, and low rural electrification are common here. The investment needed for electrifying these area is high if it relies on a centralised system, while the economics of scale is low in the small generating capacity plants needed to support distribution to isolated areas. However, as small scale renewable energy generation is preferable for electrifying isolated rural areas, improvement in small scale renewable energy generation—such as micro-hydro, solar PV, and biomass—will no doubt continue to increase, and the costs will eventually go down.

Meanwhile, access to the international market through trade is important if the indigenous production cannot meet the demand. In the case of oil, the intra-regional trade in Asia is dominated by oil producing regions in West Asia (or the Middle East), especially with China, India, Japan and Singapore. For natural gas, the access to the regional market is done through pipelines and LNG shipment. The pipeline network is well developed in mainland Asia, especially in Central Asia, Russia and China. The development of a new pipeline network is expected from the Southeast Asia region to China and from Central Asia to South Asia and East Asia. Future developments will also be linked to the development of unconventional gas in the region. The LNG trade in Asia region has intensified in the last decade, and has the largest share in the trading of natural gas in the region. Japan and South Korea are the biggest LNG importers in the region (and in the world), with China, India and other Asian countries following closely (IGU, 2013). Other Asian countries are either importing for their own use or for re-exporting. From the supply-side, Qatar (in West Asia), is the biggest LNG exporter in the world. The region is also supplied its LNG from Australia. Export from Indonesia, once the largest LNG exporter in the region, has currently fallen due to decreasing feedstock in its largest LNG refinery. Access to the LNG market for the Asian region, especially East Asia, will depend on the political situation in the exporting countries (for example, West Asia) and the availability of transportation routes. The LNG for East Asia that comes from West Asia and Africa is shipped through the Malacca strait, from Australia through the Lombok strait, and from the Southeast Asia through the South China Sea. Considering the heavy traffic in the Malacca strait as well as its shallow deep and narrow wide, LNG transportation to the East Asian region will find this strait a chokepoint. Alternative routes will increase delivery time and, eventually, the transportation costs as well (Qu and Meng, 2011).

Government policies and regulations can influence how access to energy will be developed. One example of how government policies and regulations can affect regional energy trade relates to environmental issues such as air pollution and greenhouse gases. China started to ban new coal power plants to reduce air pollution, and replaced them with nuclear and gas power plants. An increase in gas power plants will increase the demand for gas in the country, and the possibility for import may rise. At the same time, in its new national energy policy, Indonesia will increase the use of natural gas as a substitute for highly subsidised oil fuels, and to compensate for declining oil production. This means that, eventually, some of the LNG exports will be diverted for domestic consumption. The other example of government regulations that can alter energy access are export taxes. High export can discourage (for example, Indonesia's domestic market obligation or DMO), while lower taxes will encourage exports (for example, Vietnam's coal). Although the effects of this policy may not be evident in the near future, in the medium and longer term, it may affect the regional energy supply balance.

Affordability

In general, affordability in Asian region translates into on how to supply adequate and reliable energy services to the people at affordable prices. For some countries, this is interpreted further as energy price subsidy, both on the price oil fuels and electricity tariffs. The highest fuel and electricity subsidy occurs in West Asia, where the region is the biggest oil and gas producer. In Southeast Asia, only Singapore does not have an energy subsidy, while Indonesia and Malaysia have the lowest energy price in the region due to a heavy subsidy (GIZ, 2013). Although the initial idea of energy subsidy was to protect the poor, to improve the industry's competitiveness, and national economic development, in reality energy subsidy has deviated from its original purpose. The direct consequence of energy subsidy (that is, low energy price) in Asian countries has been uncontrollable energy demand growth in the few last decades. In the meantime, energy subsidy hampers the highly needed new refineries and power plants—that is, the energy infrastructure required for fulfilling the increasing demand. Consequently, energy supply reliability is low, and the number of un-served demands is increasing. In terms of energy subsidy, many Asian countries have already begun energy subsidy reform to restrain the demand, and to tackle volatile world energy prices. However, the reform will be done slowly—by considering the impacts on the whole economy and, importantly, public acceptance.

The affordability issues also links with the energy supply, especially in Asian developing countries. The exploration and production of new energy reserves (such as oil and gas) have moved away from existing low cost reserves to more remote and frontier areas, with high risk in terms of discoverable rate. Limited budgets from state-owned oil companies and the lack of technological experience will open opportunities for the entry of multinational oil companies. The other example is the cost of developing national and regional gas pipelines. The high cost is one reason for the development of Trans ASEAN Gas Pipelines (TAGP).

Acceptability

As the energy demand increases, the energy infrastructure will follow. According to many studies and reports, the Asian region will still depend on fossil fuels, especially coal and oil (see, for example, Exxon, 2013; IEA, 2012). From the environmental perspective, the future primary energy mix is quite disturbing because of potential GHG emissions and other particulates. If the demand for fossil fuels (for example coal) increases, then the possibility of opening new mining areas may also increase. The problem will arise when new mining activities take place in forest areas, especially in protected and conservation forests. A good example is coal mining in the island of Kalimantan which has been linked to deforestation in the area (Chakravarty, Ghosh, Suresh, Dey, and Shukla, 2012).

Besides fossil based energy resources, the use of renewable energy resources is also expected to increase in the future. However, the development of renewable energy will also depend on how acceptability issues will be addressed. Although it has been considered a clean renewable energy source, in reality the utilisation of geothermal energy is not always environmentally sustained/sustainable. Geothermal resources in some Asian countries are often located in protected forest or land. For example, 42 per cent of the geothermal potential in Indonesia is located in protected forests (Wardhani, Iswarayoga, and Senga, 2012). Any attempts to exploiting geothermal resources in these areas without proper guidance and regulation will result in environmental degradation, which contradicts the clean and sustainability characteristics of geothermal energy.

Social acceptance is also crucial in energy utilisation. While the social acceptability for coal power plants is clearly identified due to its pollution potential, the acceptance of renewable energy utilisation must be explored further. The social non-acceptance of solar home systems in Indonesia, for example, is not because the technology is bad but more because of the inability of the community to operate this kind of technology. Another example—also in Indonesia—is the development of micro-hydro power in the Papua region. Though the technology is quite simple, the development of micro-hydro power in this region is hindered by the lack of cultural acceptance, especially regarding land ownership that belongs to various cultural clans.

Meanwhile, the social non-acceptance of the development of nuclear plants in Asia is largely due to governance issues (Tanter, 2012). For example, the decision for developing new power plants is being conducted under secrecy, and without public participation or clear information. A good example of this is the plan to build a new 4,000 MW nuclear power plant in Indonesia. The reasons behind the decision as to why nuclear powers plant should be built are very vague since Indonesia has an abundance of other renewable energy resources that are more sustainable than nuclear power plants. The development of these power plants will increase dependency on imported uranium from other countries, noticeably its neighbor in the South: Australia. Tanter (2012) has argued that the development of nuclear power plants in Indonesia has been seen suspiciously by the people in

Australia. The development of large hydropower dam has also low social acceptance. The development of the Three Gorges dam in China is a good example of renewable energy that has low social acceptance due to displacement issues.

All of these acceptance issues must be addressed in such a way as not to hinder sustaianable energy development in the region. The failure to do so may affect access to energy resources, and may also disturb energy availability in the country.

Improving Energy Security in Asia

Maintaining and improving energy security in Asia with limited resources is challenging but achievable. The fundamental prerequisite is close cooperation between the various countries in the region. However, regional cooperation needs compatible policies and regulations in each country that are recognised by others. The cooperation should be based on mutual benefit. This will involve recognising the distinctive nature, interest and sovereignty of each country. Some examples of regional cooperation are the Trans ASEAN Gas Pipeline (TAGP) and the Trans ASEAN Power Grid (TAPG). While the existing gas and electric trade are still based on bilateral agreements, the TAGP and TAPG will work if all ASEAN countries can harmonise their policies and regulations under the cooperation framework. Such cooperation can also be done under the South Asian Association for Regional Cooperation (SAARC), Asia Pacific Economic Cooperation (APEC) as well as ADB's Central Asia Regional Economic Cooperation (CAREC) Program. The regional energy cooperation will create new perspectives on national energy security because wider and complex, but manageable, regional energy issues will be recognised and incorporated in each country's energy security policies.

Meanwhile, the depletable resource of fossil energy and the limited sustainable renewable energy utilisation are a challenge for regional energy security. Technology intervention is needed to maintain adequate and sustainable energy supply and sustainable energy demand. Some countries in Asia are already fairly advanced in the use of energy technologies, while others still rely on conventional technologies. New technologies can help Asian countries to explore new energy resources more efficiently, as well as utilise them in more efficient ways. Renewable energy technologies are more needed in this region as fossil energy will, eventually, be depleted, and disappear. Regional cooperation in research and development is required to support technology development and its utilisation. Much research on biofuels based on various feed stocks has been carried out by many countries, such as China, Japan, South Korea and Taiwan. Also, Southeast Asian countries, under ASEAN cooperation, have also conducted research on biofuel derived from cassava, jathropa, palm oil, sugarcane, etc.

The cooperation between Asian countries must also include financial and investment cooperation. The discovery of new hydrocarbon reserves is difficult and expensive, the infrastructure developments in the region need large investments, and the development of renewable energy still needs further research and development. While the regional distribution network of energy infrastructure can be developed by each country, they would need support financially and technically from other countries in the region.

Conclusion

There are many challenges facing Asian energy security. Available energy resources are more than adequate, with fossil fuel energies remaining dominant. However, energy resources, especially hydrocarbon, are not evenly distributed. Some countries have high diversity index, while others are more heavily dependent on imported fuels. Southeast Asian countries enjoy significant energy resources that have the potential of being exported to regional market, but increasing domestic demand has prevented this. This means that energy availability in the region will be affected by domestic policies, and how each country interacts with the others.

The consequence of uneven distribution of energy resources is that resources these are sometime very distant from the demand center. The demand center is currently located in Eastern Asia (with China being the largest), while the supply regions are in the Western and Southeastern part of the region. This creates the necessity to develop regional energy transportation networks. However, geographical difficulties and each country's domestic policies and regulations impede the access to the resources.

Besides the availability of, and accessibility to energy resources, Asian countries must deal with energy prices. This has resulted in many countries implementing price subsidies. The exposure to volatile world energy prices and limited budgets are preventing many countries from continuing this policy. Limited budgets and high investment costs of energy infrastructure also hinder a country's ability to provide access to their energy resources. The access to energy resources can be also limited if the acceptability of utilising those resources are low. Environmental and social acceptability must also be taken into consideration in order to avoid unnecessary problems in the future that can limit access to energy resources, and affect regional and national energy security.

NOTES

1. ASEAN: Brunei Darussalam, Cambodia, Indonesia, Lao PDR, Malaysia, Myanmar, Philippines, Singapore, Thailand and Vietnam.

REFERENCES

'Asian Population 2013', World Population Statistics, (1 January 2013).

'BP Statistical Review of World Energy 2013', British Petroleum (2013).

Chakravarty, S., Ghosh, S.K., Suresh, C.P., Dey, A.N., and Shukla, G., 'Deforestation: Causes, Effects and Control Strategies', in D.C. Okia (ed.) *Deforestation: Causes, Effects and Control Strategies, Global Perspectives on Sustainable Forest Management*, (2012), InTech. doi:10.5772/33342

EIA, International Energy Statistics. Retrieved from US Energy Information Agency (January 2013).

Exxon, '*The Outlook for Energy: A View to 2040*', Exxon (2013).

Hughes, L., and Shupe, D., 'Creating Energy Security Indexes with Decision Matrices And Quantitative Criteria', (2010, February 15). Retrieved January 2014, from Department of Electrical and Computer Engineering: lh.ece.dal.ca/enen/2010/ERG201002.pdfý

International Fuel Prices 2012/2013: Data Preview, April 2013, GIZ, (2013).

'Key Indicators for Asia and the Pacific 2012', Asian Development Bank (2012).

'Population 2013', World Bank (2013).

Priddle, R., (ed.), *World Energy Outlook : 2012*, International Energy Agency, IEA (2012).

Qu, X., and Meng, Q., 'The Economic Importance of the Straits of Malacca and Singapore: An Extreme Scenario Analysis', National University of Singapore, Department of Civil and Environmental Engineering (2011).

'Rebuilding Policy Buffers, Reinvigorating Growth', World Bank, East Asia Pacific Economic Update, October 2013. Retrieved January 2014, from World Bank: http://www.worldbank.org/en/region/eap/publication/east-asia-pacific-economic-update-october-2013

Retrieved from http://data.worldbank.org/indicator/SP.POP.TOTL

Retrieved from macha.itc.griffith.edu.au: http://macha.itc.griffith.edu.au/

Retrieved January 2014, from World Population Statistics: http://www.worldpopulationstatistics.com/asia-population-2013/

Soubbotina, T. P., and Sheram, K. A., '*Beyond Economic Growth: Meeting the Challenges of Global Development*', World Bank (2000).

Tanter, R., 'The Global Politics of Indonesian Nuclear Power', Power Point slides, (29 August 2012). Retrieved from Nautilus Institute: http://nautilus.org/wp-content/uploads/2011/12/Global-Politics-of-Indonesian-Nuclear-Power.ppt

Wardhani, I. S., Iswarayoga, N., and Senga, R. (eds.), *Igniting the Ring of Fire: A Vision for Developing Indonesia's Geothermal*, WWF Indonesia, 2012.

World Energy Resources: Survey 2013, World Energy Council (2013).

World LNG Report, 2013 edition, International Gas Union (IGU) (2013).

11

India's Resource Economy: Possible Choices and Probable Outcomes

Yashika Singh and Shamika Joshi

Introduction

The last century has witnessed a period of unprecedented economic growth in the western hemisphere of the world, with other regions playing catch up as the century drew to a close. Admittedly, the process is far from over and vast income inequalities continue to persist in the world economy. However, most instances of economic development and growth have followed a particular pattern when it comes to the usage of resources. The quantity of materials used to produce goods & services in a country has shown a rising trend in its intensity of use (ratio of materials used *to* value added, or GDP (Soile, 2013)) as the country's income it self has grown. With reference to the period between 1945 and the first oil price shock, Krausmann, F. et al., points out, *"Rapid industrialisation processes in Western industrial economies and in Japan drove global change and left their imprint on the global metabolic*[1] *system. In these 28 years alone, per capita use of materials increased by more than 50 per cent, and the use of non-renewable minerals by 340 per cent. Still, the current global level of per capita materials use is low compared to that of fully industrialised regions".* Clearly, there is remaining distance to be traversed on the intensity curve by emerging economies.

The authors gratefully acknowledge the support they received from Gunajit Kalita, Analyst—Economics & Markets, Rio Tinto India.

In a stylised system, the drivers of intensity of use of mineral resource will therefore be a function of:

- Output of each final good and service in the economy.
- Amount of mineral used (direct + indirect consumption) per unit of output of the above.

At relatively low stages of development, poor economies tend to focus on non-mechanised, subsistence agriculture, which is characterised by low intensity of use. Beyond a point, as the stage of development changes, other sectors, viz., manufacturing and construction, start to grow, and the share of agriculture in GDP declines. These new sectors are more resource-intensive, i.e., both of the bullet points referred to above start to change in an upward direction. After the initial burst of rising investment & consumption expenditures, income shares move into the services sector, which starts to therefore account for a much larger proportion of the country's GDP. Services sector by their very nature are less material intensive and each additional output in this segment uses much lesser amount of mineral to produce it. This exposition of a country's growth and development process also referred to as 'Kuznets facts' tend to broadly hold true for most countries. As the distribution of per capita income shifts amongst sectors, intensity of use of materials starts to rise in the early stages of growth, reaches an inflection point and then starts to fall and finally stabilises thus leading to the formation of an S-shaped curve. Taking into account an open economy framework, the presence of trade also presents a similar pattern of resource use. Most countries export manufactured products in the early stages of development, which are more resource intensive, and import services and technology. This trend reverses as country develops, thus, maintaining the narrative of the resource intensity curve. According to an IMF estimate, consumption of metals typically grows together with income until real GDP per capita reaches about $15,000–$20,000 per capita (in 2005 purchasing power parity adjusted U.S. dollars), as countries go through a period of industrialisation and infrastructure construction (Liu & McDonald).

This implication of an S-shaped curve of the relationship between per capita income and intensity of use should be applicable to most countries. Broadly speaking, even though this is certainly the case however there are some key caveats that need to be taken into account when moving from a stylised world to a real world. The means of production of a particular good, which may reflect the natural resource endowment or other national characteristics, may imply different intensities even at same levels of per capita income.[2] The other factor which may lead to a break in this broad trend is the structural composition of the country in question—a predominantly services led economy could well have a lower per capita resource intensity for a comparable level of per capita income.[3] In spite of the above caveats, the intensity of use hypothesis is a very useful approach to predict the possible path of a country's evolution of resource demand.

Expounding further from the above, the total demand for any mineral resource for a country will be an inverse function of its price and a positive function of the intensity of use of the economy as well the aggregate level of economic activity. The second order conditions are such that the level of economic activity will depend upon population as well as the GDP. If the structure of the economy changes or as the population or per capita incomes grows, the mineral demand curve would shift over time (Cuddington & Zellou, 2013). If we were to list some of the key drivers that impact commodity demand in a positive manner, the list (not exhaustive) would be like this:

1) Economic growth
2) Demographics
3) Structural changes such as industrialisation and urbanisation

The growth and development experience of various countries have driven their demand for minerals for different reasons. For USA, early stages of development were characterised by construction and manufacturing sectors, which drove the rising demand for minerals. In later years, consumption demand and budget was unconstrained due to a credit boom continued to drive up the demand for metal intensive and energy intensive products. In South Korea, the intensity of use of metals rose sharply, driven by predominantly manufacturing-led export orientation. China's experience of a heavy-investment led GDP growth model has had a disproportionately large impact on the world's metals and mining sector as this model has proven unprecedented in its ability to draw upon resources to support the sustained income increases. The impact of China's take-off in the early part of this century has been so significant that it is estimated "...at this point, between 40 per cent and 60 per cent of every mineral that gets dug up anywhere in the world ends up in China" (John Lichtenstein in Yale Insights, June 2013).

India, simply by virtue of being another large, populous Asian economy, has often been expected to repeat the China example in terms of growth composition and performance and hence implications for the resource economy. This expectation sometimes tends to ignore the fundamental differences between the two countries; conversely, by placing the burden of unmet expectations on India, there stands a chance that the critical changes taking place in the country might get ignored. While acknowledging the differences between the two countries, there is certain peril in ignoring the changes that are likely to take place in India's resource intensity path, and the implications that will have for the choices that the country will need to make in its policy making which in turn foster changes in managing the country's emerging resource economy. We attempt here to review the key drivers of the emerging resource economy for India, the probable path India will take along the resource path and the resultant implications.

The chapter is organised as follows: In section II, we review the China experience of economic growth, with particular emphasis on its resource intensive nature. We then review and analyse India's growth composition, both current and future in section III, and set out the implications for its resource intensity. Finally, in section IV, we attempt to set out the requisite policy implications.

I. China's Economic Growth Experience and the Impact on its Resource Economy

I.A: Anatomy of China's Economic Growth Experience

Over the past three decades, between the periods of 1980 to 2012, the Chinese economy has grown at an average growth rate of 10 per cent per annum, thus, doubling in size every eight years. This has been a truly remarkable performance, with China's real GDP per capita rising from below 4 per cent of the U.S. GDP per capita in 1980 to about 18 per cent of the U.S. GDP per capita in 2009. Given that the country is the most populous country in the world, this level of economic convergence has had a very significant impact on the world's economic growth as a whole. Broadly speaking, the three key underpinnings of the Chinese economic growth model have been *urbanisation*, *high pace and proportion of heavy investment expenditure* and a *manufacturing centric export* sector. Each of these factors have been supported by the necessary policies in the context of central planning to enable them to contribute to the steady growth of the country.

China's reform period started in the early 1980's, and in the period just preceding this landmark, proportion of China's population living in urban areas stood at 19 per cent. In the period between that and 2009, this grew by a huge 27 percentage points to touch 46 per cent. The current estimate of China's urban ratio stands at 51.8 per cent for the year 2012, and it is estimated that this will touch 56.7 per cent in the next ten years. The relationship between economic growth and urbanisation is non-linear: lower the level of GDP per capita, higher the increase in level of urbanisation for a given increase in GDP per capita. Further, the direction of causality between the two variables is perhaps best described as circular, as was the case in China. The slew of economic reforms that were put in place in the 1980s ignited a process of industrialisation, engendering expansion in capital intensity and productivity improvements, which in turn led to an increase in the demand for labour, thus attracting rural populations to the cities in search of higher wages. Reforms were also undertaken in the agricultural sector, which brought about significant productivity improvements there too, thus making the release of surplus labour an easy matter. The mass movement to cities was also an outcome of the favourable demographic conditions that prevailed in China in this period with working age population growing from 59 per cent in 1980 to 73.5 per cent in 2011. Thus, there was easy availability of cheap labour to power this growth, and in turn, urbanisation itself contributed to economic growth through rapid gains in productivity (Liu & McDonald, 2010).

Other drivers of China's economic growth are investment and exports, both of which have shown phenomenally high trends over the past couple of decades. China's investment as a share of GDP (as measured by gross fixed capital formation) stood at 47 per cent in 2012; the country has on an average invested 37 per cent of its GDP, which itself has been growing very quickly. Hence, the absolute amount of income ploughed back into the economy has been very high, supported by high levels of savings rate. China's average savings rate during the last three decades has been 41.7 per cent. A large portion of this investment has been directed towards fixed asset investment, which accounts for 72 per cent of GDP. This includes spending on the infrastructure as well as the building and construction sectors. Lastly, the final leg of the economic story has been the exports sector, which has posted a growth of 18 per cent and has, on average, contributed 26 per cent of the country's GDP over the past two decades. More significantly perhaps from the point of our central question of resource intensity, manufactured exports account for almost 86 per cent of total goods & services export of China.

I.B: The trillion-dollar question—is China an outlier in terms of its resource economy?

In many ways, the story of the $ 1.5 trillion global mining & metals industry has been the story of China during the course of this millennium. As the country industrialised, the per capita demand for natural resources has grown, much in line with the experience of other countries before it. Though *broadly* similar to other countries' experiences, the key departure in case of China was that its contribution to the global growth in resources demand was much higher than its contribution to the expansion of global economic activity. As Garnaut, 2011 points out *"China accounted for over a fifth of the increase in global demand for petroleum, steel and copper and around half for aluminium and nickel in the late years of the 1990s, straddling the Asian Financial Crisis. For the first 5 years of the new century, the Chinese share of consumption growth rose considerably for all energy and metals commodities, to over half for copper, nickel and aluminium. Between 2005 and 2010, China accounted for over four-fifths of the increase in global demand for nearly all energy and metals products. Demand for nickel, copper and aluminium fell outside China, but Chinese growth caused total global demand to be strong enough to take prices close to the highest ever"*.

Growth in World Metal Demand

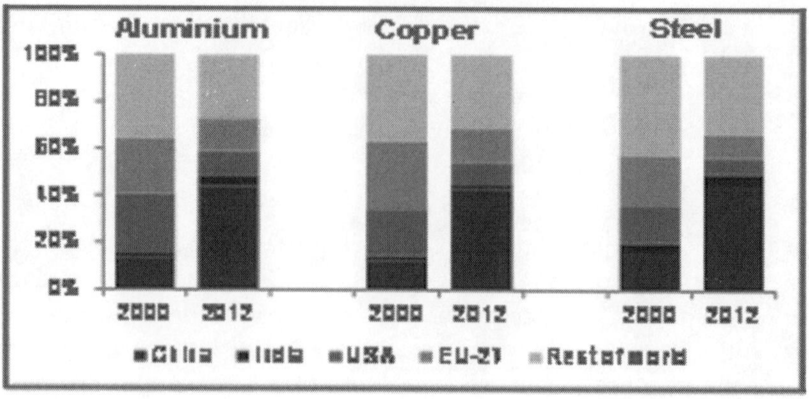

Cross Country Comparison—Per Capita Aluminium Consumption

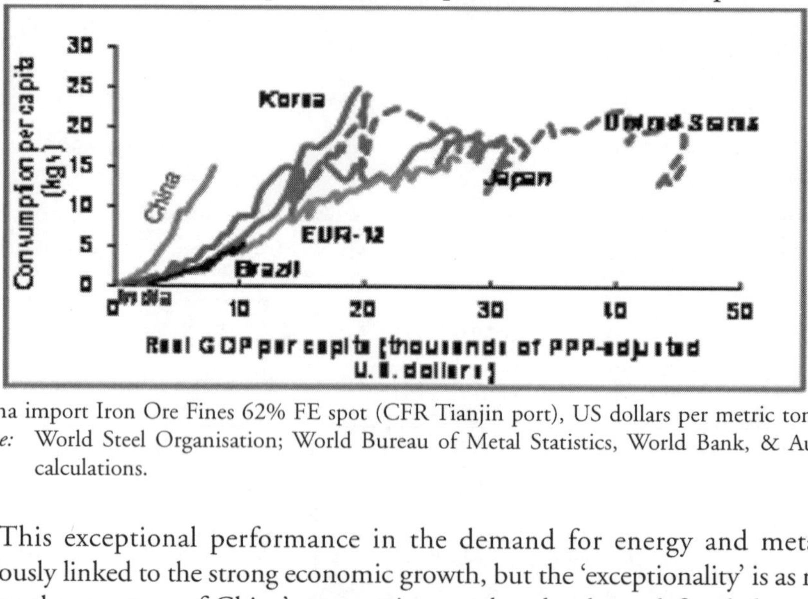

*China import Iron Ore Fines 62% FE spot (CFR Tianjin port), US dollars per metric ton

Source: World Steel Organisation; World Bureau of Metal Statistics, World Bank, & Author's calculations.

This exceptional performance in the demand for energy and metals is obviously linked to the strong economic growth, but the 'exceptionality' is as much due to the structure of China's economic growth as has been defined above. The resource-intensive manufacturing exports sector and the large-scale fixed asset investment have driven this secular increase in resource demand. It has been estimated (Ye, 2008 quoted in Roache 2012) that just over 50 per cent of China's copper usage is accounted for by infrastructure investment and construction. The question remains if this is in fact exceptional, or if this experience may in fact be replicable over time. Is China something of an outlier when it comes to the recorded global experience of countries' resource intensity?

There is some evidence to this effect, as Garnaut (2012) writes about the Chinese input-output tables, which "reveal a much higher direct and indirect metals and energy content in investment than in other components of GDP". Given the high investment share—which has been higher than any other North East Asian country and continues to grow—China's resource intensity tends to be higher than any other country at comparable levels of per capita income. As Roach (2012) explains, China's energy consumption is relatively high given its stage of economic development—it is 35 per cent higher than that of Korea, and twice that of Brazil at comparable income levels. The difference is even more stark and significant when it comes to base metals.

Structural factors as well as domestic policy distortions have been well documented by a number of studies as being responsible for China's high commodity intensity. Some of these structural factors and policy distortions may well be corrected as the country attempts its own economic rebalancing. It is fair to say that an exact replication of the conditions of China's recent history could very well replicate the Chinese experience of resource intensity as well; however, it would be also *not* be unfair to say that China has been an exceptional player in the resources sector.

I.C: Contours of China's Supply Response: Buy, Build, Acquire

Although China has sufficient reserves for thermal coal, gold, and most rare earth minerals, it is relatively constrained in metallurgical coal, iron ore and nickel. In response to the demands of its high-resource dependent economy, security of supply is quite high on China's political agenda. The Chinese approach to meeting the supply objective has been to buy—build—acquire. As we have noted above too, high proportion of the incremental demand for minerals and metals has flowed into imports, and has therefore impacted global commodity markets and prices. While the 'buy' principle has been supported by trade expansion policies, China has also aggressively built and developed mining and the requisite infrastructure internally. Since much of the mining sector in China is closed to majority ownership by foreign entities, it has been developed mostly through government enterprise and ownership. Finally, the country is spending large and increasing amounts on exploring for minerals inside China and is also reaching out to participate in the world's mining and metals industry.

Given the high resource endowment of indigenous coal reserves, it is natural that there would be a preponderance of coal in China's total energy consumption, which accounts for 70 per cent of the total. China accounts for almost 13 per cent of the world's proven coal reserves (making it the third largest) and is currently the world's largest consumer and producer of coal, including metallurgical coal (Coates & Luu, 2012). China's domestic demand-supply balance has mandated a rapid development of its coal mining and rail transport infrastructure, so that coal can be moved economically from the hinterland to the fast developing coastal regions. Environmental concerns have started to impact coal production, leading to consolidation in the industry as the government decided to shut down some of the smaller, less optimal producers. This led to a shift in the domestic balance, and required China to step into the global market, and it soon emerged as the world's second largest importer of coal (thermal and metallurgical combined).

The high demand for industrial metals to service the high infrastructure build up in the country has been matched by a rapid escalation in the production capacity for them. Achieving self-sufficiency in steel was a key aspect in the country's early stages of industrialisation, leading to the creation of a vast capacity in this area. It is today one of the largest producers of steel in the world, producing almost 716 million tons of crude steel per year. Similarly, large capacity was created in setting up aluminium smelters (although they were not very efficient in term of energy efficiency, and some were closed in 2010).

China's Demand Influence over Iron Ore Prices

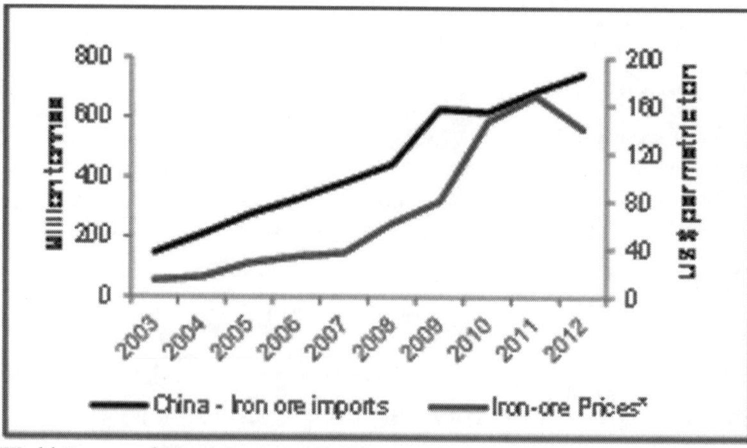

Source: World Bureau of Metal Statistics, IMF..

China's imports of intermediate inputs such as iron ore, metallurgical coal, alumina and copper ore have grown dramatically over the past few years. A case in point is the iron ore sector—although China is the fourth largest producer of iron ore in the world, demand and supply issues have been such that it has emerged as an absolute giant in the global sea borne market for iron ore. While demand soared, Chinese iron ore domestic production was beset with issues of quality and costs, as well as logistical issues which led to an increase in China's imports of iron ore from 148 million tons in 2003 to 745 million tons in 2012. Today, China accounts for 61per cent of the global imports for iron ore, even though it is the fourth largest iron ore producer in the world.

Apart from the buy and build, China has clearly entered the acquisition race across the globe. There is much evidence that the Chinese have emerged as an aggressive player in overseas investments to acquire and develop minerals and energy. As of today, the mining sector accounts for 15 per cent of China's total outward FDI,[4] having grown by as much as 28 per cent (CAGR) during the past decade. Chinese officials and representatives have expressed views that corroborate that China will continue its two pronged approach of domestic consolidation concomitantly with conducting overseas acquisitions. In 2012, China's M&A activity accounted for 21per cent of total sector M&A (in mining) globally for the year, up from 9 per cent in 2011 (EY, 2012). Chinese companies often act as strategic partners by offering to drive infrastructure development in countries of M&A targets that may have under-developed mining and metals markets. Chinese SOEs are increasingly adopting an "outward" focus, encouraged by the government to look overseas for investments and expansion of operating capabilities.

Table 1: China's Commodity Imports

Year	*Iron Ore*		*Bauxite*		*Copper*	
	China (MT)	*Share in world imports (%)*	*China (MT)*	*Share in world imports (%)*	*China (MT)*	*Share in world imports (%)*
2003	148.1	25.4	0.6	1.9	1.4	20.3
2004	208.1	31.0	0.9	2.6	1.2	16.9
2005	275.3	36.5	2.2	5.8	1.2	17.4
2006	326.3	40.6	9.3	21.5	0.8	11.7
2007	383.1	44.5	23.3	38.8	1.5	20.5
2008	443.6	47.6	25.9	41.4	1.5	20.7
2009	627.8	63.8	19.8	44.4	3.2	39.0
2010	618.6	57.8	30.4	53.1	2.9	36.7
2011	686.7	60.2	45.2	80.2	2.8	35.9
2012	745.4	61.8	40.1	58.1	3.4	41.8

Source: World Steel Organisation; World Bureau of Metal Statistic, & Author's calculations.

II. India: Current State of Play and Possible Future Trajectory

II.A: India's Growth Story: Impressive but not Resource Intensive Yet

The last decade[5] can be considered an inflexion point in India's growth trajectory given that GDP growth remained above 8 per cent for a significant part of the decade. India's average growth during the last decade stood at 7.6 per cent compared to 5.8 per cent in the earlier decade. As India leapt forward in terms of economic growth, its demand for energy and non-energy mineral resources gathered momentum. India's consumption of steel and aluminium has more than doubled between 2001 and 2010. During this period India's primary energy consumption grew at an annual average rate of 5 per cent compared 3.5 per cent in the earlier period. Apart from high GDP growth a confluence of factors including high manufacturing growth, growing per capita income (PCI), faster pace of urbanisation and infrastructure investment have been instrumental in pushing up India's resource consumption during the last decade.

Real GDP Growth*

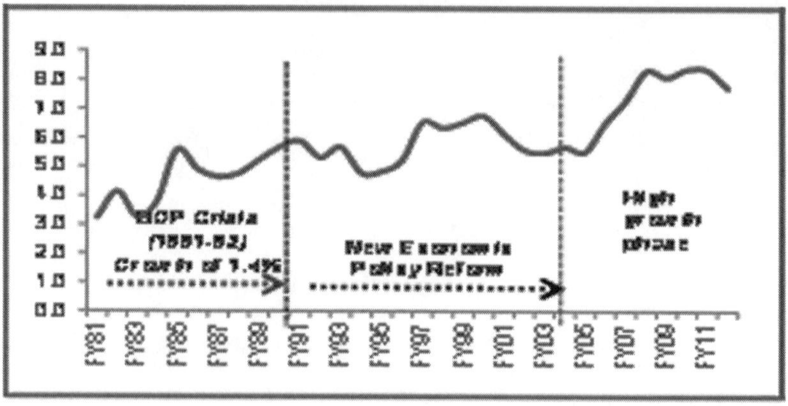

Energy and Metal Consumption

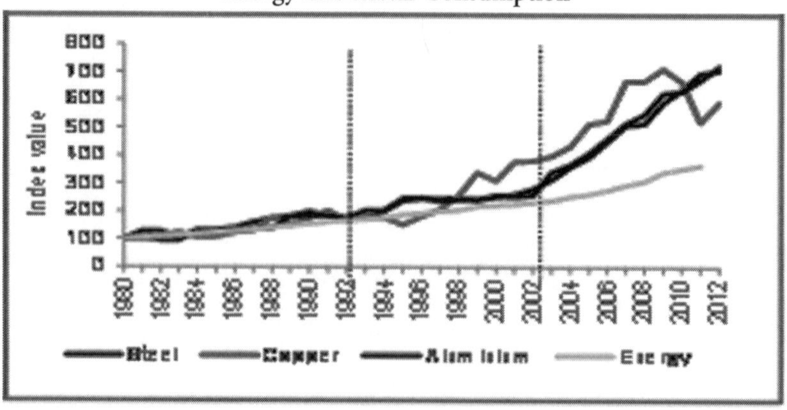

*5-year moving average GDP (factor cost, constant 2004-05 prices) growth
Source: World steel organisation; WBMS, World Bank, IMF & Author's calculations.

The impressive growth in demand of these industrial commodities, however, conceals the fact that in terms of per capita consumption India compares poorly with other emerging economies. For instance, India's per capita aluminium consumption is less than $1/10^{th}$ of aluminium consumption in China and $1/5^{th}$ of the average world per capita aluminium consumption. India's per capita energy consumption is also one of the lowest in the world and is only 30 per cent of the world's average. India being the latecomer in the development stage and given its higher share of services in GDP, its resource intensity has been quite low especially in comparison to China. India has leapfrogged over the manufacturing-led stage of development and has relied on the service sector to drive its economic growth. Contribution of the manufacturing to GDP has almost remained static at around 14-16 per cent of GDP over the last three decades and remains substantially low compared to its Asian peers. A cross country regression analysis have shown that given its per capita income, population and size, India stands out with relatively smaller manufacturing sector than expected (Francis and Winters, 2008).

India's growth so far has been consumption intensive in nature and has contributed to its relatively low resource intensity. Given the low per capita income, India's consumption pattern has been relatively less metal intensive so far. Share of expenditure on consumer durables and housing remains substantially low, though witnessing an increasing trend. Investment expenditure started to pick up in the high growth years of 2004-2008, but still remains below that which is required to bridge the infrastructure deficit in India. Although India's metal consumption remains substantially low, a cross country comparison reveals that India's consumption of some metals is in line with the international trend given its per capita GDP.

II.B: Resource Consumption Set to Take-off as Growth Accelerates through Structural Transformation

The relatively low level of consumption growth indicates huge potential for growth as Indian economy traverses on a high growth path. Notwithstanding the current slowdown in India's economic growth, the last decade highlighted India's potential to garner high growth in a conducive policy environment. As India goes forward with its reform agenda, its economic growth is expected to accelerate. This growth

Per Capita Refined Aluminium Consumption

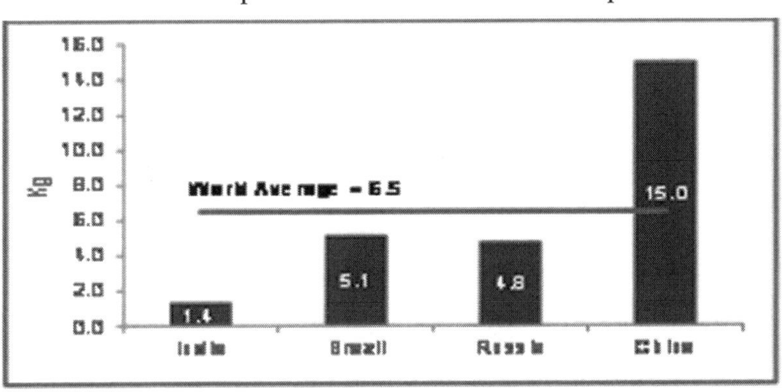

Source: WBMS, World Bank, IMF and author's calculations.

will be underpinned by favourable demographics, enormous infrastructure requirements, a transition from a rural to industrial economy and an increasing level of urbanisation and wealth. India's demand for energy and metals should rise as its economy strides forward and some rebalancing occurs in its economic structure. According to the strategy plan of Ministry of Mines, the demand for various metals and minerals will grow four to five times over the next 15 years (9-11 per cent growth per annum; see graph below). India's energy demand is also expected to increase substantially; the IEA forecasts, that India will account for one quarter of global demand growth over the next 20 years.

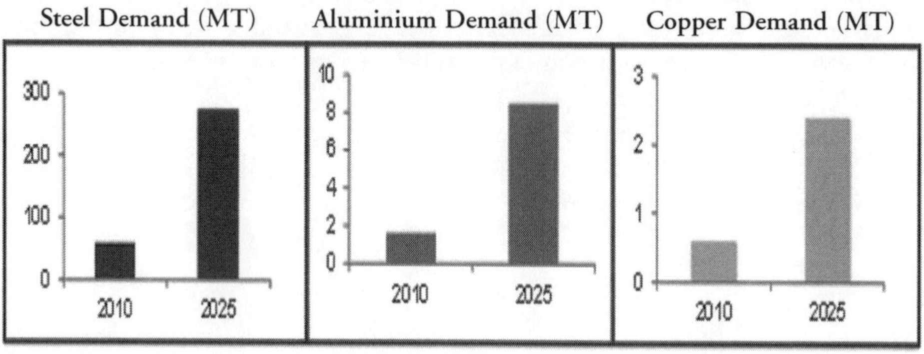

Source: Strategic plan for Ministry of Mines.

The increase in energy and metal consumption in India will be reinforced by a host of macro-economic changes that are expected to take place within the Indian economy.

Economic rebalancing in favour of manufacturing sector—Even though India will remain a services led economy, the manufacturing sector is expected to exhibit strong growth, backed by demand from a young population, growing urbanisation and a high rate of investment, particularly given the government's focus on increasing the share of manufacturing in GDP from 16 per cent to 25 per cent over the next decade. The manufacturing sector will have to grow at an annual average rate of 12-14 per cent to achieve this target. Easing of supply side bottlenecks, such as availability of skilled labour, land availability, sustained resource availability, etc. will be a key to achieving India's potential growth. The much awaited 'second generation' policy response and reform in areas of the "means of production", i.e., land, labour, resources, will be key towards demarcating the aspirational growth from the actual.

Demographic dividend & growing middle class—India's growing population especially in the working age group reinforces huge potential for growing commodity demand. India is entering demographic transition much later than many other developing countries and will relatively be a young nation even twenty years from now. The population in the working age group is expected to constitute 64 per cent of the total population by 2025, and is expected to increase through 2040. India's consumption expenditure especially for consumer durables is likely to surge given its young population, rising per capita incomes. According to an OECD[6] research paper, "India's middle class (defined as those with per-capita incomes of $10-100 a day) will expand from 5-10 per cent of the population today to 90 per cent in 2039. In other words, India will have added one billion people—almost its entire current population—to the middle class."

Shares of Global Middle-class Consumption

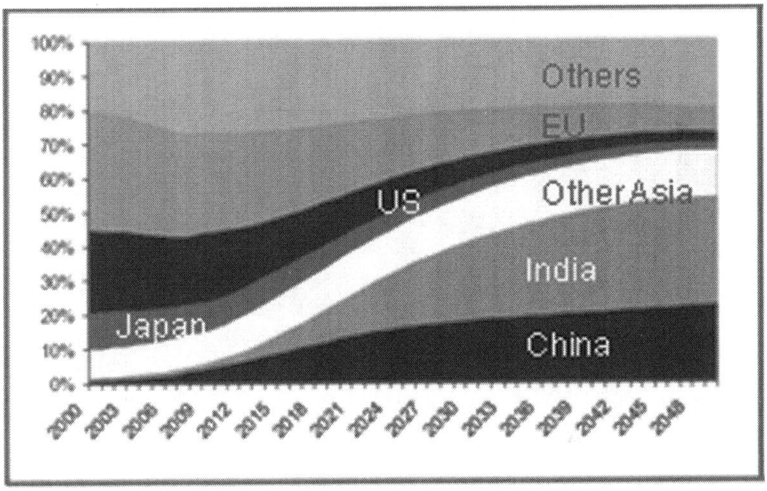

Low Car Penetration in India Portrays India's Growth Potential

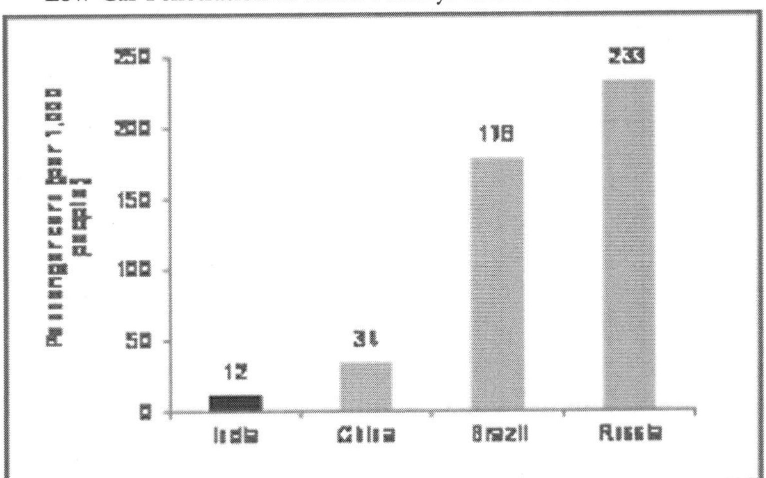

Source: OECD, EY.

Lower penetration of consumer goods indicates huge potential for growth as the middle income population rise. Penetration of white goods such as refrigerators, washing machines, televisions is fairly low in India. For instance, only 18 per cent of Indian households own refrigerators compared with 48 per cent in China.[7]

Urbanisation—According to the UN projection[8] 40 per cent of India's population is projected to live in urban areas by 2030 (from 31 per cent in 2011). This would mean 250 million additional people will live in cities by 2030. The rapid growth in urbanisation will entail significant investment to build cities and related infrastructure. Nature of urbanisation in India has been significantly different from China. In a stark contrast to China, there is almost no focussed policy-driven approach to increase urbanisation rates in India, even though there is support for its natural progression. This is reflected in much lower residential floor-space per capita in India's cities (less than 10 square meters per person) compared to China (roughly 30 square meters per urban resident).

The quality and pace of urban development differs significantly across regions and the provision of urban infrastructure is mediocre in most urban centres. As an example, it has been estimated that India is likely to suffer from a water deficit of almost 50 per cent by 2030. India will need to increase its current spend of $17 per capita on urban development by almost eight times to $134 per capita to erase the backlog and create enough capacity for future needs. This does represent an investment opportunity, and therefore will improve over the coming decades; however, it will not follow the pace or magnitude witnessed in the state-led initiatives of China.

Infrastructure investment—Infrastructure investment during the 11th five year plan (2007-12) witnessed some improvement, increasing to 7.2 per cent of GDP compared to 5.0 per cent in the 10th plan period. During the 11th plan period, India added a record 54.9 GW of power generation capacity during the 11th five year plan—about two and half times the capacity added in the 10th plan. Despite the rapid growth during the 11th plan period, infrastructure deficit remains substantially high in the country and is one of the major factors limiting investment and productivity in the economy. The 12th five year plan (2012-2017) has projected that investment in infrastructure for that period would be 9 per cent of GDP (vs. 7.2 in previous plan), implying an investment of US$ 1,025 billion. Sustained focus on reducing India's infrastructure deficit will give a boost to commodities demand going forward. It is estimated that India's power generation capacity will almost double till 2020, entailing significant increase in commodity demand especially thermal coal.

Structural Differences Between India and China

India is often compared to China, given the similarity in their population size and the fact that they have been the fastest growing economies of the world during the last decade. The two countries, however, are significantly different not only in terms of their political landscape, but also their economic structure and growth drivers. The key structural differences, such as the relatively small contribution of manufacturing to GDP (15.2 per cent in India vs. 32.4 per cent in China during the last decade) and lower reliance on exports led growth (exports constituted 21 per cent of GDP in India vs. 33 per cent in China during the last decade) have led to wide difference in their resource intensities. Even if the contribution of manufacturing to India's GDP were to increase over the next decade, India will continue to remain a services dominated economy. While dominance of services sector in Indian economy given its per capita income is contrary to historical pattern of economic development, India is a part of a new epoch where the countries in the low or middle income brackets (during 2000's) have tended to have a higher services sector contribution to GDP than that observed for countries with similar income levels in the 1990's and 1980's. India is a consumption-led economy as against the investment-led Chinese model of economic growth. China's investment rate during the last decade was 45 per cent of GDP as against 34.6 per cent in India. Other major drivers of resource-intensity, viz., infrastructure development and urbanisation, receive vastly different treatment at the policy level in India when compared to China. The Indian government has previously expressed its intention to increase investment in infrastructure to about 9 per cent of GDP over the period of the 12th Five Year Plan (2012-2017), thus implying the recognition of the task at hand. However, progress on execution is likely to be much slower as compared to China due as much to procedural issues as also because India is unlikely to 'pre-build' its infrastructure like China where as much as 20 per cent of GDP has been spent infrastructure during the past decade.

II.C: India's Supply Options: Current State of Play

India not only has robust domestic demand, but is also well endowed with most of the key minerals required for a rapidly industrialising economy such as iron-ore, bauxite, coal and several industrial minerals. However, India is highly depended on imports for some commodities such as copper, oil & gas, coking coal, diamonds et al. India produces as many as 87 minerals, which includes 4 fuel minerals, 10 metallic minerals, 47 non-metallic minerals, 3 atomic minerals and 23 minor minerals (including building and other materials). Being a part of the erstwhile 'Gondwana' basin[9] India is endowed with substantial resource of bauxite, iron ore, coal.

The country has large resources of bauxite, occupying the sixth place in the world total resources. India accounted for almost 7per cent of the world's bauxite production, most of which is consumed domestically. For iron ore, the country is estimated to have total resources of over 28.5 billion tons and occupies the fourth position in terms of iron ore production in the world. India has substantial deposits of thermal coal, with an established coal resource of around 293.5 billion tons. It is the third largest producer of coal in the world, currently producing around 557.5 million tons of thermal coal.

Given India's huge mineral potential, the last decade witnessed substantial pick up in investment in the mining sector as reflected in the increase in Gross Capital Formation in the mining sector. However, the productivity of this investment remains low since the output of the mining industry has not witnessed a commensurately sharp increase.

Slump in Iron Ore Production

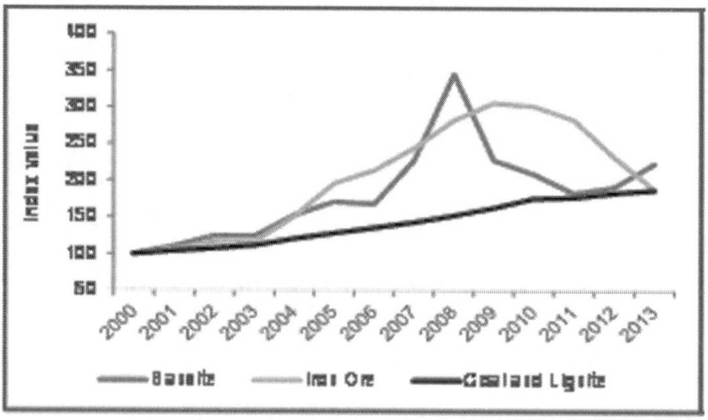

A Large Proportion of Capital Spend in the Mining Sector is Lying Unutilised

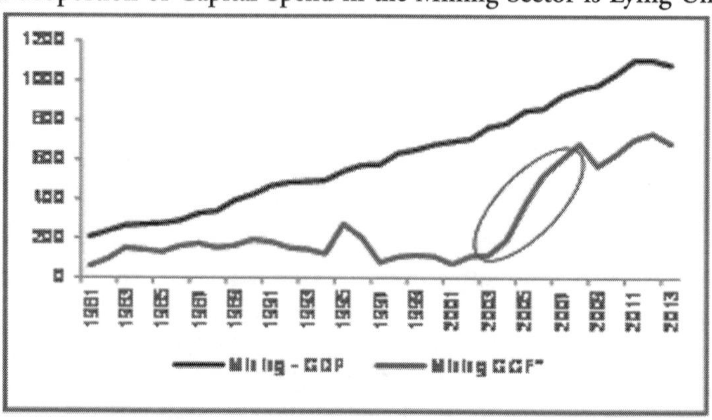

*GFC = Gross Capital Formation.

Source: World Steel Organisation; Central Statistical Organisation (GoI).

Despite extensive resources of many minerals, and high exploration potential, India's ability to meet its own resource requirements from domestic sources is being constantly challenged. The most potent example is thermal coal, where supply has been consistently falling behind demand, even though India is well endowed with thermal coal. India's thermal coal imports increased from 36 million tons in FY09 to 118 million tons in FY13, accounting for almost 20 per cent of its thermal coal consumption. Lower efficiency (low labour productivity and lack of investment in modern technology) along with delay in environmental clearances has impacted India's ability to meet its demand. Growing import dependency of thermal coal has further accentuated the concerns regarding energy security, given India's already high dependence on imports for oil & gas consumption. India has initiated several measures to resolve the logjams in the energy sector, albeit with limited success. The New Exploration Licensing Policy (NELP) rounds for exploration and development of oil resources, attracting private sector participation in power sector development, efforts to improve the availability of coal, increase investment in overseas assets have all met with lower than expected results (TERI, 2010). Ensuring security of fuel minerals remains a dominant theme in policy arena, but security of non-fuel minerals received less attention historically.

The production of iron ore and bauxite has also decelerated significantly in the last few years. Iron ore production, which grew at a CAGR of 15 per cent during FY04–FY09, today stands at 137 million tons (FY13 estimate, CEIC), which is even lower than the production levels achieved in FY05. This has hampered India's ability to export iron ore, reducing it to 28 million tons during 2012 compared to the peak of 90 million tons in 2009. Regulatory and judicial interjections to curtail illegal/irregular mining activities have been responsible for the drop in iron ore production during the last few years. Although the mining sector has witnessed substantial investment, a large proportion of capital spend is lying unutilised due to policy and regulatory impediments.

India's investment in exploration and additional productive mineral capacity has fallen or stagnated in the past few years. India's spend on exploration projects is at 0.3 per cent of the global spend (compared to 19 per cent for Canada and 12per cent for Australia). Exploration in India is mostly restricted to a depth of 50 to 100 metre vs. as deep as 300 metre in countries such as Australia. As a result, there have been few significant mineral discoveries. While the geological inventory of minerals has continued to expand and grow in places such as Western Australia, India has tended to stagnate. Substantial proportion of Indian resources remains untapped, as can be gauged from a significantly higher share of unproven resources in the total resources.

Accessibility of resource has also been limited due to a number of issues related to land acquisition, resettlement, forest preservation, environment clearances et al.

Not only accessibility, extraction of resource has had work through a number issues such as access to surface rights, preference for public sector, restrictive eligibility for mining, scant investment by government in mining & infrastructure in key mineral states. These factors have impacted India's inability to exploit its existing mineral resource base historically. In general, the mining industry in India today remains relatively low-tech, and sustainable mining practices are below established best practice internationally. While there are a small number of mines utilising large scale mechanised mining technology, these are very much in the minority, and low-tech non-mechanised mines with a heavy requirement for manual labour remain widespread. Due to low levels of investment on exploration and long-term mine planning; it is not uncommon for resources to be sub-optimally developed, with selective high-grade extraction and inadvertent sterilisation a frequent issue. Underground mining remains rare, and most open pits are relatively shallow compared to their international counterparts, rarely exceeding 100–150 m in depth.

III. Changing Paradigms and the Need to Build Capacity: Confluence of Policy, Technology and Management

From historically low levels of resource intensity per capita/unit of GDP, India may now enter a more resource intensive growth phase. With a few exceptions, the intensity of this growth is however unlikely to be equivalent to that witnessed by China during the past decade, due to a number of intrinsic structural differences such as the consumption rather than an investment-led focused economy. Nonetheless India will have to prepare itself to cater to the growing energy and mineral resources to support its economic development. The promotion of a vibrant and sustainable minerals industry represents one of the fundamental building blocks of a rapidly industrialising and urbanising economy such as India. The alternative could represent a potential brake on growth. The inter-linkages of (a) achieving a sustained high growth path through high investments and (b) achieving mineral security are well established in the China case and have some important lessons for India.

India should strive to achieve a balance between self-sufficiency based on its extensive reserves of many strategic materials and import from overseas. India needs to accord priority focus on securing better supplies from its indigenous resources. An optimal mix of policy that therefore engenders the entry of better management and technology at a wider scale is likely to drive this. Garnaut (2012) provides an excellent summary of the major drivers of supply of mineral resources. While resources may be abundantly available in nature, the main aspects of any argument which encompasses economic questions about 'limits to growth' straddle three main aspects:

1. The costs of converting naturally occurring metallic and energy minerals into suitable forms to support economic development
2. Costs of transporting them to the places of human demand
3. External environmental costs of resource use

The cost of extraction, concentration and purification of minerals will tend to vary with the varying concentrations and different chemical associations as also the depth with which it occurs in nature. Also, the natural occurring minerals will have to contend with distance and other natural barriers from places of economic activity. To summarise, the cost of ensuring supply of minerals has several elements.

1. Cost of discovery and definition of the ore bodies
2. Capital cost of building the mine and the processing facilities to convert the natural mineral into an economically valuable form
3. Recurrent cost of producing and processing the mineral from an established mine.
4. Cost of transporting the product of mining to the place where it is to be used.

As India prepares to meet its resource demand, it needs to find ways to fund each of these costs and simultaneously solve and optimise for these multiple aspects. Over and above this would be the environmental and sustainability costs that will need to be taken into account. There are manifold facets that the country will need to focus on as it creates a policy for environment that allows for the simultaneous optimisation of all the above. Capability enhancement aimed towards strengthening the governance metrics in a manner that allows and is conducive for a rule-based system to operate would be the first. Recognition of the principles of mining and the science of exploration while creating requisite rules and policies would be another. Allowing for new entrants that bring in better practices and norms, and devolve on an industry wide basis would be a third. Better and more streamlined coordination within the different arms of departments and ministries that govern mining under its various aspects would be a fourth. Creating adequate transportation & logistics framework, based upon sound transportation economic principles would be fifth.

According to the Fraser institute's report, "Survey of Mining Companies", mineral policy & infrastructure are the two major factors inhibiting the potential of India's mining industry, which is a useful pointer to the required changes to unlock India's potential supply. On the policy front, mineral exploration and mining in India is governed by the MMDR (Mines & Minerals Development Regulations) Act, 1957, and the National Mineral Policy 2008. Coal mining is covered by a separate law in India and is not under the MMDR Act. Since the nationalisation of the coal industry in the 1970's, only state owned companies are entitled to mine and trade coal in India. During the past 15 years, Indian Government has allocated around 208 coal blocks comprising ~49 billion tons of thermal coal to private and state owned companies for 'captive' consumption at pre-designated end-use plants. The policy restricts captive miners from selling coal in the open market or directing it for any-other purpose than the pre-designated end-use plants. Only a small handful of these blocks have been developed to date, with the production from captive mines restricted to around 37 million tons in 2012.

With an aim to reform the mining sector in India, a high level review committee, known as the 'Hoda Committee' was constituted in 2005 to suggest changes in the mining policy to encourage investment in public and private sector exploration and exploitation of minerals. The committee's recommendations sought to substantially improve the security of tenure and recognised that mining is a valuable standalone industry without a requirement for captive end use. Since the completion of the Hoda committee report, the draft mining law has been through numerous iterations, but has not yet been passed by Parliament. The process of getting approvals is often long drawn, with involvement of multiple agencies, leading to significant delays in acquiring mining licenses. According to the Hoda Committee report, the number of clearances for a typical mining project is 37 at the central government and 47 at the state government level (if all goes according to plan). Indian mining sector has very high tax incidence, which acts as a disincentive especially for the private sector investment. The preference for captive miners has also restricted the development of the mining industry in India. The overall track record of environmental performance and rehabilitation has been very poor and certainly below international best practice. Although there are some positive exceptions to these, they are very limited. The poor environmental performance has been compounded by illegal/irregular mining activities.

When attempting to make changes to the rule of the game (i.e., the policy regime), the desired outcome ought to the change the way the game itself is played. One of the possible ways to do it is to allow new players to come into the fray. This would imply removing entry barriers, especially in those areas where government tends to be the dominant incumbent. Although India has opened up its mining sector for foreign investors, India has not been able to attract significant foreign investment. The supply price of investment will depend upon legal and political institutions, stability of property rights, contracts, fiscal regime and the political order. India does well on many of these parameters, but could do much better on specific sectoral policies.

Mining regulation should move towards a framework that encourages and rewards scientific exploration/mining and sustainable mining best practice. This reflects a requirement to upgrade and better implement the existing regulations, but it also points to the broader issue of formulating an overall attractive investment climate for mining in India, such that those that hold the technology and expertise will feel compelled to bring this to India. As the country discusses a new mining law, it should consider a framework which substantially improves the security of tenure and recognises that mining is a valuable standalone industry without a requirement for captive end use. The law should not hamper the financial viability of the mining industry, a pre-condition for attracting sustainable investment in this sector.

If we were to create supply scenarios for the long term, India's potential supply of commodities such as iron ore and thermal coal could be two times higher in a scenario where policy reforms take place as compared to a status quo scenario. The supply options as emerged for China—Buy, Build, Acquire—are available to India as well; however, the starting point in this landscape would be to secure that which is indigenously available.

NOTES

1. Metabolic rate: Average per capita use of materials.
2. A good example of this is the use of copper in transmission sector in India, which is substantially below the levels visible in other countries. India's transmission network is dominated by overhead cables (using Aluminium). Even use of copper in underground cables remains limited due to relatively higher costs.
3. This case is true for India, and a number of other recently emerging economies, as the development epoch changes. See Box on India vs China below for more.
4. Author's calculation, based upon CEIC database.
5. Last decade refers to period between 2004-2013.
6. HomiKharas, "The emerging middle class in developing countries", Working Paper No 285, OECD Development Centre, January, 2010. http://www.oecd.org/dev/44457738.pdf
7. "India in the super cycle", Report by Standard Chartered Global Research, 2011. https://www.sc.com/en/resources/global-en/pdf/press-releases/india-expected-to-emerge-as-a-winner-in-the-third-global-super-cycle.pdf
8. UN Population Projection—Median variant.
9. India is part of mineral rich Gondwana basin caused by continental shift millions of years ago. Gondwana Basin: Australia, India, South & Central Africa and South America.

REFERENCES

Calverley, J., Jha, M., Amerasinghe, S., Caparusso, J., Henderson, C., Minikin, R., Kusuma, J. and Harr, T., "The super-cycle lives: EM growth is key", *Special Report,* Global Research, Standard Chartered, November 2013

Coates B. and Luu N., "China's emergence in global commodity markets", *Economic Roundup Issue-1,* The Treasury, Australian Government, 2012

Cuddington John T. and Zellou, Abdel M., "A Simple Mineral Market Model: Can it produce Super Cycles in prices?", *Resources Policy,* 38 (1), pp. 75-87, Elsevier, March 2013

Deverell, R., Shaw, A., Szpakowski, A. and Yu, M., "Indian Commodity Demand: On China's trail", *Fixed Income Research*, Credit Suisse, September 2011

Dobbs R. and Sankhe S., "Comparing urbanisation in China and India", *Insights & Publications,* McKinsey & Company, July 2010

EPC World, "On a quest to regain the lost shine", *Cover Story*, October 2013, at http://www.imfa.in/pdfs/EPCWorld_Cover%20Story_Oct%202013-edition.pdf

Ernst & Young, "Mergers, acquisitions and capital raising in mining and metals,2012 Trends and 2013 Outlook—When opportunity knocks, who answers?" http://www.ey.com/Publication/vwLUAssets/EY_MA_and_Capital_Raising_in_Mining_and_Metals_-_2013_trends,_2014_outlook/$FILE/EY-MA-and-capital-raising-in-mm.pdf

Hazra, Arnab K.,Chauhan, S.B.S., Gupta, A. and Sharma, E., "Development of Indian Mining Industry—The Way Forward", Federation of Indian Chambers of Commerce & Industry (FICCI), Mines and Metals Division, October 2013.

Francis M. and Winters C., "India and the Global Demand for Commodities: Is There an Elephant in the Room?", *Discussion Paper 2008-18*, Bank of Canada, December 2008.

Garnaut, R., "The contemporary China resources boom", *Australian Journal of Agricultural and Resource Economics*, 56: 222–243. doi: 10.1111/j.1467-8489.2012.00581.x, 2012

Goldman Sachs, "India revisited", *White Paper*, Asset Management, June 2010, at http://www.goldmansachs.com/gsam/docs/instgeneral/general_materials/whitepaper/india_revisited.pdf

Government of India, "Strategic plan document Ministry of Mines", Ministry of Mines, 2013 at http://mines.nic.in/writereaddata/Filelinks/e757c8a4_final%202013.pdf

International Mining Council (2012), "Trends in the mining and metals industry", *In Brief, Mining's contribution to sustainable development*, October.

Kerschner E. and Huq N., "The Emerging 21st Century Middle class", *Thematic Investing*, Global Investment Committee, Morgan Stanley Smith Barney, June 2011.

Khanna A. and Ganeshan S., "Critical non-fuel minerals security: Why India urgently needs to have a policy in place", *Policy Brief*, The Energy and Resources Institute, December 2010.

Krausmann, F., Gingrich, S., Eisenmenger, N., Erb, K., Haberl, H. and Fischer-Kowalski, M., "Growth in global materials use, GDP and population during the 20th century", *Ecological Economics*, Elsevier, 68 (10), August 2009, pp. 2696–2705,

Liu, J. and McDonald, T., "China: growth, urbanisation and mineral resource demand", *Economic Roundup Issue-2,* The Treasury, Australian Government, 2010.

Mohanty, N. and Goyal, A., "Sustainable Development—Emerging Issues in India's Mineral Sector", Institute for Studies in Industrial Development, On behalf of Planning Commission of India, Government of India, May 2012

Pichamuthu, D.V., "Note on the Evolution of India's Mineral Policy and its Impact on the Mineral Industry", *Journal of the Geological Society of India*, Vol. 78, pp. 285-289, September 2011.

Roache, Shaun K., "China's Impact on World Commodity Markets", *IMF Working Paper*, WP/12/115, May 2012.

Singh, A., Nabar, M. and N' Diaye, P., "China's Economy in Transition from External to Internal Rebalancing" *International Monetary Fund, Publication Services,* ISBN (for final edition): 9781484303931, November 2013

Soile, Ismail O., "Intensity of Use Hypothesis: Analysis of Selected Asian Countries with Structural Differences", *International Journal of Energy Economics and Policy*, 3 (1), pp.1-9, ISSN: 2146-4553, 2013.

Tiess G. and Tiewsoh L, "EU—Minerals Policy and Indian Minerals Policy: New Paradigm and Perspectives", 17th Convention of Indian Geological Congress and International Conference on 'New Paradigms of Exploration and Sustainable Mineral Development: Vision 2050 (NPESMD 2011)', 2011

Warell L. and Olsson A., "Trend and Development in Intensity of Steel use: An econometric analysis" paper presented at Securing the Future at eighth ICARD, June 23-26, Skelleftea, Sweden, 2009.

World Bank, "The Role of Emerging-Market Economy Demand during the Post-2005 boom", Contribution to G20 Commodity Markets Sub Working Group, This note was prepared by World Bank staff John Baffes (DEC), April 2012.

Wübbeke J., "China's Mineral and Metals Industry: On the Path towards Sustainable Development?, *Pacific Geographies*, July/August, 2012, at http://www.pacific-news.de/pn38/PN38_JW.pdf

Yale insights, Yale School of Management, Interview with John Lichtenstein, "How Does China Drive the Mining and Metals Business?"; June, at http://insights.som.yale.edu/insights/how-does-china-drive-mining-and-metals-business,

12

Why Water Politics Matter

Mukul Sanwal

Introduction

Climate change will impact Asia primarily with respect to reduced water availability. Water supports food production, industry and urban living, and these different uses can no longer be seen in isolation from each other. Unless these competing needs are balanced, the resulting water stress will undermine the quality of life for billions of people in the region. Technological solutions include desalination, drip irrigation, and the understanding that new crop varieties alone will not be a solution. Reduced access to water is expected to affect migration and geopolitical tensions.

The driest continent in the world is not Africa but Asia, where the availability of freshwater is not even half the global annual average of 6,380 cubic metres per inhabitant. When the estimated reserves of rivers, lakes, and aquifers are added up, Asia has less than one-tenth of the waters of South America, Australia and New Zealand, not even one-fourth of North America, almost one-third of Europe, and moderately less than Africa per inhabitant. Yet, the world's fastest-growing demand for water for food and industrial production and for municipal supply is in Asia, which now serves as the locomotive of the world economy.

Asia more than doubled its total irrigated cropland between 1960 and 2000. Once a continent of serious food shortages and recurrent famines, Asia has emerged as a net food exporter. Three sub-regions of Asia—South Asia, China, and Southeast Asia—by themselves account for about 50 per cent of the world's total irrigated land. Today, the fastest growing Asian economies are all at, or near water-stressed conditions, including China, India, South Korea, Vietnam, and Indonesia. Looking three or four decades ahead, it is clear that the water situation will only exacerbate, carrying major implications both for rapid economic growth and inter-riparian relations.

These have helped give rise to grand but environmentally questionable ideas—from China's Great Western Route to divert river waters from the Tibetan Plateau to its parched north, South Korea's politically divisive four-rivers project, to India's now-stalled proposal to link up its important rivers, and Jordan's plan to save the dying Dead Sea by bringing water from the Red Sea through a 178-kilometre-long canal which is also to serve as a source for desalinated drinking water—a significant share of which is in trans boundary water courses. As rural populations move to urban areas, consumption rises with incomes. Asia is consuming an increasing share of global resources, including water, food, oil, and energy. Dam building has only intensified intrastate and interstate water tensions, with implications for regional security and stability.

Only four of the 57 transnational river basins in Asia have a treaty covering water sharing or other institutionalised cooperation. These are the Mekong, Ganges, Indus and Jordan River basins. The absence of a cooperative arrangement in most Asian transnational basins is making trans-boundary water competition a major security risk, increasing the likelihood of geopolitical tensions.

Institutionalised cooperation on trans-boundary basin resources is needed in order to underpin strategic stability, protect continued economic growth, and promote environmental sustainability. The continent cannot continue to prosper without building political and technological partnerships to help stabilise inter-riparian relations, encourage greater water efficiency, promote environmental sustainability, take on practicable conservation strategies, and invest in clean water technologies. If Asian states are to address their water challenges, they will need to embrace good practices for the strategic planning and management of water resources.

This chapter looks at the academic and policy debate in terms of the way the issue has been framed in terms of scarcity rather than the use and distribution of scarce resources.

Analysis

The range of recent analyses—assessments, methodologies, definitions and strategic reviews —focus on the environmental aspects and the rising demand ignoring new patterns of resource use, and are much less alarming than the models that have so far been adopted to project and assess scarcity.

The strategic security dimension of water scarcity in Asia is based on the international definition of water stress which is 1,000 cubic metres of usable water per person per year, and the increasing demand in China, where the average northern Chinese has less than a fifth of that amount. China has 20 per cent of the world's population but only 7 per cent of its fresh water. This view focuses on the projects for damming or diverting rivers, and argues that such diversions have the potential to deprive other countries of their assured supply—increasing available water by capturing more of what flows through rivers or by moving water from one river to another.

The problem is also framed in terms of water security. According to the ADB's Asia Water Development Outlook 2013, 37 of the 49 countries assessed were suffering from low levels of water security, including those which lacked measures to tackle the problem. Twelve countries are shown to have established infrastructure and management systems for water security, while no country in the region was found to have reached the highest model level of water security. More than 60 per cent of households in Asia and the Pacific still live without a safe, piped water supply and improved sanitation. More than 75 per cent of Asia-Pacific countries face an imminent water crisis unless immediate steps are taken to improve resource management.

A recent strategic analysis argues that three interconnected crises—a resource crisis, an environmental crisis, and a climate crisis—are threatening Asia's economic, social, and ecological future. This analysis is based on the impacts of climate change, and argues that the Tibetan Plateau, which contains the world's third largest store of ice, is warming at almost twice the average global rate, owing to the rare convergence of high altitudes and low latitudes—with potentially serious consequences for Asia's freshwater supply.[1]

The problem is now being framed in terms of sustainable development. According to the report *Global Trends 2030,* released by the Office of National Director of Intelligence USA, demand for food, water, and energy will grow by approximately 35, 40 and 50 per cent respectively, owing to an increase in the global population and the consumption patterns of an expanding middle class. Climate change will worsen the outlook for the availability of these critical resources.

Moving on from describing what is happening to analysing the causes, the Asian Development Bank has also pointed out that the majority of Asia's water development problems are attributable to 'poor water governance and not to water scarcity'. The conservation of resources is also a societal goal—with potential to improve the quality of life around the world. According to the ADB, the important thing is a dramatic reduction in waste. The ADB has urged countries to invest in 'reduce, re-use, recycle systems' to better the use of dwindling water resources, and better sanitation and other infrastructure, mobilise additional resources to clean up rivers, and modernise irrigation systems. Governments must also step up campaigns to educate people on water scarcity, and the critical situation. This view argues that it would be better to focus on demand, reducing the consumption of water in order to make better use of limited supplies. Water is too cheap in most cities, industry recycles too little water, and agriculture wastes too much. Asia has one of the lowest levels of water efficiency and productivity in the world.

The report of the National Intelligence Council USA, also points out that scarcities in resources can be avoided, but only if steps are taken by a number of industries and economies in a coordinated manner to improve productivity and efficiency. According to this report, 'we are not necessarily headed into a world of scarcities', but policymakers and their private sector partners will need to be proactive to avoid such a future. It has also stressed that most scientists are not confident of being able to predict climatic events. Rapid changes in precipitation patterns—such as the monsoon in India and the rest of Asia—could sharply disrupt the region's ability to feed its population. At the same time, key technologies likely to be at the forefront of maintaining energy, food and water resources in the next 15-20 years are available, and will include genetically modified crops, precision agriculture, water irrigation techniques, and solar energy.

Dimensions of Climate Change

Academic debate on the impact of climate change on resource stress, or environmental security, is divided, with some concluding—on the basis either of case studies or quantitative analyses of historical and present day climate conflict relations—that anthropogenic warming is likely to exacerbate conflict dynamics, with others finding only circumstantial evidence of linkages between the two, and still others refuting the climate conflict thesis altogether.

The Tibetan Plateau

Though the amount of ice on the plateau of Tibet and its surrounding mountains, such as the Himalayas, Karakoram and Pamirs, is a lot smaller than that at the Poles, it is still huge. The area's 46,000 glaciers cover 100,000 square kilometres (40,000 square miles)—about 6 per cent of the area of the Greenland ice cap. Another 1.7m square kilometre is permafrost, which can be up to 130 metres deep. That is equivalent to 7 per cent of the Arctic's permafrost. The area is known by some as Asia's water tower, because it is the source of ten of the Continent's biggest rivers. About 1.5 billion people, in 12 countries, live in the basins of those rivers.

An unresolved issue is whether the Tibetan Plateau glaciers are retreating, as is happening in parts of the North and South Poles. The Intergovernmental Panel on Climate Change's report in 2007 incorrectly suggested that the Himalayas' glaciers could disappear as early as 2035. However, a 2012 study published in *Nature* by Thomas Jacob of the University of Colorado, in Boulder, showed that the glaciers in the Himalayas and Karakoram had lost little ice between 2003 and 2010, and that those on the Tibetan Plateau itself were growing. This assertion has been contested by Tobias Bolch of the University of Zurich on the grounds that Jacob's article was based on seven years of measurements by a satellite mission called the Gravity Recovery and Climate Experiment (GRACE). This used orbiting gravimeters to try to measure changes in the ice cover from effects on the local gravitational field.

According to Bolch, the approach suffered from two problems. One was the coarse resolving power of the satellite's instruments. These could not detect changes in features less than 200 km across. This is enough to study large regions with homogenous surfaces, such as the Arctic and the Antarctic (which GRACE did, in fact, do). But mountainous terrain has complex topography. The second, more serious problem is that the satellites cannot tell the difference between solid and liquid water. If a glacier melts but the water stays put as a lake, GRACE will see no change. Since the Tibetan Plateau contains a lot of 'closed' catchments from which melting water cannot easily escape, large amounts of melting could happen without GRACE detecting them.

An international programme (initiated in 2009) involving these countries—called the Third Pole Environment (TPE)—with lead researchers Yao Tandong of the Institute of Tibetan Plateau Research, Beijing; Lonnie Thompson of the Ohio State University; and Volker Mosbrugger of the Senckenberg World of Biodiversity, Frankfurt, is studying the Tibetan Plateau. Their work shows that the area of the glacial lakes on the plateau has increased by about 26 per cent since the 1970s. Bolch suspects that GRACE has mistaken these expanding lakes for growing glaciers. Using another satellite (called ICESat) which employs lasers to measure not only the areas of glaciers, but also the elevations of their surfaces, Bolch and his colleagues conclude that, far from advancing, many of Tibet's glaciers are in retreat.

Yao and Thompson, who have studied field reports and satellite photographs of more than 7,100 glaciers collected over the past 30 years, see a lot of regional variation. They have found that glaciers in the Karakoram and the Pamirs, in the region's west, are advancing. However, glaciers in the eastern Himalayas and in the east of the Tibetan Plateau are retreating. Those in the middle of the plateau are shrinking too, though less rapidly.

To analyse the causes, Yao and Thompson have looked at weather records. Over the decades, the Indian monsoon which brings snow to the southern part of the plateau and the eastern and central Himalayas, has been getting weaker—though no one is sure why. The westerlies that bring snow to the Karakoram and the Pamirs have, however, been getting stronger. Westerlies are caused by hot air rising from the oceans and moving north (because heat travels from warm regions to cold ones) and east (because of the Coriolis force caused by the Earth's rotation). Global warming means there is more hot air to raise, hence the stronger westerlies. The effects of these changes in wind strength on glacier growth are amplified by the season. The monsoon arrives in summer.The westerlies arrive in winter. A warming climate is more likely to stop summer snow accumulating than winter snow. Taken together, changes in wind strength and air temperature neatly account for what is going on.

The conclusion is the limited availability of data about the area. It is important to monitor bellwether glaciers every six months, and set up observatories to measure solar radiation, snowfall, melt water, and changes in the soil, as well as air temperature, pressure, humidity and wind to better understand what is happening.

The Himalayan Rivers

The Himalayas provide an interesting case study of the lack of authoritative statements on the adverse effects of climate change. With respect to water scarcity in Asia, the contribution of Himalayan and snow melt varies greatly for the rivers flowing on the Northern and Southern aspects. For example, the Yellow, Mekong and Salween rivers get less than 10 per cent of their flows from the glaciers, while the Indus and the Ganges get up to 70 per cent prior to, and during the monsoon.

For South Asia, the monsoon—including the resulting snow fall in the upper reaches—is the determining factor in water flows. Second, conclusions are usually made on the basis of a few studies, and researchers from India and China show little interest in working together with respect to the Himalayas. Third, the scientific and the intelligence community, even in the USA, differ widely in their conclusions on how environmental impacts interact with political, economic and social dynamics.

For example, the US National Research Council has adopted a sustainable development framework.[2] It recognises that the Hindu Kush Himalayan region is the location of several of Asia's great river systems which provide water for drinking, irrigation and other uses for about 1.5 billion people. The study draws upon scientific evidence to show that 'glaciers in the eastern and central regions of the Himalayas appear to be retreating at rates comparable to glaciers in other parts of the world, while in the western Himalayas glaciers are more stable and may even be increasing in size', and concludes that the consequences for the region's water supply are unclear. Their assessment is that shifts in the location, intensity, and variability of rain and snow due to climate change will likely have a greater impact on regional water supplies. The study concludes that 'social changes such as changing patterns of water use and water management decisions, are likely to have at least as much of an impact on water demand as environmental factors do on water supply'.

A recent assessment for the CIA adopts a climate-centric approach,[3] and concludes that 'it is prudent to expect that, over the course of a decade, some climate events—including single events, conjunctions of events occurring simultaneously or in sequence in particular locations, and events affecting globally integrated systems that provide for human well-being—will produce consequences that exceed the capacity of the affected societies or the global system to manage, and that have global security implications serious enough to compel international response'. Its framework is that in Asia as a whole, with 60 per cent of the world's people, there is only 36 per cent of the world's renewable freshwater, and between now and 2040, 'fresh water availability will not keep up with demand'. It assumes that the effective management of water resources will not take place with agriculture continuing to use approximately 70 per cent of the fresh water supply, thus 'posing a risk to global food markets and hobbling economic growth'. It sees the Brahmaputra basin as an area of potential conflict because of uncoordinated land use and development plans.

The academic and policy discourse that seeks to securitise water with a focus on the interaction between climate change, water and economic growth in the context of resource stress, and conflict and security has, so far, been highly climate centric, and fails to contextualise climate impacts in relation to other broader processes of economic and social change. It is also framed too narrowly around the intersection of poverty and state fragility in sub-Saharan Africa, and without understanding the complexity of interlinked processes like glacial melt and the monsoon. The strategic community has also ignored current scientific consensus on how to meet the challenge of global change, which focuses on societal dynamics as both the root of environmental problems and the potential solution to them.

Climate Change and the UN Security Council

On 17 April 2007, the UK initiated a debate in the United Nations Security Council on the relationship between energy, security and climate. Here, both the Non-Aligned Movement (NAM) and the Group of 77+China argued that the matter should be discussed within the General Assembly Economic and Social Council. On 3 June 2009, on the initiative of the small-island developing states of the Pacific Ocean, the General Assembly held a debate on climate change and its possible security implications, and requested the Secretary-General to submit a report on the possible security implications of climate change.

On 11 September 2009, the Secretary-General identified climate change as a 'threat multiplier' that exacerbates existing threats such as persistent poverty, weak institutions for resource management, and mistrust between communities. It identified five further ways in which climate change might affect security:

- climate change could threaten food security and human health, and increase exposure to extreme events;
- it could undermine the stability of states by slowing or reversing development;
- it could increase the likelihood of domestic conflict due to migration and depleting resources, with possible international ramifications;
- the disappearance of territory might raise issues of sovereignty, rights and security; and
- international conflict might be a result of climate change's impact on shared or demarcated international resources.

Further discussion in the Security Council illustrates the different perspectives, with countries focusing on those parts of this report which support their position. For example, in February 2013, the Security Council heard experts who were natural scientists talk on the 'Security dimensions of climate change'. It was a discussion initiated by Pakistan and the UK. Germany, with the strong support of Portugal, has also initiated the open debate for July 2013 on rising sea levels and its impact on coastal and small island states, which could include the loss of coastal territory, the disappearance of certain islands completely, and threats to food security due to climate change and its effects on peace and security. Brazil has stressed the livelihood and sharing aspects in the report, and argued that there is no direct link established between climate change and peace and security, and that social and economic development provides adequate tools to tackle the impact of climate change.

Long term thinking is now taking place on the relationship between climate change and access to modern energy, infrastructure and urbanisation as well as in sparking or aggravating existing tensions that could lead to conflict. The focus is now on the relationship between all these issues rather than only on conflict prevention in terms of international security

The legitimate concern of the non-permanent members of the Security Council is that sovereignty no longer exclusively protects States from foreign interference, and environmental security should not adopt the principle of 'sovereignty as responsibility' where collective action for crimes against humanity is extended to protect populations from loss of habitat, starvation and mass migration. Therefore, the emerging trend in the negotiations around the post-2015 global agenda is to stress the principle of 'sustainable development' with respect to the global impacts of natural resource use. Environmental, technological and societal transformations are interlinked and cannot be considered in isolation.

And, it would be within the mandate of the Security Council to support peace *and* security by looking at the longer term future of the planet for sharing responsibility as well as prosperity for human wellbeing.

In the case of climate change, the choice for the collective response is between rules for societal and technological transformation and intervention in the face of environmental risks and access to resources. The international community should define 'responsibility to protect' in terms of equal rights of all populations to sustainable development, with new platforms for cooperative responses to deal with longer term global change, of which climate change is only a part.

Water Footprint and Sustainable Development

Water problems are closely tied to the structure of the global economy. Interest in the water footprint is rooted in the recognition that human impacts on freshwater systems can ultimately be linked to human consumption, and that issues like water shortages and pollution can be better understood and addressed by considering production and supply chains as a whole. Many countries have significantly externalised their water footprint, importing water-intensive goods from elsewhere. This puts pressure on the water resources in the exporting regions where, too often, mechanisms for wise water governance and conservation are lacking. Not only governments, but also consumers, businesses and civil society communities need to play a role in achieving a better management of water resources.

Below are some significant examples:

- The production of one kilogram of beef requires 15 thousand litres of water, and the water footprint of a 150-gram soy burger produced in the Netherlands is about 160 litres. A beef burger from the same country consumes about 1000 litres.
- The water footprint of Chinese consumption is about 1070 cubic meter per year per capita. About 10 per cent of the Chinese water footprint falls outside China embodied in the goods exported.
- Japan with a footprint of 1380 cubic meter per year per capita, has about 77 per cent of its total water footprint outside the borders of the country. The water footprint of US citizens is 2840 cubic meter per year per capita. About 20 per cent of this water footprint is external. The largest external water footprint of US consumption lies in the Yangtze River basin, China.
- Water scarcity affects over 2.7 billion people for at least one month each year.

Recent analysis is focusing on consumption patterns as the driver of global change, and the question being asked today is: why is it generally assumed that all countries aspire to adopt the consumption patterns of the USA? An extensive land mass and low population in the USA led to an urban design and technology ignoring resource use implications. For example, getting food from the farm to a US family fork eats up 10 per cent of the total US energy budget, uses 50 per cent of the land, and swallows 80 per cent of all the freshwater consumed in the United States. Yet, 40 per cent of the food in the USA today goes uneaten, and has now been taken up as a challenge by the US Department of Agriculture.[4] The future in Asia is going to be different as the context is very different.

Reframing the Issue

Water use cannot be seen separately from emissions of carbon dioxide. Land use systems are computed to cause a quarter of total global emissions; however, half the emissions are generated subsequent to agricultural production: that is, in storage, preparation and transport. The highest impact is from livestock farming, which uses nearly three-quarters of the agricultural land, and half the water resources, while providing only 15 per cent of the global calorie supply, and contributing 18 per cent of global emissions. The lifecycle emissions of meat, dairy products, and eggs (which the city dwellers demand) are up to ten times higher than those of an equal weight of plant derived foodstuffs on which the rural population continues to depend. If urban eating habits change, global GHG emissions from agriculture can come down to below 1990 levels, even though the demand for food is expected to go up by three times during the next 20 years, as one-third of food is currently wasted.[5]

A new dimension to the debate is emerging as China plans to shift 250 million people from rural areas to dense urban clusters on the lines of New York City, where emissions are one-third of the average in the USA, and water use is nearly half. China has built 40,000 kilometers of high speed rail, equal to the length of inter-state highways in the USA, modifying earlier global trends in resource use. This explains why China, with four times the population, uses just three-fourth more energy than the USA, while the per capita energy consumption is less than half the level in the USA, and China has begun to limit vehicle ownership in major cities.

Similarly, while global livestock production was responsible for 14.5 per cent of greenhouse gas emissions, the carbon intensity is highest for beef, contributing half of those emissions This Indians do not eat at all, and neither is it a key part of the diet in China. With infrastructure reaching saturation levels, in 2012 China's emissions rose 3 per cent—well below the 10 per cent growth in the previous decade. China has set a policy of a maximum level of energy consumption by 2015, has invested nearly US$ 70 billion in renewable energy, which is 50 per cent more than the USA, and is shifting to natural gas, opening the possibility of declining global emissions (PBL, 2013).[6] Water use in China is half that in the USA. China, India and other developing countries aspire to reach the per capita levels of income of a middle level European country (like Spain), and their natural resource use will remain one-third that of the USA—a trend that has yet to be recognised by the economic and environmental models.

The implication for the trans-boundary sharing of water resources and the global rule based system is that the consumption patterns of the rich—and not just population—affects the availability of resources for others. The shift to the longer term objectives of a more equal society across the world will go beyond political boundaries, and revisit current notions of state responsibility and accountability for the environment. Instead of asking the question what action can be taken given the risk, the approach should be to maximise economic, social and environmental benefits with as little harm as possible.

For countries in Asia, the overriding question is how to move away from the historical patterns of natural resource use and design new structures for wellbeing. The types of new infrastructure will determine sustainability as they will be building the equivalent of a city of one million people every day from now until 2050. Sustainable growth will depend upon high density communities responding to the fact that land and water are becoming a scarce resource, the higher cost of commodities, and using fewer natural resources by designing living and working places close to one another, allowing people to walk rather than use cars, and providing public transportation. Other measures include mandatory energy efficiency in building, reducing waste, encouraging water reuse, and conserving rain water.

New technology will also help to reduce resource stress. For example, in Beijing, the supply of water available per person is 100 cubic metres—which is far lower than the international average of 1,000 cubic metres. China faces an annual shortfall of some 600 million cubic metres of water. To address its water shortage, China plans to double its desalination capacity to 2.6 million cubic metres of water by 2015. China is already one of the fastest growing markets in desalination, and ranks ninth in the world in terms of seawater desalination capacity. With increased urbanisation, the demand will increase. The Chinese government is looking into a project that will deliver 1 million cubic metres of desalinated water to Beijing every day by 2016. Improvements in technology have greatly reduced costs; desalination is now a viable solution to China's water shortage.

A Case Study of the Colorado River: Lessons for Asia

The Colorado River and a large number of reservoirs from the Rockies to southern Arizona are being sapped by 14 years of drought nearly unrivalled in 1,250 years. Many experts believe the current drought is a precursor of a new, drier era in which the river's flow will be substantially and permanently diminished. An intensive conservation program has slashed the region's water consumption from 2002 to 2012, even as the area has added 400,000 residents.

There is a 50-50 chance that, by 2015, Lake Mead's water will be rationed to states downstream. If Lake Mead goes below elevation 1,000" (that is, 1,000 feet above sea level), it will not be possible to serve the municipal needs of seven in 10 people in the state of Nevada. Since 2008, a tunnel is being drilled under Lake Mead—a third attempt to capture more water as two higher tunnels have become threatened by the lake's falling level.

Agriculture, California's Imperial Valley, and Wyoming's cattle herds soak up about three-quarters of the water, and produces 15 per cent of the nation's food. But 40 million people also depend upon the river and its tributaries, and their numbers are rising rapidly.

The labyrinthine rules by which the seven Colorado states share the river's water are full of potential points of conflict. And while some states have made huge strides in conserving water—and even reducing the amount they consume—they have yet to chart a united path through shortages that could last years, or even decades.

New research concludes that rising temperatures will reduce the Colorado's average flow after 2050 by five to 35 per cent, even if rainfall remains the same—and most of these studies predict that rains will diminish.

In the 1920s, the Colorado basin states tried to stave off future fights over water by splitting it, 50-50, between the upper basin states of Utah, New Mexico, Colorado and Wyoming and the lower-basin states of Arizona, Nevada and California. In fact, the deal underestimated how much water the fast-growing lower basin states would need. However, during most of the wet 20th century, the Colorado River usually produced more than enough water to offset any shortage. Now, the gap between need and supply is becoming untenable.

Lake Mead currently stands about 1,106 feet above sea level, and is expected to drop 20 feet in 2014. A continued decline would introduce a new set of problems: at 1,075 feet, rationing begins; at 1,050 feet, a more drastic rationing regime kicks in, and the uppermost water intake for Las Vegas shuts down; at 1,025 feet, rationing grows more draconian; at 1,000 feet, a second Las Vegas intake runs dry.

Carly Jerla, a geological hydrologist and the reclamation bureau's Colorado River expert, said in an interview: 'We can't depend on history to project the future anymore...The drought could end tomorrow, or it could drag on for seven more years'. This has raised questions that the states are just beginning to sort out. The river's upper basin states are worried that they might have to curb their consumption to meet their obligations downstream. However, the thorniest problems are in the lower basin where a thicket of political and legal deals has left Arizona holding the bag should the Colorado River continue to diminish.

In the 1960s, California's legislators demanded first dibs on lower basin water as a condition for supporting federal legislation to build the Central Arizona Project, a vast web of canals irrigating that state's farms and cities. Should rationing begin in 2015, Arizona would sacrifice a comparatively small fraction of its Colorado River allotment, while California's supply would remain intact. Painful as that would be, though, it could get worse. Should Lake Mead continue to fall, Arizona would lose more than half of its Colorado River water before California lost as much as a drop. This would have a cascading effect. The Central Arizona Project would lose the revenue it gets from selling water, which would raise the price of water for the remaining customers, leading farmers to return to pumping groundwater for irrigation—exactly what the Central Arizona Project was supposed to prevent. By going back to the pumps, agriculture will no longer be an industry in central Arizona.

Even Californians doubt Arizona would stand for that; but no successor to the 1960s agreement is in place. And California has a vital interest in holding on to its full allotment of water. The Southern California region using Colorado water is expected to add six million people to the existing 19 million in the next 45 years, and its other water source—the Sierra Nevada to the north—is suffering the same drought and climate problems as the Colorado basin. New technology and supplies will be insufficient to replace the lost water. Ways to live with a permanently drier Colorado are not easy. Finding more water is possible—San Diego is already building a desalination plant on the Pacific shore—but there are too few sources to make a serious dent in a shortage. This leaves conservation, a tack the lower basin states are already pursuing. Arizona farmers reduce runoff, for example, by using laser technology to ensure that their fields are table flat. The state consumes essentially as much water today as in 1955, even as its population has grown nearly twelvefold.

Working to reduce water consumption by 20 per cent per person from 2010 to 2020, Southern California's Metropolitan Water District is recycling sewage effluent, giving away high efficiency water nozzles, and subsidising items like artificial turf and zero-water urinals.

Southern Nevada's water saving measures are, in some ways, the most impressive of all: Virtually all water used indoors, from home dishwashers to the toilets and bathtubs used by the 40 million tourists who visit Las Vegas each year, is treated and returned to Lake Mead. Officials here boast that everyone could take a 20 minute shower every day without increasing the city's water consumption by a drop. Even after these measures, federal officials say that much greater conservation is possible; local officials say they have little choice to use less water.[7]

Conclusion

As population shifts to cities, the demand for water to produce food, energy and goods increases. By 2050, the world's demand for water will grow by 55 per cent. Consumption patterns, and the loss and waste of food represent a huge proportion of inefficient water use in production supply chains. Some 20 years ago, the UN International Conference on Water and the Environment had agreed that water should be recognised as an economic good. However, water is not just another commodity; it is both a public and a private good.

About 50 per cent of all available water is trans-boundary—water located in the rivers, lakes or groundwater systems of two or more countries—and cooperation over this water is often troublesome. Around two thirds of the world's trans-boundary rivers lack agreements between the countries that share them. This situation, linked to political conflicts in many of the sharing regions, has meant that trans-boundary water has been presented as a reason for violent conflicts, and even war. However, the water wars that were feared a decade ago have not materialised.

Water is increasingly becoming a source of cooperation even in situations of political tension. There are a number of benefits accruing from cooperation in trans-boundary regions: economic, environmental and social. There are also a wider range of less tangible benefits—like trust building. This suggests that the trans-boundary aspects of water generate a wide range of benefits, and resource stress is best dealt by not limiting efforts within national borders but considering them in a regional context.

NOTES

1. Brahma Chellaney, *Water, Peace, and War: Confronting the Global Water Crisis*, Maryland: Rowman and Littlefield Publishers, 2013.
2. 'Himalayan Glaciers: Climate Change, Water Resources and Water Scarcity', A Report by the National Research Council, USA, 2012.
3. 'Global Water Scarcity', Intelligence Community Assessment, ICA 2012-08, 2 February 2012, U SA.
4. 'Wasted: How America is losing up to 40 per cent of its food from farm to fork to landfill', Issue paper, Natural Resources Defence Council, USA, August 2012, IP:12-06-B.
5. 'Food Wastage Footprint: Impacts on natural Resources', Food and Agriculture Organisation, Rome, 2013.
6. 'Trends in Global Carbon Dioxide Emissions', Report, Netherlands Environmental Assessment Agency, The Hague, Netherland Environment Assessment Agency, 2013.
7. Adapted from 'Colorado River Drought Forces a Painful Reckoning for States', by Michael Wines, *The New York Times*, January 5, 2014.

13

Water Security in China

Huang Ying

Introduction

There is no universally accepted definition for "water security". For different countries at different development stages, water security may have different meanings. In China, water security has been discussed at two different levels. In the broad sense, it includes issues such as fighting natural disasters like flood and drought, food security and safe supply of fresh water. In a narrow sense, it refers to the safe supply of clean water, of which the shortage of quality water is the main problem. This paper mainly discusses the narrow sense of water security in China. It is divided into three parts. The first section, examines how serious the water situation is in China. The second gauges the effectiveness of the measures the government has taken to tackle the water challenge. The third makes suggestions on how China may improve its water security through cooperation at regional level.

Water Situation in China

China is a country with a massive population and scarce water resources. The tension between the population and water resources has been felt for decades and will intensify in the foreseeable future.

According to the World Bank statistics, China's annual freshwater storage is about 2800 km^3, which is 6 per cent of the global renewable freshwater. In terms of aggregate volume, China ranks the fourth in the world, only after Brazil, Russia and Canada. However, on a per capita basis, China is one of most water-deficient countries. According to the statistics released recently by China's Ministry of Water Resources, renewable internal freshwater resources per capita in China is as low as 2100 cubic meters, which is only about 28 per cent of the world average. It's predicted in 2030 when China's population reaches 1.6 billion, renewable internal freshwater resources per capita will drop to as low as 1700 cubic meters, which is below the internationally accepted danger level of 1800 cubic meters. According to another projection made by the International Water Management Institute (IWMI), 1.4 billion people in the world will suffer from serious water shortage in 2025.[1] About one third of China's population will live in areas defined as "absolute water scarcity", which means water resources per capita is below 500 cubic meters.

Climate change will also play a role in exacerbating the tensions between population and water resources. According to a research conducted by the Chinese Academy of Sciences, at the current melting rate, 64 per cent of the glaciers in China will disappear in 2050, adversely affecting the 300 million people who live in the west part of China.

China's rapid economic growth and accelerated urbanisation process is another factor that weighs heavily on the water situation in China. Since its GDP per capita passed the threshold of $ 5000 in 2011, China has stepped into a transitional period which is characterised by rapid economic growth, massive social and economic reforms, regional disparities, and widening income gap. Whether China can maintain the rapid and healthy growth in the next decade or not, largely depends on how china will tackle the two challenges it faces. One is energy, and the other is water.

As the urbanisation process picked up speed in China in the last decade, the rigid demand for water also increased at a stunning speed. Urbanisation of population is the main factor driving the water usage growth in the cities. It's estimated that from 2006 to 2008, the average residential water use per capita per day in the urban areas in China, including public water use, amounted to 212-215 liters. By contrast, the residential water use per capita per day in rural areas was 69-74 liters, only one third of the urban level. This means, if urban population increases by one person, urban freshwater supply will need to increase by 145 liters per day.

There is a complex relation between urbanisation process and water security. As indicated by the history, water resources are crucial in determining the fate, scale and potentials of a city. In the early stage of urbanisation, the role of water resources may be weak. However, in the mature stage of urbanisation (urbanisation rate exceeding 70 per cent), water plays a vital role. In the next decade, the tension between urbanisation and water resources in China will further intensify. On one hand, rapid urbanisation, which includes the urbanisation of both population and land will exacerbate the long-felt tensions between the water supply and demand. On the other hand, water shortage will exert a direct impact on the sustainability of economic development and the quality of life in urban areas. According to the statistics released by the Ministry of Water Resources and the Ministry of Construction, of 660 cities in China in 2009, 400 cities were "water-needy". Among them, 110 cities faced serious water shortage. In 32 big cities whose population was more than one million, 30 cities long wrestled with the problem of water shortage.

There are several factors contributing to water shortage in China. The two most salient are water pollution and water wastage.

First is water pollution. China has been obsessed by water pollution for decades. In China, water pollution is largely a by-product of economic development as the multinationals attracted by China's low labor cost and lax environmental law relocated the heavy-polluting factories from other countries to China. In the past three decades, water pollution has expanded from the eastern developed part of China to the western underdeveloped region. According to 2011 Report on National Land Resources released by the Chinese Ministry of Land and Resources in May 2012,[2] of the 4727 groundwater quality monitor posts in 200 cities, 55 per cent were at the level of "relative bad", or "very bad". According to another investigation conducted by the same ministry, 65 per cent of the residential-use water, 50 per cent of the industrial-use water, and 33 per cent of the farmland irrigation water in north China is from groundwater. Of 660 cities in China, more than 400 cities use groundwater as the main source for drinking water. Apart from the groundwater pollution, surface water is also severely contaminated. It's estimated that about 40 per cent of water courses in China were seriously (V) or very seriously polluted (V+), which means water from these rivers are not suitable for drinking, industrial use or farm irrigation. According to China's Ministry of Water Resources, 75 billion tons of sewage and waste water was discharged into them in 2011 alone.[3]

Second is water wastage. In the extensive model of economic growth, water shortage is exacerbated by both inefficient use of water and overdevelopment of land, which results in water loss and soil erosion. Water wastage, as a phenomenon, is prevalent in China. Although the government reiterated the importance to build a "water-saving" society, no hard or applicable policies were made. This contrasts sharply with the other problem that China faces, which is energy shortage. In case of water leakage for example, it's estimated that water loss from pipe leakage nationwide amounted to nearly 10 km^3 in 2005, more than the 9.5 km^3 of water that the first stage of South to North Water Diversion Project would transfer. Besides the domestic use of water, both industrial and agricultural use of water is inefficient. In 2005, water consumption per 10,000 yuan of GDP is 142 cubic meters. The irrigation efficiency is only 40-50 per cent. In 2011, water consumption per 10,000 yuan of GDP decreased to 82 cubic meters and the irrigation efficiency improved to 50 per cent. However, compared with advanced countries, whose water consumption per 10,000 yuan of GDP is less than 50 cubic meters and irrigation efficiency is 70-80 per cent, there is still a huge gap.

China's Policy to Tackle Water Challenge

The Chinese Government breaks the water security issues into five categories, such as the supply of quality drinking water; fighting flood; food security; safe supply of freshwater; and eco-system security. Challenge remains tremendous as far as the latter two are concerned. In order to ensure the safe supply of freshwater, Chinese Government has adopted various measures. Some are controversial while some need actionable policies to enforce them.

First is the water diversion project. The South to North Water Diversion Project (SNWDP) was designed to alleviate the water shortage in the northern part of China. According to the plan, the project will be able to divert a total amount of 44.8 km^3 of water from south to north annually from 2050. The project has three lines. The eastern line will provide 14.8 km^3 of water, the middle line 13 km^3 and the western line 17 km^3. China began the construction of the middle line on December 30, 2003, and completed it by the end of last year. The line will be put into use after the flood season this year. However, this project is controversial both inside and outside China. Although it can alleviate the water shortage in North China to a certain degree, it can't resolve the problem. In fact, there are three problematic trends in north China which will reduce the positive effects of the project. First, water consumption, especially the residential water use, in big cities, continues to rise. For example, between 2006 and 2011, the domestic water use in Beijing increased from 1.42 km^3 to 1.56 km^3, while industrial water use decreased from 0.6 km^3 to 0.58 km^3 and agricultural water use reduced from 1.26 km^3 to 1.1 km^3. At the same time, the amount of groundwater supply and renewable freshwater resources per capita in North China decreased. If the population in the north continues to rise, the stress on both the groundwater and the ecosystem will increase. Besides this, the water diversion project can't compare to water-saving project in terms of return on investment. For example, renewable freshwater resource per capita in Israel is only 290 m^3, which is less than that in north China. However, it successfully resolved the water problem with efficient water-saving projects. Furthermore, the water diversion project will have negative impacts on the balance and sustainability of the ecosystem where the water is diverted.

Second relates to the seawater desalinsation projects. Severe water shortage has become an important factor that restrains China's economic and social development, especially its coastal regions. China has a long coastline extending over 32,647 kilometers. Besides coastal regions, the central and western regions also boast abundant brackish groundwater. Research on seawater desalination technology in China started in 1958 and since then many small and medium-sized projects have been implemented. Seawater desalination was singled out as one of the most important emerging industries in the tenth five-year plan, the eleventh five-year plan and the twelfth five-year plan. In the period of the eleventh five-year plan (2006-2010), the handling capacity increased at an annual rate of nearly 70 per cent. By the end of 2012, 95 seawater desalination projects were established nationwide, with a production capacity of 774,000 tons of fresh water per day, of which 66 per cent was for industrial use, and 34 per cent was for domestic use. Seawater desalination is widely used in developed countries and the technology is mature. However, in China, the production cost is still relatively high. Although the industry is promising, there is still a long way to go before desalinated seawater could be widely used in China.

Third concerns pollution prevention and control. The Chinese Government made various efforts to contain water pollution. In 2008, the Water Pollution Prevention and Control Law was introduced which allowed citizens to participate in the decision-making process to prevent high-polluting firms from moving into neighborhood. The Chinese Ministry of Environmental Protection and the Ministry of Finance also made regulations prohibiting banks from lending to enterprises that were on the water pollution blacklist. However, these measures are only partly effective. As the high-polluting firms relocate to the hinterland of China, the problem of water pollution shifts from the urbanised eastern provinces to the rural inland areas.

Fourth are measures towards water-saving. In the tenth five-year plan (2001-2005), the Chinese Government proposed to establish a water-saving society for the first time. The plan pointed out that water resource should be utilised in a sustainable way and that the industrial and agricultural layout should be consistent with the bearing capacity of water resources. In the eleventh five-year plan (2006-2010), the Chinese Government stressed the importance to build a resource-saving and environmentally-friendly society. In this strategy, energy saving and water saving should enjoy equal importance, since China is both an oil-poor and water-deficient country. However, in practice, local governments paid more attention to energy-saving. Energy-saving targets are regarded as inflexible and water saving targets as flexible. For example, the eleventh five-year plan introduced four water-saving targets, which are water consumption per 10,000 yuan of GDP, irrigation efficiency, water consumption per 10,000 yuan of industrial output, water efficiency in service sector. Among the four, only water consumption per 10,000 yuan of industrial output was designed as an inflexible rule. In practice, even this target was not deemed as a must task. This hardly changed in the twelfth five-year plan (2011-2015). As a result, economic growth was achieved at the cost of water resources from coastal developed areas to mid and western underdeveloped land.

Water Situation in Asia and China's Future Role

Like China, many Asian countries face daunting water challenges. Asia is home to more than half of the world population, but freshwater resources in Asia are only more than that in the Antarctic. In the next ten years, the population in Asia is projected to grow by 500 million. While rural population may remain largely unchanged from now to 2025, urban population may increase by more than 60 per cent. Besides population growth, climate change is also a source of stress for the water situation in Asia. The Intergovernmental Panel on Climate Change (IPCC) projected that, in 2050, more than 1 billion people in Asia will be adversely affected by the decrease in freshwater resources caused by climate change. The decrease of freshwater supply may have multiple consequences, including food shortage, deteriorating quality of life, massive eco-migrants and even geopolitical tensions.

A number of regional organisations and forums endeavor to improve the water situation in Asia, but the cooperation yields little fruit. There are several reasons for this. First, for many countries, water security is not on the top agenda of domestic politics. Second, many countries lack technologies or other resources to improve water efficiency and water quality even if they recognise the importance to safeguard water security. Third, there are no effective mechanisms in the region to co-develop useful technologies and/or to share them. To tackle this common challenge, Asian countries need to stop pointing fingers at each other, and work out a regional strategy in a collective way.

China needs to work together with other Asian countries to strengthen the regional cooperation on water technology. As shown by China's own experiences, the most important weapon to tackle the water security issue is water-saving technology. A huge amount of water is squandered every year by extensive agricultural, industrial and residential use of water. If the water-saving technology were shared among the regional countries, the water situation could be greatly improved. In the past decade, regional countries have made big strides on economic cooperation, especially on trade and investment, but cooperation on water issues remains a weak link. Given the mounting water stress, most regional countries feel that water should be a public good and that regional countries with technological advantages and successful experiences need to take the leadership in fostering cooperation on water issues. China, for example, could enhance bilateral or multilateral cooperation mechanisms with interested regional countries. Joint fund, for example, could be established for technology development.

China also needs to play a more active role in bilateral and regional cooperation on international rivers. More than 40 international rivers flow from or into China. The biggest 15 account for 40 per cent of the total river runoff in

China. About 400 km^3 of water flows from China every year. Both to China and to the other riparian countries, these rivers are lifelines that have economic, social and even geopolitical importance. In the past decade, water-related cross-border disputes have been emerging as a new problem for China. Although China is more open and cooperative towards regional water cooperation, as embodied by the establishment of a number of river cooperation mechanisms, there is still a lot of work that needs to be done.

First, China needs to establish a legal framework to manage the issues related to the international rivers. At present, there are no unified regulations on how to develop international rivers in China. In practice, policies are made case by case. It's necessary for China to make domestic laws on development and protection of international rivers, guided by four principles: sovereignty principle, integrity principle, fair and reasonable use and sustainable development. It's also desirable that an integrated, open and sustainable administrative system be set up.

In 2007, National Environmental Emergencies Contingency Plan took effect in China. This plan provides a general guide on how to address environmental emergencies. As far as international rivers are concerned, two specific systems need to be put in place. First is warning system that helps to build the ability to monitor, convey, and analyse information related to the international rivers. The other important aspect is emergency handling system, which encompasses disaster forecast, emergency plan, ecological compensation and environmental impact assessment.

Second, build bilateral and regional cooperation mechanisms on development and protection of the international rivers. Most of the countries that share international rivers with China are classified as "water-poor" countries by the UN Economic and Social Council (the few exceptions are Laos and Cambodia). The water situation in these countries is most vulnerable to population growth, economic development and climate change. International rivers are resources shared by all the countries they flow through. China needs to take other countries' concerns and interests into consideration when developing the upper stream of the international rivers. China and the involved countries could enhance cooperation by forming an information-sharing mechanism. Any meaningful cooperation should be built on transparent and timely exchange of information. This is also a necessary step to boost mutual confidence on co-development and protection of the international rivers.

NOTES

1. National Bureau of Statistics of China website, http://www.stats.gov.cn/english/
2. Ministry of Land and Resources website, http://www.mlr.gov.cn/mlrenglish/
3. Ministry of Water Resources website, http://www.mwr.gov.cn/english/cpws.html

SECTION V

Ocean Governance in the Indo-Pacific

14

Time to Discipline the Sea Lawyers

Anup Singh

> *Now, as there are some things which every man enjoys in common with all other men, and as there are other things which are distinctly his and belong to no one else, just so has nature willed that some of the things which she has created for the use of mankind remain common to all, and that others through the industry and labor of each man become his own.*
>
> ***Hugo Grotius in "Mare Liberum" (1609)***

Introduction

Like no other episode in maritime history, the Mediterranean saw itself being occupied and controlled by one entity—the Roman Empire—from about 30 BCE till 117 CE. The Romans named this sea *"Mare Nostrum"* (Latin for "our sea"). Till then, the ocean was never seen as "territorial". Those days, the Mediterranean weather was found most inhospitable and dangerous for vessels during the months November to March and hence a new Latin term *"Mare Clausum"* ('closed sea'), came into use for the first time ever.[1] However, this term was not seen or used as a pejorative or as an enforcer of jurisdiction, as compared to the first term "Mare Nostrum" was. In the middle ages, states like the Republic of Genoa and Republic of Venice claimed a "closed sea" policy that led to "Mare Clausum" being seen as an aggressive, self-proclaimed law. Similarly, England and the Nordic Kingdoms used to charge 'transit fees', declare jurisdiction over fishing areas and prohibited entry of foreign ships in their respective arenas of influence. It was during the Age of Discovery that coastal sailing became oceanic, pushing sea activity outwards.

Portugal and Spain were most prominent in claiming exclusive rights over new lands discovered by them and the sea areas surrounding these. To legitimise their proclamations, even the papacy of the time helped, by ordaining bulls that prohibited others from navigating the seas 'under the possession of' these two empires. With the discovery of the sea route to India and Philippines, "Mare Clausum" came into widespread use as an enforcer of 'ownership' of certain waters. This monopoly by the Portuguese and the Spaniards was criticised by many European nations who were prohibited from trading in the affected seas.

It was under these circumstances that Hugo Grotius, the famed Dutch jurist, propounded the theory that the sea was an international domain and was free for all nations to use. His famous book, "Mare Liberum", published in 1609, demanded an end to the "Mare Clausum" practice and insisted that the oceans were a common medium for enabling trade and travel for all nations of the world. Not to be outdone, John Selden, famous British jurist and historian, wrote his treatise, *Mare Clausum*, in 1635. This was an attempt to legitimise British claims to sovereignty over waters around the British Isles and to further British ambitions of domination of world trade. Since then the larger world community was struggling to secure a set of rules that could eliminate competition between the 'haves' and make seas a peaceful territory—common to all nations.

For centuries before the Mare Clausum debate, the oceans had been free from regulation of fishing, shipping and resource exploitation. With passage of time, coastal states developed increasing interest in security of sea borders and protection of trade and marine resources. Therefore, some kind of a balance was needed to:

(a) Ensure freedom of navigation.
(b) Provide a stretch of water as a buffer zone for coastal states to secure their territorial integrity.
(c) Allow coastal states to tap marine resources in the immediate offshore zone.

By 1930, the propriety rights of coastal state over the resources of territorial sea were well established provided they did not interfere with the rights of innocent passage. Prior to 1945, there was variety in states' practice with respect to claiming maritime zones in which they could exercise full sovereignty over the seabed and subsoil, the water column and the airspace above.[2] But after World War II, this scenario changed. The scarcity of land-based resources forced states to concentrate on exploiting resources offshore. Scientific and technological progress demonstrated the importance of natural resources of sea adjoining the coastline. Also, states began to appreciate the growing importance of non-living resources of the seas as vital to their economic development. The developments resulted in the emergence of the concept of 'ownership' of the Continental Shelf. A major role in this respect was played by the United States. In 1945, President Truman issued a proclamation asserting rights to explore and exploit fossil fuels from the continental shelf outside the three nautical mile territorial sea. This proclamation was a turning point for the emergence of the Continental Shelf concept. The United States regarded the natural resources of the sub-soil and the seabed of the Continental Shelf contiguous to its coast as appertaining to the United States, subject to its jurisdiction and control. Many coastal states followed suit. The increasing demand for energy resources in the industrialised world drove advanced nations to use technology for exploitation of oil and gas from the Continental Shelf. Similarly, the sixties saw an intensive drive by the same group of nations to reach for the abundant quantity of fish known to be concentrated over the Continental Shelf. This led the U.S. Congress to enact a law declaring a 200 nautical mile fishery conservation zone (in 1976).[3]

Law of the Sea

Such unilateral declarations were bound to create conflict through counter as well as overlapping claims. As disputes mounted, the international maritime community found reason to call for a codified set of rules to "govern" the sea. Thus, was born the third UN Conference for the Law of the Sea. One of the greatest international achievements of the last century was the successful conclusion and subsequent ratification of the convention that resulted from this conference—the third United Nations Convention on the Law of the Sea, 1982 (UNCLOS III). It is considered as 'one of the greatest' because it dealt with a most contentious subject of codifying a set of rules for governing the seas including establishing maritime zones. This cleared many ambiguities leading to inequities amongst maritime nations and many conflicts over centuries. The debate on freedom of the seas, however, was finally resolved through overwhelming consensus. The convention established a comprehensive set of new rules and guidelines deliberated over a period of nine years and ended on a happy consensus on all but one article. UNCLOS III is often referred to as a package, derived from a decision made during the conference that the convention be adopted *in toto* as a "package deal" and no single issue would be adopted until all issues were settled. This decision provided an essential mechanism for reconciling the varied interests of the states participating in the conference. That is how UNCLOS III came to be known as an elaborately constructed document, built on trade-offs and consensus. The larger package consists of: a 12 nautical mile Territorial Sea; 200 nautical mile Exclusive Economic Zone; exploitation avenues for the "common heritage of mankind"; a regime for transit passage through straits used for international navigation and for archipelagic sea lanes passage; guaranteed access to and from the sea for land-locked states; protection and preservation of the marine environment; and an appropriate mechanism for settlement of disputes.

Conflict

In the1980s it appeared that a civilised maritime environment was finally established for good order to prevail at sea. Over the years, many protocols and amendments have been added to the convention, based on experience gained from disputes and incidents at sea were debated. However, two areas that still remain short of resolution include: Article XI and an ever increasing appetite amongst some coastal states to stake claims to larger pies of the ocean as part of their maritime zones. In some cases, such disputes have a historical background and are somewhat understandable; but it is those that have suddenly erupted on fallacious grounds which are now spreading a cold-war like scenario. The Indo-Pacific region, in particular, takes a majority of blame for these disputes that threaten peace which is already "fragile" in the region.

The first conspicuous case was the seemingly unending sequel of the "Cod Wars" which turned out as series of unpleasant confrontations at sea between the UK and Iceland, from late 50s till the 70s. Despite it being a well-known fact that Iceland's population was almost exclusively dependent on fishing for their survival, the British Government encouraged its trawlers to fish in the resource rich waters of Iceland, defying Iceland's declaration of a Fishery Zone (which was extended from four to 12 miles in 1958; 50 miles in 1972; and 200 miles in 1975). The British refused to recognise the Iceland Fishery Zone and openly asked its trawlers to harvest in Iceland's waters—nearly 1000 miles from the British Isles. To overcome Icelandic pressure, it started sending the Royal Navy to escort its trawlers. While Iceland used force for self-defense, the Royal Navy continued to assert its "overseas rights", leading to collisions between the trawlers and the vessels of the two nations The first Cod war lasted for two and a half months in late 1958. The second war started when Iceland expanded its zone to 50 miles in 1972. In September 1973, Iceland decided to quit NATO, lamenting that the alliance did not help in restoring the livelihood rights of the Icelandic people against illegal incursions by Britain. This tactic was not a ruse, and therefore, the then secretary general of NATO intervened asking UK to recall its forces and permitting British trawlers to fish only in certain areas, with an annual cap of 130,000 tons of fish. When this agreement expired in 1975, a third Cod war began with Iceland having declared a 200 nautical mile limit (in keeping with the emerging global trend). This war was the fiercest, with the Royal Navy's frigates, tug boats and British trawlers 'ramming' Icelandic Coast Guard vessels. Like the previous occasion, Iceland threatened closure of the NATO base at Keflavik and turned to the Soviet Union for help in acquisition of gunboats, leading to NATO mediation once again. This mediation led the third and final Cod war to end in 1976 when the British Government agreed to have its fishermen recalled outside Iceland's 200 nautical mile limit. The situation could have gone out of control had Iceland not used the NATO card on two occasions and would have remained so till signing of UNCLOS III in 1982.

The many other disputes that arose after 1982 raised the question of credibility of UNCLOS III as a mechanism for equitable distribution whereas UNCLOS is not a mechanism but a set of rules and guidelines to permit peaceful and disciplined coexistence in the maritime environment. Maritime delimitation is a complicated subject because of the complexities of the delimitation process and concerns with authority. A second issue relates to the principal methods by which delimitation is carried out, and, thirdly, there is the technical question regarding determination of the actual lines in space.[4]

Seabed resources can be crucial to the well-being of people and political stability of governments. Overlapping claims at sea (maritime zones) are as contentious as territorial disputes on land. At times they have been seen to be even more contentious than their mainland examples—because of mineral resources—particularly hydrocarbons, for example the conflicting claims in the South China Sea. China and five other countries claim some or all of its islands, rocks and waters. China has, over the years started asserting a queer claim of this sea being its "territorial waters"! It challenges the maritime world's right, even to the freedom of navigation, in some instances. Some of the primary reasons for its claims are: first, the right to exploration for what may be enormous reserves of hydrocarbons, making that sea such a 'gold mine'. Second, some of the islands in the Paracel and the Spratlys are being put to use by China as outposts for military surveillance and will be potential staging grounds for military action. The entire area—more than three quarters of the South China Sea—falls within the "nine-dashed line". This U-shaped line dates back to pre-communist era maps of the 1940s, and China claims sovereignty over it. The line has no basis in international law (not even in the pre-UNCLOS era). The entire water body (South China Sea) encompasses an area as large as 3.6 million square km. An estimated third of the global shipping worth about $ 5 trillion passes through it annually. According to a Chinese estimate, possible oil reserves in the area are as high as 213 billion barrels. U.S. estimates put proven reserves at 28 billion barrels which in itself is a huge figure. Similarly, natural gas reserves are estimated at 900 trillion cubic feet (25 trillion cubic meters).[5] The Chinese base their claims to the nine-dashed line on the "South Sea Islands Location Map" released by the (pre-Communist era) Chinese Government in February, 1948. They say that ancient Chinese mariners have discovered the Nansha (Spratly) Islands as early as the second century BCE. The moot point, however, is how come these claims are not being annulled by any international body and why China never staked claims at the time of its first delimitation exercise? UNCLOS cannot deal with such dispute resolution and China has made it clear that it will settle disputes only bilaterally with respective claimants and not multi-laterally or through international mediation. To the international community, the issue is one of freedom of navigation and hegemonistic tendencies with dangerous portents for the future.

Dispute Resolution

The increasing incidence of sovereignty disputes has now assumed alarming proportions. To resolve such disputes, only customary international law can be applied which may have been template out of judgments for territorial disputes delivered by international courts and tribunals. Sovereignty disputes can be subjected to third party dispute settlement only through consent of the disputing parties. Given the national sensitivities associated with sovereignty disputes in regions like the South China Sea, it is unlikely that the disputes will be resolved in the near future through third party dispute settlement.

It is widely believed that one of the most viable interim solutions is for the claimants to set aside sovereignty disputes and jointly develop the natural resources. Such agreements can take the form of provisional arrangements of a practical nature, as called for in Articles 74 and 83 of the United Nations Convention on the Law of the Sea (UNCLOS III).[6]

UNCLOS makes provision for the fact that it may be extremely difficult for states to reach agreements on maritime delimitation in areas of overlapping EEZ and continental shelf claims and it purports to provide a temporary solution to this situation in paragraph three of Articles 74 and 83.2. However, there are obligations contained in these articles that require the disputing states to make every effort to enter into provisional arrangements of a practical nature and during the transitional period, not to jeopardise the final agreement. Also, such arrangements are supposed to be without prejudice to the final delimitation.

The Way Forward

While cooperating to manage and exploit shared resources may be a preferred route to settle the overlapping maritime claims (rather than wait for long before an agreement to divide is made), the conditions necessary before such an arrangement is decided are almost utopian. These include trust amongst claimants; political will to withstand domestic politics and changes in the government. Exploration and subsequent exploitation of resources like oil and gas normally have a timetable measured in decades. Joint agreements for such purposes will therefore have to provide for continuity and stability far beyond the likely tenure of the governments that enter such an arrangement. Disputes in the South China Sea have become potent symbols of nationalism for the citizens of claimant states. Therefore, such an arrangement is not easily negotiable. Though entering into a joint development arrangement is the second best option to having a defined maritime boundary but it is significantly less attractive than the preferred option of having exclusive rights on a defined maritime boundary. Therefore it is natural that the contesting states who may have agreed to a joint development arrangement will wish to maintain their respective legal positions. Also, joint development arrangements are provisional arrangements—without prejudice to the final delimitation. The question therefore is what is the way out of the series of imbroglios that seem to only multiply with each passing year? Is there some light at the end of the tunnel? Will the business of UNCLOS be once again respected as a credible compendium of rules and guidelines? The answers unfortunately state the negative. Therefore, it is time to review and renew the convention (UNCLOS III). The only way forward lies in disciplining all the stakeholders—the sea lawyers who are in the business of staking claims on the principle of "might is right". The answer to this lies in calling for an UNCLOS IV that must include a degree of predictability. UNCLOS III sets forth the objective to achieve maritime delimitation but falls short in enunciating the principles and final methods for achieving equitable results. As maritime delimitation cases differ, consideration must be given to factors including geography, historical linkages and predictability in the affairs of states in the new convention. Otherwise, disputes will not only be restricted to the South China Sea; but will extend to the Arctic and Southern Oceans as the next hotbeds. The casualties in such cases are not just victim nations and their reputations, but the global economy (through threatened shipping), the fishing community and peace and good order at sea. It is time to discipline the sea lawyers amongst nations who have expansionist designs based on current prowess.

NOTES

1. Olga Tellegen-Couperus, *Short History of Roman Law,* Routledge, 1993, pp.32
2. Nugzar Dundua, "Delimitation of Maritime Boundaries Between Adjacent States", the United Nations-Nippon Foundation, 2006-2007. http://www.un.org/depts/los/nippon/unnff_programme_home/fellows_pages/fellows_papers/dundua_0607_georgia.pdf
3. "History of the Maritime Zones under International Law, Law of the Sea", NOAA Office Coast Survey, http://www.nauticalcharts.noaa.gov/staff/law_of_sea.html
4. Alexander L.M., "The Delimitation of Maritime Boundaries", *Political Geography quarterly,* Vol.5, 1986, pp. 1-2
5. "South China Sea Issue Explained", at http://www.china.org.cn/china/2012-07/18/content_25941294.htm
6. Leonardo Bernard, "Prospect for Joint Development of Hydrocarbon Resources in the South China Sea", http://cil.nus.edu.sg/wp/wp-content/uploads/2013/08/Bernard-ASPI-Draft-6-Aug-2013-Prospect-for-Joint-Development-in-the-SCS.pdf

15

Chinese Response to Maritime Disorder in the Indo-Pacific Region

You Ji

Introduction

Currently there is no viable governance model for managing maritime security challenges in the Indo-Pacific region. This dangerous reality has existed for a long time, but is being worsened amidst mounting territorial disputes, rivalry in safeguarding Sea Lanes of Communications (SLOCs), and resources extraction. Sovereignty clashes in the East and South China Seas (ESCSs) have an enduring feature due to their connection with domestic politics driven by nationalism and election cycles, and defy the deepening trend of economic interdependence/integration in the region. In the race between regional efforts to formulate mechanisms of crisis prevention in dealing with overlapping territorial claims, for example, the Sino-ASEAN negotiation for establishing a Code of Conduct in the South China Sea (SCS), and envelope pushing by certain disputants, the former is a lot weaker and slower than the latter, and heralds a further escalation of tension in the maritime domain. This demonstrates the urgency for creating an abiding oceanic governance regime on the one hand, and a mission-impossible reality on the other, thanks to the rigidness of sovereignty issues. This essay argues that the situation will become more tense before a turnaround is achieved due to a crisis that forces all parties to seek commonly acceptable rules of the game—that is, the basics needed for an institutionalised governance system in the Indo-Pacific maritime region.

The US Pivot policy focuses on continuing maritime dominance, especially vis-à-vis China's rising naval power, to the effect of squeezing China's strategic space in the maritime domains from the near-sea areas (the ESCSs) to the Indian Ocean/West Africa regions. The US naval Pivot strategy gives rise to an island chain strategy embedded in geostrategic features of the first and second island chains in the Pacific. Through enhanced allied force redeployment, a horizontal S-Shape string of pearls stretching from Alaska to West Africa becomes increasingly visible, readily made usable for blockading Chinese strategic waterways. Threats to Chinese SLOC safety are both realistic and serious. In a way, USA's advocacy of freedom of navigation is legally undisputable; but it is also part of its control of the maritime security of other nations—for example, through close-in spy activities near Chinese strategic military bases—and thus perpetuates Asian maritime governance disorder.

China's imposition of an East China Sea Air Defence Identification Zone (ADIZ) is part of an answer to its disadvantaged position in the existing maritime security status quo. It highlights the *à la carte* nature of the Asia-Pacific maritime order that is biased against rising powers. The US-centric ADIZ arrangements as part of the oceanic governance regimes are currently unfair to certain countries as also unsustainable in themselves in the long run. The changing balance of economic power induces alteration in the hierarchy of state military influence, with regional naval strength rebalanced. However, as overlapping areas in the ADIZ are being enlarged amidst intensified territorial disputes, accidental mid-air clashes above the sea, or planned brinkmanship acts, will mount due to lingering historical animosity, and to the lack of effective governance to manage the ADIZ overlapping.

These security hazards in the Indo-Pacific region will be addressed by this essay, mainly from a Chinese perspective. While there is no easy solution for any one of them, the cheerful side of the challenge is that no regional state wants war, and all of them hope to establish some mechanisms of governance to avoid worst case scenarios. Therefore, the hope lies in the management of the maritime security challenge, which is inherently easier than seeking solutions. This is part of building a governance model for crisis prevention, the topmost task for all countries in maritime Asia to engage seriously.

Beijing's Maritime Strategy: the Pre-emption of Dispute Escalation

Nowhere in the global maritime domains more competing sovereignty claims been registered than in the Indo-Pacific region.[1] Moreover, the lack of commonly agreed rules of the game underlines the lack of governance. The rise and fall of ESCS disputes form cycles of Asian maritime tension since the 1970s. It is now in a new cycle characterised by a rise in intensity.[2]

Making Sense of Chinese Assertive Response to Changed ESCS Games

Recently, assertiveness has been the buzz word to characterise China's ESCS behaviour, which has been interpreted as anti-status quo. Yet, this word is too encompassing to allow any nuanced understanding of Beijing's maritime policy. Clearly, assertiveness serves no Chinese vital interests at home and abroad, and Beijing is well aware of it.[3] This essay argues that Chinese assertiveness is mainly a hardened response to the evolving situation in the ESCS disputes. Generally speaking, China is reactive by nature—but through a proportionally asymmetrical strategy to protect Chinese sovereignty claims. In other words, it is best explained by Xi Jinping's One-Plus strategy aimed at pre-empting dispute escalation against China's maritime security interests.

Beijing faces a tough choice between adopting a firm stance to safeguard its maritime rights and the search for an acceptable governance mechanism to avert standoffs on island disputes, which hurt China more than other claimants. However, to Chinese strategists, the construction of such a mechanism should not be solely based on the existing legal framework of the UNCLOS because some elements of the legality of UNCLOS clashes with Chinese territorial claims which are rooted in history. This is testified by Beijing's 3-No principle with reference to Filipino law suits regarding the ownership of the Huangyan/ Scarborough Shoal: 'no response, no participation, and no implementation'.[4] Indeed, the UNCLOS may have created more confusion and problems in resolving ESCS disputes—the reason why Manila chose to resort to an international court process. The à la carte situation in maritime Asia is not due to the lack of a legal body that can be used to tackle the dispute, but due to its problematic existence.

Domestic politics is another reason for the difficulty in creating a governance mechanism in the Indo-Pacific region. For instance, a tough position on the Spratly dispute has been a useful weapon to win votes in Manila, and elsewhere. Beijing's concern of state stability always outweighs that of international perception. As a result, assertiveness is irrational to China watchers, but rational to Beijing: if state stability is threatened, what is the use of a benign external image?[5] The policy relevance for Washington and ESCS claimants is the assumption that China has to yield to collective pressure, if it is heavy enough. However, this interpretation underestimates Chinese resolve under domestic constraints.[6]

Moreover, Chinese assertiveness is a response to the changed security environment in the ESCS, which is due to the causes listed below.

- The claimants' demarcation of their EEZ boundary requested by the UN in 2009 eliminated the space for ambiguity that helped them keep a precarious status quo in the previous decade.

- US Pivot to Asia takes the form of picking sides in ESCS disputes that encourages some claimants to stand up to China.
- Regime change in Manila in 2010 visibly altered its Spratly approach vis-à-vis Beijing.
- Mounting territorial nationalism narrows policy choices for the claimants to accommodate their differences.
- The Diaoyu-Senkaku nationalisation opened a Pandora Box that can be hardly fixed again.

As China rises further, some claimants may feel that time is not on their side and that it is necessary to push the envelope now.[7]

The nature of the ESCS dispute has also changed. While any unilateral change of the status quo on occupied islands is hard to realise, the 'war zone' has shifted to surrounding waters where resource exploration leads to the erection of permanent features that allow de facto control of the areas in dispute. In turn, de facto control can be translated into legal possession. If this is so, then China would lose its claim for all practical purposes. This underlines Beijing's response to the commercial pursuits of Vietnam and the Philippines in disputed areas as these are more about sovereignty than oil. In addition, law enforcement through military means by some countries has been stepped up to enhance their claims.[8] This evolution puts Beijing in a corner under nationalist pressure at home. Ordinary Chinese question the wisdom of Beijing's maritime policy centred on Deng Xiaoping's admonition of 'shelving dispute and jointly developing'. They ridicule this as 'shelving China' while others enlarge their presence.

If this trend remains unchecked, Beijing sees the eventual use of force as inevitable as the room for compromise and ambiguity vanishes. If China's assertive reactions can deter the further moves of others, it would be a cost effective way of crisis management, saving actual military action in the end. Generally, assertiveness is pursued in a retaliatory manner, and in proportion to perceived encroachment. Yet, the price paid for this method is high. Assertiveness has hurt China's charming diplomacy,[9] which contributed to Beijing's success in persuading ASEAN to adopt a China policy based on cooperation rather than a balance of power in the 2000s. One example is ASEAN's strong reaction to Beijing's relentless pressure on Cambodia to omit the mention of SCS in the communiqué of the 2012 ASEAN summit. On the surface, China attained diplomatic gains in this event; but it also strategically weakened its long term position in Southeast Asia. Having said this, China will continue its reactive assertiveness in protecting its core interests. Any other option may put the government in an awkward position in the eyes of the population.

China's assertiveness toward Japan's nationalisation of the Diaoyu Islands was more forcefully exercised; but it did not go beyond the category of response. State purchase was regarded as a major game changer that breached a 'gentleman's agreement' between Zhou Enlai and Tanaka in 1972. Shelving the dispute was necessary for both to address their more urgent strategic concern.[10] Japan's acquiescence on this ambiguity was traded with Chinese acquiescence on Japan's de facto administration over the islands. Beijing has been sincere on this status quo, which gave it breathing space to attend to more urgent matters in world politics. When the status quo was maintained, not only was the Diaoyu dispute a non-'core interest' issue but was also low in Beijing's overall foreign policy hierarchy.[11]

China reacted assertively to Japan's move of nationalisation for several reasons.

- Noda's announcement of the purchase only one day after his corridor meeting with Hu Jintao enormously hurt the President's prestige and Chinese feelings.
- The procurement occurred at the most sensitive time of the year in Sino-Japanese relations, which could easily have been manipulated into popular riots.
- State ownership allows for more effective state administration, logically enhancing a process of translating de facto control into legal possession.[12]
- In Beijing's strategic calculus, only through assertive reaction could Japan's follow up measures have been pre-empted. Noda's justification against Ishihara's purchase proposal should not be taken at face value. The fact was that his government had 8 point plan for the development of Senkaku after nationalisation. This included keeping the current state of affairs, building ports and facilitates, setting up a government post, the extraction of resources and human inhabitation. Noda personally preferred Plan B that advocated creation of a government post in the Island.[13] Were these plans put into practice Sino-Japanese tension would have been worse than Ishihara's act. Beijing's reaction may have deterred his first choice, which was also Abe's (being conveyed in his national election campaign in 2012).[14] What prevented Noda from attempting more after the buying were not just the riots in China, but the rioters. A large proportion of them were urban consumers who may make a difference to Japanese economic interests in China.
- China's history-based strategic culture leaves little levy for its leaders to manage domestic uproar when they make Japan policy.

The question that arises here is: What alternative does Beijing have instead of reactive assertiveness under domestic pressure, and when faced with envelope pushing from other claimants? Hu Jintao adopted a passive way to calm down Vietnam and the Philippines during his term in office. This turned out to be a decade of lost control over the process of dispute management in the ESCSs. In addition, the US Pivot strategy involved picking sides in the dispute which narrowed the space for continued passivity even further. Washington made itself a key stakeholder of ESCS disputes by shifting from its previous position of ambiguity to that of partial clarity. It supports the ASEAN claimants' call for a collective approach vis-à-vis China, insists on dispute resolution based on international law against the 9-dotted line, and extends the coverage of US-Japan defence treaty to the Senkakus in more clear terms. Washington as a game changer has emboldened some disputants in facing up to China and has, thus, made the Spratly dispute fully internationalised.

Xi's One-Plus Strategy: Dealing with Rising Maritime Challenges

Under Xi's new leadership, continued passivity would have put Beijing in a more losing position in the battle for control over rule setting. He initiated key changes in China's approach toward territorial disputes. Specifically, he has executed the One-Plus strategy to protect China's maritime claims since he took charge of Beijing's foreign affairs in 2012. The strategy means that, in the game of envelope pushing, if the initiator moves one inch, Beijing would react by moving one-plus. If the initiator moves two inches, Beijing would retaliate it by two-plus. In concrete terms, China responded to Manila's use of naval force against Chinese fishermen in April 2012 with a semi-permanent patrol in the Scarborough Shoal area—something it was unable to do in the past. When Vietnam promulgated its maritime territorial law in June 2012, China quickly responded by creating the Sansha Municipality in charge of SCS affairs—a government office that China formed in 2007 but never officially opened for fear of escalating Spratly tensions.[15] Now, Beijing has seized the opportunity. Days after the nationalisation of Diaoyu/ Senkaku, Beijing announced maritime boundary lines around the islands. Since then, it has routinely patrolled the waters within the islands' 12 nm, something it was unable to do previously. To PLA analysts, this routine patrol simply means the joint control of the island group by China and Japan.[16] In all these events, China was reactive; but its reaction went an extra mile in pressing sovereignty claims. This level of assertiveness is unprecedented.

On the other hand, China's One-Plus strategy is one of retaliation rather than seeking to up the ante by its own choice.[17] Secondly, it is no irredentist, entailing no plan to eject other claimants from their occupied islets by force. Thirdly, it is non-military—that is, seeking no armed confrontation.[18] Last, but not the least, it designs reactive moves which try not to be too excessive (more on this in later sections). Under these guidelines, Beijing would make sure that SCS disputes remain tactical and largely free of armed rifts, as none of others is capable of challenging China in a strategic way. Moreover, Washington would not allow this to happen in the first place. This is why, despite the on-going stand-offs, Beijing understands that if it restrains itself from excessive moves to escalate tensions, the probability of sizeable ESCS confrontation is low.

The guiding principle of China's maritime policy is to react to territorial disputes in the ESCSs in an asymmetric but proportional way. This is the key for Xi's One-Plus strategy to work. The emphasis here is proportional, which means that if the other claimants make one inch, Beijing would react by one-plus, and not by two inches. Beijing has followed several self-imposed red-lines in managing enhanced levels of dispute. The primary one is to avoid actions that would force Washington to intervene directly. A second one is to prevent cohesive collective action—for example, by ASEAN—against China's overall regional standing. For example, a proportional response to the Senkaku purchase is to pursue civilian maritime patrols as sovereignty statements, but not for law reinforcement. This is why the Chinese side has not moved to expel any Japanese ships in the disputed area.

On the other hand, China also deems it necessary to take some asymmetric counter measures in order to secure its maritime security interests. Asymmetry is the way to regain initiative as the defender, as also the way to deter further moves of others. Yet, according to a Beijing's foreign policy principle, asymmetry should not be used excessively. It should be used only on just ground; it should be to Chinese advantage; and should be used with constraint. Without constraints, even a just move triggers damaging backlash against Chinese overall interests, and the high cost would erase any gains Beijing may obtain. Striking the right balance needs subtlety. Thus, the line between asymmetric and proportional response is often times very thin. Furthermore, China's marine deployment in the SCS, and its frequent patrols, are perceived by other claimants not as being reactive by nature but aggressive enough to arouse concerns.

So far, Beijing has sensibly set red lines in exercising assertiveness. The following shows how careful it is in managing ESCS standoffs so that direct US intervention and collective ASEAN opposition is avoided.

- The PLAN has not been used to handling stand-offs, although 'the navy is behind the civilian ships that hold the first line of defence'.[19]
- Swamping the disputed waters with a large number of fishing boats is an effective means of applying pressure; but risks escalation of tension. China has chosen not to do this, as it may cause Japan's massive expelling actions with US support. Hundreds of Chinese fishing ships did approach the Diaoyu area in October 2012; but Beijing quickly called the game off.
- The interception of a Chinese civilian surveillance aircraft en route to the Diaoyu area by a dozen Japanese F-15s on 22 December 2012 stimulated calls of military escort for the civilian aircraft. Xi ignored them lest that such an act may increase the chances of a military clash.[20]

- PLA aircraft does not enter Japan's ADIZ casually. The entry is often symbolically indicative of Beijing's displeasure certain actions undertaken by Tokyo. This is something the PLA has learnt from Russia's attitudes to the idea of ADIZ.[21] Yet, such behaviour only demonstrates 'an attitude of opposition', not a pattern of actions to avoid military standoffs.[22]
- Xi vetoed advice to target Japanese economic interests as a way of forcing Tokyo to rescind the nationalisation of Diaoyu.[23] This indicates that Beijing's maritime policy guidance is to compartmentalise territorial disputes away from overall bilateral relations as much as possible, although some negative implications are inevitable. Economic leverage has only been selectively used, such as against the Philippines in 2012. Yet, economic sanctions are more of a weapon in reserve than one that can be invoked casually.
- Serious law reinforcement is executed only in disputed areas where China's boundary base line is announced. This differentiates Chinese actions in the Paracel islands and in the Spratly islands. It is useful to point out that the Hainan Provincial Maritime Law is not for the Spratlys where China has not promulgated the basic maritime boundary and points.[24]

Perhaps the best test case is the Chinese response to the Philippines' recent attempt to consolidate its beached landing ship in the Second Thomas Shoal. The beaching act in 1999 was Manila's design to occupy the uninhabited reef with soldiers stationed in the ship constantly. It was the last act of occupation among disputants. Yet, the occupation is not complete, as no permanent structure has been built to support a de jure presence. Now Manila's attempt to build a civil engineering foundation for the sinking ship has moved the occupation further towards creating a permanent structure there. To the Chinese this amounts to a unilateral change of the status quo, and has to be answered. The question then arises is: What kind of response will be regarded as being proportional? Blockading ships carrying building materials to the area can be defined as proportional in the light of status quo maintenance; but pulling the beached ship away is not. Still less proportional would be a Chinese own occupation initiative. Beijing's decision to allow logistical supplies for the beached ship is appropriate. Yet, all this is not only dependent on Beijing's cautiousness; Manila too has to decide what the best choice would be for it.

The rationale behind the One-Plus strategy is that between US supporting other claimants as a way to constrain China, and US reluctance to confront China militarily, Beijing has larger room to manoeuvre than other disputants. Chinese strategists believe that America's goal in East Asia is to pursue a level of controllable tension. A level of territorial tension is desirable to prohibit China, and highlights regional security dependence on the USA. Yet, if the tension gets out of hand, it may drag US troops into an unwanted war with another nuclear power. Similarly,

US strategists argue that Washington has to work out a delicate balance between pressurising China and not doing so overtly.[25] Indeed, China has achieved gains in the ESCSs under the One-Plus strategy and gotten away with it, testifying to the meaning of 'China is a major power'—in the words of Yang Jiechi to his ASEAN counterparts in July 2011. For instance, any US decisive move against China's de facto control in the Huangyan area, and its routine patrol in the Diaoyu area, will seriously hurt Sino-US relationship which is vital to the USA. Rocks in the ESCSs test US commitment to its allies, which is important enough, but are not core US interests. Its vigilance against footing a blank cheque has been well exploited by Beijing.

Crisis Prevention and the Management of Territorial Disputes

Short of an acceptable governance model to resolve competing sovereignty claims, dispute control and confrontation prevention then become paramount for regional security-making. This parallels Beijing's current concern and short-term objective of a maritime policy of crisis management. However, the possibility of an armed rift in the ESCS cannot be dismissed altogether.[26] At the strategic level, if Tokyo decides to use naval vessels to expel Chinese civilian surveillance ships—as suggested by the LDP's official defence guideline—Beijing would have no choice but to escort civilian ships with PLAN ships. A major escalation would then become inevitable. In the SCS, an accidental clash is a constant possibility. In April 2012, a Filipino commander tried to arrest Chinese fishermen on his personal initiative. The captains of Chinese surveillance ships were much on their own to stop the Philippine naval action.[27] Therefore, crisis management is top priority for Beijing's maritime policy. This can be analysed with a case study of China's participation in the code of conduct (CoC) negotiations.

Beijing has long, though reluctantly, acknowledged the internationalisation of the Spratly dispute. This fact rectifies a commonly held erroneous view that China selects to deal with other SCS claimants on a one-to-one basis, which advantages Beijing as a stronger power.[28] The fact is that China does not reject multilateralism as a mechanism for crisis management and prevention; this is the reason why it signed the DoC, and engages ASEAN for the CoC.[29] Beijing insists on bilateralism in seeking sovereignty resolution because it is impossible for a multi-party dispute to be resolved collectively. China does not see the Spratly dispute as Sino-ASEAN because only four ASEAN states are involved. Moreover, it perceives that ESCS issues have been leveraged as part of the US geo-political coalescing to marginalise Beijing in the settlement process. Yet, since sovereignty issue is widely regarded as unresolvable,[30] emphasis on bilateralism is more a policy preference than a policy of substance. The most urgent regional concern over the SCS dispute is about crisis prevention that has to be worked out through multilateral forums. China has taken an active part in them.

In fact, China conditionally welcomes a CoC arrangement. As its title suggests, it is about conduct control rather than a sovereignty resolution. If the CoC would help ease envelope pushing by all parties, it would save China from continuing assertive practices, which undermine its overall global status. What Beijing hopes in the SCS is to restore the Spratly status quo up to 2009. Status quo in the ESCSs is essential to China's 'strategic opportunity period' mentioned earlier. If nobody stirs the boat, the ESCS dispute is low on Beijing's diplomatic priority list.[31] In fact, maritime disputes fall to the bottom in the PLA's top five most serious national security threats, following: (1) a nuclear strike against China; (2) a conspiracy of hostile domestic and international forces to topple the PRC government; (3) Taiwan independence; (4) limited border wars due to foreign encroachment of Chinese land territories; and (5) harassment and intrusion into Chinese claimed islands in the ESCSs.[32] The CoC serves Beijing's status-quo hope by preventing stand-offs and, thus, serves its core interests by providing precious breathing space for it to tackle other priority threats. Stand-offs are convenient stimulants for regional coalescing against Beijing. China has generally accepted the six-point guidance for Sino-ASEAN CoC negotiations under Indonesian auspices. Chinese foreign minister Wang Yi restated this approach during his recent ASEAN trip in July.

The challenge for formulating a mutually acceptable CoC is to set a legal scope for it to regulate actions of the claimants. Some ASEAN states want the CoC to tackle Chinese sovereignty claims, that is, the 9-dotted line. Further, since the CoC is for crisis management, it should not deal with the issue of EEZ demarcation. This is what I mean by Beijing's conditional support of CoC negotiations. To Beijing, 9-dotted line and EEZ demarcation would render the CoC a zero-sum game. Even if ASEAN reaches a CoC accord on these, and demands that China sign—as urged by US strategists—Beijing would regard it as 'a piece of toilet paper' (remarks of a senior Chinese scholar on ASEAN affairs).[33] Then the CoC negotiations would not go anywhere. Under the circumstances, the delaying tactics is simply an understatement.

For Beijing, if the sovereignty issue can be shelved following the status quo principle and politics of ambiguity, it is possible for an abiding CoC to be arrived at as a mechanism for crisis prevention. This would not be satisfactory to all; but it would be acceptable at a minimum level. There are many obstacles for this to materialise—such as outstanding standoffs in the ESCS. This highlights the value of the CoC as a viable and interim ingredient for an Asian maritime governance arrangement, even if it avoids the sovereignty dispute.

Therefore, the maintenance of the *status quo* and the avoidance of the premature tackling of the sovereignty issue are keys to the construction of a governance model for the sake of regional stability. However, eventually China has to face sovereignty issues such as the 9-dotted line.[34] A clear clarification of it is in Chinese interests. The current obstacle is more from China's domestic politics than from diplomatic considerations. China has already removed two lines from it, and also had a debate on it in 1996. In short, an Asian maritime governance model cannot be constructed without looking into the issue of defining the 9-dotted line.

US Island-Chain Strategy against Chinese Naval Expansion

From Beijing's perspective, the US Pivot strategy strengthened US naval deployment along the two island-chains in the West Pacific that can be used to blockade Chinese SLOCs.[35] In July 2013, Herbert Carlisle, Chief of the US Pacific Air Force Command, revealed a plan to enhance US forward presence in the Indo-Pacific region as part of the US Asia Pivot strategy. It included the reopening of suspended military bases, such as Saipan; more regular troop visits to allies and partners to secure semi-permanent basing facilities; and quickened transfers of strategic and tactical capabilities to places close to Asian hot spots. In addition to US marine deployment in Darwin, the US Air Force will send jets to Changi air base in Singapore, Korat air base in Thailand, Trivandrum in India, and possibly bases at Kubi Point and Puerto Princesa in the Philippines and airfields in Indonesia and Malaysia.[36] Clearly, these efforts will translate the geographically convenient islands chains into naval containment belts against China's commercial SLOCs and its naval westward and southward movements.[37] Rekindling a Cold War island chain strategy reflects a Cold War mentality and behaviour, which is at odds with regional efforts to erect a viable institution of maritime governance because the strategy makes some feel safe but others insecure.[38] This sense was substantiated by Carlisle's allusion that '…back in the late, great days of the Cold War, we had a thing called *Checkered Flag*: we rotated almost every CONUS (Continental United States) unit to Europe, we're turning to that in the Pacific.'[39] In a way, the US island chain strategy serves as an impediment for a workable governance mechanism to ensure stability in the Indo-Pacific region so that it can be a driver to generate an action-reaction arms build-up dynamic.

The Perceived US Islands Chain Strategy against China

Militarising the island chains through enhancing old bases and creating new ones represents the true 'strings of pearls' in US military planning. Indeed, this island-chain strategy incrementally erodes PLAN space of manoeuvring beyond its normal areas of activity, and puts Chinese SLOC safety at great risks. It confirms a long time PLA concern that the forward basing chains along the island chains make a natural geographic constraint on the PLAN's combat reach, worse.[40]

Yet, constructing an encirclement chain around China is rooted in the US perception of a Chinese naval challenge to its maritime dominance. US sea power requires a robust constellation of bases to support power projection and the Asia Pivot strategy.[41] An islands chain strategy is the US response to a visible increase in PLAN sails through the narrow passes in the West Pacific. To Beijing, however, it is an offensive move to consolidate US naval superiority against the PLAN's inevitable expeditionary missions in the region and beyond. Moreover, it translates Pentagon's ASB doctrinal guidance into war planning and force development.[42] ASB is conceptualised as an effective way to maintain US military edge against the PLA, but its effectiveness depends on new posturing, new basing facilities, and new troop deployment. Matching forward deployment with geographic advantage is a cost-effective way to hedge PLAN power projection.

Therefore, the islands chain strategy is designed to operationalise the island-chain concept into combat readiness. This concept was the brainchild of Secretary Dulles in 1951, but its implementation against China has not been visible. Objectively, the PLAN has, until recently, confined its major activities within its adjacent waters (500 km from the coast) due to its slow growth in war fighting capability. 'Breaking' the first islands chain was not its immediate strategic goal in transformation in the 20th century. The PLA design to undo any islands chain blockade was more in the form of air and missile strikes than naval intrusions.[43] This reality did not raise any urgency for the US to substantiate the islands chain offense.

Geographically, therefore, there are natural faulty spots in the two islands chains as employable lines of blockade against China. For instance, PLA analysts have lately talked about the third islands chain radiating from Hawaii. However, it is more like points than a line. The second islands chain is quite short, with few islands turned into military assets. The first islands chain can be an effective line of offense, defence, and blockade. However, it is marked with broken and vulnerable sections. Consequently, PLA planners see that the islands chains contain both strategic merits and perils.[44] When the geographic features are translated into viable combat guidance, their usefulness cannot be ideally realised if those 'short plates in a basket' are not fixed.

Constructive Measures of the USA and its Allies

Restructuring basing arrangements concretely materialise the US military Pivot strategy embedded in an Indo-Pacific notion that brings South Asia into the geostrategic network against China.[45] Generally speaking, it is about thickening the first islands chain defence with new basing facilities along crucial waterways, and stretching it south eastwards to link the Indian Ocean; strengthening the second islands chain in the north, and extending it southward to connect Australia;

and arranging necessary joints between the first and the second, and the second and the third islands chains to create more strategic depth for the first and second island chains. PLA strategists see this as the new battlefield construction by the USA and its allies to deal with the scenario where the PLAN is able to break the first island chain, and engage them in major naval warfare between the first and second island chains. The purpose is still to contain Chinese naval expansion in the West Pacific.[46]

In the first islands chain, the USA and its allies have taken a number of measures to address vulnerable points, including strengthening US presence in the weakest link in the first line of conflict, that is, the Philippines. This has been done primarily under the troop visit agreement which facilitates US military's return to the Subic Bay. The Filipino navy will build a new pier and harbour at its naval base in Palawan. Basing facilities are also proposed in the Mindanao Island (another X-Band Radar station?).[47] These form a Subic-centred strategic triangle, sustaining not only the US Pivot strategy but also endangering Chinese SLOCs through the SCS. Now, the frequent visits of US nuclear submarines and carrier groups, the semi-permanent stationing of US marines, and regular US surveillance flights in the SCS regions, and their routine patrols in the dispute areas have put the Chinese under constant pressure. For instance, compared with Japanese controlled waterways, the Bushi Strait is a relatively easier passage corridor, which is crucial for the PLAN South Sea Fleet to get to the West Pacific. The Taiwan side of the Strait presents no serious threat when the KMT is in power, and the weak Filipino navy poses no realistic challenge to the effort. However, this situation may change soon.[48]

Another seemingly soft spot in the first islands chain defence line is Japan's south western islands. The SDF Cold War deployment prioritised the northern tip in the chain, with the USSR as the targeted adversary. The effect of this was that the islands beyond Okinawa were deprived of necessary defence assets. In the wake of the Diaoyus standoffs, routine Chinese patrols in the ECS and the increase in the regular PLA 'passing through' activities in the West Pacific, Tokyo has endeavoured to enhance SDF basing arrangements in the southwest direction—partially out of its own security needs and partially for matching the US islands chain strategy. Among these efforts are six intelligence/signal imagery stations in Japan's main islands, as well as a new X-Band radar station in Kyoto. The Southwest offshore islands are designated as hosts for SDF troop relocation to quicken reaction for a Senkakus crisis. For instance, air force and naval facilities—such as the radar stations in Yonaguni Jima, Naha Jima or Ishigaki Island—can help control strategic waterways south of Miyako Jima. The likely deployment of Marine corps and supporting equipment—such as the Global Eagles and the MV-22s—will effectively rectify potential 'void points' in the

Japanese section of the first island chain[49] Simultaneously, the SDF's improved rapid response capabilities against an ECS scenario weaken PLA combat effectiveness in times of confrontation, much to the worry of PLA strategists. For example, PLAN experts point out that since there are very few water-ways from the Tsugru Strait in the north to the Miyayuko Jima in the south, enhanced SDF surveillance facilities around the narrow passes in between (for example, patrols by P-8As), will greatly increase the vulnerability of PLA nuclear submarines entering the vast expanses of waters in the Pacific for launching SLBMs.[50] More specifically, the Miyayuko Strait offers a short cut access for surface combatants of the PLAN South Sea Fleet to reach the West Pacific. Now, the SDF has deployed Type-88 surface-to-ship missiles in the islands located on both sides of the Strait—accidentally in line with RAND advice to conceal Chinese SLOCs by land based anti-ship missiles. Then, the PLA will have to use long range precision strikes to neutralise these assets to clear the way for its vessels in time of war.[51]

The first islands chain phases out below the Philippines in its narrow definition. Strategically, this relatively incomplete line may cause disruption of the US blockade of China in times of crisis. US efforts to strengthen this chain line since its Pivot strategy has expanded the previously narrow purview of the chain further to the Indian Ocean (IO); this has enriched Pentagon's new island chain strategy. The permanent deployment of Littoral Combat Ships in Singapore can conceal the Malacca Strait in a major Sino-US strife that will amount to choking China's economic life line. The routine visits of US ships to Camranh Bay in Vietnam would help restrict PLAN's manoeuvrings in the semi-closed SCS should the Spratly dispute evolve into confrontation. Further east, the USA has sought to rent a strategically positioned island from India to enhance its air strike capability for SLOC operations in the IO.[52] Militarily, this addition can match the US air base in Diego Garcia.

The islands chain strategy requires a more ambitious construction for the second islands chain. Reopening the Saipan Airport for US strategic bombers will significantly reinforce the Guan base into a greater Guan military region that forms the core of the second islands chain line of defence vis-à-vis PLAN's projection of power. Here, the Guan is home for US forward naval deployment, and Saipan is the extension of the Guan base, which specialises in hosting strategic and tactical air force. As it can operate strategic bombers, F-22s, and drones, it serves as a supporting pillar for US offensive campaigns in the region and, in terms of defence, it constitutes an impenetrable fire wall shielding Hawaii. More importantly, the value of the Guan and Saipan Islands lies in their retrenching the fist for better punches: their distance from the continent of Asia protects them from direct attack; but its long punches can still reach the enemy.

Another prospect of the second islands chain blockade is its southward extension to Australia's northwest waters, where a large number of Chinese ships sail densely in the southern route. The presence of 2,500 marines in Darwin cannot just be symbolic. As expeditionary units, they can serve as crack force for rapid reactions in SCS situations.[53] Moreover, the institutionalised visits by US carrier groups and strategic bombers to Perth and Brisbane will enhance the second islands chain bases.[54] The Indo-Pacific concept that forms a component of ASB guidance with regard to SLOC warfare will be also further substantiated, as the added forces and basing facilities conveniently put the crucial joints of the two Oceans under tighter allied control. The SCS combat zones and the IO region are, thus, geo-strategically linked.[55]

The islands chain strategy is a true 'string of pears' strategy, with well-defined objectives and supporting measures. Although it largely remains as an unfinished project, once completed, the various chains will get connected and form one huge S-shape snake starting from Alaska, through the South and West Pacific, the SCS, Malacca Strait, to the IO, ending in Africa.[56] A big financial gap exists between a functioning islands chain strategy and the required capabilities put in place in the wake of US budget reduction in the years ahead. Yet, the USA's allies and partners can collectively help narrow the gap. The PLA sees the endeavour as a cost-effective one when the needs are inflated but the means are structurally short.[57] The Pentagon may not create new bases, but it may re-use those already there. Geographic advantages and allied help present the US an economical way to make up the balance. Then, the choice for the PLAN becomes narrow: it has to substantially enlarge its sea power in order to offset the constraining effect of the strategy. Yet, the result is not only a more à la carte maritime order in the making but an energised naval race in the region in the form of 'flying geese'.[58]

Air Defence Identification Zone: Conflict's New Territories

The Cold War legacy of the US-centric ADIZ arrangement is the clearest sign of an à la carte security disorder; it stands in the way of building a governance model for managing maritime conflicts in the region. China's ADIZ announcement in November 2013 may have been criticised for the wrong reasons: what it did was not different to what Washington and Tokyo have always done. For a while there seemed to emerge a new united front against the Chinese ADIZ initiative, with a strategic effect similar to that of the reaction of the allies to the PLA missile tests in 1996. Now, Beijing is still busy absorbing the negative ADIZ impact lest history may repeat itself.

Biden's China visit in December 2013 may have relieved Beijing. Tokyo's request to have three joint US-Japanese responses: a joint communiqué, US-Japanese demand on Beijing to withdraw the ADIZ; and a mutual agreement on no prior flight report of civilian aircraft to China, did not materialise. This was what Beijing was worried about most before Biden's visit to Toky. Xi personally engaged Biden to pre-empt such a development. Moreover, Beijing's vigorous diplomacy resulted in Washington's acquiescence on US civilian airlines reporting their flights to China, something that Tokyo still disallows. Generally, Beijing perceived that an 'agree to disagree' understanding was accorded out of the Xi-Biden talks. Its worst fears did not come true.

However, the negative after effects of the ADIZ imposition will last—in the sense that the US and its allies/partners may have arrived at a new assessment of what China may do with regard to the existing world and regional security order, as it increases its military clout. The US Pivot strategy will accelerate, especially in forms of troop redeployment and allied cooperation. On the other hand, as far as Beijing is concerned, the previous ADIZ status quo hurt China's security interests strongly, and it could not sit idle about it. It will continue to challenge the existing ADIZ arrangements (for example, announcing a SCS ADIZ in due time), not unaware of its consequences in regional power politics. As pointed out by major general Qian Liang, an act such as ADIZ imposition is the natural behaviour of the top powers. Eventually, other states will have to get used to it.[59] Yet, Beijing's current strategic concerns are expressed in its efforts to absorb the ADIZ storm quickly so that China's strategic standing in the region would not be adversely affected too much. Beijing's control over the ADIZ conflict from this new strategic turning point is limited; but it will try its utmost to prevent the worst from occurring.

Why ADIZ now?

In their long close-door meeting, Xi told Biden that the ADIZ measure was not meant to challenge the US-centred status quo in Asia. It was mainly aimed at Japan's ADIZ that extends close to Chinese boundaries. Yet, this is not the exact purpose for Beijing setting up the ADIZ, although the Japan factor was relevant. China's ADIZ initiative can be defined in both narrow and broad terms. The former is about its true meaning, which is a concept of early warning for air defence; it is a tactical military issue at a relatively low level of importance. The latter conveys a revisionist attempt against US and Japanese ADIZs, which is a part of the US-centric security order in the region. The strong US reaction is well understood when the second defining feature of Chinese ADIZ is factored in.

The fact is that the primary target of Chinese ADIZ is largely tactical: it is to counter US spy activities near coastal PLA facilities and bases; the aim of these activities is to gather military imagery intelligence as well as electronic signatures and signals.[60] The ADIZ is specifically a PLA response to foreign aircraft coming near to high valued PLA assets with a hostile intent. From the PLA perspective, this violates China's core national interests: US aerial spy activity within 50 kilo meters of a Chinese strategic naval base (near the Yalong Base in the Hainan part of the SCS), is a kind of war without smoke that may cause PLA defeat in future wars. The painful lesson of EP-3 and *USS Impeccable* incidents was that the PLA had no effective way of dealing with US aircraft in China's adjacent airspace. All it could do was to scramble airplanes to shallow US planes under the EEZ claims. Yet, the US has never recognised the EEZ. The US argument of the freedom of aviation in international space cannot be legally rebuked. So, the PLA copied the ADIZ idea from the US to justify its counter actions. PLAAF chief Xu Qiliang called for a study of the feasibility of a Chinese ADIZ as early as 2009.[61] A consensus emerged that the ADIZ was a viable way to counter US spy flights in open air space, with a sub-legal guidance for PLA aircraft to engage US planes according to US practice.[62] The ADIZ was, thus, not a prompt act, but one after serious assessment (深思熟虑), as Xi told Bidan.[63]

However, the trigger for the ADIZ announcement was the intrusion of a Japanese destroyer 107 into the zone where the three PLAN Fleets were conducting *Mobile-5* war drills in October 2013. The destroyer stayed right in the area for 70 hours, forcing the PLA to cut short the exercise.[64] Beijing sources revealed that such an intrusion outraged the PLA top command, and ended a debate on the timing for the ADIZ announcement. Xi approved the PLA motion.[65] For some time, the PLAAF has contemplated various measures against the SDAF, often tailing its aircraft at a close range in Japan's ADIZ. Regular announcement about the times SDF aircraft are shadowing Chinese planes gives people an impression that China is to blame for entering Japan's ADIZ. While the PLA follows Russia's way of disregarding Japan's ADIZ, it designs its own ADIZ according to US and Japanese formulas. The SDF aircraft and destroyers in the PLAN's exercise zone in November 2013 accidentally facilitated Beijing's decision making process.

Thus, the primary consideration of Chinese ADIZ is not Japan but the USA; this is currently derived more from a tactical and battle field calculus than from an assessment of its geo-strategic consequences. This may be a miscalculated move. Japan's shadowing of PLA aircraft and ships in the ECS is an irritant; but it is not any immediate threat to Chinese national security. This raises a question: What is the ADIZ? It is about creating a mechanism of preventative or pre-emptive crisis control/management; it is not about sovereignty imposition or resolution. No doubt territorial factors lie behind it being set up; but it is not the primary focus. As the Japanese ADIZ has the Senkaku/Diaoyu area covered, China's inclusion of the area in its ADIZ is, thus, more of a political and diplomatic gesture—and meant largely for domestic consumption. Therefore, the ADIZ idea is not equivalent to an irredentist attempt. Beijing had no plan to capture the Senkakus before the declaration; nor does it have any after, as this may trigger a war involving top powers.

Here, the real test is whether Beijing will enforce the ADIZ in the Senkaku area. This is not likely. Significant here are Xi's 5-Nos listed earlier with regard to China's management of the Diaoyu dispute: no military aircraft into the area; no naval vessels into the area; no sizeable clusters of fishing ships into the area; no real law reinforcement by civilian surveillance ships in the area (no expelling actions); and no punitive acts against Japanese economic interests in China.[66] This is the kind of proportional response to Japan's nationalisation of the islands, although in an asymmetric form. If the PLA indeed dispatches military aircraft or vessels into the area for ADIZ enforcement, it would be excessive; it would also alter the status quo in escalating the dispute to a military level, and thus cross US red lines on dispute control. Xi is very cautious about acts of such brinkmanship. So far, there has been no Chinese ADIZ enforcement in the Senkaku/Diaoyu area, and there will probably be none for a long time to come, although some symbolic moves may be mounted. To some extent, the fundamental status quo has not been upset there with the ADIZ announcement—at least not for now.

Future Prognosis

The ADIZ promulgation clearly raised the level of security worries of Asian states as a consequence of which they have become involved in territorial tension. The Chinese ADIZ document is a mission statement covering all possible scenarios in an ADIZ dispute, although, as mentioned earlier, its purpose is narrowly dual: against US spy planes peering into Chinese waters, and justifying Chinese flights through Japanese ADIZ in a mirror image. Yet, Beijing cannot openly state these real aims, especially with regard to US spy activities near Chinese airspace, which is a defining feature of the Asian status quo—at least this is what the PLA always complains about.[67]

The dilemma for China is that it has to have necessary prescriptions—such as 'emergence defensive measures'—in the document to cope with worst case scenarios against China's security. It is clear to everyone, including PLA commanders, that US spy aircraft have no intention of entering Chinese air space. However, this raises many questions: How should the PLA deal with P-8A which is often only 15 nm from Chinese air space? And, how should this scenario be dealt with in written language in the ADIZ declaration? This is something that can only be treated with ambiguity. There are also other independent or dependent variables which are hard to cover for a short document. For instance, it is difficult for the document to specify in clear terms how the PLA should react to a military plane flying parallel to Chinese air borders within the ADIZ, as also one that flying towards Chinese borders.

Moreover, it is difficult for the PLA to have a well-defined ADIZ protocol to specify how it should react to one aircraft flying toward Chinese air borders but still 200 kilometres away, and another already 50 kilometres from the border. The phrase included in the document is 'emergency defensive measures', and the requirement to report of all foreign aircraft entering the zone are standard provisions of the ADIZ provisions of most countries. Yet, given the complicated security situation in which China finds itself (as for example, territorial disputes with its neighbours, and the unusually narrow airspace shared by China, Japan and South Korea in the ECS), the intended ambiguity proves to be a PR disaster, leaving much space for misunderstanding and/or misinterpretation. It was not until a huge storm gathered did a PLA spokesman issue a relatively detailed explanation of what its ADIZ was, and was not. However, by then it was too late to clear the confusion in the minds of foreign observers.

For instance, as long as the sentence of 'emergency defensive measures' is there, the US would worry that PLA aircraft would expel US spy planes at a much extended range—that is, 100 kilometres away from their current operational zones— raising the possibility of repeating the EP-3 clash. And, as long as China's ADIZ overlaps Japan's with the Senkaku area inside China's ADIZ, Tokyo would have to factor in the scenario of the PLA enforcing the ADIZ for sovereignty claims. Such concerns cannot be explicitly addressed by the ADIZ protocol, or by a PLA spokesman. Only through behind doors diplomacy (as the one between Xi and Biden), would the two sides secure acquiescence on the rules of engagement that would help mitigate the strategic impact of the ADIZ on the regional balance of power. However, the Sino-Japanese political impasse prevents the two states from starting diplomacy on mutually acceptable rules of engagement over the overlapping ADIZ areas. The ADIZ is not a cause for war; but, as mentioned earlier, it increases chances for accidental confrontation if a mutual understanding of each other's rules of engagement is not secured.

What Chinese rules of engagement are in place to prevent a military standoff in the air? The Xi-Biden meeting may have resulted in some tacit understanding that US spy aircraft would continue to come close to Chinese air space, and PLA aircraft would continue to follow and accompany them, even at a close range; but, there would be no forceful expulsion. The SDF has never dispatched aircraft to locations sensitive to Chinese national defence. The PLA would reciprocate. This should be an important rule for China and Japan while handling ADIZ conflict. PLA analysts have explained why no aircraft was scrambled on 26 November 2013 to shadow US B-52s and Japanese planes inside the declared ADIZ by saying that the aircraft were adequately monitored by PLA AWACs as well as land-based long-range radar systems.[68] This kind of radar surveillance is the standard method for enforcing ADIZ. To the PLA, this is far from satisfactory; but it does constitute an acceptable justification under the circumstances of the

US military's determination to stay close to Chinese air space. PLA aircraft will continue to be dispatched to follow the intruders from time to time, with bilateral no-contact acquiescence.

A major uncertainty with profound security implications is whether PLA aircraft should continue patrolling the Senkaku/Diaoyu area in the aftermath of the ADIZ. This is quite unlikely, as this was not an ADIZ design in the first place.[69] The SDF confirmed that the PLA was capable of electronically monitoring SDF flights around the Senkakus. This surveillance saves PLA aircraft at close range in the overlapping areas.[70] Certainly, if Sino-Japanese tension escalates continuously, the possibility of PLA aircraft entering the Diaoyu area—as a sovereignty statement—cannot be entirely excluded due to domestic pressure and diplomatic needs. Therefore, it is urgent that Beijing and Tokyo formulate some measures of crisis prevention.

More generally, the Chinese rules of engagement can be specified under the following scenarios.

- If foreign planes enter the ADIZ briefly but keep a long distance from Chinese air space, no action is necessary as the distance maintained and brevity of the flight inside the zone convey no hostile intent.
- If foreign planes are inside the zone for an extended period of time but show no hostile intent (for example, no weapons carried or a decent distance is kept keeping from Chinese borders, PLA aircraft will only keep radio contact, or stage an accompanying flight within the general vicinity.
- If the foreign aircraft demonstrates hostile intent and its penetration into the zone is deep, PLA aircraft would continue to warn them through radio contact and try to edge them some amount of distance away from Chinese air space; but they would, generally, not indulge in aggressive actions, as these planes are in the international air space.

In this way, the ADIZ is understood as a zone to provide more early warning time (through electronic signals and radar surveillance), and not suggest a no-flight zone; as such, this does not change the status quo in a substantial way.[71] Shooting the intruding aircraft down is out of the question. Following this principle, the entry of B-52s into the zone on 26 November 2013 was regarded as a challenge to China's ADIZ; but not one to its defence security. It was provocative, but not dangerous; and so were SDF aircraft. What the Chinese did toward them heralds a pattern of reaction for future ADIZ enforcement.

Conclusion

As there is no commonly accepted governance mechanism in the Indo-Pacific region, especially with regard to territorial disputes, China will continue to protect its sovereignty interests through seemingly assertive behaviour. Yet, its maritime policy is oriented toward crisis management rather than any irredentist intent. The calculated assertiveness serves a number of purposes: it is there primarily for domestic consumption; for pre-empting further moves by other disputants; and for leaving space for political negotiations in order to restore the *status quo*.

In protecting its core national interests, China does enjoy critical breathing time and space for manoeuvring. China's maritime policy is currently status quo based, although its response to the game-changers of other claimants may have tactically altered the status quo, as it was originally understood. Beijing is in no hurry to resolve sovereignty disputes.[72] This policy choice also serves US interests. Under such rationale, Beijing is confident that it has enough leverage against envelope-pushing by other ESCS claimants, while being careful enough not to over-react to its own disadvantage. This subtle game will continue to be played out, and no doubt cause standoffs. Yet, without any armed confrontation of a scale, the standoffs would be basically tactical and manageable.

To Chinese naval commanders, the US island chain strategy poses a fatal threat to China's critical SLOCs, and then to its economic lifeline. Moreover, facing geographic constraints and the prospects of a naval blockade, Beijing is developing a carrier-embedded expeditionary navy which is capable of breaking islands chains as also of launching SLOC campaigns in the far seas. Its catch-up mentality and strategy vis-à-vis the US will stimulate an already visible arms race in the region. Under the circumstances, a regional maritime governance regime is hard to achieve.

The unexpected ADIZ imposition will produce a far reaching strategic impact on the regional status quo in the years ahead. While China sees it simply as a copy of ADIZ practices of Japan, Australia, and a number of countries that require the flight report of all aircraft transiting their ADIZs, and thus address the unfair status quo,[73] many of its neighbours get worried over this move, and see strategic ambition behind it. This endeavour will exert long term security consequences. Despite China's ADIZ rationality in regard to its long term maritime interests, it appears to have been a premature decision, given the backlashes it has generated. There is no urgent need to have it right now. Yet, with careful and expedient enforcement, the Chinese ADIZ may not escalate tension in the short run, as observers fear. If this is indeed the case, the US-centric status quo in the regional security order will not be seriously upset in the foreseeable future. Yet, the ADIZ serves a notice to the region that the *status quo* has to change in due time.

NOTES

1. In this essay, 'Indo-Pacific' is used more as a geostrategic concept in association with the US Pivot strategy and China's rise. The term has become popular among Australian scholars,

such as Rory Medclaf of the Lowy Institute. For an academic analysis of the concept, see Chengxin Pan, 'The Indo-Pacific and Geostrategic Anxieties about China's Rise in the Asian Regional Order', *Australian Journal of International Affairs*, Vol. 68, No.4, 2014, pp. 453-469.

2. You Ji, 'The Spratlys: A Test Case for China's Defence and Foreign Policy', *Contemporary Southeast Asia*, Vol. 16, No. 4, March 1995, pp. 375-403.
3. On this assertiveness, see Li, M., 'Reconcile Assertiveness and Cooperation?: China's Changing Approach to the South China Sea Dispute', *Security Challenges*, Vol. 6, No. 2, 2010.
4. Wu Shicuan's remarks to the weekly Yihu Debate, on the Phoenix TV, 26 January 2014.
5. Da, W., 'Has China Becomes Tough', *China Security*, Vol. 6, No. 3, pp. 97-102.
6. Michael Auslin (of the US Enterprise Institute) argues that the 'US government is unable to force Beijing to yield even if it exercises more pressure. It would harden the dispute'. Voice of America, 11 May 2013. On Beijing's resolve, Chinese Minister of Defence, Chang Wanquan, made it clear in his talk with his US counterpart in Pentagon, on 15 August 2013, that nobody should expect Beijing to swallow bitter fruit with regard to sovereignty—the actual words of Xi.
7. The unanimous view by ASEAN participants to the conference titled 'Security Outlook of the Asia Pacific Countries', National Institute for Defence Studies, Tokyo, 15-16 January 2013.
8. The killing of a Taiwanese fisherman by the Filipino Coastal Guard in May 2013 is the latest incident that has produced a profound impact on the maritime dispute in the region.
9. Kurlantzick, J., *Charming offensive: How China's Soft Power is transforming the World*, New York: Yale University Press, 2007, pp. 129-132.
10. *Ashasi Shimbun*, 12 July 2012; also, Kevin Rudd, 'Asia's own Balkans: a Tinderbox', *The Australian*, 2-3 February 2013.
11. In the 1970s, Deng said 'we leave it to the future generations to deal with'. This remains the policy guidance for the current Chinese government. According to Major General Qiao Liang, the Spratly and Diaoyu issues are only tactical as compared with China's rise, which is strategic. The untimely resolution of a tactical challenge to the detriment of a strategic goal is not a sensible policy choice. *Global Times*, 12 September 2012.
12. Hall, S., *The Principles of International Law*, LexisNexis, 2011, pp. 347-349.
13. 'Review of the decision on Senkaku nationalisation', *Ashasi Shimbun*, 27 September 2012.
14. Noda admitted that he was hugely surprised by China's reaction. He might have miscalculated under the conviction that the rules of the game in territorial dispute are those of the occupiers, as he had to swallow what South Korea did on the Dockit/Bamboo Island during his office. *Ashasi Shimbun*, 27 September 2012. Shigeru Ishiba, a leading LDP politician, told reporters (on 7 September 2012) that 'ports should be built in Senkakus as a means of lifting levels of control. And we should dispatch officials to the islands permanently'; *Bloomberg News*, 15 September 2012.
15. Major General Jin Yinan's comments, 'National Defence Skyline', on the Voice of China, 9 August 2012.
16. Senior Colonel Fan Bing's comments in Military Decoding, on Beijing TV, 17 September 2013.
17. Minister Zhang Zhijun's speech, 8th Blue Hull Forum, Beijing, 27 December 2012.
18. General Qi Jiangguo reiterated official Chinese military policy toward ESCS disputes (in the Shangri-la Dialogue on 1 June 2013) that 'Beijing would not use force to settle Spratly disputes but would use necessary measures to roll back the provocations of others'.
19. Major General Xu Yan, 'Several decades of Sino-Pilipino disputes in the South China Sea', *Study Times*, 21 May 2012

20. Information gleaned from senior PLA officers at the PLA National Defence University in Beijing, in January 2013.
21. Senior Colonel Hu Siyuan's words in Global Zero Distance, on Guangdong TV, 15 September 2013.
22. Western analysts see this as a turn for the situation to get worse. Michael Cole, 'Japan, China Scramble military jets in the East China Sea', the *Diplomat*, 11 January 2013.
23. This was a decision by the Maritime Response Leading Group in September 2012. Oral sources in Beijing, obtained in January 2013.
24. Rear Admiral Zhang Zhaozhong's comments in Focus in the News Today, on China Central TV-4, 25 November 2012.
25. RAND Report: *US President Can Maintain US-China Peace through Dedicate Deterrence*, RAND, 6 November 2012.
26. The Chinese Academy of Social Science (ed.), 2012, p. 125.
27. Li Mingjiang's speech, RSIS 'International Conference on Security Challenges in Southeast Asia', Nanyang University of Technology, 15 November 2012.
28. Keith Bradsher, 'Philippine Leader Sounds Alarm on China', *New York Times*, 4 February 2014.
29. In his Southeast Asian trip in May 2013, Foreign Minister Wang Yi reiterated Beijing's willingness to work with ASEAN for a mutually acceptable CoC.
30. Australian Foreign Minister, Bob Carr's keynote speech, CSIS, 22 March 2013, Washington D.C., USA.
31. General Zhu Chenghou's speech to the International Forum on the South China Sea Dispute, organised by Asian Society and National University of Singapore, New York City, 14-15 March 2013.
32. Xu Yan, 'How to rank our national interests', *Journal of the PLA*, National Defence University, No. 1, 2000, p. 14.
33. In an RSIS/Stanford University 'Conference on Southeast Asian Security', 14 November 2012, in Singapore, Donald Emmerson called ASEAN to present a CoC document to Beijing, and said 'sign it'. The 'toilet paper' remark was from a Chinese ASEAN specialist in Singapore in November 2012.
34. In a summit meeting between Jiang Zemin and Suharto Jakarta in 1994, Suharto asked Jiang to clarify why the dotted line got into Indonesia's EEZ. Jiang assured Suharto that China had only claimed the islets and their adjacent waters (12 nm) within the dotted lines, and not all the waters, so that there was no territorial dispute between the two countries. Suharto further required Jiang to have this written in a diplomatic document. Jiang immediately concurred. The Ministry of Foreign Affairs presented the document to Jakarta in 1992. In 1995 and 1996, the Foreign Minister Qian Qishen officially announced this Chinese stance on his tour to Southeast Asia.
35. The chain starts from Japan to Liuqu islands to Taiwan to the Philippines. It is strategically backed up by the second islands chain from Japan's Ogasawa-gunto islands to the Io-retto islands to the Mariana Islands.
36. John Reed, 'US deploying jets around Asia to keep China surrounded', *Foreign Policy Magazine*, 29 July 2013.
37. Senior Colonel Li Li's comments to New Defence Watch, on the CCTV Military Channel (7), 31 August 2013.
38. Li Jie and Liu Weixing, 'The strategic status of the islands chains and their impact', *Journal of the PLA*, National Defence University, No. 12, 2000, p. 24.
39. John Reed, 'US Deploying Jets around Asia to Keep China Surrounded', *Foreign Policy Magazine*, 29 July 2013.
40. Major general Jin Yinan, 'National eunification and national sustainable development',

Journal of the PLA, National Defence University, No. 12, 2000, p. 24.

41. Carnes Lord and Andrew Erickson (eds), Rebalancing U.S. Forces: Basing and Forward Presence in the Asia-Pacific, Annapolis, Naval Institute Press, 2014.
42. Andrew Krepinevich, 'Why AirSea Battle?' Centre for Strategic and Budgetary Assessment, 2010.
43. You Ji, 'The Chinese Navy, its Regional Power and Global Reach', *Strategic Analysis*, Vol. 36, No. 3, 2012, pp. 477-488.
44. Li Jie and Liu Weixing, p. 25.
45. Michael McDevitt, 'America's New Security Strategy and its Military Dimension', *Global Asia*, Vol. 7, No. 4, 2012.
46. Interview with Senior Colonel Li Li
47. *Kyodo News*, 20 November 2013.
48. Comments made by senior Colonel Fang Bing, the National Defence University, to Taiwan Strait Watch on CCTV-4, 19 November 2013.
49. Editorial, *Nikkei Daily*, 21 May 2013, quoted by Sun Xiuping, ('Japanese monitoring troops to enter Yonaguni Jima') in *Global Times*, 23 May 2013.
50. Interview with PLA expert, Song Xinzhi in 'Military Decoding', Beijing TV Station, 18 October 2013.
51. Senior Colonel Fang Bing, to CCTV-4, 19 November 2013; and also to Channel NewsAsia, 7 November 2013.
52. 'Military Decoding', on Beijing TV, 30 August 2013.
53. Comments by Rear Admiral Yin Zuo, in 'Deep Analysis of World Affairs', 26 November 2012.
54. CSIS Report, 'Strategic US Military Posture in the Asia-Pacific Region', cited in *Sydney Morning Herald*, 1 August 2012.
55. On SLOC warfare in the Indian-Pacific region in the ASB guidance, see Andrew Krepinevich, 'Why AirSea Battle', Centre for Strategic and Budgetary Assessment, 2010.
56. Senior Colonel Fang Bing's comments in 'Cross the Taiwan Strait', on CCTV-4, 8 October 2013.
57. For instance, using land-based anti-ship missiles to conceal Chinese SLOCs is only one of the methods that US allies can help with, as suggested by RAND. It is only a supplement to other methods that the US is capable of, such as submarine warfare and air superiority. Comments by Senior Colonel Du Wenlong, New Defense Observer (防务新时空), on Shanghai Satellite TV, 9 December 2013.
58. You Ji, 'China's Response to the Deadly Triangle: Arms Race, Territorial Disputes and Energy Security', *CLAWS Journal*, Summer 2010, pp. 35-52.
59. 'Deep Analysis of World Affairs', 6 December 2013.
60. Major General Qian Lihua's talk in a closed door 'Conference on Taiwan Relations and Regional Security', organised by the Institute of International Relations, National Chengchi University, Taipei, 19 December 2013.
61. *Asahi Shimbun*, 28 November 2013.
62. Comments by Major Chai Lidan, of the PLA Air Force Command Academy in Beijing, in 'Daily Affairs of the Chinese World', on Phoenix TV, 25 November 2013.
63. 'The Voice of America', 4 December 2013.
64. According to Chinese MoD spokesman Colonel Li Yujun, China served a notice through the International Maritime Organisation (18 October 2013) that the PLA would conduct war drills in the East China Sea from 24 October to 3 November 2013. The notice reminded ships and aircraft to keep a certain amount of distance from the exercising zone.
65. 'Xi Jinping Gave the Ultimate Order to Move on the Japanese', *Asian Weekly*, 29 November 2013.

66. You Ji, 'Decipher Beijing's Maritime Security Policy and Strategy in Managing Sovereignty Disputes in the China Seas', Policy Brief, RSIS, Nanyang Technological University, Singapore, October 2013.
67. Jane Perlez, 'American and Chinese Navy Ships Nearly Collided in SCS', *New York Times*, 14 December 2013.
68. 'How to monitor ADIZ, Japan's aircraft can be monitored through radar', *Global Times*, 26 November 2013.
69. Ibid.
70. Comments by Senior Colonel Du Wenlong, 'Deep Analysis of World Affairs', 8 December 2013.
71. Senior Colonel Du Wenlong, 8 December 2013.
72. General Qi Jianguo conveyed this message at the 12th Shangri-la Dialogue on 1 June 2013. He echoed Deng's remark that the dispute could be to be handled by future generations, which is now Beijing's official policy.
73. When it announced the ADIZ in 1969, Japan made it clear that all aircraft flying through its ADIZ must report their plan beforehand. For a long time, Chinese civil aviation planes detoured the area (at increased costs) to avoid potential trouble. Even today, Taiwan's civil aviation flights are electronically inspected when they pass the Japanese ADIZ which, according to Taiwan's civil aviation administration, could be risky, as their communication with the home airport could be interference mid-air. *China Post*, Taiwan, 3 December 2013.

16

Quest for Effective Ocean Management in the South China Sea

T. Lan Anh Nguyen

Introduction

In managing the ocean, it is always challenging for states to find mechanisms to harmonise different interests and to exploit the resources in the most sustainable manner. The South China Sea, one of the largest semi-enclosed sea in the world is not only rich in marine environment but also contains complicated sovereignty and maritime disputes, making the quest for effective ocean management is even more imperative. In an effort to find the most feasible options for ocean management in the South China Sea, this paper will first examine the elements that call for better ocean management of the South China Sea. It then considers available options for managing the South China Sea from best practices of the region and the world. Each option will be analysed to assert its feasibility. The paper concludes by suggesting the most feasible option to better manage the South China Sea in its own context.

The Need for Ocean Management in the South China Sea

The need for better ocean management in the South China Sea comes from at least three sources because the South China Sea is (1) a sea of proven and potentially very rich resources; (2) a sea of complicated disputes; and (3) a sea of potential conflict.

A Sea of Rich Resources

The South China Sea is one of the largest semi-enclosed seas with rich natural resources, and is ranked fourth among the nineteenth richest world fishing zones. In the waters around the Spratlys alone, fishing capacity is estimated at 7.5 tones per square kilometer a year.[1] Annually, the South China Sea states and entity produce over eight million metric tonnes live weight of marine fish, accounting for 10 per cent of the total world catch and 23 per cent of Asia, making it extremely important to the fishing industries of nearby countries.[2] Fish not only brings exporting advantages, but also provides about 25per cent of the protein necessary for the 500 million people of littoral states.[3] The South China Sea is believed to contain a large quantity of oil and gas reserves. In November 2012, the Chinese National Offshore Oil Company (CNOOC) estimated that the South China Sea has 125 billions barrels of oil and 500 trillion cubic feet of natural gas in undiscovered resources. In the most recent report, the Energy Information Administration estimated that the South China Sea contains approximately 11 billion barrels of oil and 190 trillion cubic feet of natural gas in proven and provable reserves. Particularly, the Spratlys area may contain significant deposits of undiscovered hydrocarbon resources of up to 2.5 barrels of oil and 25.5 trillion cubic feet of natural gas in undiscovered resources.[4]

Besides natural resources, the unique and diversified ecosystem in the South China Sea also offers a promising opportunity for littoral states to develop tourism. Some countries in the region have as well explored the tourism potential of the South China Sea, for example, Malaysia is operating a dive resource in the disputed Swallow Reef; China plans to develop tourism in the disputed Paracels. Vietnam also sent a tourist group to the Spratlys.

A Sea of Complicated Disputes

With rich resources, the South China Sea is also a sea of disputes, which falls into two broad categories: disputes on sovereignty of the features in the South China Sea and disputes on jurisdictions over the maritime zones.

Sovereignty disputes: the sovereignty disputes in the South China Sea mainly relate to some mid-ocean islands. China, Taiwan, Vietnam, Philippines, Malaysia and Brunei have different claims over different features. Due to the long history and complicated claims from multiple parties, many issues in international law concerning territory acquisition arise. International law on territory acquisition is well established in international customary law and consists of five legal modes, namely occupation, prescription, cession, conquest and accession. Unfortunately, some claimants do not base their sovereignty claims on these legal grounds, but rather on the discovery of the islands by individual—the fishermen—not the activities of their government, which is not supported by modern international law thus further complicating the disputes. Another party based its claim on the ground that when they discovered the islands they were so-called *terra nullius,* or territory which belongs to no one, although other parties had evidence of establishing sovereignty over those islands before that.

Not only what is claimed is disputed, what can be claimed is also a subject under dispute in the South China Sea. In general, under the United Nation Convention on the Law of the Sea (UNCLOS) 1982, seabed elevations are classified into three legal groups: islands, low tide elevations and others which are always under the water even at low tide. Of the three groups, only islands allow states to generate title, and thus are subjects of sovereignty claims. Low tide elevations cannot be fully assimilated with islands and other land territory thus cannot be subjects of sovereignty claims.[5] In addition to islands and low title elevations, no other feature in the Spratlys has any impact on questions concerning territorial sovereignty. However, the practice of the parties to the South China Sea dispute suggest that some elevations, although submerged at high tide or low tide are still objects of occupation and claims for both territorial issues and maritime zones. The parties have fortified these claims by constructing structures such as lighthouses, military structures and weather stations in order to make the elevations stand above water at high tide.

Maritime disputes: the maritime disputes in the South China Sea come from three sources: overlapping maritime zones generated from the mainland of littoral states; the maritime zones of the disputed islands; and other maritime claims.

In line with the provisions of the UNCLOS, all coastal states in the South China Sea claim maritime zones including 200 nautical miles of exclusive economic zone and continental shelf. These claims result in overlapping zones between those generated from adjacent and opposite coasts of the littoral states.

The second source of maritime dispute is generated from the mid-ocean islands. The regime of islands is currently provided for under Article 121 of UNCLOS. Accordingly, an island is entitled to generate full maritime zone if it can sustain human habitation or have economic life of its own.[6] The wording of this article is a topic of controversy[7] and even more controversial in applying to the case of the Paracels and Spratlys where all features are very small in size, having no habitation of ordinary people and limited natural resources in the islands themselves. Vietnam by its *note verbale* in 2009 responded to the opposition of China and the Philippines to their extended continental shelves implying that Spratlys and the Paracels produce no exclusive economic zone and continental shelf of their own. Meanwhile, China has lodged its claim to the United Nations to generate exclusive economic zone and continental shelf for the Spratlys,[8] resulting in significant overlapping with maritime zones of littoral states from their mainland.

The third source of maritime dispute comes from the so called China 9 dashed line. The claim first appeared in Republic of China in 1947, then 11 dashed line, covering a large area of the South China Sea extending southward from 15 to 4 degrees North latitude to include the entire the Paracel, Spratlys and even a submerged feature, the James Shoal at the southernmost.[9] There was no explanation from China and Taiwan, even to this day, given for the reasons or purpose of drawing the dashed lines on the map. Due to its ambiguity, various possible explanations for what the dashed line can notate have aroused, even among Chinese scholars and officials. These include: (1) the line shows the territorial claims of China to the islands within the line;[10] (2) the water within the line is China's historic water; (3) the water within the line is the limit of the historical rights of China; (4) the line shows the potential maritime delimitation line between China and littoral states.[11] Of the four possible explanations, only the first could survive under international law. No legal foundation under modern international law could be found for the other three explanations.

A Sea of Potential Conflicts

Armed conflict and military clashes in the South China Sea have happened in the past and the risk for further conflict is rising. Countries in the South China Sea have been modernising their militaries. By 2012, China's military budget has risen to $ 103 billion.[12] A nuclear submarine base was built at Sanya (Hainan Island) homing the newly launched Liaoning air-craft carrier and other modern weapons. Vietnam is modernising its navy with the purchase of six Russian-built kilo-class submarines and other surface vessels. Singapore, Indonesia, Malaysia are also adding submarines to their fleet.[13] Concern for conflict became more imminent when China harassed seismic survey vessels of coastal states[14] and warned other littoral states to "prepare for the sounds of cannons if they remain at loggerheads with Beijing".[15]

Concern for conflict worries non-claimants and extra-regional countries because the South China Sea is a popular navigation route for goods and cargo transportation by sea, carrying annually more than 50 per cent of the world merchant fleet tonnage, in which approximately a third of global crude oil and over half of global liquefied natural gas passes through the three straits of the South China Sea, namely the Malacca, Sunda and Lombok.[16] Approximately 41,000 ships, accounting for half of the global shipping annually sails though the South China Sea.[17] Freedom of navigation and over flight in the South China Sea are of great concern for the international community. The incidents of EP3 and USNS Impeccable[18] and the recent near collision between the U.S. and Chinese warships[19] revealed that even in the situation of no armed conflict in the South China Sea, the interpretation and application of various legal provisions could still create a negative impact and impede vessels and aircrafts enjoying the freedom of navigation and over flight as provided for under international law. The declaration of China on the establishment of an Air Defense Identification Zone (ADIZ) on November 23, 2013 highlighted this concern.[20]

Since all parties concerned have conducted activities to exercise their sovereign rights and jurisdiction to fortify the claims, number of disputes rose, incidences became more frequent and widespread and the risk of conflicts even higher. In 2009, incidences were only confined in the Northern part of the South China Sea near the Paracels (i.e. the harassment of the Impeccable, the arrest of Vietnamese fishing vessels, and the unilateral fishing ban laid by China). In subsequent years, more incidences occurred deeper to the South and closer to the coastlines of the Philippines, Vietnam, Malaysia, escalating the intensity and seriousness of the incidences.

Options for a More Effective Ocean Management in the South China Sea

Resources Management

Countries in the South China Sea region are among the most dynamic economic development regions of the world. China, in particular, enjoyed continued high economic growth for at least two decades. With one fourth of the world population and a booming economy, China needs oil to fuel the many industries of the country like textile, transportation, metallurgy and to produce fertiliser to guarantee sufficient agricultural production to feed its population.[21] ASEAN countries also have a great demand for hydrocarbon, fishery and other resources of the South China Sea in order to develop their equally dynamic economies.[22]

Besides economic reasons, it is also noteworthy that the South China Sea is a semi-enclosed sea in which the marine system is naturally unified. Littoral states are all parties to the 1982 UNCLOS who have the obligation to cooperate under Article 123 of the 1982 UNCLOS. The obligation is to cooperate in exploration and exploitation of living resources, protection of the marine environment and scientific research to which, primarily, is the need for building a fishery management regime to protect the resources and maintain the security in the region.[23]

In addition, given the maritime dispute in the South China Sea, the claimant states are obliged to find a temporary arrangement while pending for final solutions under the provisions of Article 74(3) and 83(3).[24] UNCLOS does not prescribe specific forms of interim arrangements, however, it is submitted that any model for resources management is well fit within these obligations.

So far, joint development/cooperation as cooperative state practices in the exploitation of resources has grown significantly and showed its effectiveness in disputed maritime zones. In the South China Sea, the success of fishery cooperation between China and Vietnam in the Gulf of Tonkin, joint development of hydrocarbon resources between Malaysia and Vietnam give hopes for further cooperation in other areas of the South China Sea. Experiences from these successful practices show that the parties' first need political will to enter cooperation, at the same time, need to exercise restraint and make reasonable proposal on the specific area and fields of joint development/cooperation. The next condition is to agree on a fair management mechanism including the choice of proper applicable law, equal sharing of obligations as well as interests and the emphasis on the prejudice clause on sovereignty issues. Last but not least is to be flexible in establishing the management institutions by using either a simple form of joint commission or a more comprehensive and well structure organisation.[25]

Dispute Management

Dispute management can be undertaken in a two-step process. The parties concerned first need to clarify their claims and second create a forum for narrowing the gaps of differences and settle the disputes.

So far, there are encouraging signals from state practices in the South China Sea in this regard. ***China,*** in 2009, in a series of *note verbale* concerning the submissions of the extended continental shelf of Vietnam and Malaysia, expressed the position that China "enjoys the sovereign rights and jurisdiction over the relevant water as well as the seabed and subsoil thereof" and attached the nine-dash line map.[26] In another *note verbale* in 2011, China repeated this statement and made another position that under the relevant provisions of UNCLOS, as well as the Law on Territorial Sea and Contiguous Zone (1992) and the Law on the EEZ and Continental Shelf (1998), the Spratlys is fully entitled to territorial sea, EEZ and continental shelf.[27] China also clarified that "the dotted line was formally announced by the Chinese government in 1948" and that "China's sovereignty, rights and claims in the South China Sea were established and developed in the long course of history"[28] and "the UNCLOS ...does not restrain or deny a country's right which is formed in history and abidingly upheld."[29] Notwithstanding the debate on historical basis, China will need to further clarify its sovereignty claims and the meaning of the nine-dashed line.

Malaysia has not made any official maritime claims from the mid-ocean features of the South China Sea. However, from the joint submission on extended continental shelf with Vietnam where the continental shelf was only projected from its mainland, it was inferred that Malaysia considered the features in the South China Sea as only rocks and thus has no EEZ and continental shelf.

The Philippines has a general approach to the legal regime of islands. Article 2 of Act No. 9522 provides that the Kalayaan Island Group (Spratlys) will be determined as "regime of islands", i.e. the waters shall be according to Article

121 of UNCLOS. However, with the recent initiatives on a Zone of peace, cooperation and friendship (ZoPFF/C), the Philippines argued that the disputed maritime zones can be enclaved by 12 nautical miles, and the submerged Reed Bank is not a part of the Spratly islands. This argument shows that the Philippines considers the islands of the Spratlys as rocks, having no exclusive economic zone and continental shelf of themselves.

This position is further endorsed by the statement of the Philippine in the Note Verbal dated on April 5, 2011, that since the adjacent waters of the relevant geological features are definite and subject to legal and technical measurement, the claims by China on the 'relevant waters as well as seabed and subsoil thereof' outside of the aforementioned relevant geological feature in the Kalayaan Island Group and their "adjacent waters" would have no basis under international law, especially UNCLOS.

Vietnam, similar to Malaysia, on its own and joint submission with Malaysia has defined the baseline, the boundaries of the exclusive economic zone and continental shelf extension. However, Vietnam did not make any claims to the exclusive economic zone and continental shelf of the Paracel and Spratly Islands. Therefore, many scholars argued that Vietnam also considers the islands of the Spratly and Paracel islands as rocks, which cannot generate full maritime zones.[30]

Given the significance of proper application of the legal regime of islands in the South China Sea as well as the current different views on this issue, the parties may exchange point of views on this issues or seek an advisory opinions of a third and credible party like the International Court of Justice or the International Tribunal on the Law of the Sea. However, in order to clarify the claims, the parties concerned are required to have good faith in using international law, particularly the 1982 UNCLOS as the common legal basis.

Once the sovereignty and maritime claims are clarified, the parties may proceed to dispute settlement. Disputes may be settled directly in the form of negotiations or international conference. Meanwhile, disputes can also be settled by accepting the assistance of third parties in ways of mediators, conciliators or even by submitting the disputes to international judicial bodies.

Conflict Management

The possibility of conflicts in the South China Sea comes from two main sources including (1) the lack of information and communication across agencies operating and navigating in the South China Sea and (2) the escalation of activities to exercise their sovereign rights and jurisdiction to fortify the claims.

The first option to address these issues is to increase dialogues for information sharing. Information sharing can be fostered by exchanging point of views in various forums. Experience from the conclusion of the Regional Cooperation

Agreement on Combating Piracy and Arms Robbery against Ships in Asia (ReCAAP) or the establishment of the Singapore Chanqi Command and Control Center show that creating information sharing center is the best way to maintain transparency and thus not only reduces misunderstanding, but also nurtures initiatives for cooperation. Information sharing can also be increased by conducting joint activities between cross agencies. Joint patrol, joint exercise, training course for maritime law enforcement officials and technical assistance are among the joint activities that the parties in the South China Sea may take into consideration.

The second option for dispute management in the South China Sea is to develop rules of engagement for various forces of different countries operating and navigating in the South China Sea. In this regard, there are suggestions to follow the models and lessons from other similar arrangements such as the 1972 U.S.-USSR Agreement on Prevention Incidents at Sea (INCSEA), Western Pacific Naval Symposium (WPNS), Codes for Unalerted Encounters at Sea (CUES) and Convention on International Regulations for Preventing Collisions at Sea 1972 (COLREGS) to develop rules of engagement for naval communication, cooperation and due regard to obligations to avoid unintended incidences at sea.[31] There are also some ideas to integrate such rules of engagement into a Code of Conduct which is currently under formal consultation between ASEAN and China.[32]

The Most Feasible Way Forward

There are several levels and models for better ocean management in the South China Sea available as options for the parties in the South China Sea. The lowest level is to conduct dialogue to identify the issues, share information and initiatives, learn from good practices and lessons through which to narrow the gaps of differences and foster cooperation in the three aspects, i.e. resource, disputes and conflict management. The higher level is enhancing ocean management through a rule-based approach. This includes joint activities, coordination on policy making and implementation as well as cooperation in interpretation and compliance with international rules. The highest level involves institution and mechanism development to enforce those rules and ensure smooth dialogue and cooperation at all levels and in all areas.

Of the three aspects requiring better management in the South China Sea, resource management will require the development of all three levels. At the first level, there are indications that all parties are open for discussion on joint development/cooperation initiatives. However, discussions may be deadlocked on sovereignty issues, for example, if one party continues to insist that "sovereignty is indisputable" and makes any discussion impossible to conclude, thus preventing further management at the second and third levels. This, unfortunately, is what has happened since the last two decades, shelving any possibility for joint development/cooperation.

Dispute management shares similar difficulties with resources management. The parties in the South China Sea dispute have not yet formed any forum for discussion on sovereignty and maritime claims, let alone reaching consensus on joint actions to seek unified interpretation of the law governing the claims or submission to judicial bodies. Most recently, for example, the act of the Philippines in submitting certain aspects of the disputes in the South China Sea to an arbitration formed under Annex VII of UNCLOS faced strong criticism from other party.

Given the stalemate of the two aspects in management of the South China Sea, the only hope is to examine the possibility of conflict management. However, one may argue that the matter in the South China Sea is not lack of rules but improper enforcement of rules. The context in which the U.S. and former USSR concluded INCSEA is different because China's naval capacity today is not yet compatible to that of the former USSR and the current rules have fully developed. States now have the WPNS, COLREGS and CUES.[33] WPNS creates multilateral cooperation framework for navy forces of 20 members and observers of the Western Pacific. COLREGS emphasised on due regard obligation in which "due regard shall be adhered to all dangers of navigation and collision and to any special circumstances, including the limitations of the vessels involved".[34] CUES also emphasises on due regard obligation of COLREGS with the addition of due regard to safety of navigation of civil aircrafts. CUES applies to naval, public ships, submarines and aircraft. In addition, China and the U.S. also have Military Maritime Consultative Agreement (MMCA), a forum facilitating consultations between the U.S. Department of Defense and the PRC Ministry of National Defense for the "purpose of promoting common understandings regarding activities undertaken by their respective maritime and air forces."[35]

Notwithstanding the availability of those rules, it is submitted that they are insufficient to prevent potential conflicts in the South China Sea even in the case that they are well enforced. The WPNS has limited applicable scope to foster communication and cooperation among naval forces. Meanwhile, in South China Sea, operational forces vary and mainly marine law enforcement forces which are beyond the applicable scope of the naval forces of WPNS. COLREGS covers all kinds of vessels but only those navigate in the high sea. In the South China Sea, the overlapping of maritime claims may result in the non-existence of high sea and thus make COLREGS inapplicable. CUES has the most suitable applicable scope, but unfortunately is not yet formally endorsed by WPNS members and is only suggestive. MMCA was used as a platform to criticise the U.S. on arms sales to Taiwan and conducting military activities in Chinese EEZ.

Given that all the above rules are either not applicable, inappropriate or insufficient to regulate the South China Sea, a specifically developed set of rules is still in need for the South China Sea in order to prevent incidences and potential conflicts.

For the set of rules to be developed, adopted and enforced, it might be most viable to make use of the existing regional mechanism such as ASEAN or WPNS. ASEAN has the advantage of being a flexible forum and is already engaging China in developing a Regional Code of Conduct. A set of rules of engagement will well fit a part in the COC. While waiting for progress of the COC process, WPSN may be another ideal option. The WPSN has wider membership and more focused interests in maritime issues, and thus may better serve the purpose of developing such rules. The WPSN also have greater convergence of interests and expertise on these issues and is already working on CUES. Given such balanced membership, mandate and expertise, the WPSN could have more influence on its members on this particular issue. In developing such rules for the South China Sea, all existing regimes and best practices should be taken into account. Extra-regional countries will play significant roles by sharing technical expertise, give political support to the direct stakeholders in the South China Sea and help ensure that any rules developed for the South China Sea meet international standard and are in accordance with international law. China, as the host of WPNS in 2014, may take the lead for the endorsement of CUES. India, a leading member in Indian Ocean Naval Symposium (IONS) and an observer in WPNS may also help by sharing experiences and best practices of conflict management in the Indian Ocean.

Located in the central of the Indo-Pacific, the South China Sea is not only a sea of rich resources, but also a sea of disputes and potential conflicts. Managing the South China Sea for regional stability and sustainable development has long been the quest and desire of the littoral states. State practices offer variety of options for ocean management in the South China Sea. Joint development models, joint fishing and cooperation in marine environment protection are among the models that can be applied for resource management. Establishing forum for discussion and clarification of claims, mediation or conciliation and mechanism for dispute settlement are the ways for dispute management. Rules of engagement, procedures for contingency and channel for communication have proved their success in conflict management in many parts of the world. Despite various options from good practices, the sensitivity of the sovereignty claims still stands as the main obstacle to hinder effort for ocean management in the South China Sea. In such a context, conflict management that does not involve the sovereignty issues may be the most feasible way forward. Countries sharing the common interests of a stable South China Sea may join hands to raise initiative and help the littoral states build rules and mechanisms for better conflict management.

NOTES

1. Alan Dupont, The Environment and Security in Pacific Asia, Oxford University Press, Adelphi Paper, No. 319, 1998, p.53.
2. Ibid.
3. Scott Snyder, Brad Glosserman, and Ralph A. Cossa, "Confidence Building Measures in the South China Sea, Issues and Insight"s, No 2-01, Pacific Forum CSIS, 2001, p.19.
4. Ibid.
5. ICJ Report, 2001, para.202. http://www.icj-cij.org/court/en/reports/report_2000-2001.pdf
6. Article 121 provides:
   1. An island is a naturally formed area of land, surrounded by water, which is above water at high tide.
   2. Except as provided for in paragraph 3, the territorial sea, the contiguous zone, the exclusive economic zone and the continental shelf of an island are determined in accordance with the provisions of this Convention applicable to other land territory.
   3. Rocks which cannot sustain human habitation or economic life of their own shall have no exclusive economic zone or continental shelf.
7. For some discussion of the difficulty in interpreting this Article, see Charney, "Rocks Cannot Sustainable Human Habitation" 93 (1999) AJIL, pp. 863-77 and Kwiatkowska and Soons, "Entitlement to Maritime Areas of Rocks which Cannot Sustain Human Habitation or Economic Life of their Own" 21 (1990) NYIL, 174, pp.139-181. Brown commented on the wording of Article 121(3) that "in its present form, Article 121(3) appears to be perfect recipe for confusion and conflict". For further reference, see Brown E.D., "Rockall and the Limits of National Jurisdiction of the UK" (Part I) (1978) *Marine Policy*, p. 181.
8. Note Verbale of China dated on April 14, 2011, at www.un.org/Depts/los/clcs_new/submissions_files/mysvnm33_09/chn_2011_re_phl_e.pdf
9. The earliest compiled map was found in 1914. For details of the origin and evolution of the map, see Li Jinming and Li Dexia, "The Dotted Line on the Chinese Map of the South China Sea: A Note", 2003, 34, ODIL, p. 287.
10. This is the opinion of some Chinese scholars quoted in Cheng-yi Lin, "Taiwan's South China Sea Policy", 1997, *Asian Survey*, 37(4), p. 323.
11. Bin Bin Jia and Gao Zhiguo, 'The Nine-Dash Line in the South China Sea: History, Status and Implications', *American Journal of International Law,* 107, 2013, pp. 98-124.
12. 660.6 billion in yuan according to the Report on the implementation of central and local budget in 2012 and on draft central and local budgets for 2013. http://news.xinhuanet.com/english/china/2013-03/19/c_132246270.htm However, according to some western sources, this number did not cover the expenditure for importing military equipment. The Department of Defense of the United States reveals that the total military expenditure of China for 2012 falls between $135-215 billion (See Annual Report to Congress: Military and Security Developments Involving the People's Republic of China, 2013, pp.45. http://www.defense.gov/pubs/2013_china_report_final.pdf
13. V. Saighal, 'Is Time Running Out: The Urgency for Full, Final and Equitable Resolution of the South China Sea Imbroglio', Presentation at The South China Sea: Towards a region of Peace, Security and Cooperation.
14. The harassment to Philippines seismic surveys vessel in the Reed Bank in March 2011 and the cut of seismic cable of the Bình Minh 02 and Viking of Vietnam in May and June 2011.
15. *Global Times*, November 25, 2011. Although Chinese spokesman announce that the opinion of Global Times is not the official of Chinese government, the fact that an official voice of the Chinese Communist Party cover this view indicated that at least this was the view of

majority leaders of Beijing or this can be considered as threaten policy of the country. Earlier in June, the Global Times already transmitted a similar message to Vietnam.

16. Report of the United State Energy Information Administration on February 7, 2013. http://www.eia.gov/countries/analysisbriefs/South_China_Sea/south_china_sea.pdf
17. S. Snyder, B. Glosserman, and R.A. Cossa, "Confidence Building Measures in the South China Sea, Issues and Insights", *Pacific Forum CSIS*, 2001, No 2-01, p.4
18. The first incident related to the crash between Chinese aircraft and the military EP3 of the United States on location of 70 miles away from Hainan Island on April 1, 2001. The second concerned the incident between Chinese navy ship and the Impeccable of the United States on the location of 75 nautical miles from the base lines of China on March 8, 2009.
19. Barbara Starr, "US, Chinese warships come dangerously close", *CNN News*, December 13, 2013 at http://edition.cnn.com/2013/12/13/politics/us-china-confrontation/
20. Full text of the declaration at http://news.xinhuanet.com/english/china/2013-11/23/c_132911635.htm
21. It was estimated that by 2010, China will need to import 100 million tonnes of crude oil annually if no large oil fields are found. The oil demand of China has been increasing between 5-5.5 per cent annually since the 1990s, *op. cit.*, note 16.
22. Ulf Linderfalk, *On the Interpretation of Treaties: The Modern International Law As Expressed in the 1969 Vienna Convention of the Law of the Treaties,* Dordrecht, Springer, 2009, p. 6
23. So far, fishing activities in the South China Sea were out of control and led to the fish stock shortage and clashes among fishermen and soldiers among the littoral states. See details, supra, Chapter 1, Section 2.1.
24. Articles 74(3) và 83(3) stipulated that pending final solution, "the States concerned, in a spirit of understanding and cooperation, shall make every effort to enter into provisional arrangements of a practical nature and, during this transitional period, not to jeopardise or hamper the reaching of the final agreement. Such arrangements shall be without prejudice to the final delimitation."
25. For a survey of successful elements for joint development in Asia see Tara Davenport, "Joint Development in Asia: Lessons for sustainable peace in the South China Sea", Presentation at Law in a Sustainable Asia, 8th Asian Law Institution Conference, 2011, Japan, pp.34-39
26. Para.2 of the *Note Verbale* dated on May 7, 2010 of China.
27. *Note Verbale* of China dated on April 14, 2011.
28. Remarks by Foreign Minister Yang Jiechi at the ARF Foreign Ministers' Meeting, at http://www.fmprc.gov.cn/eng/zxxx/t842183.htm
29. Foreign Ministry Spokesperson Jiang Yu's Regular Press Conference on September 15, 2011 at http://www.fmprc.gov.cn/eng/xwfw/s2510/t860126.htm
30. Beckman, Presentation at the second International Workshop "The South China Sea: Towards a Region of Peace, Security and Development", Ho Chi Minh City, 2010.
31. Sam Bateman, "Managing Incidents at Sea", The Strategist, available online at http://www.aspistrategist.org.au/managing-incidents-at-sea/ (Accessed on February 10, 2014); Raul Pedrozo, "Close Encounter at Sea: the USNS Impeccable Incident", *Naval World College Review*, 2009, 62(3), p. 109.
32. Sam Bateman, "Cooperation or Trust in the South China Sea", *RSIS Commentaries*, October 1, 2013.
33. Pete Pedrozo, "The US-China At Sea Incident Agreement: A Recipe for Disater", *Journal of National Security Law and Policy*, Vol. 6, 2012, pp. 207-226.
34. Rule 2 of the Convention.
35. Article 1 of Military Maritime Consultative Agreement (MMCA). This is an agreement between US and China on establishing a consultation mechanism to strengthen military maritime safety.

SECTION VI

Assessing Risks: Cyber and Critical Infrastructure

17

Risk and Resilience: International Approaches to Vulnerable Infrastructure Protection

Tim Legrand and Saskia Hufnagel

Introduction

Modern society is a complex and delicate matrix of individuals, communities, institutions and infrastructures. The health and vitality of society and its political and economic processes is partly a function of its capacity to withstand and rebound from internal and external risks. In recent years, governments have sought to understand and improve this capacity via the voguish concept of 'resilience'. Communities and critical infrastructure operators alike have been enjoined to increase their ability to withstand and rebound from natural and manmade hazards. The threats to the state and society are very real. The flooding that paralysed Queensland, Australia (in late 2010 and early 2011) covered a geographical area that was larger than France and Germany combined. Few who saw the impact and aftermath of the earthquake and tsunami that struck Japan in 2011 could be left in any doubt that modern society is far from impervious from the whims of nature. The Tôhoku earthquake and tsunami killed more than 15,000 people, and devastated the eastern seaboard of Japan to a cost of US$ 235 billion, according to World Bank estimates. What is more, the still unresolved nuclear crisis at the Fukushima nuclear power plant that resulted from the natural disaster has further emphasised the thin line between manmade and natural disasters, and illustrated the interdependencies of modern society and technology. It is apparent that 'Many contemporary disasters follow the lead of complex technology, common-mode design, and multifunctional use of infrastructures' (Rosenthal, 1998, p.152). Ulrich Beck's seminal work on 'risk society' (1992) points out that the process of modernisation itself induces increased vulnerability to society. Society is, thus, increasingly beholden to what Anthony Giddens labels 'manufactured risks' (2003).

Challenges of Globalisation, Government and Society: A Changed Policy Environment

The international dynamics of disasters and crises cannot be neglected. The processes of globalisation bring a suite of benefits and burdens for policy officials charged with responding to man-made threats from terrorism, cyber-attack or industrial accidents and natural threats. On the one hand, increased connectedness brought by frequent and low-cost global travel and communications offers government officials far more opportunities to learn from the experiences of other countries in preparing for disasters. In the acute phase of a disaster, countries benefit from modern capabilities in logistical planning and transport with the deployment of rapid and specialised assistance for disasters. Within hours of an earthquake, or other natural disasters, well-equipped teams of specialised teams—with well-established operating protocols—can be flown in from anywhere in the world; so can search-and-rescue teams, medical teams, food distribution organisations, and so on. The influx of international support has become the norm in the aftermath of a natural disaster, especially in the developing world: the 2004 tsunami in South East Asia and the 2010 Haiti earthquake saw global donations, from governments as well as civil society, surge.

On the other hand, the spill-over effects of disasters can wreak havoc overseas. The global matrix of financial, economic and industrial infrastructures and support lines is becoming increasing interconnected (that is, there are more points of contact, overlap and interaction than ever before), and interdependent (that is, normal modes of operation in one domain are reliant on one or more processes in another domain). For example, an outbreak of salmonella on one farm in Germany in 2011 infected more than 2,000 people across Europe; a dispute over energy contracts in Russia in 2009 stemmed energy supplies across 18 of 27 EU states. Disasters are also often a function of human technology, whether caused by technology's failure, or compounded by a natural event. These include the nuclear disasters of Fukushima and Chernobyl; global climate change; the Avian Bird Flu epidemic, the BP Oil Spill in the Gulf of Mexico; the Global Financial Crisis (2007-8). In one particularly alarming instance, electricity blackouts in Ontario had cascading effects across sectors, knocking out airports, banks, trains and the New York Stock Exchange (Whitman 2005). The global context can be regarded as a double-edged sword for emergency policy officials (Legrand and McConnell, 2012). The benefits brought by enhanced international cooperation, learning, and support is balanced by the increased vulnerabilities wrought by global technology and travel.

This chapter explores the vulnerabilities and strengths brought by increased global inter-connectedness. It pays particular attention to those risks that are particularly *internationalised*: that is (i) the recent rise of international terrorist threat, and (ii) the increased opportunities for and instances of attacks emanating from the cyber sphere. It begins with a conceptual survey of the literature concerned with how institutions learn from one another in the emergency and crisis management sphere. It contends that 'soft' modes of learning and cooperation are more readily adopted than 'hard' regulatory structures. It then develops this conceptual discussion of 'soft' policy collaboration via two case studies of risk management. The first explores the collaborative approach to risk management of terrorism threats that has developed between jurisdictions of different levels: (i) internationally, and (ii) domestically in Australia. The second explores the manner in which the newly internationalised digital commons, cyberspace, has introduced a host of new technical and political risks to the United Kingdom, and highlights the way UK governments have developed risk management strategies in collaboration with the private sector. In each we show that the trend in managing internationalised threats is increasingly reliant on informal cooperation rather than on formal regulatory instruments, both across states and between the public and private sector.

Institutional Learning about Crisis Management

Public policy literature has recently been animated in debate over the mechanisms and explanations of how and why policy ideas, such as emergency policy, are transmitted. For some authors, crises spur organisational learning and change (Boin et al., 2006; Deverall, 2009; Brändström et al., 2004). A number of authors further seek to unpack this process of learning about crisis. For example, Deverall (2009) explores the mechanisms and processes by which officials learn from crisis. Following the work of Rose (1991) on lesson-drawing, Deverall suggest that a lesson is constructed on the 'basis of experience and thus "requires a cause-and-effect model", which shows how the lesson can achieve a desired goal if adopted' (2009, p.180). Elliot and Macpherson warn that learning about crisis remains a uncertain undertaking: 'enacting learning successfully is difficult given the unpredictable nature of crisis, the variety of contexts, and the array of people who interpret such ambiguous situations' (2010, pp. 572-3). Moreover, the vernacular of crisis and disasters remains somewhat nebulous. Indeed, one of the most prominent scholars in this area comments that 'some issues and questions in the disaster area—including the basic one of what constitutes a disaster—are not primarily matters of empirical determination; rather they rest fundamentally on conceptual definitions and theoretical approaches used, either explicitly or implicitly' (Quarantelli, 1985, p.42). This ambiguity has not stopped the recent flow of articles seeking to draw out and communicate lessons from disasters. For example, Schwartz and Schwartz draw out a series of lessons for the USA from the example of China's management of the SARS outbreak that began in 2002 (2010). Aimed at informing the global governance of disasters, Takeda and Helms similarly distil a series of insights from the management of the Asian Tsunami of 2004 (2006), while Farazmand (2007), Pyles (2009) and Moore et al. (2009) derive lessons for government from the organisational responses to Hurricane Katrina in 2005.

Largely, the literature looking at the lessons arising from disasters focuses on the substantive rather than theoretical element of learning. For example, Miccoli and Destefano (2010) offer a model of transnational and interdisciplinary sharing of lessons arising from disasters 'to improve the ability to control, reduce or eliminate risk and to establish a common strategy between different countries' (2010, p.411). While their approach is focused on deriving themes for an international audience, the theoretical frame of reference of international policy learning, however, is neglected. Authors who directly address the international dynamic of learning from disaster, such as Moore et al. (2009), similarly fail to assert a theoretical framework for international learning. Moore et al., for example, in an otherwise comprehensive overview of lessons learned from a series of case studies, provide a 'synthesis of exemplary practices' (2009, p.16), yet do not locate this synthesis within an explicit theoretical approach to how organisations learn from overseas. Tierney argues that research on disaster is in a fractured state, and focuses primarily on building knowledge of disasters via a case-by-case approach. Research, Tierney claims, 'must locate the study of disasters within broader theoretical frameworks, including in particular those concerned with risk, organisations and institutions, and society-environment interactions' (Tierney 2007, p. 520-21, cited in Williams, 2009, p. 1119).

Case Study 1: International and Australian Cooperative Approaches to Delivering Security

Internationally, regionally, and within national federal systems, terrorism has had a considerable impact on the formation of law enforcement cooperation strategies between jurisdictions. The strategies applied to achieve cooperation differ with regard to the level of formalisation and their reliance on existing political structures. Within the international sphere, the main institution to coordinate efforts is Interpol; regionally, the Europol agency is a prominent player; and nationally the Australian Federal Police (AFP) will be addressed in this essay with a view to the fight against terrorism.

With regard to terminology, the terms 'formal' and 'informal' cooperation strategies to combat terrorism across jurisdictional borders have been attributed particular meanings. 'Formal' strategies are defined as those based on binding legal frameworks, while 'informal' strategies are those based on non-binding legal frameworks, or on no valid legal basis at all. One could claim that the crossing from formal to informal is equal to the transition from legal to illegal. However, in the cross-border policing of terrorism, the distinction is not that simple. Informality is not necessarily illegal, although there is often only a fine line between the two. This chapter puts a focus on the hazy distinction between formality, legality, informality and illegality, and assesses how they could be more constructively balanced.

International Cooperation

At the international level, the preferred models of cooperation between sovereign nation states involve informal structures. These rely on police-to-police cooperation through informal networks and informal police cooperation mechanisms, most prominently Interpol. However, formalisation has, to a certain degree, taken place through the use of liaison officers between different police forces, whose deployment is usually based on bilateral formal agreements and regulated through unilateral national legislation.[1]

With regard to the development of international police cooperation mechanisms, terrorism can be considered one of the main drivers throughout history. An example for an international cooperation mechanism that was, at least in its very beginnings, intended to support the fight against 'terrorism'—in those days it was termed a response to 'radical political opposition'—was Interpol. Interpol could generally be considered the first manifestation of a coordinated multilateral effort in the fight against international crime, and its establishment can be traced to the late 19th century.[2] Interpol was created as the first permanent international body of security cooperation in 1923, and established in Vienna as the International Criminal Police Commission (ICPC).[3] The aim of the organisation was the creation of stability in Western Europe in the aftermath of the effects of World War I and the Russian Revolution.[4] In 1946, following the Nazification of the ICPC, the organisation was re-established in Paris, and emerged, in its current form, after 1989 in Lyon.[5] Interpol is not a 'formal' police cooperation initiative as its constitution is not binding, and its members are not states but police forces.

Interpol today has limited competence in relation to the fight against terrorism, although the sphere of its duties has shifted in that direction after the terrorist events in the 1970s and 1980s in Europe. According to Deflem, the goal of ICPC (and later Interpol), as expressed at the Vienna Congress of 1923, was to 'establish and enhance mutual assistance between all police within the framework of the laws of their respective states and to establish all institutions suited to fight against "ordinary crime".'[6] It is, therefore, much broader than Europol today, which focuses mainly on 'organised crime, terrorism and other forms of serious crime'.[7] However, Interpol, unlike Europol, is considered a truly international cooperation mechanism for the purpose of this essay since membership is open to all nations of the world. The limitation of Interpol to 'ordinary crime' exists because Article 3 of the Interpol Constitution[8] forbids involvement in political, military, religious and racial matters. As a result, unlike Europol, Interpol could initially not play a prominent role in the fight against terrorism.[9] However, the heightened sensitivity towards terrorism in the late 1970s and 1980s intensified global efforts to promote cross-border police cooperation, for example, by re-interpreting Article 3 of the Interpol Convention to enable co-operation in the investigation of terrorism as a category of 'political crime'.[10] Today, Interpol participates in terrorism investigations due to a changed interpretation of Article 3 of its Constitution, and has, since 2002, formed its own taskforce to assist member states.

Interpol can be considered the most prominent international police cooperation mechanism. Its nature is informal as the agreement of police forces to cooperate, considering the diverse standards of the police participants, cannot be enforced in the same way as between a more homogenous group of states with similar standards of policing and criminal justice, as well as common value systems (such as within the EU). This argument can also be more directly linked to human rights standards. Countries with a strong commitment to high human rights standards cannot (at least legally) commit their police forces to cooperate with countries or police with considerably lower standards. It could hence be said that, rather than human rights standards themselves, the differences between these standards have become a legal impediment to international police cooperation.

Another international strategy that was from the outset influenced by 'terrorism' and is now employed to deal with a vast array of serious crimes is the 'liaison officer' mechanism. Before becoming an official strategy for police cooperation in many countries, police-to-police cooperation between different nations was an informal strategy, restricted more by sovereignty than human rights concerns. In the 19th century, police action across borders was mostly related to so-called 'political offences' and many covert operations in foreign countries at the time were not even cooperative but rather operated as unilateral espionage operations.[11] However, such political policing must have involved at least some bilateral and multilateral contacts between police, for example, through the 'personal correspondence system' between police officials and the distribution of alerts relating to wanted suspects.[12]

In Europe, the practice of deploying police liaison officers to other countries only started in the 1970s.[13] The establishment and initial need for liaison officers differed according to the historical and political context of each country establishing them. In Germany, Sweden and the Netherlands, for example, the establishment of police liaisons was closely linked to drug law enforcement, and their first officers were posted to Thailand.[14]

From the legal perspective, liaison officers are subject to the national legislation of their home country. They are not part of the police of the receiving state, hence they cannot exercise enforcement powers on foreign territory; but their main task is to exchange information and coordinate investigation efforts.[15] Their deployment can be based on specific bilateral or multilateral treaties and agreements, depending on whether the liaison is deployed to one or more countries or is derived from more general bilateral agreements on diplomatic relations.[16] The binding international legal frameworks (where they are specific) can, in addition to the national legislation, determine the scope of the deployment, and can either limit or broaden the liaison officer's tasks. With a view to human rights protection, at least from a purely legal perspective, it could be concluded that no information can be exchanged or investigation supported that would infringe such rights in the liaison's home or host country. Of course, this view is rather legal and theoretical as liaison officers are equipped with extensive professional discretion to enable them to adapt to situational factors in different systems. A major advantage of their employment is considered to be the informality with which they can cooperate with other jurisdictions.[17] However, as a cooperation strategy, international police liaison officers are legally bound by national, bilateral and/or multilateral legal frameworks, which aim at safeguarding the respective procedural rules of deploying and hosting nations.

It can be concluded that the two international police cooperation strategies examined here with regard to the policing of terrorism are governed by a high degree of informality. Under the mode of deployment, the number of liaison officers within EU member states alone has risen exponentially in the past 40 years.[18] This indicates that the strategy is considered beneficial to cross-border law enforcement. While bound by national legislation, there seems to be a high degree of professional autonomy and informality afforded to these missions. It could even be claimed that cooperation with countries with considerably different human rights standards would not be possible without a certain degree of informality and a certain risk of human rights infringements. However, countries with high human rights standards (such as EU member states), seem to accept this risk in the fight against terrorism and other cross-border crime. However, instruments limiting the risk of human rights abuses are also in place, such as the UK Foreign and Commonwealth Office, Overseas Security Justice Assistance (OSJA) Human Rights Guidance 2011.[19]

In the case of Interpol, it could be said that cooperation between such a large number of state parties would not be possible on a formal level. While two or three states with similar legal systems, policing and human rights standards might agree on binding legal rules to enable police cooperation and prevent human rights abuses, this is less likely for all nations of the world working within Interpol. The problem here is not whether information exchange through this informal international strategy has the potential to infringe human rights (which it has without a doubt), but whether the efficiency of the agency is from the start limited by contradictory national standards that will restrain police from using the agency under national legislation. It could, therefore, be said that the more international a cooperation strategy is, the less formal it has to be.

Regarding the interaction between terrorism and international police cooperation, it can be concluded that while the two strategies discussed have terrorism as an incentive for their earliest periods of establishment, it is only one of their many tasks today. However, it can be said for international cooperation in general, and for terrorism in particular, that the safeguarding of human rights protection remains a serious issue in this field.[20]

Australian Strategies for Police Cooperation

Another tier of interaction between police cooperation in the area of terrorism and the protection of procedural rights is observed in the Australian federal system. As an example of a national jurisdiction, Australia is a federation of states comprised of six states, two territories, and a federal jurisdiction, each of which has its own criminal and criminal procedure laws, and is policed by its own police force. The Constitution gives the power to legislate in the area of criminal law and policing to the states. Police cooperation between the states and territories takes place predominantly at the informal police-to-police level though, in the last decade, a small number of bilateral and multilateral formal initiatives have evolved. None of these initiatives have, however, been adopted at the federal level, as has happened in the EU context.

At the Australian federal level, policing across various jurisdictions is facilitated by two federal law enforcement agencies: the Australian Federal Police (AFP) and the Australian Crime Commission (ACC).[21] It is surprising to see that in the Australian interstate context, fewer attempts to harmonise the cooperation mechanism and cross-border policing practices—both formal and informal—exist than in the EU between sovereign nation states.

Since Australia became a federation in 1901, different strategies have been created to enable the policing of terrorism offences across internal jurisdictions. The most prominent federal strategy to overcome cross-jurisdictional issues closely linked to terrorist events is the creation of federal law enforcement agencies. While this essay focuses on federal strategies, it needs to be stressed that informal, agency-to-agency cooperation has always existed in Australia. However, the policing of terrorism offences falls under the competences of federal agencies, which is why informal cross-jurisdictional cooperation is not discussed.

Similar to the international and EU cooperation strategies, Australia's first 'federal' law enforcement agencies had a rather weak, if any, legal basis. The first federal agency to be established was the Commonwealth Police Force, and its creation is the subject of many stories. A common account is that Prime Minister William 'Billy' Hughes initiated it in 1917, after he was struck by an egg in the Queensland town of Warwick (the famous 'Warwick egg').[22] Becoming frustrated with the lack of investigative efforts of the 'terrorist' incident by the Queensland police, he promptly created a Commonwealth Police Force, competent to investigate offences against federal law contained in the War Precautions Act, 1914.[23] More complex accounts of the political forces that led to the creation of the Commonwealth Police have highlighted the national government's concern to exercise surveillance over political opponents, particularly during the First and Second World Wars.[24] However, the legal basis for such a law enforcement strategy would only be created 40 years later by the Commonwealth Police Act, 1957.

Like the EU, Australia has experienced an increased emphasis on the importance of coordinating policing efforts between jurisdictions during the second half of the 20th century.[25] A particularly important stimulus for this development in the Australian context followed the bombing of the Hilton Hotel in Sydney, in 1978. This is when the Australian government realised that an organisation was needed to deal with issues such as terrorism at a national level.[26] The result was the creation of the AFP and several other national common police services.[27] Unlike its less stable predecessors, the AFP was established with a solid legal basis, the Australian Federal Police Act, 1979 (Cth). In this way, similar to the creation of TREVI, terrorism was a main driver for establishing new policing institutions in Australia.

While there are some informal police cooperation mechanisms at the national level,[28] and even some bilateral and multilateral mostly informal initiatives,[29] federal agencies—and the AFP in particular—are the most prominent cross-jurisdictional institutions to fight terrorism in Australia. Cross-border cooperation between state and territory police is, however, also supported by harmonisation initiatives in the area of criminal procedure and the federalisation of terrorism offences. Model laws were developed by a Joint Working Group (JWG) on National Investigative Powers, and published in a Report of the Leader's Summit on Terrorism and Multijurisdictional Crime: *Cross-Border Investigative Powers for Law Enforcement* in November 2003. The JWG had envisaged a much broader range of model laws extending beyond mutual recognition of forensic procedures and search warrants to include surveillance devices and controlled operations.

The informal modes of police cooperation are increasingly relevant given that there is no one model of legal harmonisation in Australia. In relation to terrorism, federal law predominates, and has involved the referral of powers by the States to the Commonwealth. That said, the federal definition of 'terrorism' has been incorporated into legislation enacted to combat terrorism at the State level. In relation to the federal serious and organised crime laws introduced by the Crimes Legislation Amendment (Serious and Organised Crime) Act, 2010 (Cth), these have been promoted to the States as a 'model law' to criminalise conduct that falls outside the jurisdiction of the 'federal' offences.

Focusing on the competences of the AFP in the area of terrorism investigations across state borders, it needs to be conceded that, despite the AFP being a fully formalised strategy bound by procedural rules and high human rights standards, problems have arisen in relation to terrorism investigations. The most prominent example is the case of the Indian national and Muslim, Mohamed Haneef, a Gold Coast doctor, related to two terrorist suspects allegedly involved in attempted bombings in London and Glasgow on 28-30 June 2007. Haneef was arrested on 2 July 2007, detained under terrorism powers for 12 days, charged with terrorism offences—which later collapsed—his visa was consequently cancelled, and he was transferred to immigration detention where he was held for another 15 days before being released and allowed to leave the country.[30] The alleged slackness of the police investigation was blamed for producing a rather weak case against the suspect. More than any other case in the history of the AFP, this event—and the ensuing highly embarrassing public inquiry into the conduct of the investigation—led to an enormous wave of criticism towards the federal agency, and to a critique of its role, functions, and powers.[31]

Australian State police did not 'blame' the AFP for these errors but stressed that the investigative experience of AFP officers might not have matched their breadth of duties and responsibilities in such investigations.[32] The issue in this example was neither the diversity of procedural rules and human rights safeguards in relation to counter-terrorism investigations in the Australian system, nor a resulting lack of trust and reluctance to cooperate by the different police forces, but the inability of the competent police force to adhere to national standards. With a view to the formalisation of trans-jurisdictional terrorism investigations, and in particular the comparison between the different international, regional and domestic strategies addressed in this essay, it can be concluded that even the highly formalised and centralised nature of a cross-border policing strategy, such as a federal agency, does not prevent the occurrence of human rights abuses, and that police competences and cultures will always play a role. Thus, as with international policing cooperation, efforts at collaboration between Australian policing agencies are being led, in the first instance, by informal agreements. This is partly a consequence of the necessity to find ways for inter-state agencies to work together to find a balance between security and the upholding of respective state laws.

Case Study 2: Managing the Diversifying Cyber Threat in the UK

The potential economic gains offered by an interconnected cyber economy is offset by a buoyant online criminal economy, and a swathe of overseas groups, including state-agencies, taking advantage of the anonymity of cyberspace.[33] Cornish et al. call attention to this 'heterogeneous nature of cyber threats' (2011, p. ix), which represent a widening array of risks in today's digital economy. Recognising these threats, the UK government has expressed concerns over the growth of cyber crimes including data and identity theft, money laundering, fraud, and intellectual property theft. Meanwhile, the age-old games of state espionage continue to manifest in attempts by hostile intelligence agencies to gain illicit access into government and private ICT systems to gain intelligence on or even attack critical infrastructure. In addition, the UK government has expressed fears that non-state entities might seek to hack into corporate and government networks to 'steal information or damage computer systems to serve political agendas' (NAO, 2013, p. 6). Some, such as the former director of the US National Security Agency, Michael Hayden, have been contemptuous of such groups, describing them as 'nihilists, anarchists, activists, Lulzsec, Anonymous, twentysomethings who haven't talked to the opposite sex in five or six years'.[34]

The itinerant cyber threats seem to be as diverse as they are pervasive and ambiguous. It is difficult to come by clarity over the precise character of the individuals and groups concerned in cyber attacks, whether or not they are of a criminal or political nature. Often, familiar caricatures are easier to draw on: As the US Assistant Secretary of Defence, William Lynn, put it: 'a couple dozen talented programmers wearing flip-flops and drinking Red Bull can do a lot of damage'.[35] However, the reality may be markedly different. With considerably greater resources, the most prolific actors involved in cyber attacks are state-sponsored groups operating within a quasi-legal mandate. For example, the digital security firm Mandiant (2013) detected a distinctive pattern in a series of cyber attacks on US government and corporate systems that corresponded to a Monday to Friday, 9am to 5pm working week in Shanghai, China. The protagonists of the attacks were identified as 2nd Bureau of the People's Liberation Army (PLA) General Staff Department's (GSD) 3rd Department or Unit 61398.

The widening array of threats in cyber space continues to pose a heightened risk to government, society and business. As individuals spend an increasing proportion of time socialising, communicating and shopping online, the opportunities to fall victim to cyber crime also increase. And so individuals are becoming increasingly familiar with warnings to protect themselves from digital identity theft, online credit card fraud, computer viruses and malware designed to corrupt home computers. The UK government also suffers considerable and regular cyber attacks: as many as 33,000 cyber attacks a month from criminals and state-sponsored groups, according to the Minister for Political and Constitutional Reform, Chloe Smith.[36] Criminal groups regularly attack companies' servers and intranets to exfiltrate intellectual property, research, financial data and much more. For example, in September 2013, the Metropolitan Police's Central e-Crime Unit reportedly foiled an attempt by several individuals to gain remote control of the computers of a London branch of the bank Santander, and steal vast sums of money. A report by the Cabinet Office calculated the cumulative financial impact of cyber crime to the UK costs to be around £27 billion annually (Cabinet Office, 2011a), including an estimated £9.2 billion loss from the theft of Intellectual Property from UK businesses. Significantly, the 2011 report argued that across government and civil society 'efforts to tackle [cyber crime] seem to be more tactical than strategic' (2011a, p. 3) and, moreover: 'The problem is compounded by the lack of a clear reporting mechanism and the perception that, even if crimes were reported, little can be done' (2011a, p.3).

One of the major fears associated with cyberspace is the prospect of cyber-terrorism. The concern, and it is one that has not manifested to date, is that politically-motivated non-state groups might, through use illicit use of digital systems, sabotage or disrupt critical infrastructures and potentially cause physical injury to individuals. Though at the present time we are more likely to find cyber-terror plots in the imaginations of Hollywood script-writers than in the real world, there are some indications that such attacks might be possible. According to the digital security company McAfee, 'nearly two-thirds of critical infrastructure companies report regularly finding malware designed to sabotage their systems' (2011, p.6).[37] The prospect of cyber-terrorism also seems to occupy the fears of IT professionals: A 2012 survey by Ixia of the Information Systems Security Association's membership,[38] found that 79 per cent expected a major cyber terror attack within 2013. Though 2013 passed without any such attacks (that are known to the public, at least), the Ixia survey underlines the very real concern amongst those most concerned in the protection of cyber systems that not only might such attacks be attempted, but that they might be successful.

To date, the UK government's strategy to counter cyber threats has been predicated on a risk-based approach:

> In a globalised world where all networked systems are potentially vulnerable and where cyber attacks are difficult to detect, there can be no such thing

> as absolute security. We will therefore apply a risk-based approach to prioritising our response (Cabinet Office, 2011b, p. 22)

Crucially, the strategy to defend government and corporate systems using a risk-based approach requires an unprecedented level of collaboration between the public and private sectors. The astonishing rise and evolution of cyber-space has occurred within a space of just thirty years and has been driven almost entirely by non-government actors. As a result, governments around the world must rely only the private sector to provide information on emerging cyber threats. This perspective is underlined by the UK's Cabinet Office: 'Much of the infrastructure we need to protect is owned and operated by the private sector. The expertise and innovation required to keep pace with the threat will be business-driven' (Cabinet Office, 2011b, p. 22). As such, the nation's digital security has become a shared responsibility between the public and private sectors and dominated by the language of 'risk assessment'. Whether or not the risk-based approach will substantially decrease material threats is contested. According to Amoore and de Goode, governments' deployment of 'risk assessment' as a means to address contemporary threats is merely a means to ensure that 'the appearance of securability and manageability is maintained' (2008, p. 9). Given that few, if any, governments have a firm grasp on the nature and potential of threats in cyberspace, it might not be surprising if policy officials attempt to put the burden of security provision onto the private sector. Indeed, the UK government certainly recognises that its prevailing governance instruments are not quite up to the job:

> Today, information and cyber security threats are becoming increasingly complex and are evolving at a rapid pace. At the same time, traditional risk management regimes used by government are no longer adequate to mitigate against this threat (Cabinet Office, 2011c, p. 53).

One of the UK government's earliest descriptions of cyber threats underlines how policy officials struggled to accurately articulate the unfamiliar parlance of cyber-space: 'Hacking or "cyber-terrorism" can also be done for political reasons by terrorist groups, agencies of foreign states or activist groups' (CSIA, Cabinet Office, 2004, p. 7). The inaccurate conflation of 'hacking' and 'cyber-terrorism' is illustrative of how, just ten years ago, policy officials were still grappling with the fundamental concepts of the new digital economy and its incumbent risks. As a result, policy on the subject has avoided nuance and complexity and, instead, opted to subsume the range of threats together within the same governance framework:

> Activity in cyberspace will continue to evolve as a direct national security and economic threat, as it is reined as a means of espionage and crime, and continues to grow as a terrorist enabler, as well as a military weapon for use by states and possibly others (UK Cabinet Office, 2011b, p. 29).

In other areas of policy, such as industry, education or health, the government has had decades of experience and experiment to draw upon to develop its governance strategies. Indeed, even in these portfolios, governance mistakes occur regularly. Yet, the nascent form of digitisation and its influence on the economy, society and politics has forced government to urgently develop new policies without the benefit of experience. Nevertheless, in terms of its role as the principal agent of national security, the UK government has developed an entirely new governance architecture in little more than ten years. In 2001, the Communications-Electronics Security Group (CESG) undertook a review of government data systems and, in its recommendations, laid the foundations for the first whole-of-government digital data protection strategy. The CESG recommended the creation of a 'central sponsor' for digital security.[39] To meet the CESG's recommendation, the government created a governance architecture specified in the 2003 Information Assurance (IA) strategy, later in 2007 to become the National Information Assurance Strategy (NIAS). Oversight of the strategy was maintained by the Central Sponsor for Information Assurance (CSIA), based in the Cabinet Office, which had responsibility to ensure 'risks to the information systems underpinning key public interests are appropriately managed'.[40] The NIAS was revamped in 2009 with the publication of the UK's first Cyber Security Strategy.[41] The Strategy described cyberspace as the latest vector of security in the international landscape:

> Just as in the 19th century we had to secure the seas for our national safety and prosperity, and in the 20th century we had to secure the air, in the 21st century we also have to secure our advantage in cyber space (2009, p. 5).

The Strategy recognised both the bounty of economic and social rewards offered by cyber space and the associated uncertainty and threats in the new environment:

> The low cost and largely anonymous nature of cyber space makes it an attractive domain for use by those who seek to use cyber space for malicious purposes. These include criminals, terrorists, and states, whether for reasons of espionage, influence or even warfare (2009, p.12).

Along with the new 2009 Strategy, the UK government established the Cyber Security Operations Centre (CSOC) and the Office of Cyber Security (now the Office of Cyber Security and Information Assurance (OCSIA)). CSOC operates as a multi-agency unit with a mandate to 'monitor developments in cyberspace...analyse trends and to improve technical response coordination to cyber incidents' (p. 17), while the role of OSCIA is to oversee the Cyber Security Strategy and its constituent cross-government programmes from within the UK Cabinet Office. In 2010, the government published its 2010 National Security Strategy (NSS) and Strategic Defence and Security Review (SDSR), in which cyber threats were described for the first time as a Tier 1 threat to the UK. The SDSR boosted the resources available to cyber security with a 4-year allocation of £860 million to a cross-government National Cyber Security Programme (NCSP) tasked to enhance the resilience of the UK's digital architecture. The National Cyber Security Programme is led by the Office of Cyber Security and Information Assurance (OCSIA) within the Cabinet Office.

In 2011, the UK published an updated UK Cyber Security Strategy (Cabinet Office, 2011b). This strategy, which may be updated in 2015, sets out the full programme of government initiatives to address threats emanating from cyber space, and sets out the responsibility for implementing the Cyber Security Strategy (CSS). Six central departments and nine further government organisations have shared responsibilities for delivering elements of the CSS. Recognising that 'much of the UK's critical infrastructure is not in Government hands but is owned and managed by the private sector' (Cabinet Office, 2011b, p. 28), the CSS articulates the future of the governance of the UK's digital architecture, especially in terms of critical national infrastructure (CNI). Since the 1980s, the landscape of CNI in the UK has changed markedly through the process of privatisation. With the majority of CNI owned by private enterprise, there is no longer a *common* strategy to ensure the integrity of infrastructure security. Indeed, the digital control systems that are a fundamental operational element of CNI systems across utilities, communications, transport, and so on, are diverse, do not use common digital security protocols, and are embedded in a fragmented array of enterprise management systems. As a consequence, there is little prospect of government developing a unified digital border to protect all CNI from cyber attacks. To overcome this problem, the government has instead instituted a programme of government technical advice on security (against digital and physical threats) for owners and operators of national infrastructure. The Centre for the Protection of National Infrastructure (CPNI) core aim is to provide, 'advice on protective security measures and direct technical support to organisations within the national infrastructure' and achieves this aim in two ways.

The first is the Information Exchange Mechanism. This is a process by which government and owners/operators of critical infrastructure can share information on emerging cyber threats between one another. There are 14 IEMs grouped via their sectors: aerospace and defence manufacturers, communications industry personnel security, civil nuclear sector SCADA, financial services, managed service providers, Northern Ireland, network security, pharmaceutical industries, SCADA and control systems, space industries, security researchers, transport sector, vendor security and water security. The CPNI uses the IEMs to deliver both general and specific advice on emerging threats to the sectors. Crucially, it is reliant on the active participation of the private sector owners/operators, who enjoy a collective benefit in pooling their intelligence.

The second, announced in August 2013, is the Cyber Incident Response Scheme. The scheme involves (i) the development of industry-wide cyber-security standards managed by the Council of Registered Ethical Security Testers, and (ii) the deployment of a team dedicated to 'responding to sophisticated, targeted attacks against networks of national significance'.[42]

The development of the UK's strategy for protecting, in particular, critical infrastructure reflects the broader dilemma posed by cyber threats. The development of a whole-of-government programme of cyber security is a natural means of consolidating security resources: it has allowed the government to bring all government services within one 'citadel' of protection under the mandate of a single office, OCSIA. Yet the fragmentation of digital security across the private sector makes it unfeasible for government to directly provide the same protection against hostile cyber threats. As a consequence, the decision to *facilitate* security via intelligence advice through the CPNI, and only *ad hoc* support for specific threats, reflects a new era for infrastructure management.

This new era of infrastructure protection was foreshadowed in the 2011 Cyber Security Strategy, which stated that 'government capacity...is not sufficient or sufficiently scaled to meet the growing security challenges of the digital age' (emphasis in original, Cabinet Office, 2011b, p. 18). Thus the onus of security is placed firmly not only on individual owners/operators of critical infrastructure but on whole sectors to act collectively to provide mutual support through IEMs. Yet the intention, while laudable and potentially inevitable given the challenges of digital security governance, rests on some unstable and unproven assumptions that private sectors owners/operators will always choose to share information. As the OECD has claimed:

> The reluctance of some private owners of critical infrastructure to disclose information beyond what is required by industry regulations presents a challenge to country risk managers who are tasked with taking accurate account of the capabilities of critical infrastructure systems to withstand disasters.[43]

Conclusion

There is a clear urgency for the state to respond to the growing internationalisation of threats to civil society from terrorism, crime, and cyberspace. Yet, the marked expansion and diffusion of these threats across the world has left the legal and regulatory capacity of the state far behind to tackle these. As a consequence, informal cooperation between states, agencies and the private sector has led the way. Our first case study has shown that it has become manifest that terrorism and police cooperation are closely interlinked. Many international, regional and national police cooperation strategies that exist today had their basis in some 'terrorist' event or the 'policing of violent political opponents'.[44]

However, significant differences remain between international, regional and federal cooperation mechanisms. The result of the comparison is partly logical and partly surprising. While it would have been expected that the Australian federal system, due to its similarity of procedural rules, language, police standards, organisational cultures, human rights values and, most of all, a highly formalised and centralised common police agency with enforcement powers, would have had the most congruent relationship between the trans-jurisdictional policing of terrorism and human rights, problems became apparent that equally create the potential for human rights infringements. More generally, this insight leads to the conclusion that the more states with differing procedural and human rights standards are involved in a counter-terrorism police cooperation initiative, the less cooperation can rely on highly formalised legal structures, leading to an inherent threat to the maintenance of procedural rules and human rights. Even when cooperation mechanisms are formalised, they are frequently supplemented with informal cooperation structures. This becomes particularly apparent in the example of international liaison officers where informal methods are embedded to assure swift and flexible information exchange for practitioners.

Likewise, in the cyber sphere, the diminished capacity of the state to directly deliver or control outcomes for the public interest is clearly reflected in current approaches to tackling cyber-threats and cyber-terrorism. With much of the national critical infrastructure now firmly held in private hands, government's power to manage external threats to the resilience of these systems carrying significant public interest has been diminished, with the worrying repercussion that government is now reliant on voluntary compliance: there is no legal obligation for corporate owners to disclose cyber-security vulnerabilities or even security breaches. Though the UK government has sought to manage this relationship by providing secure threat information-sharing channels, it is far from clear whether these will become effective. Second, research by Chatham House on how cyber risks are managed by owners and operators of national critical infrastructure shows extant tensions between security, accountability and profitability.

> ...these same organisations were willing, for a variety of resource and other reasons, to accept an unexpectedly high level of cyber security-related risk. There was even a tendency, as noted earlier, to distance the handling of this risk from the authority and responsibility of the board or senior management (Cornish et al, 2011, p.13).

So, while informal cooperation holds a host of benefits in combating internationalised threats, there remain potential trade-offs. In the policing and counter-terrorism sphere, there are clear vulnerabilities to human rights that emerge in the milieu of differing legal standards across states. Meanwhile, the informal cooperation between the state and the private sector in protecting against cyber threats is unable to overcome the potential for businesses to privilege profitability over critical infrastructure security. These remaining challenges, we contend, portend a future of *changed* rather than *reduced* vulnerabilities to the threats to civil society from belligerents operating in terrorist cells or cyber-space.

NOTES

1. L. Block, *From Politics to Policing: The Rationality Gap in EU Council Policy-Making* (Eleven International Publishing, 2011), pp. 166-182.
2. C. Fijnaut, 'International Policing in Europe: Its Present Situation and Future' in J. P. Brodeur (ed.), *Comparisons in Policing: An International Perspective* (Aldershot, 1995), pp. 115, 116.
3. J. Occhipinti, *The Politics of EU Police Cooperation: Towards an European FBI?* (Lynne Rieners Publishers, 2003), p. 29.
4. C. Fijnaut, ibid. p. 2, p. 116.
5. M. Deflem, *Policing World Society* (Oxford University Press, 2002), p. 179; J. Occhipinti, ibid. pp. 3, 29.
6. M. Deflem, ibid. pp. 5, 127; W.J. Leamy, 'International Co-operation through the Interpol System to Counter Illicit Drug Trafficking' (1983), 35 *Bulletin on Narcotics* 55.
7. See Art 3 of the Council Decision of 06 April 2009, 'Establishing the European Police Office (Europol)', [2009] OJ L 121/37 (the 'Europol Decision'). Previously, under Art 2 of the Europol Convention, 'terrorism, unlawful drug trafficking and other serious forms of international crime' (Council Act of 26 July 1995, Drawing up the Convention based on Art K.3 of the Treaty on European Union on the Establishment of a European Police Office (Europol Convention), [1995] OJ C316/2).
8. See Art 3 of the International Criminal Police Organisation-INTERPOL Constitution, adopted 1956.
9. See, in relation to the competences of Interpol, C. Fijnaut, 'Policing Western Europe: Interpol, Trevi and Europol' (1992), 15 *Police Studies International Review*, p. 102.
10. See Art 3 of the International Criminal Police Organisation-INTERPOL Constitution (adopted 1956): 'It is strictly forbidden for the Organisation to undertake any intervention or activities of a political, military, religious or racial character.' See also, the interpretation of Art 3: INTERPOL, *Neutrality: Article 3 of the Interpol Constitution*, http://www.interpol.int/About-INTERPOL/Legal-materials/Neutrality-Article-3-of-the-Constitution, accessed 7 November 2011. See further, M. Deflem and L.C. Maybin, 'Interpol and the Policing of International Terrorism: Developments and Dynamics since September 11', in L. L. Snowden and B. C. Whitsel (eds.), *Terrorism: Research, Readings and Realities* (Pearson, 2005), pp. 176-178.
11. M. Deflem, ibid. pp. 5, 47; L. Clutterbuck, 'Countering Irish Republican Terrorism in Britain: Its Origin as a Police Function' (2006), 18 *Terrorism and Political Violence*, pp. 95, 97.
12. M. Deflem, ibid. pp. 5, 47.
13. L. Block, ibid. pp. 1, 170-171.
14. Ibid at 171; see in relation to Germany Bundeskriminalamt, 'Verbindungsbeamte des BKA im Ausland', at http://www.bka.de/DE/DasBKA/Aufgaben/InternationaleFunktion/

Verbindungsbea mte/verbindungsbeamte__node.html?__nnn=true, accessed 26 December 2011.

15. Ibid. p. 166.
16. The use of liaison officers posted abroad by law enforcement agencies of Member States of the European Union is commonly encouraged and facilitated (Decision 2003/170/JHA, 27 February 2003). The Nordic States also collectively send liaison officers to host States.
17. L. Block, ibid. pp. 1, 170.
18. Ibid. p. 172: from the first deployment in 1971 to 541 posted liaison officers in 2008.
19. See http://www.fco.gov.uk/resources/en/pdf/global-issues/human-rights/osja-guidance-51211.pdf, accessed 5 September 2012.
20. See examples for the lack of communication and coordination between law enforcement agencies leading to human rights abuses and breaches of sovereignty: *R (Mohamed) vs Secretary of State for Foreign and Commonwealth Affairs* [2010] EWCA Civ 158; Council of Europe, Committee on Legal Affairs and Human Rights Report, *Alleged Secret Detentions and Unlawful Inter-State Transfer of Detainees Involving Council of Europe Member States* (2006) Doc. 10957, pp. 42-45; Maher Arar Case in the same document, pp. 40-42; and Abu Omar Case, p. 37.
21. See Australian Federal Police Act, 1979 (Cth); Australian Crime Commission Act, 2002 (Cth).
22. See Australian Dictionary of Biography (Online Edition), *Hughes, William Morris (Billy) (1862-1952)*,http://adb.anu.edu.au/biography/hughes-william-morris-billy-6761 accessed 18/09/2012).
23. K.L. Milte and T.A. Weber, *Police in Australia: Development Functions and Procedures* (Butterworths, 1977), pp. 29-30.
24. Ibid, p. 30; B. Dupont, *Construction et Réformes d'une Police: Le Cas Australien (1788-2000)* (L'Harmattan, 2002), pp, 144-145.
25. See B. Etter, 'Policing: Reflecting on the Past, Projecting into the Future' in M. Enders and B. Dupont (eds.), *Policing the Lucky Country* (Hawkins Press, 2001), pp. 22, 23-24.
26. For a detailed background, see Commonwealth, Royal Commission on Intelligence and Security, *First Report* (Australian Government, Canberra, 1977). See also, J Hocking, *Beyond Terrorism: the Development of the Australian Security State* (Allen and Unwin, 1993), Ch. 9.
27. See Sir Robert Mark, *Report to the Minister for Administrative Services on the Organisation of Police Resources in the Commonwealth Area and Other Related Matters* (Australian Government Publishing Service, 1978).
28. The earliest and probably most significant informal Australian police co-operation strategy at the national level was the 1903 Conference of Australian Police Commissioners, which continues to this day, but has changed its name and constitution several times. Most recently, it has been rebadged from the 'Conference of Commissioners of Police in Australasia and the South West Pacific Region' to the 'Australia and New Zealand Police Commissioner's Forum'.
29. See S. Hufnagel, 'Cross-Border Police Cooperation: Traversing International and Domestic Frontiers' (2011), *Criminal Law Journal*, pp. 333, 339-342.
30. See *Haneef vs Minister for Immigration and Citizenship* [2007] FCA 1273; *Clarke Inquiry into the case of Dr Mohamed Haneef* (Commonwealth of Australia, Canberra, 2008); J. Ransley and L. Mazzerolle, 'Policing in an Era of Uncertainty' (2009) *Police Practice and Research*, pp. 1, 13.
31. Ibid. See also, from an AFP practitioner perspective, J. McFarlane, 'The Thin Blue Line: The Strategic Role of the Australian Federal Police' (2007), *Security Challenges*, pp. 91, 102.
32. S. Hufnagel, *Policing Cooperation across Borders: Comparative Perspectives on Law Enforcement*

within the EU and Australia (forthcoming Ashgate, 2012).

33. For a further elaboration of these claims, see T. Legrand, 'The citadel and its sentinels: state strategies for contesting cyberterrorism in the UK', in T. Chen, L. Jarvis and S. Macdonald (eds), *Cyberterrorism, Understanding Assessment and Response* (Springer, 2015).
34. Michael Hayden, speech to the Bipartisan Policy Center, reported in *The Guardian*, 6 August 2013. http://www.theguardian.com/technology/2013/aug/06/nsa-director-cyber-terrorism-snowden
35. Remarks on Cyber at the RSA Conference as Delivered by William J. Lynn, III, San Francisco, California, Tuesday, 15 February 2011. http://www.defense.gov/speeches/speech.aspx?speechid=1535
36. Quoted in http://www.independent.co.uk/news/uk/politics/government-faces-around-33000-cyber-attacks-a-month-reveals-cabinet-office-minister-chloe-smith-8584636.html
37. McAfee Critical Infrastructure Protection Report, March 2011.
38. Reported at http://blogs.ixiacom.com/ixia-blog/cyber-terrorism-going-happen-whoe28099s-responsible-protecting-us-part-1/
39. The UK cyber security strategy: Landscape review. Report by the Comptroller and Auditor General, 5 February 2013.
40. Central Sponsor for Information Assurance (2004), 'Protecting our information systems: Working in partnership for a secure and resilient UK information infrastructure'.
41. Cabinet Office (2009), 'Cyber Security Strategy of the United Kingdom: Safety, Security and Resilience in Cyber Space'.
42. Government Communications Headquarters, Press Release, 'Cyber Incident Response Scheme',launched 13 Aug 2013. http://www.gchq.gov.uk/Press/Pages/CIR_Scheme_Launched.aspx
43. OECD (2009), 'Innovation in Country Risk Management', OECD Studies in Risk Management. Paris: OECD.
44. C. Fijnaut, ibid. pp. 2, 115, 116.

18

Use of Lethal Force and Military Aid to Civil Power in India and Australia: Sharing Lessons in Counter Terrorism

Simon Bronitt and Ashutosh Misra

Introduction

Australia-India relations have come a long way since the 1990s when bilateral ties lacked warmth, political understanding and mutual appreciation. Over the last decade, bilateral engagement has intensified in the fields of trade and commerce, education, energy, science and technology, defence and security cooperation. Marking a major leap in bilateral cooperation, the then Australian Prime Minister Kevin Rudd visited India in November 2009, during which diplomatic ties were upgraded to a "strategic partnership" that was underpinned by a joint declaration in security cooperation that established a cooperation framework for counter-terrorism, defence, disarmament, non-proliferation and maritime security. The declaration also established the Joint Working Group on Counter-Terrorism with a comprehensive mandate aimed at buttressing cooperation between the security and intelligence agencies of Australia and India (Government of India, 2009). In July 2010, the Australia Federal Police (AFP), in the lead up to the New Delhi Commonwealth Games (2011), opened an office in New Delhi to strengthen the law enforcement relationship with Indian counterparts. During the Commonwealth Games, the AFP deployed its personnel to support local security arrangements amidst rising concerns over possible terror attacks and concerns for the safety of Australian athletes (Herald Sun, 2011).

Both nations are victims of terrorism and share the political commitment to establish a counter-terrorism strategy that not only safeguards national borders from external threats, but also extends a curtain of protection to its globally dispersed citizenry. In fact, one of the earliest acts of international terrorism in Australia was targeted at India—in Canberra in September 1977—when a member of the Ananda Marga kidnapped the Indian Defence Attache, Colonel Iqbal Singh and his wife Darshan kaur Singh to avenge the arrest of their leader Prahat Rajan Sarkar by the Indian Government. Fortunately, both managed to overpower the kidnapper and rescued themselves to safety (The Sydney Morning Herald, 1977). Other major terrorist attacks include the 1972 bombing of the Yugoslav General Trade Agency in Sydney; the 1978 bombing of the Sydney Hilton hotel during a Commonwealth Heads of Government Regional Meeting; the 1980 assassination of the Turkish Consul General in Sydney; 1982 bombing of the Israeli Consulate at the Hakoah Club in Sydney; and the 1986 bombing at the Turkish Consulate in Melbourne. Post 9/11, Australians have suffered terrorism related casualties, most notably the Bali bombings in Indonesia that killed 88 Australians on October 12, 2002. The attack established an ongoing security and law enforcement partnership between Australia and Indonesia and the establishment of the Jakarta Centre for Law Enforcement Cooperation (JCLEC). It also led the Australian Parliament to move swiftly to enact a raft of new offences prohibiting 'harming Australian citizens or residents abroad'.[1] These new offences were novel in two respects: first, the new offences applied extra-territorially and secondly, they were intended to have retrospective application.[2] Ultimately, the offences were not prosecuted in the case as Bali bombers were successfully prosecuted in Indonesia (with some being executed).

Australia's large, diverse and globally dispersed migrant communities as well as the involvement of the Australian Defence Force in many theatres of conflict in the world make Australia and its citizens vulnerable to the risk of both national and international acts of terrorism. Australia's involvement in the 'war on terror' in Afghanistan and Iraq has made it a more likely target of global terror groups such as the Al-Qaida and its affiliates. The Australian Defence Force's deployment post-9/11 in Afghanistan has resulted in 40 soldiers being killed and another 261 injured (Australian Government, 2013). Overall, 100 Australians have been killed in terrorist strikes the world over and Australia has now a clear and present threat inside its borders too. A number of 'home-grown' terrorist attacks have been foiled within Australia, leading to the prosecution and conviction of 35 people for terrorism offences and more than 40 people have had their passports cancelled or denied for security reasons (Australian Government, 2010)

Since the 1980s, India's battle with terrorism has resulted in the death of over 63,000 people, including civilian, security forces and terrorists and left wing extremists (South Asia Terrorism Portal, 2014). The country remains a target of several groups including the *Lashkar-e-Toiba* (LET) and *Jaish-e-Muhammad* (JeM) and *Harkat-ul Jihadi e-Islami* (HUJI). In recent years, the advent of 'home-grown' terrorism and left-wing extremism has added new dimensions to its internal security concerns. The lessons of 1999 still sear in Indian memory when the ill-fated Indian Airlines IC 814 was hijacked from Nepal carrying 176 passengers. The plane eventually landed in Kandahar and after hectic negotiations with the hijackers, the government secured the release of the hostages, in lieu of three terrorists, serving imprisonment in India—Mushtaq Ahmed Zargar, Omar Saeed Sheikh (Daniel Pearl murder accused) and Maulana Masood Azhar (leader of group Jaish-e-Muhammad based in Pakistan).

Following the Mumbai terrorist siege of 2008, India has to now counter a triad of possible terrorist attacks from the land, air and the seas. Besieged with a myriad of terrorism threats and insurgencies, the Indian Government has deployed its armed forces in the North Eastern states (to counter insurgency) and in Jammu and Kashmir (J&K) (to counter cross-border terrorism and internal disturbances). The prolonged deployment of armed forces has fuelled bitter acrimony and tension between New Delhi and the North Eastern States and J&K. The ensuing debate in the government, media and strategic circles has intensified in recent years, pitting the local communities into a protracted confrontation with New Delhi. Consequently, the Indian Government has not only been reviewing the feasibility of amending or repealing the Armed Forces (Special Powers) Act, 1958 but also tightening its anti-hijacking laws. As India strengthens its counter-terrorism legislations and strategies to deal with internal and external threats, it faces the difficult task of preserving its integrity and national interests on one hand and assuaging international concerns on the other expressed by the international human rights groups and bodies over the alleged human rights violations by the security forces. Understandably, the Indian Prime Minister Manmohan Singh has said the country is keen to learn from international experience in this regard (PM's address, 2011).

Despite the divergence in internal security threats, both in nature and scale between India and Australia, parallels can be drawn from the respective legislative frameworks that facilitates the domestic deployment of armed forces in crisis situations to aid civil power and from the safeguards (if any) that serve to place limits on the conduct of the military during such operations and uphold human rights to the maximum extent.

The most salient policy lesson which applies equally in Australia and India is that the aftermath of an act of terrorism is rarely conducive to the development of sound legal and policy responses. In the aftermath of an attack, the overwhelming domestic political pressure to respond swiftly and effectively, invariably leads to emergency powers legislation, with scant attention to cost-effectiveness, reasonableness and proportionality of the response (Legrand and Bronitt, 2012). Human rights are well known to be a first casualty in the 'war on terror' in many countries and that temporary emergency measures in both Australia and the UK have tended to become normalised and even extended further over time (Bronitt, 2008).

In this context, this paper focuses on two issues related to the use of emergency powers to combat terrorism and insurgencies: (a) the legal/constitutional frameworks authorising the domestic deployment of the military in aid of civil power and (b) the legislation that authorises the military to use lethal force against hijacked planes pre-emptively to counter attacks of the type used to devastating effect in the United States on September 11, 2001. Our aim is to draw out lessons from the Australian responses for policy-makers in India. The key Indian counter-terrorism legislation examined include: the Armed Forces (Special Powers) Act, 1958 (AFSPA), the Anti-Hijacking Act, 1982, and Unlawful Activities (Prevention) Amendment Act, 2008. After discussing the Indian Legislations, we present an overview of the key comparable Australian legislative provisions, drawing lessons from the evolution and deployment of these special powers.

The objective of our paper is to analyse how can modern democracies like India and Australia combat internal security challenges effectively, while remaining compliant with the relevant international treaties and conventions, constitutional and domestic laws relating to human rights, as well as fundamental liberal ideals related to the Rule of Law and separation of powers. In fact, India may be at one advantage with respect to human rights protection: unlike most common law jurisdiction, Australia continues to lack a constitutional Bill of Rights or comprehensive national human rights legislation—the protection of the rights to human dignity, life, liberty and property rest upon an independent judiciary, robust defence bar and innovative approaches to the judicial development of the common law, which has (to date at least) been reasonably effective in tempering the most repressive aspects of the 'war on terror' (Bronitt, 2011).

Calling Out the Troops in India: The Armed Forces (Special Powers) Act, 1958 (AFSPA)

Following India's partition and independence in 1947, in order to deal with the arising security situation in the country, four ordinances were passed viz., the Bengal Disturbed Areas (Special Powers of Armed Forces) Ordinance 1947, the Assam Disturbed Areas (Special Powers of Armed Forces) Ordinance 1947, the East Punjab and Delhi Disturbed Areas (Special Powers of Armed Forces) Ordinance and the United Provinces Disturbed Areas (Special Powers of Armed Forces) Ordinance

1947. These ordinances were shortly replaced by the Armed Forces (Special Powers) Act of 1948 (Act 3 of 1948). A decade later the Armed Forces (Assam and Manipur) Special Powers Act, 1958 was passed by the Indian Parliament which was applied to other states of the North East—Arunachal Pradesh, Meghalaya, Mizoram and Nagaland later. The Act was also implemented in the state of J&K in the wake of growing insurgency in 1990. The Act has been invoked ever since to facilitate the deployment of the Indian Armed Forces, the para military and the Indian Reserve Battalions in the North East following the approval of the 1958 Act, in Punjab between 1982 and 1992 and in Jammu and Kashmir since 1990. The AFSPA 1958 was first invoked in Assam and Manipur which were declared as "disturbed areas" and subsequently amended in 1960, and then in 1970 (with reference to Tripura), in 1972 (with reference to Assam and Manipur), in 1986 (with reference to Mizoram and Arunachal Pradesh). The description in the Act does not specify the characteristics of a "disturbed area", but only refers to "dangerous condition" as declared by the Governor, or the Administrator of the Union Territory or the Central Government, that would necessitate the "use of armed forces in aid of the civil power" and "maintenance of public order" (Government of India, 1958). The Disturbed Areas Act, 1976 describes the "disturbed area"—as when a state is having "extensive disturbance of the public peace and tranquillity, by reason of differences or disputes between members of different religious, racial, language or regional groups or castes or communities" (The Disturbed Areas (Special Courts) Act, 1976).

The AFSPA confers special powers upon the armed forces (military, air force and other union forces) in the entire region of the North East (Arunachal Pradesh, Assam, Manipur, Meghalaya, Mizoram, Nagaland and Tripura) to operate in the area declared as "disturbed area" (Government of India, 1958). In 2004 the Manipur Government had revoked the application of Act from some parts of the state, in spite of the objections raised by the Centre. The Act therein empowers the security forces to employ 'use of force' and carry out arrests and searches without warrant, effectively suspending *habeas corpus* (Ibid). The Act, as noted above, was extended to the State of Jammu and Kashmir as well in 1990 from where it has continued to receive vehement opposition (The Gazette of India, 1990).

The AFSPA empowers any "commissioned officer, warrant office, non-commissioned officer or other person of equivalent rank" to (a) fire upon or otherwise use force, even to the causing of death (having given due warning); prohibiting the assembly of five or more persons; or carrying of weapons or of fire-arms, ammunition or explosive substances; and (b) destroy any arms dump, or fortified position, or any structure used as training camp or hideout. But what has drawn most criticism, both nationally and internationally, is the powers that AFSPA confers on the security forces to arrest, enter and search without a warrant.

The Act also says that "any person arrested and taken into custody under this Act shall be made over to the officer in charge of the nearest police station with the least possible delay, together with the report of the circumstances occasioning the arrest" but the Act does not clearly specify what constitutes "least possible delay" (Government of India, 1958). Also, the Act provides that "no prosecution, suit or other legal proceeding shall be instituted, except with the previous sanction of the Central Government, against any person in respect of anything done or purported to be done in exercise of the powers conferred by this Act" (Government of India, 1958). It is this derogation from the right to be brought before a competent court to answer charges without delay and to contest the legality of detention, and sweeping powers conferred upon the security forces operating in a disturbed area lie at the core of the increasing criticism of the Act both in and outside India.

Opinion is deeply divided over the dilution of the powers of the security forces. The Indian Army Chief General Bikram Singh while referring to the situation in J&K says, "We need to look at the developments in Afghanistan in 2014 before we can look at the perhaps tampering with or diluting the disturbed areas (Act)" (Press Trust of India, 2014). While refraining from recommending the AFSPA's indefinite extension, he says that "As per the military's perspective, the situation prevailing in the valley, we should wait for a while to see whether the situation remains the same, worsens or improves" (Ibid). General V.R. Raghavan, former Director General Military Operation (DGMO) who was also member of the Jeevan Reddy Committee which was constituted to review the AFSPA provisions and relevance, says, "If AFSPA's enabling powers are to be revoked, diluted or made subject to normal processes of law, the military will conduct operations not on the basis of military judgment, but on the need to defend its actions in courts...They will have a lasting and debilitating effect on the ability of the Indian state to apply military force as a last resort in the defence of its citizens, against internal and foreign inspired armed groups determined to destroy the values that the Indian nation stand for" (V.R. Raghavan, 2010). However, the Indian Prime Minister, former Union Home Minister Mr. P. Chidambaram and J&K Chief Minister Omar Abdullah have alluded to reviewing the AFSPA (Vishwa Mohan, 2011). The Prime Minister's working group on Confidence-Building measures had also recommended reviewing both the Disturbed Areas Act as well as the AFSPA and suggested a "possible lifting of the former and revoking the latter". The Ministry of Home has also recommended aligning the AFSPA provisions with the Criminal Procedure Code, but also providing protection for the armed forces. In the light of the dip in militancy the group has recommended phased withdrawal of the army and transferring civilian policing duties to the paramilitary and the J&K Police eventually (Special correspondent, 2012). The Defence Minister A.K. Antony, however, remains opposed to lifting the AFSPA in J&K (Press Trust of India, 2011). The right-wing Rashtriya Swayam Sevak Sangh (RSS) has also argued against lifting the AFSPA in J&K and Manipur (Times News Network, 2013).

A large number of civil society groups, students, lawyers and activists from the North East have been over the years protesting for the repeal of the AFSPA in the region, angered by the allegations of excesses and rapes committed by the security forces. In July 2004, a young Manipuri girl, Thangjam Manorama, was detained by members of the Assam Rifles. She had been suspected of being a rebel. The next day her body was found in a field, having been shot several times, with an autopsy suggesting she had been sexually assaulted. The Assam Rifles claimed that she was shot while trying to escape custody. The failure to prosecute those responsible, hampered by the application of the APSA in the region, caused public outcry, including a daring protest by 12 naked women seeking to highlight the sexual violence against women committed by the security forces in that state. Irom Sharmila's fast unto death since 2000 is however most powerful and persistent symbol of anti-AFSPA voice from the State. Unfortunately, the AFSPA was lifted briefly in the state in August 2004, but was reimposed following a grenade attack by suspected militant on a religious congregation (Iboyaima Laithangbam, 2013).

Rising protests and allegations of human rights violations have persistently resonated abroad drawing criticisms of the Indian Government's decision to continue with the Act in North East and J&K. At the invitation of the Indian Government, Christof Heyns, the United Nations Special Rapporteur on Extra Judicial Summary of Arbitrary Executions, visited several Indian states including J&K and Assam in March 2012. The subsequent report of the Rapporteur, apart from commenting on violence against women, minorities and social activists also spoke about the AFSPA related issues. The Special Rapporteur drew attention to two major concerns related to AFSPA: first, the use of lethal force by the security forces under Section four and secondly, the broad protection provided to officers against prosecution (without prior sanction) under section six (AFSPA) and Section seven (J&K AFSPA). It also endorsed the Supreme Court of India's judgment in 1997 in the *Naga People's Movement of Human Rights v Union of Indian And Others* that the declaration of a "disturbed area" under AFSPA must be "for a limited duration and there should be periodic review of the declaration before the expiry of the six months" (United National General Assembly, 2013). It also shared the recommendations of the 2004 Jeevan Reddy Committee. The report concluded that although the Supreme Court judgment did spell out some dos and don'ts, it failed to bring the AFSPA in compliance with international standards. The report also noted that the AFSPA confers more powers to forces than what is prescribed in emergency situations and widespread employment becomes 'the rule rather than exception' with use of military force viewed as the primary response. The Special Rapporteur sent a strong message to the Indian Government that "retaining a law such as the AFSPA runs counter to the principles of democracy and human rights. Its repeal will bring domestic law more in line with international standards and send a strong message that the government is committed to respect the right to life of all the people in the country" (Ibid). In response the then Home Minister Chidambaram said that the report highlighted both positive and negative aspects of the India's policies and that such criticism was also surfacing at home in various quarters. He noted that the Home Ministry itself conveyed looking into three recommendations (without specifying) of the Jeevan Reddy Committee (Times News Network, 2012).

The Justice (Retd.) B.P. Jeevan Reddy Committee was constituted in November 2004 by the Ministry of Home Affairs in the wake of the widespread agitation following the rape and death of Thangjam Manorama, to review the provisions and continuation of the AFSPA in the North Eastern Region. The Committee made several significant recommendations including the following:

1. The deployment of the armed forces to restore public order ought to be an exception and not the rule. Deployment for too long, carries the danger of the troops losing their moorings and leading to brutalisation of such forces;
2. it is equally necessary to ensure that where they (armed forces) knowingly abuse or misuse their powers, they must be held accountable therefore and must be dealt with according to law applicable to them;
3. the AFSPA 1958 should be repealed and the continuation of the Act with or without the amendments does not arise. The Supreme Court has upheld the constitutionality of the Act but it is not the endorsement of the desirability or advisability of the Act;
4. the Act has become a symbol of oppression, an object of hate and an instrument of discrimination and high handedness;
5. in place of AFSPA, appropriate legal mechanisms should be devised by inserting necessary provisions in the Unlawful Activities (Prevention) Act, 1967. Since the ULP applies to the entire country, it will erase the feeling of discrimination and alienation among the North Eastern states;
6. the new provisions in the ULP should be clear, unambiguous and must specify the powers of the armed forces during operations;
7. there is a need for forming a "Grievances Cell" comprising of a local administrative official (as the Chair), a captain of the armed/security forces and senior police official, to deal with the complaints in order to infuse confidence and trust among the local communities; and
8. the extension of the deployment of the armed forces should be tabled

before the both houses of the Parliament within one month of the notification of the extension (Government of India, 2005).

The Unlawful Activities (Prevention) Amendment Act, 2008

The Unlawful Activities (Prevention) Act was passed in December 1967. The Act empowered the Indian Parliament "to impose, by law, reasonable restrictions in the interest of the sovereignty and integrity of India, on the—(i) freedom of speech and expression; (ii) right to assemble peaceably and without arms; and (iii) right to form associations or unions" (Government of India, 2008). The Act applied to the whole of India and was applicable to Indian citizens in and outside the country, government personnel and persons on ships registered in India. The Act was amended in 2008 and 2013. The amendments invoked several United Nations Security Council Resolutions including 1373 (2001) which requires all States "to take actions against certain terrorist organisations, to freeze the assets and other economic resources, to prevent the entry into or transit through their territory and prevent the direct or indirect supply, sale or transfer of arms and ammunitions to the individuals or entities..." (Government of India, 2013). The 2008 amendments to the Act substituted section 15 related to 'terrorist act' and included bombs and explosives (biological radioactive, nuclear or otherwise), assassinations and kidnappings and destruction of property, funding and organisation of terrorist camps in the definition (Government of India, 2008). It also inserted new powers and procedure to arrest, search and seizure' (Government of India, 2008). Later, the 2012 amendment inserted "economic security" in the act including "financial, monetary and fiscal stability, security of means of production and distribution, food security, livelihood security, energy security, ecological and environmental security" (The Gazette of India, 2013).

The Anti-Hijacking Act, 1982

Acceding to the convention for the suppression of unlawful seizure of aircraft, signed at the Hague in 1970, India passed the Anti-Hijacking Act, 1982 which was applied to entire India. The Anti-Hijacking Act made hijacking (of aircrafts registered in and outside India) and related offences punishable with life imprisonment and also a fine (Government of India, 1982). The Act was amended in 1994 to 'confer on any officer of the central government, power to arrest, investigate and prosecute exercised by a police officer under the Code of Criminal Procedure, 1973'. The amendment also provided for 'speedy trial' by a 'designated court' with the 'concurrence of the Chief Justice of the High Court' (Government of India, 1994). In 2010, further amendments were made to the Anti-Hijacking Act, 1982, at the recommendation of the group of ministers, headed by the home minister five years after the cabinet committee on security approved the amendments in 2005. The new changes now empower the Indian Air Force (IAF) in the Indian airspace to force or shoot down a "hostile plane if there is conclusive evidence that it is likely to be used as a missile to blow up strategic establishments". The new laws also establish a coordinated chain of command network between the Air Traffic Control, the IAF and the Cabinet Committee on Security (CCS) (Times New Network, 2010). The IAF is now also empowered to take steps for scrambling fighters to guard and guide a hijacked plane and force it to land. The new laws also direct the airports to immobilise the 'hostile' aircraft and prevent it from taking off, a lesson learnt from the 1999 hijacking during which the Indian security forces could not immobilise the plane during its brief stopover in Amritsar (Ibid). The new laws contain a 'no negotiation' policy with terrorists and death penalty for the hijackers, amending the 1982 Act which previously only contained imprisonment and fine (Special Correspondent, 2010).

The amendments to The Anti-Hijacking Act, 1982 triggered a debate in the media over the new powers to shoot down a hijacked plane carrying innocent passengers, and the wisdom of a blanket 'no negotiation' policy with hijackers. While an SMS poll showed 80 per cent in favour of the death penalty for the hijackers, opinions were divided over the shooting down of a place and 'no negotiation policy. In a media debate, one of the hostage survivors from 1999 hijacking, disagreed with the no negotiation policy and argued that the hijackers are usually on a suicide mission and in 1999 hundreds of lives were saved because of the negotiations between the government and the hijackers (IBN Live, 2008). Brahma Chellaney, a strategic expert, says that instead of no negotiations, the governments should adopt a "no capitulation policy" (Ibid). Vrinda Grover, a human rights lawyer says that "we need to unpackage national security and understand that it is completely removed from human security....A series of lapses led to what Kandahar was. And governance is about protecting the citizens of the country. Shoot at sight in a country like India—where there is no vigilance, no alertness, no protocols in place and where fake encounters rule the day—is a recipe for disasters" (Ibid.).

Calling Out the Troops in Australia: From Prerogative Martial Law to Prospective Legislative Immunities

The history of calling out the troops has been the subject of extensive examination in Australia (Head, 2009). The Hilton bombing in 1978 was the first time since Federation (1901) that the Australian Defence Force (ADF) had been deployed militarily on Australian soil to deal with a domestic security threat. The Hilton bombing revealed the lack of clarity over the precise legal basis for the troop call out: at that time, the powers of the federal government to seek military assistance, through the office of the governor general, rested on a complex web of general constitutional powers, as well as the right of individual states to make a formal request to the federal government to combat 'domestic violence' (O'Donnell and Bronitt, 2014). As in India there were also executive prerogative powers related to martial law inherited from the common law, though invoking these powers would be politically unattractive since they were not invoked in living memory.

Security concerns in the lead up to the 2000 Sydney Olympic Games stimulated a legislative review and the call out powers were further expanded in the post-9/11 era. After 9/11, a review of the Defence Act of 1903 (Utilisation of Defence Force to protect Commonwealth interest and States and self-governing Territories) in 2004 exposed the further concern that the existing powers were too reactive (modeled around a hostage siege situation) and there needed to be a more proactive model—the 2006 amendments in Part IIIAAA now provide that legislative basis. Part IIIAAA created a legislative framework for prospective authorisation of force by the military including the power to destroy an aircraft. It enables a 'call out' of the ADF to respond to incidents or threats to commonwealth incidents in the air environment, as well as ensuring that 'powers conferred on the ADF under Part IIIAAA can be accorded to the ADF in the course of dealing with a mobile terrorist incident and a range of threats to Australia's security' (Australian Government, 1903). The underlying principles that inform the operation of Part IIIAAA were identified as follows:

- the ADF should only be called out as a last resort where civilian authorities are unable to deal with an incident;
- where the ADF is called out the civil power remains paramount;
- ADF members remain under military command;
- if called out ADF members can only use force that is reasonable and necessary in the circumstances; and
- ADF personnel remain subject to the law and are accountable for their actions. (Explanatory Memorandum, 2005).

Part IIIAAA of the Defence Act, 1903 also authorises, the governor-general, the prime minister and ministers to call out and direct the ulilisation of the defence force in the following purposes:

(a) to protect Commonwealth interests against domestic violence;
(b) to protect commonwealth interests in the offshore area;
(c) to protect Commonwealth interests against violence if specified circumstances arise;
(d) to protect State against domestic violence; and
(e) to protect self-governing Territory against domestic violence (Australian Government 1903).

The Act authorises the governor-general, by written order to call out the ADF and direct the chief of defence force to utilise the forces to protect commonwealth interests. In common with the Indian framework, the head of state (in Australia's case the Governor-General) may make the order whether or not the government of the state or the self-governing territories has made the request. It is important to highlight that the governor-general makes the order when the authorising ministers (the prime minister, the minister and the attorney-general are satisfied that the domestic violence likely to imperil the commonwealth, states or self-governing territories or the internal waters of Australia (Ibid.). 51CA also in situations of urgent circumstances authorises the prime minister, the other two authorising ministers which include the deputy prime minister and the foreign affairs ministers or the treasurer to make an order of a kind that the governor general is empowered to make (Ibid). At the same time section 51G also enshrines restrictions, "in accordance with section 51D, that the Chief of the Defence Force must not stop or restrict any protest, dissent, assembly or industrial action, except where there is a reasonable likelihood of the death of, or serious injury to, persons or serious damage to property" (Ibid). It is interesting to note that Article 51I specifies that the defence forces can "detain the person for the purpose of placing the person in the custody of a member of a police force at the earliest practicable time" (Ibid). The AFSPA has similar provisions that direct the armed forces to hand over the detained person to the police with "the least possible delay".

The ADF is now regularly domestically deployed in aid of civil power in Australia—the ADF have engaged in highly controversial policing and security operations, including in 2007, when the federal government called out the troops, as part of the Northern Territory National Emergency Response to deal with a range of endemic violence and child abuse problems in the aboriginal communities. The ADF operation involved more than 600 soldiers and detachments, concluding on October 21, 2008 (Wallis, 2011). The use of ADF to support law enforcement operations has become a regular occurrence; for example, the ADF were used to assist operations to support Victoria Police in raids against organised criminal "bikie" groups (ABC, 2013; Vogler and Donna, 2013).

A key feature of the Part IIIAAA framework is clarifying the specific powers available to the ADF in protecting the states against terrorist threats. Part IIIAAA, however, more controversially, *immunises* the ADF from civil and criminal liability (under certain conditions. It is striking that these powers though broad and subject to some academic critique, has not generated much public controversy or debate in Australia (Bronitt and Stephens, 2009).

Combating Aviation Security Incidents in Australia

Part IIIAAA of the Defence Act, 1903, sets out the framework to control the military use of force against civilian aircraft which poses a security threat domestically. The purpose of the new provisions in relation to aviation security incidents is to provide clear legal authority for the military to act decisively, rather than force ADF members to engage in the deliberative exercise of weighing interests in necessity or self defence or resort to the vagaries of executive powers or martial law to defend the realm! The provisions seek to structure the decision-making process—and also to move beyond the reactive call out model, to designate a set of circumstances where the chief of defence is already pre-authorised or prospectively authorised to act (whether in Australia or offshore). In these cases, the military can act without ministerial authorisation or governor general order.

Section 51SE, also allows ADF members operating under orders given by the chief of the defence force to do certain things in relation to persons, vessels, aircraft or offshore facilities, including destroying a vessel or aircraft (or ordering it to be destroyed) and preventing or putting an end to acts of violence. In using force or other measures against a vessel or aircraft or ordering such, the ADF member must conform to the requirements of section 51 SE(2) or (3). Amongst other things, the ADF member cannot use force unless satisfied that:

- the order was not manifestly unlawful;
- the member has no reason to believe that circumstances have changed in a material way since the relevant order was given;
- the member has no reason to believe that the order was based on a mistake as to a material fact; and
- taking the measures was reasonable and necessary to give effect to the order.

Section 51 SE confers special powers on the defence force members to 'use reasonable and necessary force when protecting critical infrastructure designated by the authorising ministers'. This means that the right to life (of those innocent persons on the aircraft or on the ground) is trumped by the importance of the designated critical infrastructure to be protected. It can be concluded that even if the plane threatens to crash into an empty building (eg., unmanned power plant or government facility so designated) the aircraft may be destroyed, killing innocent passengers although this does not serve to save a greater number of people from death or serious injury.

By way of comparative analysis, equivalent powers conferred on the police to shoot down hijacked aircraft were ruled unconstitutional in Germany as being incompatible with the fundamental right to human dignity of the innocent passengers under the *Basic Law*. The right to human dignity is elevated to an overriding constitutional value in the Federal Constitution of Germany (*Grundgesetz*) which prevents the state authorising and conferring immunity on state officials who use torture or pre-emptive lethal force against hijacked aircraft (Hufnagel 2008). In Germany, the fundamental ideal that human beings cannot be used as instruments of state action trumps the utilitarian logic of weighing lesser evils inherent within the common law defences of necessity, duress and self defence (Hufnagel 2008 and 2012).

It is noteworthy that the legal regime governing hijacked aircraft now being expanded and structured for effective functioning in India. As in Australia, India acceded to the convention for the suppression of unlawful seizure of aircraft in 1970, implementing its obligations through the Anti-Hijacking Act, 1982. The Anti-Hijacking Act, which was applied to whole of India, made hijacking (of aircrafts registered in and outside India) and connected offences punishable with life imprisonment and also fine (Government of India, 1982). The Act was amended in 1994 to 'confer on any officer of the central government, power of arrest, investigation and prosecution exercisable by a police officer under the Code of Criminal Procedure, 1973'. The amendment also provided for 'speedy trial' by a 'designated court' with the 'concurrence of the Chief Justice of the High Court' (Government of India, 1994). There are no provisions comparable to Part IIIAAA in India that seeks to regulate and control the use of force by the military in hijack scenarios.

In addition, any action, or giving of orders, must be authorised by the relevant minister beforehand [s 51SE(4)], unless the ADF member believes on reasonable grounds that there is insufficient time to obtain the authorisation because a sudden and extraordinary emergency exists [s 51SE(5)]. In relation to action against aircraft specifically the action must be reasonable and necessary, though these powers are more extensive than other powers to use force otherwise available under Part IIIAAA. The key provisions governing reasonable and necessary force are as follows:

Section 51T—Use of Reasonable and Necessary Force

(1) A member of the defence force may in exercising any power under Division 2, 2A, 3, 3A or 3B or this division uses such force against persons and things as is reasonable and necessary in the circumstances.

(1A) However, subsection (1) does not apply to the powers under subdivision E of Division 3A.

(1B) In order to avoid doubt, any use of force by a member of the defence force under this part must be in accordance with this section.

Further Restrictions on Use of Force

(2B) Despite subsection (1), in exercising powers under subparagraph 51SE(1)(a)(i) or (ii) or Division 3B [action against aircraft], a member of the defence force must not, in using force against a person or thing, do anything that is likely to cause the death of, or grievous bodily harm to the person unless the member believes on reasonable grounds that:

(a) doing that thing is necessary to protect the life of, or to prevent serious injury to, another person (including the member); or
(b) doing that thing is necessary to protect designated critical infrastructure against a threat of damage or disruption to its operation; or
(c) doing that thing is necessary and reasonable to give effect to the order under which, or under the authority of which, the member is acting (Australian Government, 1903).

At the same time Part IIIAAA also provides immunity from otherwise applicable state or territory criminal law (murder, manslaughter, endangerment etc.) and does not relate to any criminal act of a defence force personnel (Australian Government, 1903). The ADF personnel will be dealt with only by reference to offences under the commonwealth criminal law or the Jervis Bay Territory law and applicable military offences. State police can still investigate the incident and liaise with the Commonwealth Directorate of Public Prosecutions (DPP), which interestingly has been given the power to prosecute illegal action by the military who are exercising powers under the act. There is a defence of military prosecutions department within the ministry of defence which handles all cases related to 'unlawful conduct of the defence force personnel and all charges under S5A of the Defence Force Discipline Act (DFDA) 1982. In the case of general court martial, there would be a president and four representatives of the armed forces who are above the ranks of the accused. The objective is to establish a due process where the competent court martial bench can adjudicate the case by relating to the context and the situation in which an 'unlawful conduct' would have occurred.

Conclusion

Comparative analysis of counter-terrorism and security legislation is not without challenges. Not only does it demand technical knowledge of other systems of law, it also requires a serious commitment to understanding the history and context of these powers and an appreciation that there is not one simple answer which is universally applicable. That said, there are some common observations one can draw from the analysis: the role of the modern military within domestic borders are changing and are being increasingly called upon by government to combat a wider range of challenges in the 21st century from disaster response to adjunct policing and public order roles. The presence of the military on the streets is not a sign that civilian authority has been displaced, merely that some threats are beyond the capabilities of other governmental agencies; for example, countering serious threats to people and critical infrastructure posed by hijacked aircraft. It is vital that democracies like India and Australia have modern legislation that sets the parameters of military powers and immunities, as well as systems of holding the military to account. There is a commonality between India and Australia in terms of legislative provisions which authorises the designated authority on the ground to use discretion to take immediate action when there is insufficient time to secure authorisation from higher officials. But it is critical to note that blanket immunities often lead to impunity, as noted by the Jeevan Reddy Committee as well, which cannot be accepted. It is also imperative that the troops on the ground are sensitised and trained adequately which would enable them to conduct their duties without impinging upon the liberties to which the communities are entitled. Human rights consideration must be designed into the legislative framework at the outset which has been the approach taken in Australia, and is also being addressed in India as reflected in the reports of various committees and government proclamations. In fact, India is better placed with respect to human rights protection than Australia which still continues to be one of the few common law jurisdictions which lacks a constitutional bill of rights or comprehensive national human rights legislation. Old colonial-style emergency powers inherited from Britain—what may be called the 'Martial Law' model—simply do not pass muster today. We hope that our reflections may assist policy makers and practitioners reflect on these key challenges, and to develop a legislative framework that is not only effective but also legitimate.

NOTES

1. Four offences were inserted into Divsion 104 of the *Criminal Code* (Commonwealth): murder of an Australian citizen or a resident of Australia (s 104.1); manslaughter of an Australian citizen or a resident of Australia (s 104.2); intentionally causing serious harm to an Australian citizen or a resident of Australia (s 104.3) and recklessly causing serious harm to an Australian citizen or a resident of Australia (s 104.4). The offences attract the following maximum penalties: murder, life imprisonment; manslaughter, 25 years imprisonment; intentionally causing serious harm, 20 years imprisonment; and recklessly causing serious harm, 15 years imprisonment.
2. The offences were expressly intended by the drafters to apply retrospectively, from October 1, 2002: Parliament of the Commonwealth of Australia, House of Representatives, Criminal Code Amendment (Offences Against Australians) Bill, 2002, Second Reading.

REFERENCES

Legislation and Official Reports

Australian Government, "Battle Casualties in Afghanistan", Department of Defence, 2013, at http://www.defence.gov.au/operations/afghanistan/personnel.asp

Australian Government, Counter-Terrorism White Paper 2010, Department of Defence, at http://www.dsto.defence.gov.au/national-security/page/6905/

Commonwealth Parliament, Explanatory Memorandum, Defence Legislation Amendment (Aid to Civilian Authorities) Bill 2005, at http://www.austlii.edu.au/au/legis /cth/bill_em/dlatcab2005507/memo_0.html

Government of India, 'India-Australia Joint Declaration on Security Cooperation during visit of Prime Minister Kevin Rudd', Bilateral/multilateral documents, Ministry of External Affairs, November 12, 2009, at http://www.mea.gov.in/bilateral-documents.htm?dtl/5035/India

Australia+Joint+Declaration+on+Security+Cooperation+during+visit+of+Prime+Minister+Kevin+Rudd,
Government of India, 'The Unlawful Activities (Prevention) Act, 1967 and 'The unlawful Activities (Prevention) amendment act, 2008', Ministry of Home Affairs, December 2008, att http://mha.nic.in/hindi/sites/upload_files/mhahindi/files/pdf/UAPA-1967.pdf,

Government of India, 'The Armed Forces (Special Powers) Act, 1958, Ministry of Home Affairs, September 11, 1958. At http://mha.nic.in/sites/upload_files/mha/files/pdf/armed_forces_special_powers_act1958.pdf

Government of India, "Report of the Committee to Review the Armed Forces (Special Powers) Act, 1958", *Ministry of Home Affairs*, June 2005, at http://www.hindu.com/nic/afa/ afa-part-i.pdf

The Gazette of India, 'The Armed Forces (Jammu and Kashmir) Special Powers Act, 1990, Ministry of Law and Justice, September 10, 1990, at http://mha.nic.in/sites/upload_files /mha/files/pdf/Armedforces%20_J&K_%20Splpowersact1990.pdf

The Gazette of India, 'The National Security Act, 1980', Ministry of Home Affairs, December 27, 1980, athttp://mha.nic.in/sites/upload_files/mha/files/pdf/National_Security_Act1980.pdf

The Gazette of India, 'The Unlawful Activities (Prevention) Amendment Act, 2012', Ministry of Law and Justice, January 3, 2013, at http://indiacode.nic.in/acts-in-pdf/032013.pdf

The Government of India, 'The Anti-Hijacking (Amendment) Act, 1994 (39 of 1994)', 1994, Ministry of Law and Justice, at http://lawmin.nic.in/legislative/textofcentralacts/1994.pdf

The Government of India, 'The Anti-Hijacking Act, 1982 (65 of 1982)', 1982, Directorate General of Civil Aviation, at http://dgca.nic.in/nat_conv/NatConv_Chap9.pdf

United National General Assembly, 'Report of the Special Rapporteur on Extrajudicial, Summary or Arbitrary executions, Christof Heyns', Human Rights Council, twenty third session, Agenda Item 3, Promotion and Protection of all Human Rights, Civil, political, Economic, Social and Cultural Rights, including the right to Development, April 26, 2013, A/HRC/23/47/Add.1, at http://daccess-dds-ny.un.org/doc/UNDOC/GEN/G13/134/53/PDF/G1313453.pdf?OpenElement.

Books and Journal Articles

Australian Government, "Defence Act, 1903, Act No. 20 of 1903 as amended", *Ministry of Defence,* at http://www.comlaw.gov.au/Details/C2013C00078/Html/Text#_Toc347491970

Bronitt, S. and Donkin, S., "Australian responses to 9/11: New world legal hybrids?" in A. Masferrer (ed.), *Post 9/11 and the State of Permanent Legal Emergency Security and Human Rights in Countering Terrorism,* Chapter 10,Dordecht: Springer, 2012, pp. 223-240.

Bronitt, S., "Balancing Liberty and Security: Critical Perspectives on Terrorism Law Reform" in M. Gani and P. Mathew (eds), *Fresh Perspectives on the 'War on Terror',* 2008.

Bronitt, S., "The Common Law and Human Dignity" in J Brohmer (ed.), *The German Constitution Turns 60: Basic Law and Commonwealth Constitution—German and Australian Perspectives,* Peter Lang, Internationaler Verlag der Wissenschaften, 2011, Publication, pp. 77-88.

Head, M., *Calling Out the Troops: The Australian Military and Civil Unrest: The Legal and Constitutional Issues,* The Federation Press, 2009.

Hufnagel, S., "German Perspectives on the Right to Life and Human Dignity in the 'War on Terror'" *Criminal Law Journal* 100, (2008).

Iboyaima Laithangbam, "AFSPA here to Stay?" *The Hindu*, 25 August 2013, at http://www.thehindu.com/news/national/other-states/afspa-is-here-to-stay/article5058559.ece

Legrand, T. and Bronitt, S., "Policing to a Different Beat: Measuring Police Performance" in T. Prenzler (ed), *Policing and Security in Practice—Challenges and Achievements,* Palgrave McMillan, 2012, pp 1-19.

O'Donnell, K. and Bronitt, S., "Philip's Brief—The Hilton Bombing, Calling Out The Troops and Turning Points in History",*Criminal Law Journal,* 38 (1), 2013.

South Asian Terrorism Portal (SATP), "India Fatalities: 1994-2014", at http://www.satp.org/satporgtp/countries/india/database/indiafatalities.htm

'The Disturbed Areas (Special Courts Act), 1976', South Asia Terrorism Portal, at http://www.satp.org/satporgtp/countries/india/document/actandordinances/DistributedAct.htm

Vishwa Mohan, "PM, Chidambaram "Receptive" on AFSPA: Omar", *The Times of India*, November 14, 2011, at http://articles.timesofindia.indiatimes.com/2011-11-14/india/30396955_1_afspa-home-minister-omar-abdullah

Wallis, R., "Legislation Comment: The role of the Australian Crime Commission in policing Indigenous violence and child abuse", *Criminal Law Journal,* 35(6), 2011, pp. 398-402.

Media Reports

ABC News, "Army, Police Raid Melbourne Property in Ongoing Operation Targeting Outlaw Motorcycle Gangs",12 October 12, 2013.

Anon, "Anti-hijack law dilemma: Lives first or national first", *Ibn Live*, February 15, 2008, at http://ibnlive.in.com/news/antihijack-law-dilemma-lives-first-or-nation-first/58999-11.html

Anon, "Attache Kidnap Case: Man on Remand, *The Sydney Morning Herald*, September 20, 1977, pp. 3, at http://news.google.com/newspapers?nid=1301&dat=19770920&id=bYRWAAAAIBA J&sjid=ZeYDAAAAIBAJ&pg=6352,6493261

Press Trust of India, "Kashmir Valley Not Conducive for Dilution of AFSPA", *Indian Express,* January 13, 2014, http://indianexpress.com/article/india/politics/the-jammu-and-kashmir-valley-not-conducive-for-dilution-of-afspa-army-chief/

Press Trust of India, "No Deadline on Lifting AFSPA from Jammu and Kashmir Says Defence Minister", *Hindustan Times*, November 14, 2011.

Raghvan, V.R., "Don't Blame the Law", *Indian Express,* September 16, 2013, at http: //www.indianexpress.com/story-print/681580/

Special Correspondent, "Defence Ministry must Respond Positively to Move to Amend AFSPA", *The Hindu*, April 14, 2012, http://www.thehindu.com/todays-paper/tp-national /defence-ministry-must-respond-positively-to-move-to-amend-afspa/article3313299

Times News Network, "Changes Likely in Armed Forces Law", *The Times of India*, 1 April 1, 2013, at http://articles.timesofindia.indiatimes.com/2012-04-01/india/31269701_1_afspa-excessive-state-power-justice-jeevan-reddy-report

Times News Network, "RSS Says No to AFSPA Repeal from Manipur", *The Times of India*, December 8, 2014, http://timesofindia.indiatimes.com/city/guwahati/RSS-says-no-to-AFSPA-repeal-from-Manipur/articleshow/27040173.cms

Vogler S. and Donna K., "Army could join Queensland Police to Help Bikie Crackdown", *The Courier Mail*, October 13, 2013, http://www.couriermail.com.au/news /queensland/army-could-join-queensland-police-to-help-bikie-crackdown/story-fnihsrf2-1226738926916

Index